Word 2000 Expert Course

Brian Favro

Russel Stolins

Developmental Editor: Brian Favro
Marketing Director: David Gauny
Production Management, Design and
    Publishing Consultation: The Cowans
Copy Editing: Nick Murray

Composition: The Cowans
Index: Bayside Indexing Service
Proofreading: Laura Lionello
Manufacturing Coordinator: The Cowans
Printer and Binder: Courier, Kendallville

LABYRINTH
PUBLICATIONS®
3314 Morningside Drive, El Sobrante, California   94803
(800) 522-9746   www.labyrinth-pub.com

Contents

From the Keyboard Summary Sheet—Word 2000 Expert Course

NAVIGATION

Beginning of document . . . . `CTRL`+`HOME`

Beginning of line . . . . `HOME`

Browse object menu
  (displaying) . . . . `ALT`+`CTRL`+`HOME`

End of document . . . . `CTRL`+`END`

End of line . . . . `END`

Go To . . . . `CTRL`+G

Next paragraph . . . . `CTRL`+↓

Next word . . . . `CTRL`+←

Previous paragraph . . . . `CTRL`+↑

Previous word . . . . `CTRL`+→

SELECTING

Beginning of line . . . . `SHIFT`+`HOME`

Document . . . . `CTRL`+A

End of line . . . . `SHIFT`+`END`

Text . . . . `SHIFT` while tapping arrow keys

EDITING

Copy while dragging . . . . `CTRL`

Copy . . . . `CTRL`+C

Cut . . . . `CTRL`+X

Delete to beginning of word . . . . . . `CTRL`+`BACKSPACE`

Delete to end of word . . . . `CTRL`+`DELETE`

Find . . . . `CTRL`+F

Paste . . . . `CTRL`+V

Redo . . . . `CTRL`+Y

Repeat . . . . `CTRL`+Y

Replace . . . . `CTRL`+H

Show/hide nonprinting characters . . `CTRL`+`SHIFT`+8

Spell check . . . . `F7`

Spike (cutting to) . . . . `CTRL`+`F3`

Spike (pasting contents) . . . . `CTRL`+`SHIFT`+`F3`

Thesaurus . . . . `SHIFT`+`F7`

Undo . . . . `CTRL`+Z

FORMATTING

Bold . . . . `CTRL`+B

Decrease font size one point . . . . `CTRL`+[

Increase font size one point . . . . `CTRL`+]

Indent (hanging) . . . . `CTRL`+T

Indent (left) . . . . `CTRL`+M

Indent (removing hanging) . . . . `CTRL`+`SHIFT`+T

Indent (removing left) . . . . `CTRL`+`SHIFT`+M

Italics . . . . `CTRL`+I

Line spacing (1.5) . . . . `CTRL`+5

Line spacing (double) . . . . `CTRL`+2

Line spacing (single) . . . . `CTRL`+1

Outline-style numbered list (demote) . . . . `TAB`

Outline-style numbered list (promote) `SHIFT`+`TAB`

Underline . . . . `CTRL`+U

DIALOG BOXES

Hyperlink . . . . `CTRL`+K

Office Assistant (displaying) . . . . `F1`

Office Assistant (hiding speech balloon) . . . . . . `ESC`

Open . . . . `CTRL`+O

Print . . . . `CTRL`+P

Save As . . . . `CTRL`+S

VBA editor window . . . . `ALT`+`F11`

INSERTING AND UPDATING

Date (inserting) . . . . `ALT`+`SHIFT`+D

Endnote (inserting) . . . . `ALT`+`CTRL`+D

Footnote (inserting) . . . . `ALT`+`CTRL`+F

Index entries (marking) . . . . `ALT`+`SHIFT`+X

Nonbreaking hyphens (inserting) . . . . . `CTRL`+`SHIFT`

Nonbreaking spaces
  (inserting) . . . . `CTRL`+`SHIFT`+`SPACE BAR`

Style list (displaying full
  list) . . . . `SHIFT` while clicking style list button

Table of contents (updating) . . . . `F9`

Time (inserting) . . . . `ALT`+`SHIFT`+T

MAIL MERGE

Data form (displaying) . . . .⌈ALT⌉+⌈SHIFT⌉+E

Insert Merge Fields box
   (displaying) . . . .⌈ALT⌉+⌈SHIFT⌉+F

Merge to new document . . . .⌈ALT⌉+⌈SHIFT⌉+N

Merge to printer . . . .⌈ALT⌉+⌈SHIFT⌉+M

TABLES AND COLUMNS

Column break . . . .⌈CTRL⌉+⌈SHIFT⌉+⌈ENTER⌉

Display column measurements
   . . . .⌈ALT⌉ while dragging column boundaries

Move back one cell . . . .⌈SHIFT⌉+⌈TAB⌉

Move forward one cell . . . .⌈TAB⌉

Use tabs within tables . . . .⌈CTRL⌉+⌈TAB⌉

DRAWING OBJECTS

Draw circle . . . .⌈SHIFT⌉ while drawing new oval

Draw lines at 15-degree
   increments . . . .⌈SHIFT⌉ while drawing new line

Draw square . . . ⌈SHIFT⌉ while drawing new rectangle

Maintain proportions of existing
   oval . . . .⌈SHIFT⌉ while sizing existing oval

Maintain proportions of existing
   rectangle . . . .⌈SHIFT⌉ while sizing existing rectangle

Nudge object . . . .⌈CTRL⌉ while tapping arrow keys

Prevent object from snapping
   to grid . . . .⌈ALT⌉ while dragging object

Size object while maintaining
   proportions . . . .⌈SHIFT⌉ while sizing object

Quick Reference Index

Visual Conventions

This book uses many visual and typographic cues to guide you through the lessons. This page provides examples and describes the function of each.

Typographic Cue	What It Indicates
Ⓐ Ⓑ Ⓒ	These characters indicate the order in which tasks should be performed in a Hands-On exercise.
Type this text	Anything you should type at the keyboard is printed in this typeface.
TIP!	This is an important tip which usually contains shortcuts or reminders.
Note!	This contains information that will help you understand a concept or a feature.
Warning!	Read and consider each warning before continuing with the lesson.
Command→Command	Indicates multiple selections to be made from a menu bar. For example: **File→Save** means you should click the **File** command in the menu bar, then click the **Save** command from the drop-down menu.
From the Keyboard **From the Keyboard** (CTRL)+S to Save	These margin notes indicate shortcut keys for executing a task described in the text. For example, (CTRL)+S to save your work in an application program.

Special Section	Purpose
Quick Reference	These sections contain generic procedures you can use to accomplish a task at any time. *Note: As you work through a lesson, you should not perform instructions in Quick Reference sections unless you are told to do so in a Hands-On exercise instruction.*
Hands-On Exercise	This section contains specific instructions for the exercise you are working on. You should always work through the Hands-On exercises. These exercises will guide you step-by-step through the topics. You will be told exactly what to do, which keys to press, and other steps to try out a new skill or feature.
Concepts Review	This section contains questions that help you gauge your mastery of the concepts covered in the lesson.
Skill Builders	This section contains additional exercises that provide opportunities for review.
Assessment	This section contains a test on the material covered in the lesson.
Critical Thinking	Critical Thinking exercises give you the opportunity to apply your knowledge to solve a realistic problem with minimal guidance. Some of these exercises are performed on your own, others are performed in groups.

LESSON 1

Creating and Editing Business Letters

In this lesson, you will learn the basics of word processing using Microsoft Word 2000. You will create a variety of business letters while learning proper business document formatting. You will also learn fundamental techniques of entering and editing text, saving documents, and using Word 2000 commands. This lesson is designed to provide you with a solid foundation of word processing skills to prepare you for the advanced features introduced in later lessons.

In This Lesson

Case Study

Susan Adams is the top sales representative for Western Office Supplies. Western Office Supplies distributes office equipment, including copy machines, laser printers, fax machines, and digital scanners to customers throughout the Western United States. Susan and her manager Richard Jones have just delivered a dynamic presentation to Sandra Evans, Vice President of Integrated Office Solutions. Like all top-notch sales representatives, Susan provides excellent follow-through and customer support. As a follow-up to her sales presentation, Susan writes a formal business letter to Sandra Evans thanking her for her time and preparing the next step in the sales process. Susan uses Word 2000 to create and edit her business letter.

June 26, 1999

Ms. Sandra Evans
Vice President
Integrated Office Solutions
2756 Industrial Lane
Los Angeles, CA 90024

Dear Ms. Evans:

It was a pleasure meeting with you and the rest of your staff yesterday. Both Richard Jones and I were quite impressed with your facilities and the quality of your team. You certainly have a group of hard working and creative people.

Our presentation was designed to give you an overview of our high-performance copiers, laser printers, fax machines, and digital scanners. We would like to follow up our presentation with a live demonstration. You must see our products in action to truly appreciate their benefits.

I will contact you early next week to arrange a demonstration. In the meantime, feel free to contact me if I can be of further assistance.

Sincerely,

Susan Adams
Sales Representative

xx

What Is Microsoft Word 2000?

Microsoft Word 2000 is a program that makes word processing a pleasure instead of a chore. Word's powerful suite of tools lets you easily create and modify a variety of documents. Word provides tools to assist you in virtually every aspect of document creation. From desktop publishing to Web publishing, Word has the right tool for the job. For these and many other reasons, Word is the most widely used word processing program in both homes and businesses.

Why Use Word?

Word provides a number of important features and benefits that make it a smart choice to use.

- **IntelliSense Technology**—Word's IntelliSense technology includes automated tools like AutoCorrect to assist you in creating, editing, and formatting documents. This speeds up the process of creating and formatting documents, so that you can focus on content.

- **GUI**—Word's Graphical User Interface is so easy to use that even beginning computer users find it simple. The interface reduces the need to memorize commands, and it will make you more productive.

- **Writing Tools**—Word has powerful writing tools, including automatic grammar checking and spell checking, as you type. These and other tools will help you improve your writing skills.

- **Widely Used**—Word is the most widely used word processing software. Word is the right choice if you are trying to develop marketable skills and find employment.

- **Integration with Other Office Programs**—Word 2000 is part of the Microsoft Office 2000 suite of programs, which also includes Excel, Access, PowerPoint, Outlook, PhotoDraw, and others. The ability to exchange data with these programs is one of the most powerful and attractive features of Word.

- **Web Integration**—Word 2000 lets you easily publish your documents to Web sites on the World Wide Web or to your company Intranet.

It's Time to Master Word!

It's time to put your fears behind and master this wonderful program. You will be amazed at the power and simplicity of Word and how easy it is to learn. The knowledge you are about to gain will give you a marketable skill and make you a master of Word.

Starting Word 2000

The method you use to start Word and other Office programs depends in large part upon whether you intend to create a new document or open an existing document. If you intend to create a new document, then use one of the following methods to start Word. Once the Word program has started, you can begin working in the new document window that appears.

- Click the Start button, and choose Microsoft Word from the Programs menu.

- Click the Microsoft Word 🔲 button on the Quick Launch toolbar (located near the Taskbar).

- Click the Start button, choose New Office Document, choose the General tab, and double-click the Blank Document icon.

Use one of the following methods if you intend to open an existing Word document. Once the Word program has started, the desired document will open in a Word window.

- Navigate to the desired document using Windows Explorer or My Computer, and double-click the document.
- Click the ⓡ Start button and point to Documents. You can choose the desired document from the Documents list. The Documents list displays the most recently used documents.

Hands-On 1.1 Start Word

1. If necessary, start your computer, and the Windows Desktop will be displayed.

2. **Click** the ⓡ Start button, and choose **Programs.**

3. Choose **Microsoft Word** from the Programs menu.
   The Word program will load, and the document window shown below will appear. Don't be concerned if your document window appears different from this example.

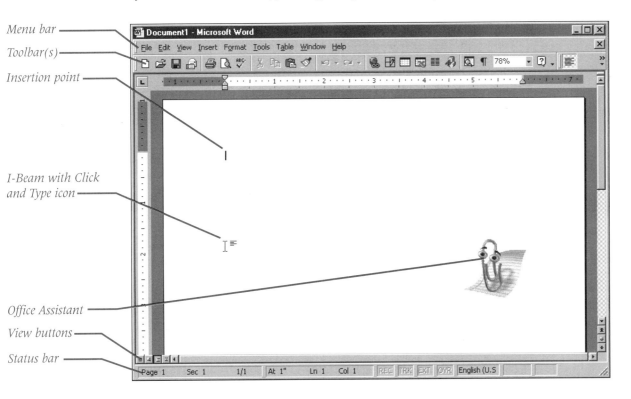

Menu bar
Toolbar(s)
Insertion point
I-Beam with Click and Type icon
Office Assistant
View buttons
Status bar

The document window is where you type information into Word. The document window allows you to access Word commands, and it can be customized to suit your particular needs. You will learn how to modify the document window at a later time.

Business Letter Styles

There are several acceptable styles of business letters. The styles discussed in this text include block, modified block, and personal. All business letters contain the same, or similar, elements but with varied formatting.

Block Style Letter

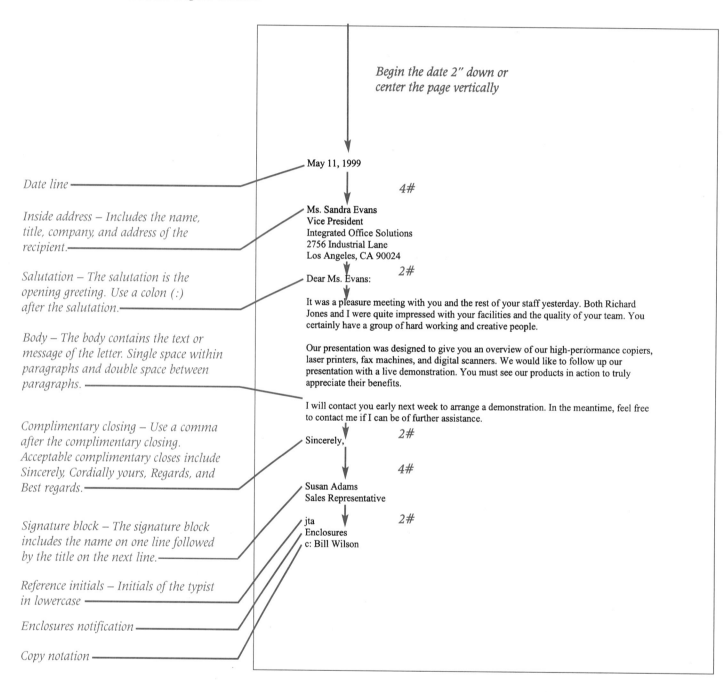

Begin the date 2" down or center the page vertically

May 11, 1999

4#

Ms. Sandra Evans
Vice President
Integrated Office Solutions
2756 Industrial Lane
Los Angeles, CA 90024

2#

Dear Ms. Evans:

It was a pleasure meeting with you and the rest of your staff yesterday. Both Richard Jones and I were quite impressed with your facilities and the quality of your team. You certainly have a group of hard working and creative people.

Our presentation was designed to give you an overview of our high-performance copiers, laser printers, fax machines, and digital scanners. We would like to follow up our presentation with a live demonstration. You must see our products in action to truly appreciate their benefits.

I will contact you early next week to arrange a demonstration. In the meantime, feel free to contact me if I can be of further assistance.

Sincerely,

2#

4#

Susan Adams
Sales Representative

2#

jta
Enclosures
c: Bill Wilson

Date line

Inside address – Includes the name, title, company, and address of the recipient.

Salutation – The salutation is the opening greeting. Use a colon (:) after the salutation.

Body – The body contains the text or message of the letter. Single space within paragraphs and double space between paragraphs.

Complimentary closing – Use a comma after the complimentary closing. Acceptable complimentary closes include Sincerely, Cordially yours, Regards, and Best regards.

Signature block – The signature block includes the name on one line followed by the title on the next line.

Reference initials – Initials of the typist in lowercase

Enclosures notification

Copy notation

Modified Block Style Letter

The modified block style has the same elements and spacing between paragraphs as the block style. However, the date line, complimentary closing, and signature block begin near the center of the lines as shown below.

Tab or indent dateline, complimentary closing, and signature block to approximately 4.25" (3" on the ruler).

May 11, 1999

Ms. Sandra Evans
Vice President
Integrated Office Solutions
2756 Industrial Lane
Los Angeles, CA 90024

Dear Ms. Evans:

It was a pleasure meeting with you and the rest of your staff yesterday. Both Richard Jones and I were quite impressed with your facilities and the quality of your team. You certainly have a group of hard working and creative people.

Our presentation was designed to give you an overview of our high-performance copiers, laser printers, fax machines, and digital scanners. We would like to follow up our presentation with a live demonstration. You must see our products in action to truly appreciate their benefits.

I will contact you early next week to arrange a demonstration. In the meantime, feel free to contact me if I can be of further assistance.

Sincerely,

Susan Adams
Sales Representative

jta
Enclosures
c: Bill Wilson

Personal Business Letter (Block Style)

Personal business letters are used when an individual representing himself or herself sends a letter to a recipient in a business. Personal business letters can be composed using either the block or modified block style.

Today's Date

Mr. Jake Wilson
Rebate Manager
Sierra Snowboards
4200 University Avenue
Berkeley, CA 94702

Dear Mr. Wilson:

Thank you for your excellent advice on the snowboarding equipment I recently purchased. Sierra Snowboards certainly has the best equipment in the business.

I would like to know when I can expect the rebate on the board I purchased. I mailed in my rebate coupon last month and I have yet to hear from the company. Do rebates normally take this long? Please contact me as soon as possible at (510) 223-3344. Thank you for your assistance.

Sincerely,

Melissa Jackson
1223 Appian Way
El Sobrante, CA 94803

In a personal business letter, the signature block includes the sender's address.

Inserting Text

Text is always inserted into a Word document at the flashing **insertion point.** For this reason, it is important to position the insertion point at the desired location before inserting text. You will learn how to position the insertion point later in this lesson.

Other Ways to Insert Text

Most users insert text using the keyboard. In fact, keyboarding is arguably the most important skill an office user can possess. However, if you have a physical disability or suffer from an ailment such as carpal tunnel syndrome, you may want to invest in voice dictation software such as **IBM's Via Voice.** Via Voice is highly accurate and lets you enter text by dictating into a microphone connected to your computer. You can also insert text with techniques such as Copy and Paste. Later in this course, you will use the Copy and Paste commands to insert text from another document and from a Web page.

Word Wrap

If you continue typing after the insertion point reaches the end of a line, Word automatically wraps the insertion point to the beginning of the next line. This feature is known as **word wrap.** If you are creating a paragraph with two or more lines, then you should let word wrap do its job. Just keep typing until the entire paragraph is complete. Word wrap will format the paragraph by wrapping the lines at the appropriate location. If you let word wrap format the paragraph initially, then the paragraph will also be reformatted as you insert or delete text.

Taking Control With the (ENTER) Key

You use the (ENTER) key to begin a new paragraph or to insert blank lines in a document. (ENTER) inserts a hard carriage return that can only be removed by the user.

AutoComplete and Other Automated Features

Word 2000 has numerous features to assist you in entering text and creating documents. AutoComplete recognizes certain phrases, such as dates and company names, and offers to complete them for you. You accept a phrase that AutoComplete proposes by tapping (ENTER). You can increase the number of phrases that AutoComplete recognizes by adding new AutoText entries to the system. You will learn more about AutoComplete and AutoText later in this course. For now, you will use AutoComplete to enter today's date in a business letter.

Hands-On 1.2 Begin Typing a Business Letter

Use AutoComplete

1. Tap (ENTER) six times.

   Each time you tap (ENTER), the insertion point moves down one line. (ENTER) is used to insert blank lines in documents.

2. Notice the vertical position indicator on the status bar as shown below.

   The vertical position indicator shows the vertical postiton of the insertion point within the document.

   | Page 1 | Sec 1 | 1/1 | At 2.1" | Ln 7 | Col 1 |

3. Type today's date, but stop typing when AutoComplete displays a yellow date tip as shown at the right.

   June 26, 1999

   June

   The example at the right uses the date June 26, 1999, but you should type today's date. Also, AutoComplete may not display the date tip. This is because AutoComplete may not be set up to automatically display tips.

4. If AutoComplete displays the date tip, then tap (ENTER) to complete the date. Otherwise, complete today's date by typing it.

   You can always accept an item that AutoComplete proposes by tapping (ENTER).

Complete the Inside Address

5. Tap (ENTER) four times.

   Business letters require four returns after the date.

6. Now type the following inside address and salutation.

   Only tap (ENTER) in the locations indicated. The Office Assistant may appear when you tap (ENTER) after typing the salutation. The Office Assistant will be discussed in a moment.

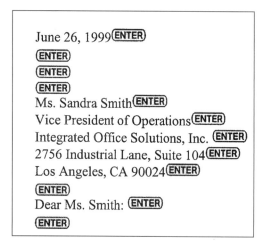

June 26, 1999(ENTER)
(ENTER)
(ENTER)
(ENTER)
Ms. Sandra Smith(ENTER)
Vice President of Operations(ENTER)
Integrated Office Solutions, Inc. (ENTER)
2756 Industrial Lane, Suite 104(ENTER)
Los Angeles, CA 90024(ENTER)
(ENTER)
Dear Ms. Smith: (ENTER)
(ENTER)

The Office Assistant

The Office Assistant is an interactive Help tool that monitors your activities and provides suggestions whenever it assumes you need assistance. The Office Assistant has a balloon window that pops up, allowing you to ask questions and get assistance.

TIP!

You can click anywhere in the document window to close the Office Assistant balloon.

7. If the Office Assistant balloon pops up as shown here, then click the **Cancel** button to close it.
You will work with the Office Assistant and online Help in the next lesson.

8. Now complete the letter as shown in the following illustration. Only tap ⒺⓃⓉⒺⓇ in the indicated locations. Use ⒷⒶⒸⓀⓈⓅⒶⒸⒺ to correct any typing mistakes. Word 2000 automatically checks spelling and grammar as you type. Word underlines misspelled words with wavy red underlines and grammar errors with wavy green underlines. For now, ignore any red or green underlining that may appear.

Dear Ms. Smith:

It was a pleasure meeting with you yesterday. Both Richard Brown and I were quite impressed with your facilities and the quality of your team. You certainly have a group of hard working people.(ENTER)
(ENTER)
Our meeting was designed to give you an overview of our copiers, laser printers, fax machines, and digital scanners. We would like to follow up our presentation with a live demonstration. You must see our products in action to truly appreciate their benefits. I will contact you early next week to arrange a demonstration.(ENTER)
(ENTER)
In the meantime, please feel free to contact us if we can be of further assistance.(ENTER)
(ENTER)
Sincerely,(ENTER)
(ENTER)
(ENTER)
(ENTER)
Susan Adams(ENTER)
Sales Representative

Save Concepts

One important lesson to learn is to save your documents frequently! Power outages and careless accidents can result in lost data. The best protection is to save your documents every 10 or 15 minutes, or after making significant changes. Documents are saved to storage locations such as floppy disks, hard disks, or to Web sites on the World Wide Web.

Save Command

From the Keyboard
(CTRL)+S for save

The Save 🖫 button on the Standard toolbar and the **File→Save** command initiate the Save command. If the document had previously been saved, then Word replaces the previous version with the new edited version. If the document had never been saved, then Word displays the **Save As** dialog box. The Save As dialog box has been significantly enhanced in Word 2000. The Save As dialog box lets you specify the name and storage location of the document. You can also use the Save As dialog box to make a copy of a document by saving it under a new name or to a different location. You can use filenames containing as many as 255 characters. The following illustration describes the Save As dialog box.

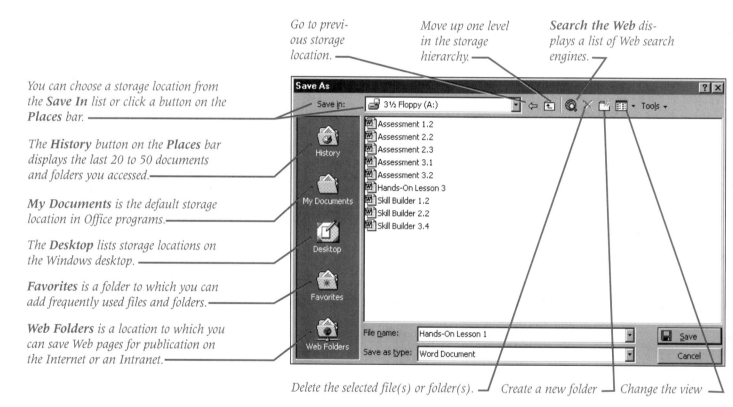

Go to previous storage location.

Move up one level in the storage hierarchy.

Search the Web *displays a list of Web search engines.*

*You can choose a storage location from the **Save In** list or click a button on the **Places** bar.*

*The **History** button on the **Places** bar displays the last 20 to 50 documents and folders you accessed.*

My Documents is the default storage location in Office programs.

*The **Desktop** lists storage locations on the Windows desktop.*

Favorites is a folder to which you can add frequently used files and folders.

Web Folders is a location to which you can save Web pages for publication on the Internet or an Intranet.

Delete the selected file(s) or folder(s).   *Create a new folder*   *Change the view*

 **Hands-On 1.3 Save the Letter**

In this exercise, you will save the letter that was created in the previous exercise. Your instructor will most likely want you to save your documents onto the exercise diskettes that are provided with this course. You will most likely be saving documents onto the A: disk drive.

1. Click the Save 🖫 button and the Save As dialog box will appear.

2. Follow these steps to save the letter.
   Keep in mind that your dialog box will contain more files than shown here.

Ⓐ *Click here and choose the disk drive with your exercise diskette. It is most likely 3½ Floppy (A:).*

Ⓑ *Notice that Word proposes the first part of the date as the name. Word always proposes the first line of text as the filename.*

Ⓒ *Type the name* **Hands-On Lesson 1** *and it will replace the proposed name. (If you switched disk drives, then you may need to click in the* **File name** *box, delete the proposed name with the (DELETE) and/or (BACKSPACE) key, then type the new name.)*

Ⓓ *Click the Save button.*

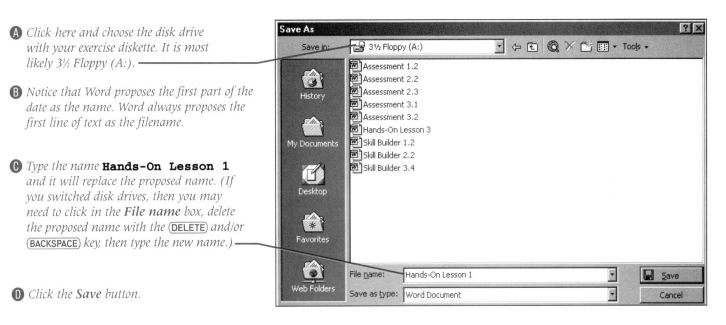

Notice that the letter was saved and remains on the screen. You will continue to use the letter throughout this lesson.

Scrolling Documents and Repositioning the Insertion Point

The vertical and horizontal **scroll bars** let you browse through documents. However, scrolling does not move the insertion point. You must click in the document to reposition the insertion point. The vertical scroll bar is on the right side of the document window and the horizontal scroll bar is at the bottom of the document window. Scroll bars also appear in many dialog boxes. The following illustration shows the scroll bars and their components.

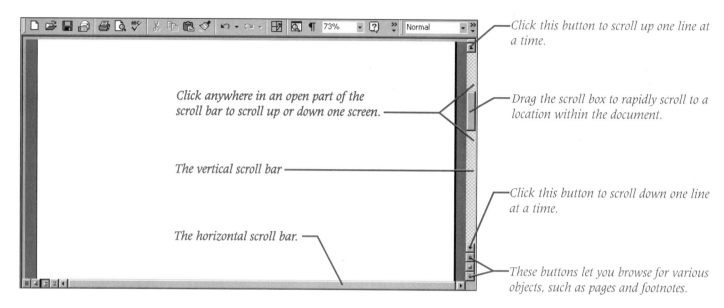

Click this button to scroll up one line at a time.

Click anywhere in an open part of the scroll bar to scroll up or down one screen.

Drag the scroll box to rapidly scroll to a location within the document.

The vertical scroll bar

Click this button to scroll down one line at a time.

The horizontal scroll bar.

These buttons let you browse for various objects, such as pages and footnotes.

 ## Hands-On 1.4 Practice Scrolling

1. Click the Scroll Down 🔽 button five times.
   Notice that the document scrolls down, but the insertion point does not move.

2. Click the Scroll Up 🔼 button until the date is visible at the top of the letter.

3. Slide the mouse; the pointer will have an I-Beam I shape when it is in the typing area.
   The pointer must have this I-Beam shape before the insertion point can be repositioned.

4. Click the I-Beam anywhere on the date, and the blinking insertion point will be positioned there.

5. Move the I-Beam into the left margin area, and it will become an arrow 🔄.
   This arrow should not be present if you are trying to reposition the insertion point.

6. Position the I-Beam on the first line of the inside address just in front of Ms., and click the left mouse button.
   The insertion point should be positioned just in front of Ms. If a black background appears behind the text, then you have accidentally selected it. Selecting is discussed later in this lesson. If you accidentally selected the text, then deselect it by clicking the mouse pointer outside of it.

7. Take a few minutes to practice scrolling and repositioning the insertion point.

Inserting and Overtyping Text

TIP!

You will almost always work in Insert mode.

Insert mode is the default editing mode in Word. In insert mode, existing text moves to the right as new text is typed. The new text is thus inserted into the document. Thus far, you have been working in insert mode. In **overtype mode,** existing text is replaced as new text is typed. You switch between insert mode and overtype mode by double-clicking the OVR (overtype) indicator on the status bar as shown in the following illustration.

*Double-clicking the **OVR** (overtype) indicator switches between insert mode and overtype mode. The mode is set to overtype when the **OVR** indicator is bold as shown here.*

Hands-On 1.5 Inserting and Overtyping Text

Insert Text

1. Click just in front of the word **yesterday** in the first body paragraph as shown below.

   —*Click here*

   It was a pleasure meeting with you yesterday.

2. Type the phrase **and the rest of your staff**, and tap the (SPACE BAR) once.

3. Use the technique in Steps 1 and 2 to insert the phrase **and creative** in front of the word **people** at the end of the paragraph. The completed paragraph is shown below.

   > It was a pleasure meeting with you and the rest of your staff yesterday. Both Richard Brown and I were quite impressed with your facilities and the quality of your team. You certainly have a group of hard working and creative people.

Overtype Text

4. Position the insertion point in the inside address in front of the S in Smith.

5. Double-click the **OVR** button on the status bar.
   The OVR button should now appear bold.

6. Type the word **Evans**, and Smith should be replaced by Evans.
   If insert mode had been active, the name Smith would have moved to the right, making room for Evans.

7. Now click in front of the name Smith in the salutation line, and type **Evans**.

8. Double-click the **OVR** button on the status bar when you have finished.
   The letters OVR will be dimmed on the status bar, indicating that insert mode is active.

9. Click the Save 🖫 button to save the changes to your exercise diskette.

Selecting Text

You must select text if you wish to perform some action on that text. Suppose you want to delete an entire paragraph. You would select the paragraph first and then tap the (DELETE) key. Selected text is usually displayed in white on a black background. The illustration to the right shows a selected paragraph in the inside address of your letter.

Ms. Sandra Evans
Vice President of Operations
Integrated Office Solutions, Inc.

Selection Techniques

Word provides many selection techniques using both the mouse and keyboard. The mouse techniques are usually more intuitive; however, beginners may find it difficult to control the mouse. The keyboard techniques tend to provide greater control. You can use the keyboard techniques if you have difficulty controlling the mouse. The following quick reference table illustrates the available selection techniques.

SELECTION TECHNIQUES

Item to be Selected	Mouse Technique	Keyboard Technique
One word	Double-click the desired word.	Click at beginning of word, press and hold (SHIFT) and (CTRL) while tapping →.
A phrase or continuous section of text	Drag the I-beam I in any direction over the desired text.	Click at beginning of phrase, press and hold (SHIFT) while tapping any arrow keys. You can also click at beginning of phrase, press and hold (SHIFT), and then click at end of phrase.
A line	Position the mouse pointer to the left of the line, and click when the pointer has an arrow shape.	Press (SHIFT) + (END) to select from insertion point to end of line. Press (SHIFT) + (HOME) to select from insertion point to beginning of line.
One paragraph	Triple-click anywhere on the paragraph. You can also position the mouse pointer to the left of the paragraph in the margin and double-click when the pointer has an arrow shape.	
Multiple paragraphs	Drag the I-beam I over the desired paragraphs. You can also position the mouse pointer to the left of the paragraphs and drag up or down when the pointer has an arrow shape.	
Entire document	Triple-click to the left of any paragraph, or press and hold (CTRL) and click to the left of any paragraph.	Press (CTRL) + A to execute Select All command, or press (CTRL) and click in left margin.

Select Using the Left Margin

1. Follow these steps to select text using the left margin.

Ⓐ *Place the mouse pointer to the left of this line and it will have this shape. Click the mouse button to select the entire line.*

> **Ms. Sandra Evans**
> Vice President of Operations
> Integrated Office Solutions, Inc.
> 2756 Industrial Lane, Suite 104
> **Los Angeles, CA 90024**

Ⓑ *Click here to select this line. Notice that the previously select-ed paragraph is no longer selected.*

> Dear Ms. Evans:

Ⓒ *Select this paragraph by double-clicking in front of it.*

> **It was a pleasure meeting with you and the rest of your staff yesterday. Both Richard Brown and I were quite impressed with your facilities and the quality of your team. You certainly have a group of hard working and creative people.**

2. Try dragging the mouse pointer down in the left margin.
   Be sure to press and hold the left mouse button as you drag, and multiple lines will be selected.

3. Try triple-clicking the mouse pointer anywhere in the left margin.
   The entire document will become selected. Triple clicking can be tricky, so you may need to try it several times. Also, you can select the entire document by pressing (CTRL) and clicking in the left margin.

4. Deselect the document by clicking anywhere on the selected text.

Select Words

5. Double-click the I-beam I on any word.
   The word should become selected.

6. Double-click a different word, and notice that the previous word has been deselected.

7. Select five different words one after another by double-clicking them.

8. Deselect the last word you selected by clicking the I-Beam I anywhere outside of it.

(Continued on the next page)

Drag Select

9. Follow these steps to drag select a phrase.

Ⓐ *Position the I-beam here just in front of* It was a pleasure . . .

Dear Ms. Evans:

I ▌It was a pleasure meeting with you▐ and the rest of your staff Brown and I were quite impressed with your facilities and th certainly have a group of hard working and creative people.

Ⓑ *Press and hold the left mouse button, then drag to the right until the phrase* It was a pleasure meeting with you *is selected.*

Ⓒ *Release the mouse button and the text will remain selected.*

TIP!

Use Undo if you accidentally move text.

10. Practice drag selecting text in the second large paragraph. Try dragging the mouse in all directions.
    Notice how the selection block expands and contracts as you move the mouse.

11. Deselect by clicking anywhere on the selected text.

12. Take two minutes to practice selecting text using the drag technique.

13. Take five minutes to practice selecting text using all of the techniques discussed in the table at the beginning of this topic. In particular, try using the keystroke techniques discussed in the Quick Reference Selection Techniques table.

Editing Text

From the Keyboard

(CTRL)+(BACKSPACE) to delete from insertion point to beginning of word.

(CTRL)+(DELETE) to delete from insertion point to end of word.

The (DELETE) and (BACKSPACE) keys are used to remove text from a document. (DELETE) removes the character to the right of the insertion point and (BACKSPACE) removes the character to the left of the insertion point. You can also remove an entire selection by tapping (DELETE) or (BACKSPACE). If you are removing just a few characters, it is usually more efficient to click in front of the characters and tap (DELETE) one or more times. If you are removing a word, phrase, or paragraph, it is more efficient to select the desired text and then tap (DELETE) to remove the selection.

You can replace text by selecting the desired text and then typing the replacement text. Selected text is removed as you begin typing replacement text. The replacement text is then inserted in the document as you continue to type.

Undo and Redo

From the Keyboard

(CTRL)+Z to undo
(CTRL)+Y to redo

Word's Undo [↶] button lets you reverse your last editing action(s). You can reverse simple actions such as accidental text deletions, or you can reverse more complex actions such as margin changes. Most actions can be undone. Actions that cannot be undone include commands such as printing documents and saving documents.

The Redo [↷] button reverses Undo. Use Redo when you Undo an action but decide to go through with that action after all.

Undoing and Redoing Multiple Actions

The arrows on the Undo and Redo buttons display lists of actions that can be undone or redone. You can undo or redo multiple actions by dragging the mouse over the desired actions. You can undo or redo an almost unlimited number of actions using this method. However, you must undo or redo actions in the order in which they appear on the drop-down list.

Repeat

The **Edit→Repeat** command lets you repeat your last action. For example, imagine you want to change the font size at several locations in a document. To accomplish this, you could change the font size at one location, reposition the insertion point, and then issue the Repeat command. The Repeat command would set the font size at the new location to the same size you set at the previous location. You can repeat an action as many times as desired. However, the Repeat command is only available when the Redo button is unavailable. The **Edit→Repeat** command changes to **Edit→Redo** as soon as you undo an action.

From the Keyboard
CTRL +Y to repeat.

Hands-On 1.7 Edit the Letter and Use Undo

Delete Several Words

1. Follow these steps to delete text from the inside address block.

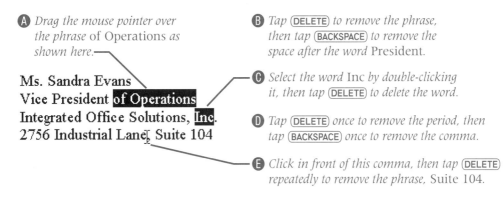

Ⓐ *Drag the mouse pointer over the phrase* of Operations *as shown here.*

Ⓑ *Tap* (DELETE) *to remove the phrase, then tap* (BACKSPACE) *to remove the space after the word* President.

Ⓒ *Select the word* Inc *by double-clicking it, then tap* (DELETE) *to delete the word.*

Ⓓ *Tap* (DELETE) *once to remove the period, then tap* (BACKSPACE) *once to remove the comma.*

Ⓔ *Click in front of this comma, then tap* (DELETE) *repeatedly to remove the phrase,* Suite 104.

Ms. Sandra Evans
Vice President of Operations
Integrated Office Solutions, Inc.
2756 Industrial Lane, Suite 104

Select and Replace Words

2. Follow these steps to select and replace several words and to insert a phrase.

Ⓐ *Double-click the last name* Brown *and type the replacement name* **Jones**.

Ⓑ *Double-click the word* meeting *and type the replacement word* **presentation**.

Ⓒ *Click in front of the word* copiers, *type the phrase* **high-performance**, *and tap* (SPACE BAR). *The new phrase should be inserted in front of the word* copiers.

It was a pleasure meeting with you and the rest of your staff yesterday. Brown and I were quite impressed with your facilities and the quality of certainly have a group of hard working and creative people.

Our meeting was designed to give you an overview of our copiers, laser machines, and digital scanners. We would like to follow up our present demonstration. You must see our products in action to truly appreciate will contact you early next week to arrange a demonstration.

In the meantime, please feel free to contact us if we can be of further as:

Ⓓ *Select the word* us *and type the replacement word* **me**.

Ⓔ *Replace* we *with* **I.**

(Continued on the next page)

TIP!

*To turn off Auto
capitalization,
choose
Tools→AutoCorrect
and uncheck the
Capitalize first
letter of sentences
box.*

Use Undo to Override AutoCorrect

AutoCorrect is a Word 2000 tool that automatically corrects many common spelling errors, and looks for other potential problems. One of these potential problems is the lack of capitalization at the start of a sentence. AutoCorrect will automatically capitalize the first letter of a sentence if you fail to capitalize it yourself. This is acceptable most of the time, but there are occasions when you may want to override AutoCorrect.

3. Scroll to the bottom of the document, and click to the right of the title Sales Representative in the signature block.

4. Tap (ENTER) twice.

5. Type your initials in lowercase, and then type a colon (**:**).
   AutoCorrect should spring into action, capitalizing your first initial. Unfortunately, typists initials should appear in lowercase in business correspondence.

6. Click Undo, 🔄 and the capital letter should return to lowercase.
   You can always use Undo to override AutoCorrect.

7. Tap (SPACE BAR), and type the document name **Hands-On Lesson 1**.
   The completed signature block should be xx: Hands-On Lesson 1, where xx are your initials.

8. Click Save 💾 to save the changes to your document.

IMPORTANT!

   It is important to save now because you will experiment with Undo and Redo in the remainder of this exercise.

Practice Using Undo and Redo

9. Delete any word in the letter.

10. Click Undo 🔄 and the word will be restored.

11. Select any paragraph, then tap (DELETE) to remove the paragraph.

12. Click Undo 🔄 to restore the paragraph.

13. Click Redo 🔁 and the paragraph will vanish again.
    Redo always reverses the most recent Undo.

14. Click Undo 🔄 again to restore the paragraph.

Undo and Redo Multiple Actions

15. Follow these steps to explore the Undo actions list, and to delete three items.

Ⓐ *Click the drop-down button next to **Undo**, and a list of all preceding actions will be displayed. Don't worry if your list does not match the list in this illustration.*

Ⓑ *Use the scroll bar to browse through the list of actions. Scroll to the top of the list when you are finished browsing and make a mental note of the first three or four actions on the list.*

Ⓒ *Tap the (ESC) key to close the list.*

Ⓓ *Select the month, and delete it.*

Ⓔ *Delete the word* Vice *from the title* Vice President.

Ⓕ *Select the street number 2756, and type the replacement number **2989**.*

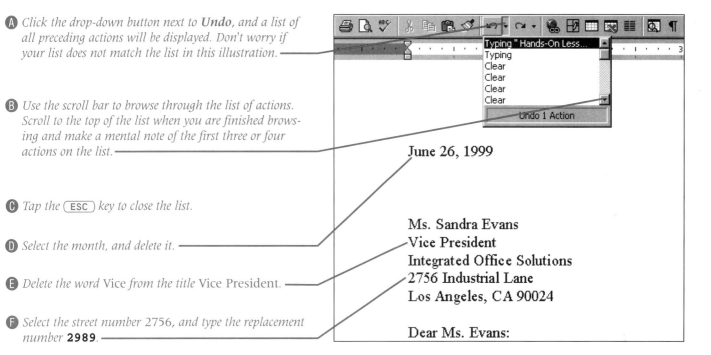

16. Follow these steps to undo the last three actions:

Ⓐ *Click the **Undo** drop-down button, and notice that there are three new actions at the top of the list. Your most recent action was typing the number 2989, so it appears on top of the list. Each action is given a descriptive name to help identify it.*

Ⓑ *Position the mouse pointer on the first action, Typing "2989," then slide the mouse down (there is no need to press the mouse button) highlighting the first three actions as shown here.*

Ⓒ *Click when the actions are selected, and all three actions will be undone. Your document should be exactly as it was prior to making the changes.*

17. Feel free to experiment with Undo and Redo.

Closing Documents

The **File→Close** command is used to close an open document. When you close a document, Word prompts you to save the changes. If you choose Yes at the prompt and the document had previously been saved, then Word saves the changes. If the document is new, Word displays the Save As dialog box, allowing you to assign a name and storage location to the document.

Hands-On 1.8 Close the Document

1. Choose **File→Close** from the menu bar.

2. Click the **No** button if Word asks you to save the changes.
   You can always close without saving to eliminate changes that have occurred since the last save. The next exercise will instruct you to open the letter. You will notice that the most recent changes have not been saved.

3. Finally, notice that there is no document in the document window.
   The document window always has this appearance when all documents have been closed.

Opening Documents

The Open 🖝 button on the Standard toolbar and the **File→Open** command display the Open dialog box. The Open dialog box lets you navigate to any storage location and open previously saved documents. Once a document is open, you can browse it, print it, or even make editing changes. The organization and layout of the Open dialog box is similar to the Save dialog box discussed earlier in this lesson.

From the Keyboard
(CTRL)+O to display open dialog box.

Hands-On 1.9 Open the Letter

1. Click Open 🗁 on the Standard toolbar.

2. Follow these steps to open the Hands-On Lesson 1 document.
   Keep in mind that your dialog box will contain more files than shown here.

Ⓐ *Choose the disk drive containing your exercise diskette. It is most likely in 3½ Floppy (A:).*

Ⓑ *Choose* Hands-On Lesson 1.

Ⓒ *Click the* **Open** *button.*

TIP!

You can also double-click a document on the list.

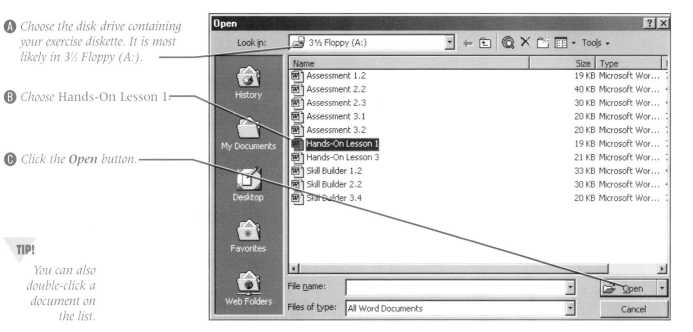

3. Take a few moments to scroll through the letter. Notice that the most recent changes were not saved (because you closed without saving).

Showing Nonprinting Characters

The Show All ¶ button on the Standard toolbar shows or hides all nonprinting characters in a document. Nonprinting characters include spaces, tab characters, and carriage returns that do not appear on the printed page. Showing these characters can be important, especially when editing a document. For example, you may need to display the nonprinting characters to determine whether the space between two words was created with (SPACE BAR) or (TAB). The following illustration shows the location of the Show All button and the characters that are inserted whenever (SPACE BAR) and (ENTER) are tapped.

From the Keyboard

(CTRL)+(SHIFT)+8 to show or hide characters

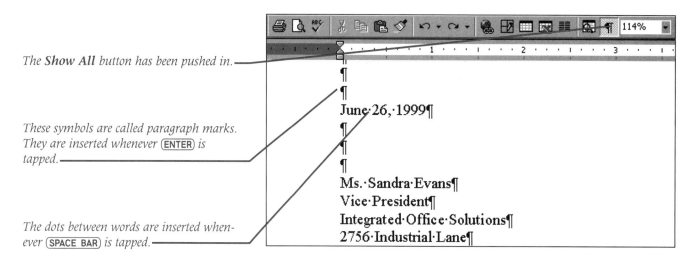

*The **Show All** button has been pushed in.*

These symbols are called paragraph marks. They are inserted whenever (ENTER) is tapped.

The dots between words are inserted whenever (SPACE BAR) is tapped.

Inserting and Deleting Paragraph Marks

Paragraph marks ¶ (or carriage returns) play an important role in Word documents. Every paragraph ends with a paragraph mark. A paragraph mark is inserted whenever (ENTER) is tapped. Paragraph marks affect the appearance and format of documents. You may need to delete paragraph marks as you edit and format documents. For example, suppose you want to combine two paragraphs into one large paragraph. To accomplish this, you would delete the paragraph mark separating the paragraphs. It is usually best to display the nonprinting characters with the Show All button before deleting paragraph marks and other nonprinting characters. You can delete the paragraph mark to the right of the insertion point using (DELETE). Likewise, the paragraph mark to the left of the insertion can be removed with (BACKSPACE).

Hands-On 1.10 Insert and Delete Paragraph Marks

In this exercise, you will restructure several paragraphs in the letter. Remember to use Undo if you make a mistake.

Combine Two Paragraphs

1. Click Show All ¶ to display the symbols.

2. Position the insertion point in front of the paragraph mark at the end of the second main paragraph as shown here.

presentation·with·a·live·demonstration.·You·must·see·our·products·in·action·to·truly·
appreciate·their·benefits.·I·will·contact·you·early·next·week·to·arrange·a·demonstration.|¶
¶
In·the·meantime,·please·feel·free·to·contact·me·if·I·can·be·of·further·assistance.¶

*⎯Position **insertion point** here.*

3. Tap (DELETE) once.
   The paragraph mark to the right of the insertion point will be deleted. The mark below the paragraph will immediately move up to take its place. Notice that the gap between the paragraphs is no longer a double space.

4. Tap (DELETE) again, and the paragraphs will be joined together.

5. Tap (SPACE BAR) once to create space between the two sentences in the combined paragraph.

Split the Combined Paragraph

6. Follow these steps to split the paragraph into two smaller paragraphs.

Our·presentation·was·designed·to·give·you·an·overview·of·our·high-performance·copiers,·
laser·printers,·fax·machines,·and·digital·scanners.·We·would·like·to·follow·up·our·
presentation·with·a·live·demonstration.·You·must·see·our·products·in·action·to·truly·
appreciate·their·benefits.·I·will·contact·you·early·next·week·to·arrange·a·demonstration.·In·
the·meantime,·please·feel·free·to·contact·me·if·I·can·be·of·further·assistance.¶

Ⓐ *Click here just in front of the word I.⎯*

Ⓑ *Tap (ENTER) twice to push the last two sentences down and to form a new paragraph.*

7. Click Show All ¶ to turn off the symbols.
   At this point, your letter should match the example shown in the case study at the start of this lesson (except for the date).

Inserting and Deleting Paragraph Marks   **25**

Print Preview

The Print Preview button and the **File→Print Preview** command display the Print Preview window, which shows how a document will look when it is printed. Print Preview can save time, paper, and wear-and-tear on your printer. Print Preview is especially useful when printing long documents, or with documents containing intricate graphics and formatting. It is always wise to preview a long or complex document before sending it to the printer.

When you display the Print Preview window, the standard toolbars are replaced by the Print Preview toolbar. The following illustration explains the important buttons on the Print Preview toolbar.

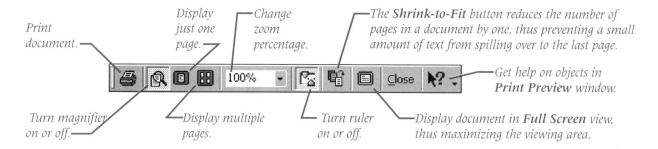

Hands-On 1.11 Use Print Preview

1. Click Print Preview on the Standard toolbar.

2. Make sure the Magnifier button is pushed in on the toolbar.

3. Position the mouse pointer over the document, and the pointer will look like a magnifying glass.

4. Zoom in by clicking anywhere on the document.

5. Zoom out by clicking anywhere on the document.
   You can zoom in and out whenever the magnifier is on. When the magnifier is off, the mouse pointer functions normally, allowing you to edit the document in Print Preview mode.

6. Feel free to experiment with the other buttons on the Print Preview toolbar.

7. When you have finished, click the **Close** button on the Print Preview toolbar to exit from Print Preview.

Printing

The Print button on the Standard toolbar sends the entire document to the current printer. You must display the Print dialog box if you want to change printers, specify the number of copies to be printed, print selected pages, and to set other printing options. The Print dialog box is displayed with the **File→Print** command. When you print a document, a printer icon appears on the status bar. The Printer icon indicates that Word is processing the print job and is preparing to send the job to the printer. The following illustration explains the most important options available in the Print dialog box.

From the Keyboard

CTRL+P to display
Print dialog box

You choose printers from this drop-down list.

You can specify the number of copies here. The Collate option is useful when you are printing more than one copy of a multiple page document. If the Collate box is checked, the first copy is printed before the second copy begins printing, etc.

You can choose to print all pages, the current page, or a range of pages. You specify a range of pages by typing the desired range in the Pages box. The example text below the Pages box shows the entry required to print pages 1, 3, and 5 through 12.

You can choose to print odd or even pages only with the Print option.

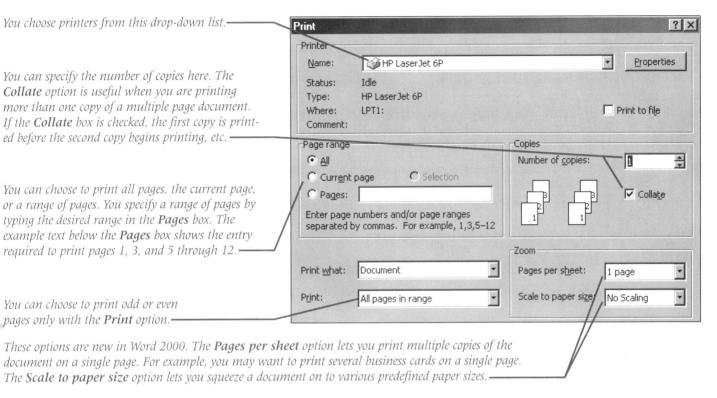

These options are new in Word 2000. The Pages per sheet option lets you print multiple copies of the document on a single page. For example, you may want to print several business cards on a single page. The Scale to paper size option lets you squeeze a document on to various predefined paper sizes.

Hands-On 1.12 Print the Document

1. Choose **File→Print** to display the Print dialog box.

2. Take a few moments to check out the dialog box options.

3. When you are ready to print, make sure the options are set as shown in the preceding illustration, and click the **OK** button.
   Keep in mind that your printer will probably be different than the printer shown in the Name box in the illustration.

4. Retrieve your document from the printer.

Canceling Print Jobs

Sometimes you will want to cancel a print job after issuing the Print command. When you print a document, Word processes the print job and sends it to the printer. Most modern printers contain memory where the Print job is stored while it is being printed. For this reason, it is not always possible to terminate a print job from Word or other Office programs. The difficult work of canceling the print job must often be done at the printer. This is especially true with newer computers. Newer computers are so fast that the print job is often sent to the printer before you have time to cancel it from within the application. The following quick reference steps can be used to effectively cancel print jobs. This sequence of steps is designed to save paper, prevent jamming of the printer, and effectively terminate the print job.

CANCELLING PRINT JOBS

■ Remove the paper stack from the printer, or remove the paper tray. You should be able to do this even if the printer is in the middle of printing a page.

■ Double-click the Printer icon on the status bar. This will terminate further processing of the job by Word. The Printer icon won't be visible if Word has finished processing the job.

■ If a page was being printed when you pulled out the paper tray, make sure it has finished printing.

■ Switch off the power on the printer. This will clear the job out of the printer's memory.

■ Pause 30 seconds and turn the printer back on.

■ Reinsert the paper stack or the paper tray.

▼ **WARNING!**

Turning off the printer may disrupt other users in a networked computer lab or office environment.

Exiting From Word

The **File→Exit** command is used to close the Word program. You should close Word and other programs if you are certain you won't be using them for some time. This will free up memory for other programs. When you close Word, you will be prompted to save any documents that have unsaved edits.

Hands-On 1.13 Exit from Word

1. Choose **File→Exit** from the menu bar.

2. Choose **Yes** when Word asks if you would like to save the changes.
   Word will close, and the Windows desktop will appear. Continue with the questions and exercises on the following pages.

Concepts Review

True/False Questions

1. The insertion point is automatically repositioned when you scroll through a document.   TRUE   FALSE

2. (ENTER) can be used to end one paragraph and begin another.   TRUE   FALSE

3. The Show All button is used to display nonprinting characters, such as paragraph marks.   TRUE   FALSE

4. The OVR button toggles Word between insert mode and overtype mode.   TRUE   FALSE

5. A single word can be selected by clicking once on the word.   TRUE   FALSE

6. Paragraph marks cannot be deleted once they have been inserted in a document.   TRUE   FALSE

7. (BACKSPACE) deletes the character to the right of the insertion point.   TRUE   FALSE

8. Overtype mode is the default editing mode in Word.   TRUE   FALSE

Multiple-Choice Questions

1. Which shape does the mouse pointer have when it is in the text area?
   a. Right-pointing arrow
   b. I-beam
   c. Left-pointing arrow
   d. None of the above

2. Which of the following methods can be used to select a paragraph?
   a. Double-click anywhere in the paragraph.
   b. Triple-click anywhere in the paragraph.
   c. Triple-click anywhere in the left margin.
   d. None of the above

3. What is happening if your existing text is disappearing as you type new text?
   a. You are in overtype mode.
   b. You are in insert mode.
   c. You are tapping (DELETE) by accident.
   d. None of the above

4. Which of the following statements is true?
   a. Undo is only available if Redo has been used.
   b. Redo is only available if Undo has been used.
   c. Both a and b
   d. Neither a nor b

Skill Builders

Skill Builder 1.1 Create a Block Style Letter

1. Start Word, and a new document window will appear. If you did not exit Word at the end of the last exercise, then click the New button on the Standard toolbar (first button on the toolbar). The New button is used to open a new document.

2. Type the following letter, tapping (ENTER) only as indicated. Notice the six hard returns shown at the top of the document. These hard returns position the date at approximately the 2″ position.

(ENTER)
(ENTER)
(ENTER)
(ENTER)
(ENTER)
(ENTER)
June 26, 1999(ENTER)
(ENTER)
(ENTER)
(ENTER)
Ms. Melissa Thompson(ENTER)
Customer Service Representative(ENTER)
Urbana Software Services(ENTER)
810 Ivanhoe Way(ENTER)
Urbana, IL 61801(ENTER)
(ENTER)
Dear Ms. Thompson:(ENTER)
(ENTER)
I would like to take this opportunity to thank you for your excellent customer service. You were patient, courteous, and very helpful. The installation assistance you provided was invaluable.(ENTER)
(ENTER)
I have already put your program to good use. As you know, application programs can boost personal productivity. Your program has allowed me to manage my business much more effectively. I have enclosed the $45 fee you requested.(ENTER)
(ENTER)
Please send me a receipt and a catalog.(ENTER)
(ENTER)
Sincerely,(ENTER)
(ENTER)
(ENTER)
(ENTER)
Denise Smith(ENTER)
Administrative Assistant(ENTER)

---

3. Use Show All ¶ to display the hidden characters.

4. Position the insertion point just in front of the sentence **I have enclosed the $45 . . .** in the second paragraph, and tap (ENTER) twice to create a new paragraph.

5. Position the insertion point at the end of the new paragraph just in front of the paragraph mark.

6. Tap (DELETE) twice to remove the two paragraph marks separating the new paragraph from the following paragraph.

7. Tap (SPACE BAR) once to insert a space between the two sentences in the combined paragraph.

8. Position the insertion point just to the right of the sentence **The installation assistance . . .** at the end of the first paragraph. The insertion point should be just to the right of the period ending the sentence.

9. Tap (SPACE BAR), and then type the sentence **I also appreciate the overnight delivery.**

10. Type **The program is also a lot of fun.** at the end of the second paragraph.

11. Insert your initials, below the signature block.

12. Save the document to your exercise diskette with the name **Skill Builder 1.1;** then close the document.

Skill Builder 1.2 Edit a Document

1. Click Open 📂 on the Standard toolbar.

2. Navigate to your exercise diskette, and double-click the file named **Skill Builder 1.2.**
   You will edit this document during this exercise. Notice that this document contains formatting that you have not yet learned about. For example, the title is centered and bold, and the paragraphs are formatted with double line spacing. This document is formatted like this because it is a report. You will learn about reports and formatting documents as you progress through this course.

(Continued on the next page)

3. Use these guidelines to make the editing changes shown in the following document.

- If only one or two characters require deletion, then position the insertion point in front of the character(s) and use (DELETE) to remove them.

- If one or more words require deletion, then select the text and use (DELETE) to remove the selected text.

- If a word or phrase needs to be replaced with another word or phrase, then select the desired text and type the replacement text.

- Use Undo ⟲ if you make mistakes.

4. When you have finished, **Save** the changes, and **Close** the document.

MAINE – THE PINE TREE STATE

Maine is recognized as one of the most ~~healthy~~ *healthful* states in the nation with temperatures averaging 70°F and winter temperatures averaging 20°F. It has 3,~~7~~500 miles of coastline, is about 320 miles long and 210 miles wide, with a total area of 33,215 square miles or about as big as all of the other five New England States combined. It comprises 16 counties with 22 cities, 424 towns, 51 plantations, and 416 unorganized townships. Aroostook county is so large (6,453 square miles) that it covers an area greater than the combined size of Connecticut *and* ^*Rhode Island*.

Maine abounds in natural assets—542,629 acres of state and national parks, including the 92-mile Allagash Wilderness Waterway, Acadia National Park (second most visited national park in the United States), and Baxter State Park (location of Mt. Katahdin and the northern end of the Appalachian Trail). Maine has one mountain ~~which~~ *that* is approximately one mile high—Mt. Katahdin (5,268 ft. above sea level) and also claims America's first chartered city: York, 1641.

Maine's blueberry crop is the largest ~~blueberry crop~~ in the nation—98% of the low-bush blueberries. Potatoes rank third in acreage and third in production nationally. Maine is nationally famed for its shellfish; over 46 million pounds of ~~shellfish~~ *lobster* were harvested *in the United States* in 1997. The total of all shellfish and fin fish harvested was approximately 237 million pounds with a total value of $273 million *in 1997* ~~during the 1997 fishing season.~~

Skill Builder 1.3 **Create a Modified Block Style Letter**

A modified block style letter has the same elements and similar formatting as a block style letter. However, the modified block style positions the date, complimentary close, and signature block near the center of the lines.

1. Click New ▣ to open a new document window.

2. Type the following modified block style letter. Start the letter approximately 2″ down from the top of the page. Tap ⟨ TAB ⟩ seven times to begin the date, complimentary close, and signature block just past the center of the lines. Finally, use the correct number of hard returns between the various paragraphs so that you have a properly formatted business letter.

3. When you have finished, save the document with the name **Skill Builder 1.3,** and then close the document.

Today's Date

Ms. Jessica Simms
811 Fairview Drive
Kansas City, MO 64106

Dear Ms. Simms:

I am pleased to inform you that you had excellent scores on all of your placement tests. You scored 98% on the word processing test, 97% on the spreadsheet test, and 99% on the office procedures test. These scores were far above average and are a testament to the quality of the vocational training program you recently completed.

I am pleased to offer you employment with Wilkinson Legal Services. Sarah Adams is looking forward to working with you should you decide to accept our offer.

I know you have several other job offers, and I hope you will give Wilkinson serious consideration. Sarah has already expressed an interest in having you train our staff members due to your excellent knowledge in Word and Excel. You will certainly have a bright future at Wilkinson.

Ms. Simms, please contact me soon. We look forward to having you as part of the Wilkinson team.

Sincerely,

Cynthia Lentz
Director, Human Resources

xx

Skill Builder 1.4 **Create a Personal Style Business Letter**

Personal business letters are used when an individual representing himself or herself sends a letter to a recipient in a business. Personal business letters can be composed using either the block or modified block style. Notice below that the return address is included in the signature block.

1. Start a new ⬜ document, space down 2″, and type the letter shown below.

2. When you have finished, save the document with the name **Skill Builder 1.4,** and then close the document.

Today's Date

Mr. Richard Johnson
Customer Service Manager
Colonial Credit Corporation
1000 Sherwood Place
East Brunswick, NJ 08816

Dear Mr. Johnson:

I have been with Colonial Credit for three years, and I have always paid my bills promptly. My annual income has also increased 30% in the past three years. For these reasons, I would like my credit limit raised to $3,000. The increase is necessary because I am traveling on business quite often.

Please respond as soon as possible. I appreciate your assistance.

Sincerely,

Jill Simms
2010 Washington Way
Racine, WI 53403

Assessments

Assessment 1.1 **Block Style Letter**

1. Create the block style business letter shown below. Space down the proper distance from the top of the page, and use proper spacing between paragraphs.

2. Save the letter to your exercise diskette with the name **Assessment 1.1.**

3. Print the letter, and then close the document.

Today's Date

Mrs. Suzanne Lee
8445 South Princeton Street
Chicago, IL 60628

Dear Mrs. Lee:

Thank you for your interest in the Back Bay Users Group. We will be holding an orientation for new members on the first Thursday in April at our headquarters.

Please let us know if you can attend by calling the phone number on this letterhead. Or, if you prefer, you may respond in writing or via email.

Sincerely,

Jack Bell
Membership Chair

xx

Assessment 1.2 Editing Skills

1. Open 📂 the document on your exercise diskette named **Assessment 1.2.**

2. Make the editing changes shown in the following document.

3. Use (ENTER) to push the entire document down so that the date is positioned at approximately the 2″ position.

4. Use (TAB) to move the date, complimentary close, and signature block to approximately the 3″ position on the ruler. This will convert the letter from block style to modified block style.

5. When you have finished, save the changes, print the letter, and close the document.

Today's Date

~~Ms. Cynthia Wilson~~ Mr. Roosevelt Jackson
~~118 Upper Terrace~~ 8 Spring street
~~Freehold, NJ 08845~~ Martinville, NJ 08836

Dear ~~Ms. Wilson~~:
    Mr. Jackson
                                          back
Thank you for your recent letter concerning back injuries in your office. Yes, ^injuries are a common problem for office workers today. It was estimated by the U. S. Bureau of Labor Statistics that in one year over ~~490~~,000 employees took time from work due to back injuries.
                                580

Encourage your office employees to make certain their work surface is at a ~~suitable~~ height. They should also be encouraged to take frequent breaks from their desks.   comfortable

Please
~~Feel free to~~ contact my office if you would like more information.

Sincerely,

Elaine Boudreau
Ergonomics Specialist

Assessment 1.3 Personal Style Business Letter

1. Create the personal style business letter shown below.

2. Save the letter to your exercise diskette with the name **Assessment 1.3.**

3. Print the letter, and then close the document.

Today's Date

Mr. Jake Wilson
Rebate Manager
Sierra Snowboards
4200 University Avenue
Berkeley, CA 94702

Dear Mr. Wilson:

Thank you for your excellent advice on the snowboarding equipment I recently
purchased. Sierra Snowboards certainly has the best equipment in the business.

I would like to know when I can expect the rebate on the board I purchased. I mailed in
my rebate coupon last month and I have yet to hear from the company. Do rebates
normally take this long? Please contact me as soon as possible at (510) 223-3344. Thank
you for your assistance.

Sincerely,

Melissa Jackson
1223 Appian Way
El Sobrante, CA 94803

Critical Thinking

Critical Thinking 1.1 On Your Own

Cathy Jacobson is an Administrative Assistant in the Marketing Department of Big Time Video Distributors. Big Time distributes videos to small video stores throughout the local area. Cathy works for Donald Livingston, the Director of Marketing. Donald and his marketing team have decided to offer promotional discounts to customers depending upon their sales volume in the previous quarter. The discounts are designed to encourage customers to order all of their videos from Big Time and to entice larger accounts to begin ordering from Big Time. Donald has instructed Cathy to prepare a letter to be sent to all Big Time customers.

Follow these guidelines to prepare a formal business letter announcing the promotional offer.

- Use the following generic text for the inside address.

   Name
   Company
   Address
   City, State Zip

- Let the customers know that the promotion will begin on the first day of the coming month. Use the date for the first day of the month following the preparation date of the letter.

- The discount schedule is shown below. You can describe the discount schedule in a paragraph, or you can lay it out as shown below using the ⎯TAB⎯ key to create a column effect.

Volume in Previous Quarter	Discount Percentage
$50,000	10%
$100,000	15%
$200,000	25%

- Inform the customers that in order to get the discount they must respond within 30 days by returning the enclosed card. Your letter should include an enclosure notation indicating that there is an enclosure.

Save your completed letter as **Critical Thinking 1.1.**

Critical Thinking 1.2 On Your Own

Compose a personal business letter to Donna Wilson, the Loan Manager of Citizen's Bank. The address of Citizen's bank is 12300 West Washington Avenue, Los Angeles, CA 90024. The purpose of the letter is to thank Donna for approving your $15,000 automobile loan. Donna worked hard to secure the best interest rate and terms for your loan, so you should let her know just how much you appreciate her excellent service. Save your completed letter as **Critical Thinking 1.2,** and then close it.

Critical Thinking 1.3 On Your Own

Open the Critical Thinking 1.2 letter that you composed in the previous exercise. Insert a new paragraph requesting that Donna send you information on Citizen Bank's new Small Business Credit Line program. Let Donna know that you are starting a new business venture (you choose the venture), and you are interested in obtaining financing from the bank. Save the completed letter as **Critical Thinking 1.3.**

Critical Thinking 1.4 Web Research

George Wilson is a certified financial planner and the owner of PlanRight Retirement Services. George sends correspondence to his clientele quite often and he usually includes one or more helpful hints on ways they can save money. Use Internet Explorer and a search engine of your choice to locate the Web site URLs of American Airlines, United Airlines, and Southwest Airlines. Compose a letter from George to his clientele letting them know that their 2000 tax packages are ready and available for pickup or mailing. In addition, include a paragraph describing the savings that can be realized by booking airline reservations through the Web sites of United, American, and Southwest airlines. Include the Web site URLs so that George's customers can visit the sites. Use the same generic text for the inside address that you used in Critical Thinking 1.1. Save your completed letter as **Critical Thinking 1.4.**

Critical Thinking 1.5 With a Group

Choose a classmate whom you will work with on the With a Group critical thinking exercises throughout this course. You and your classmate have started a new Web-based business named Health-e-Meals.com. Health-e-Meals.com delivers healthy, nutritious meals directly to homes, businesses, and school lunch programs. Together, compose a business letter to Donna Wilson at Citizen's Bank using the address information for Donna from Critical Thinking 1.2. Let Donna know that you are interested in establishing a $100,000 credit line with the bank and that you would like to schedule an appointment to meet with her. You compose a short paragraph describing the clientele and the product/service you are offering. Have your classmate compose a paragraph describing the current monthly sales, expenses, and growth rate of the company. Save your completed letter as **Critical Thinking 1.5.**

LESSON 2

Creating a Memorandum and Press Release

In this lesson, you will expand upon the basic skills you developed in the previous lesson. You will create a two-page document that uses a page break to separate the pages. Paragraph formatting is an important technique in Word. This lesson introduces paragraph formatting and paragraph alignment techniques. You will learn how to apply various text formats, and you will use Cut, Copy, and Paste to rearrange text and paragraphs. Word has powerful editing tools that go beyond the traditional Cut, Copy, and Paste tools. This lesson introduces three of those tools: the new Office Clipboard, the Spike, and document scraps. Finally, you will unleash the power of Word's Format Painter—a powerful tool that is used to rapidly format text and ensure formatting consistency throughout a document.

In This Lesson

Case Study

Lashanda Robertson is the Public Affairs Representative for Flexico, Inc., a fabrics manufacturer specializing in materials for active wear. Image and public perception are important determinants of success in the high-profile world of fashion design. Flexico is a progressive company that understands the importance of image. As the Public Affairs Representative for Flexico, Lashanda's responsibilities include issuing press releases to inform clothing manufacturers and other potential customers of forthcoming fabrics and materials. Lashanda creates a memorandum to which she attaches her latest press release announcing the new FlexMax line of fabrics for active wear. Memorandums are used for internal communication within a company or organization, whereas business letters are used for external communication. A sample of the memorandum and press release are shown below.

MEMO TO: Bill Watson

FROM: Lashanda Robertson

DATE: April 25, 1999

SUBJECT: Flexico® Press Release

I have attached a press release to announce the launch of our new FlexMax™ line of fabrics. Please review the press release and let me know if you have comments or suggestions. I will submit this press release to the media organizations next week.

xx
Attachment

Flexico,® Inc.

Press Release

Flexico Announces FlexMax™ Fabric

Announcement
San Francisco, Ca.—July 10, 1999—Flexico, Inc. today announced the FlexMax fabric for active wear. This revolutionary fabric is designed by Flexico and allows for maximum range of motion while providing support, comfort, and moisture protection. Flexmax fabric is ideally suited for active wear such as biking, hiking, and aerobics attire.

Delivery and Availability
FlexMax products are expected to reach retailers shelves by the third quarter of this year. Look for the distinctive Flexico logo and the FlexMax trademark. FlexMax products will be available at most quality sporting goods stores.

FlexMax Styles
Initially, FlexMax fabric will be available in two weights and a variety of colors. Contact Flexico or your distributor for information and samples.

About Flexico
Founded in 1988, Flexico is a leading manufacturer of fabrics for active wear and outdoor activities. Flexico fabrics are used in fine active wear products worldwide.

Memorandum Styles

There are a variety of acceptable memorandum styles in use today. All memorandum styles contain the same elements but with varied formatting. Many new formats have emerged since the widespread use of computer and word processing technology. The style illustrated below is a traditional memorandum style with minimal formatting.

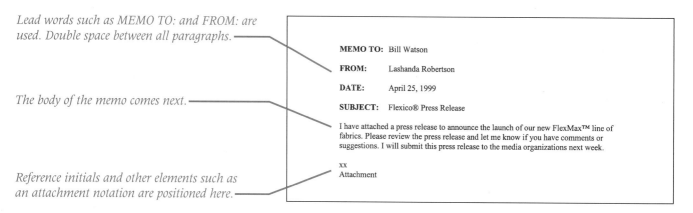

Lead words such as MEMO TO: and FROM: are used. Double space between all paragraphs.

The body of the memo comes next.

Reference initials and other elements such as an attachment notation are positioned here.

MEMO TO: Bill Watson

FROM: Lashanda Robertson

DATE: April 25, 1999

SUBJECT: Flexico® Press Release

I have attached a press release to announce the launch of our new FlexMax™ line of fabrics. Please review the press release and let me know if you have comments or suggestions. I will submit this press release to the media organizations next week.

xx
Attachment

Adaptive Menus

Word's menus now consist of a short section containing the commands you use most frequently and an expanded section containing commands that are rarely used. These adaptive menus reduce the number of commands on the main (short) menu, thereby reducing screen clutter. The following illustrations outline the adaptive menus in Word 2000.

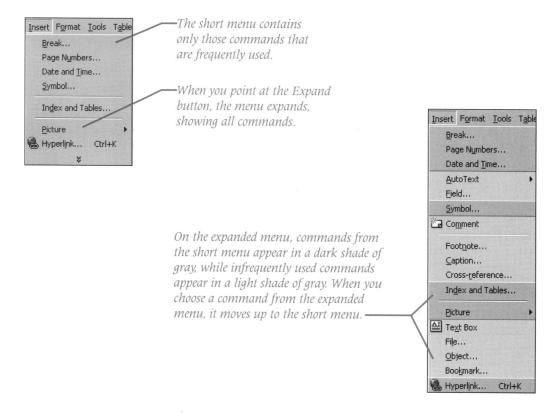

The short menu contains only those commands that are frequently used.

When you point at the Expand button, the menu expands, showing all commands.

On the expanded menu, commands from the short menu appear in a dark shade of gray, while infrequently used commands appear in a light shade of gray. When you choose a command from the expanded menu, it moves up to the short menu.

Working with Toolbars

In Word 2000, the Standard toolbar and Formatting toolbar are placed side by side on a single row just below the menu bar. This is a change from earlier versions of Word, where the Formatting toolbar was positioned below the Standard toolbar. In addition to the Standard toolbar and Formatting toolbar, Word has approximately 20 additional toolbars that are used with various program features.

Adaptive Toolbars

Like adaptive menus, adaptive toolbars may change depending upon how you use Word. Buttons may automatically be added to or removed from these toolbars. The right end of each Word toolbar now contains a button named More Buttons. You use this button to display buttons not currently visible on the toolbar and to add or remove buttons from a toolbar. The following illustration uses the Formatting toolbar to discuss adaptive toolbars in Word 2000.

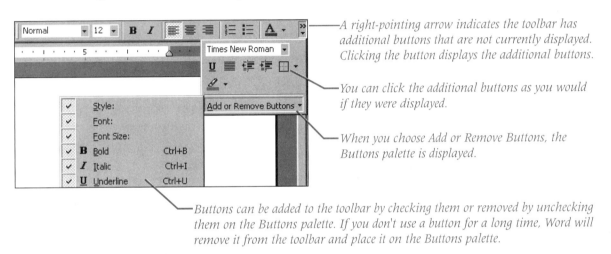

A right-pointing arrow indicates the toolbar has additional buttons that are not currently displayed. Clicking the button displays the additional buttons.

You can click the additional buttons as you would if they were displayed.

When you choose Add or Remove Buttons, the Buttons palette is displayed.

Buttons can be added to the toolbar by checking them or removed by unchecking them on the Buttons palette. If you don't use a button for a long time, Word will remove it from the toolbar and place it on the Buttons palette.

Displaying and Hiding Toolbars

You can display and hide toolbars by choosing **View→Toolbars** from the menu bar and checking or unchecking the desired toolbars. You can also display or hide toolbars by right-clicking any toolbar on the screen and checking or unchecking the desired toolbar.

Moving Toolbars

You can move a toolbar to any screen location. For example, many users prefer to move the Formatting toolbar below the Standard toolbar as in previous versions of Word. You move toolbars by dragging the Move handle located on the left end of the toolbar.

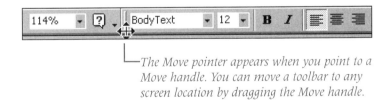

The Move pointer appears when you point to a Move handle. You can move a toolbar to any screen location by dragging the Move handle.

Displaying the Formatting Toolbar on a Separate Row

Dragging the Formatting toolbar below the Standard toolbar can be tricky. Fortunately, Word provides an easier way to display the Standard and Formatting toolbars on separate rows.

 Hands-On 2.1 Display the Formatting Toolbar on a Separate Row

 From this point forward, the instructions in this text will assume the Standard and Formatting toolbars are displayed on separate rows. This will make it easier for you to locate buttons when instructed to do so.

1. Start Word, and choose **View→Toolbars→Customize** from the menu bar.

2. Click the Options tab in the Customize dialog box.

3. Uncheck the **Standard and Formatting toolbars share one row** checkbox.

4. Click the **Close** button, and the Formatting toolbar should be positioned below the Standard toolbar.

Inserting the Date and Time

From the Keyboard

ALT +SHIFT+D to insert date

ALT +SHIFT+T to insert time

Word lets you insert the current date and time using a variety of formats. For example, the date could be inserted as 4/25/99, April 25, 1999 or 25 April 1999. You insert the date and time with the **Insert→Date and Time** command.

Update Automatically Option

You can insert the date and time as **text** or as a **field.** Inserting the date as text has the same effect as typing the date into a document. Fields, however, are updated whenever a document is opened or printed. For example, imagine you created a document on April 25, 1999, and you inserted the date as a field. If you had opened the document the next day, then the date would have automatically been updated to April 26, 1999. The date and time are inserted as fields whenever the Update Automatically box is checked, as shown to the right.

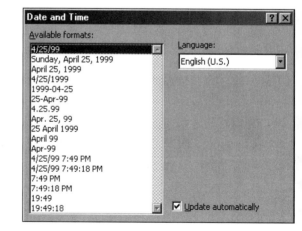

When to Use the Update Automatically Option

Maintaining the original date in a document may be important. For example, the date is important in documents such as business letters and legal agreements. If you insert the date in such documents using the Update Automatically option, then you will lose the original date the next time you open the document.

TIP!

To find the original date that a document was created, right-click the document in My Computer or Windows Explorer, choose Properties, and click the General tab.

Hands-On 2.2 Set Up the Memo and Insert the Date

Set Up the Memo

1. Use (ENTER) to space down to approximately the 2″ position.
   Memorandums generally begin 2″ down from the top of the page.

2. Type **MEMO TO:** and tap the (TAB) key.

3. Type **Bill Watson,** and tap (ENTER) twice.

4. Type **FROM:** and tap the (TAB) key.

5. Type **Lashanda Robertson,** and tap (ENTER) twice.

6. Type **DATE:** and tap the (TAB) key **twice.**
   It was necessary to tap (TAB) twice to align the date with the names. The first tab aligned the insertion point with the ½″ mark on the ruler (located just above the document). The second tab aligned the insertion point with the 1″ position on the ruler.

Insert the Date

TIP!

If the date and time are not accurate on your computer, double-click the clock on the right end of the Taskbar, set the correct date and time, and click OK.

7. Choose **Insert→Date and Time** from the menu bar.

8. Make sure the Update Automatically box is checked at the bottom of the dialog box.
   This option instructs Word to insert the date as a field. Once again, be careful when using this option. It is being used in this memorandum for instructional purposes only. You may want to avoid using this feature in business correspondence.

9. Choose the third date format on the list, and click OK.
   Notice that the date appears to be in a shaded box. The shaded box indicates that the date has been inserted as a field.

(Continued on the next page)

10. Complete the remainder of the memorandum as shown in the following illustration.
    Make sure you double-space after the date line, the subject line, and after the main paragraph. Also, use TAB *to line up the phrase Flexico Press Release after the SUBJECT: lead word.*

MEMO TO: Bill Watson

FROM: Lashanda Robertson

DATE: April 25, 1999

SUBJECT: Flexico Press Release

I have attached a press release to announce the launch of our new FlexMax line of fabrics. Please review the press release and let me know if you have comments or suggestions. I will submit this press release to the media organizations next week.

xx
Attachment

---

11. Click the Save button, and save the memorandum as **Hands-On Lesson 2**.
    You will continue to enhance the memorandum throughout this lesson.

Inserting Symbols

Word lets you insert a variety of symbols, typographic characters, and international characters not found on the keyboard. Most symbols are inserted by using the **Insert→Symbol** command and choosing the desired symbols from the Symbol dialog box. You can also use keystrokes to insert common typographic symbols such as the Registered ® symbol and some international characters. The following illustration shows the organization of the Symbol dialog box.

The special characters tab contains commonly used characters such as the Registered ® symbol, and various English language symbols.

There are several symbol fonts from which you can choose. Each font displays different symbols in the dialog box. Some fonts, such as Windings, contain interesting symbols.

Hands-On 2.3 Insert Symbols

1. Position the insertion point to the right of the word Flexico on the SUBJECT: line.
   You will insert a Registered Trademark ® symbol in the next few steps. A registered trademark gives a company the exclusive right to use a trademark (Flexico in this case) nationwide.

2. Choose **Insert→Symbol** from the menu bar.

3. Click the Special Characters tab.

4. Choose the Registered symbol, and click the Insert button.
   Notice that the Registered ® symbol appears in your document, and the Symbol dialog box remains open. Word leaves the dialog box open in case you wish to insert additional symbols.

5. Click the insertion point to the right of the word FlexMax in the main paragraph (you may need to drag the dialog box out of the way in order to see the word).

6. Insert the Trademark ™ symbol.
   The Trademark symbol indicates that a company claims a phrase or icon as their trademark, but they have not received federal protection (indicated by the Registered ® symbol).

(Continued on the next page)

7. Click the Symbols tab on the Symbol dialog box.

8. Click any symbol, and it will be magnified.

9. Try choosing a different font from the Font list, and you will see a new set of symbols.

10. When you have finished experimenting, click the Close button to close the dialog box.

11. Click the Save button to save the changes.

Views

Word lets you view documents in several ways. Each view is optimized for specific types of work, thus allowing you to work efficiently. The views change the way documents appear onscreen but have no impact on the appearance of printed documents. You can choose the desired view from the View menu or from the View bar at the left end of the horizontal scroll bar as shown to the right. The following table outlines the views available in Word 2000.

VIEWS	
View	**Description**
Print Layout	Print Layout is the default view in Word 2000. In Print Layout, documents look almost exactly as they will when printed. Print Layout is the most versatile view, allowing you to see text, graphics, headers and footers, and other types of objects. You will probably use Print Layout view most of the time.
Normal	Normal view simplifies page layout by eliminating page numbers, page breaks, and a few other elements from the view. Normal view can be useful if you want to concentrate on the text in your document. Normal view may also speed up scrolling and other tasks, especially if you have an older computer or large documents with many graphics.
Web Layout	Web Layout displays your document, as it would look on a Web page. Text, graphics, and background patterns are visible. The document is displayed on one long page without page breaks.
Outline	Outline view is useful for organizing documents.

Hands-On 2.4 Experiment with Views

1. Locate the Views  bar on the left end of the horizontal scroll bar.

2. Position the insertion point over each button, and a descriptive ScreenTip will pop up.

3. Click each button to see how the appearance of the document changes.
   You may not notice much of a difference because your document lacks graphics and other more advanced elements.

4. Switch to Print Layout view when you have finished experimenting.

Zooming

The Zoom Control lets you "zoom in" to get a close-up view of a document or "zoom out" to see the "big picture." Zooming changes the size of onscreen text and graphics but has no affect on printed text and graphics. You can zoom from 10% to 500%.

You can type a zoom percentage in the Zoom box and tap Enter, or . . .

. . . you can click the drop-down button . . . and choose an option from the list.

Notice how large the onscreen text appears; however, it will print in the normal size.

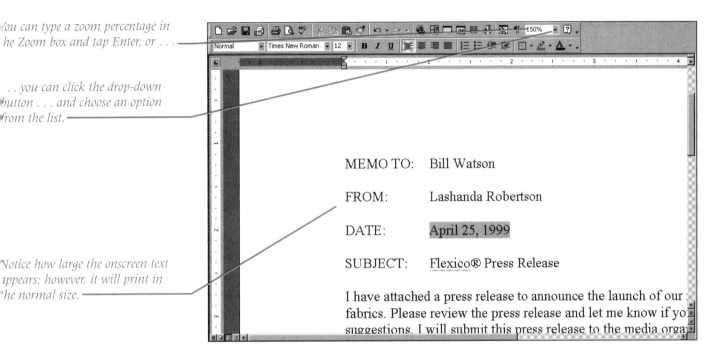

MEMO TO: Bill Watson

FROM: Lashanda Robertson

DATE: April 25, 1999

SUBJECT: Flexico® Press Release

I have attached a press release to announce the launch of our fabrics. Please review the press release and let me know if yo suggestions. I will submit this press release to the media orga

Hands-On 2.5 Use the Zoom Control

1. Follow these steps to experiment with the zoom control.

Ⓐ *Click in this box, type* **123***, and then tap* (ENTER)*. You can zoom to any percentage between 10 and 500.*

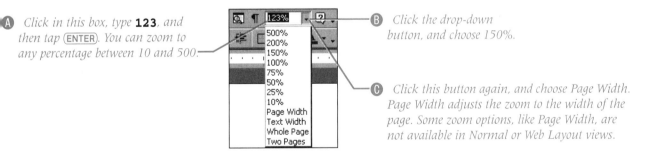

500%
200%
150%
100%
75%
50%
25%
10%
Page Width
Text Width
Whole Page
Two Pages

Ⓑ *Click the drop-down button, and choose 150%.*

Ⓒ *Click this button again, and choose Page Width. Page Width adjusts the zoom to the width of the page. Some zoom options, like Page Width, are not available in Normal or Web Layout views.*

2. Use the zoom control to select the following three zoom settings: Whole Page, 75%, and Page Width. Feel free to experiment with the zoom control.

Page Breaks

If you are typing text and the insertion point reaches the bottom of a page, Word automatically breaks the page and begins a new page. This is known as an **automatic page break.** The location of automatic page breaks may change as text is added to or deleted from a document. Automatic page breaks are convenient when working with long documents that have continuously flowing text. For example, imagine you were writing a novel, and you decided to insert a new paragraph in the middle of a chapter. With automatic page breaks, you could insert the paragraph, and Word would automatically repaginate the entire chapter.

From the Keyboard
(CTRL)+(ENTER) to insert page break

You can force a page break to occur at any location in a document by inserting a **manual page break.** A manual page break remains in place unless you remove the break. You insert manual page breaks whenever you want to control the starting point of a new page. You can insert a manual page break with the **Insert→Break** command.

Removing Manual Page Breaks

In Normal view, manual page breaks appear as a horizontal line with the phrase Page Break appearing on the line. The page break line also appears in Print Layout view if you click the Show All button. You can remove a manual page break by positioning the insertion point on the page break line and tapping (DELETE), as shown in the following illustration.

You can remove a manual page break by showing the nonprinting characters, clicking on the Page Break line, and tapping (DELETE).

> I·have·attached·a·press·release·to·announce·the·launch·of·our·new
> fabrics.·Please·review·the·press·release·and·let·me·know·if·you·ha
> suggestions.·I·will·submit·this·press·release·to·the·media·organiza
> ¶
> xx:Hands-On·Lesson·2¶
> Attachment¶
> --Page Break--

 ## Hands-On 2.6 Page Breaks

Insert a Page Break

1. Make sure you are in Print Layout view.

2. Position the insertion point to the right of the word *Attachment* on the attachment line.

3. Choose **Insert→Break** from the menu bar. If the Break option is not on the menu, you will need to click the Expand button at the bottom of the Insert menu, and then choose Break. *Notice that several types of breaks are listed on the Breaks menu. This lesson only introduces page breaks.*

4. Make sure **Page break** is chosen, and click **OK.** *You should be able to see the bottom portion of page 1 and the top of page 2.*

5. Look at the Status bar at the bottom of the screen; it will show the insertion point is on Page 2.

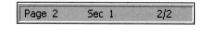

TIP!

You can remove a break without showing the nonprinting characters. However, this takes a little practice.

Remove the Page Break

6. Scroll up until the attachment line is visible.

7. Click the Show All ¶ button, and a Page Break line will appear.

8. Click on the Page Break line, and tap (DELETE).

9. Try scrolling down to the second page, and you will see that it has been removed.

Reinsert the Break

10. Scroll up, and the insertion point should be just below the attachment line.

11. Press (CTRL)+(ENTER) to reinsert the page break.
    This shortcut keystroke is useful to remember because page breaks are inserted often.

12. Click Show All ¶ to hide the nonprinting characters.
    The insertion point should be positioned at the top of the second page.

Paragraph Concepts

The word paragraph has a special meaning in Word. A paragraph includes any text, graphics, or objects followed by a paragraph mark. Word lets you format paragraphs in a variety of ways. For example, you can change paragraph alignment, add bullets and numbering to paragraphs, and indent paragraphs.

A paragraph mark

You can click anywhere in a paragraph and apply the desired formats. When you tap (ENTER), the formats from the current paragraph are applied to the new paragraph. For example, if a heading is centered and you tap (ENTER), then the new paragraph will also be centered. You can format several paragraphs by first selecting the desired paragraphs and then applying the formats.

Aligning Text

The alignment buttons on the Formatting toolbar allow you to align paragraphs horizontally. Text can be left or right-aligned, centered, or justified. The alignment commands affect all text in a paragraph. To mix alignments within a line, you must use customized tab stops or tables.

From the Keyboard

(CTRL)+L Align Left
(CTRL)+E for Center
(CTRL)+R for Align Right
(CTRL)+J for Justify

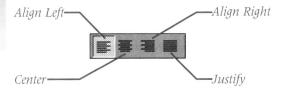

Align Left ——— *Align Right*

Center ——— *Justify*

In this exercise, you will set up a press release. A press release is a type of announcement, so you will begin the first line 2" down from the top of the page.

Set Up the Title Lines

1. Make sure the insertion point is at the top of the new page, and tap (ENTER) several times to space down to approximately the 2" position.

2. Locate the alignment buttons on the Formatting toolbar, and notice that the Align Left button is pushed in.
    Left alignment is the default setting in Word.

3. Click the Center button.
    The insertion point moves to the center of the line.

4. Type the title **Flexico Announces FlexMax™ Fabric**, inserting the Trademark symbol as shown.

5. Tap (ENTER) twice, and notice that the center alignment is still in effect.
    Paragraph formats (including alignments) are copied to the next paragraph when (ENTER) is tapped.

6. Type **Press Release**, and tap (ENTER) twice.

7. Type **Flexico,® Inc.** inserting the Registered symbol as shown.

8. Tap (ENTER) twice; then click Align Left to restore left alignment.
    You are now ready to set up the body of the press release.

Set Up the Body

9. Type the heading **Announcement**, and tap (ENTER).

10. Type the phrase **San Francisco, Ca**.
    In the next step, you will insert an em dash. Em dashes are used as connectors within sentences and are available on the Symbols dialog box.

From the Keyboard

Type two hyphens with no spaces before or after hyphens. Word will convert hyphens to em dash when (SPACE BAR) is tapped after typing second connector word.

11. Display the Symbols dialog box, choose Em Dash from the Special Characters tab, and click Insert.

12. If necessary, move the Symbol dialog box out of the way, and click in the document to the right of the em dash.

13. Type **Today's Date**, and insert another em dash.

14. Close the Symbol dialog box, and complete the press release as shown below.

Flexico Announces FlexMax™ Fabric

Press Release

Flexico,® Inc.

Announcement
San Francisco, Ca.—April 25, 1999—Flexico, Inc. today announced the FlexMax fabric for active wear. Flexmax fabric is ideally suited for active wear such as biking, hiking, and aerobics attire. This revolutionary fabric is designed by Flexico and allows for maximum range of motion while providing support, comfort, and moisture protection.

About Flexico
Founded in 1988, Flexico is a leading manufacturer of fabrics for active wear and outdoor activities. Flexico fabrics are used in fine active wear products worldwide.

FlexMax Styles
Initially, FlexMax fabric will be available in two weights and a variety of colors. Contact Flexico or your distributor for information and samples.

Delivery and Availability
FlexMax products are expected to reach retailers shelves by the third quarter of this year. Look for the distinctive Flexico logo and the FlexMax trademark. FlexMax products will be available at most quality sporting goods stores.

---

15. Save ▣ the changes, and continue with the next topic.

Formatting Text

From the Keyboard

CTRL+B for Bold
CTRL+U for Underline
CTRL+I for Italics
CTRL+] to increase
size one point
CTRL+[to decrease
size one point

In Word and other Office programs, you can format text by changing the font, font size, and color. You can also apply various font formats including bold, italics, and underline. If no text is selected, the format settings take effect from that point forward or until you change them again. If you wish to format existing text, you must select the text and then apply the desired formats. You can format text with buttons on the Formatting toolbar, as shown in the following illustration.

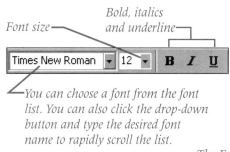

Font size

Bold, italics and underline

You can choose a font from the font list. You can also click the drop-down button and type the desired font name to rapidly scroll the list.

The Font Color button is on the right end of the Formatting toolbar. The color palette appears when you click the drop-down button. Once you choose a color, the color is displayed on the button. From that point forward, you can rapidly apply the color by clicking the button.

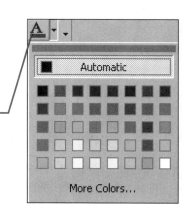

Character Effects and Animation

The **Format→Font** command displays the Font dialog box. Any text formats that can be applied with the Formatting toolbar can also be applied using the Font dialog box. In addition, the font dialog box lets you apply underlining options, character effects (such as superscript and strikethrough), and animation. The Font dialog box also provides a Preview window that lets you preview the formatted text before it is applied. The Preview window is helpful if you want to experiment with various font and effect combinations.

Format the Press Release Title Lines

1. Follow this step to select the press release title lines.

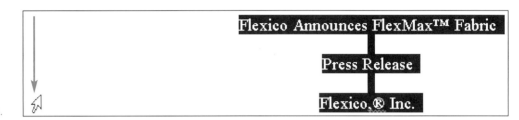

Ⓐ *Position the mouse pointer in the left margin, and drag down.*

2. Follow these steps to format the title lines.

Ⓐ *Click this button to drop down the font list.*

Ⓑ *Notice this dividing line. The names of recently used fonts are placed above the dividing line at the top of the menu. This makes it easy to choose the fonts you use most often.*

Ⓒ *If necessary, scroll down the list, and choose Arial.*

Ⓓ *Click the Font Size button, and choose 14.*

Ⓔ *Click the Bold button to apply bold.*

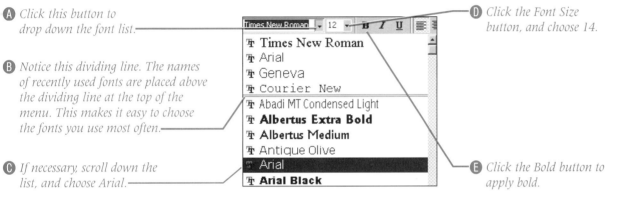

3. Click the drop-down button on the Font Color 🅰️▾ button (on the right end of the Formatting toolbar), and choose your favorite color.

Use Keystrokes to Select and Format

The following steps show you how to select using the keyboard. In some situations, keyboard selecting can give you greater precision and control.

4. Scroll up to the first page of the document to view the memorandum.

5. Follow these steps to select the phrase MEMO TO:

Ⓐ *Click just in front of the word MEMO when the mouse pointer has an I-beam shape as shown here.*

Ⓑ *Press and hold the (SHIFT) key, and tap the → key until the phrase MEMO TO: is selected as shown here.*

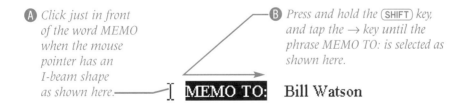

6. Press (CTRL)+B to apply bold to the phrase.

7. Use the techniques in the previous two steps to apply bold to the next lead word, **FROM:**.

(Continued on the next page)

8. Now apply bold to the lead word **DATE:**. You should see the date move one tab stop to the right, thus throwing off the alignment.

    This occurred because the bold format increased the size of the lead word DATE:. The increased size pushed the lead word past the tab stop at the ½" position on the ruler. This in turn pushed the date past the tab stop at the 1" position. In the next few steps, you will solve this dilemma by removing a tab stop.

Remove a Tab Stop

9. Click the Show All ¶ button to display the nonprinting characters.

10. Notice the tab → symbols between DATE: and the date.
    The tab symbols show each location where the (TAB) key was tapped.

11. Click between the tab → symbols, and tap (DELETE) to remove the second symbol.
    The date will move to the left, restoring proper alignment.

12. Click Show All ¶ to hide the nonprinting characters.

13. Now apply bold to the **SUBJECT:** heading.

14. Save the changes, and continue with the next topic.

Cut, Copy, and Paste

Cut, Copy, and Paste are available in all Office 2000 applications. With Cut, Copy, and Paste you can move or copy text within a document, between documents, or between different Office applications. For example, you could use the Copy command to copy an important paragraph from one document, and the Paste command to paste the paragraph to another document. Cut, Copy, and Paste are most efficient for moving or copying text a long distance within a document or between documents. Cut, Copy, and Paste are easy to use if you remember the following concepts:

- You must **select text** before issuing a Cut or Copy command.

- You must **position the insertion point** at the desired location before issuing the Paste command. Otherwise, you will paste at the wrong location.

USING CUT, COPY, AND PASTE

Command	Description	How to Issue the Command
Cut	The Cut command removes selected text from its original location and places it on the Office Clipboard.	Click the Cut ✂ button, or press (CTRL)+X.
Copy	The Copy command also places selected text on the Office Clipboard, but it leaves a copy of the text in the original location.	Click the Copy 🗐 button, or press (CTRL)+C.
Paste	The Paste command pastes the most recently cut or copied text into the document at the insertion point location.	Click the Paste 📋 button, or press (CTRL)+V.

The Office 2000 Clipboard

Office 2000 introduces a new clipboard that can hold up to 12 cut or copied items. The Clipboard toolbar appears once you have cut or copied two or more items. The Clipboard toolbar displays an icon representing each cut or copied item. You can paste any item by choosing it from the Clipboard toolbar. You can paste all items from the toolbar by clicking the Paste All button. The items are pasted in the order in which they were cut or copied to the toolbar.

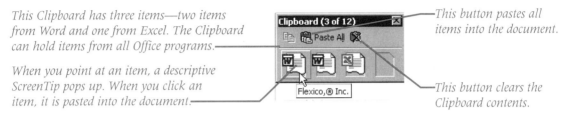

This Clipboard has three items—two items from Word and one from Excel. The Clipboard can hold items from all Office programs.

When you point at an item, a descriptive ScreenTip pops up. When you click an item, it is pasted into the document.

This button pastes all items into the document.

This button clears the Clipboard contents.

Hands-On 2.9 Use Cut and Paste

In this exercise, you will use Cut and Paste to rearrange the title lines in the press release.

1. Scroll down to the press release page.

2. Follow these steps to Cut and Paste a title line.

Ⓐ *Select this title line and the empty paragraph below it by dragging in the left margin.*

Ⓑ *Click the Cut [✂] button on the Standard toolbar. The text will be removed and placed on the Office Clipboard.*

Ⓒ *Click the I-beam just in front of the first title line as shown here.*

Flexico Announces FlexMax™ Fabric

Press Release

Flexico,® Inc.

Ⓓ *Click the Paste [📋] button.*

The Press Release *title and the paragraph mark below it should have pushed the* Flexico Announces *heading down, maintaining the double-spacing of the title lines. This occurred because of the way you selected the text prior to issuing the Cut command. By dragging in the margin to the left of the text, you selected both the text and the paragraph marks. The paragraph marks were pasted along with the text. The paragraph marks pushed the* Flexico Announces *paragraph down, maintaining the double-spacing. This was, by the way, the intended result.*

3. Now select the third title line, **Flexico,® Inc.,** and the empty paragraph below it by dragging in the left margin.

4. Click the Cut [✂] button, and the Clipboard toolbar should appear. If the Clipboard toolbar did not appear, then choose **View→Toolbars→Clipboard** from the menu bar.
   You will use the Clipboard toolbar in a moment.

(Continued on the next page)

5. Position the insertion point just in front of the first heading, **Press Release**.

6. Click the Paste 📋 button on the Standard toolbar (not the Clipboard toolbar).
   Your headings should now have the arrangement shown to the right.

> Flexico,® Inc.
>
> **Press Release**
>
> **Flexico Announces FlexMax™ Fabric**

Use the Clipboard Toolbar

7. Click the drop-down ▾ button on the Undo ↶▾ button.
   If you performed the preceding steps correctly, the first four items on the Undo list should be Paste, Cut, Paste, Cut.

8. Slide the mouse pointer over the first four items to select them, and click the mouse button.
   The press release headings should be in the same order they were in prior to cutting and pasting.

9. Click the Clear Clipboard 🗙 button on the Clipboard toolbar.
   The two icons should be cleared from the Clipboard.

10. Select the **Press Release** heading and the empty paragraph below it.

11. Click the Cut ✂ button.

12. Select the **Flexico,® Inc.** heading and the empty paragraph below it.

13. Click the Cut ✂ button.
    The Clipboard toolbar should display two icons.

14. Position the insertion point just in front of the **Flexico Announces** title line.

15. Point at the first icon on the Clipboard toolbar, and the ScreenTip shown to the right should pop up.
    This heading was the first heading you cut to the Clipboard so it is in the first position on the Clipboard.

16. Click the icon; the **Press Release** heading and empty paragraph should be pasted above the **Flexico Announces** title line.
    If you selected the title line and the paragraph mark following it prior to cutting, then the Flexico Announces *heading should be pushed down to the second line.*

17. Position the insertion point just in front of the **Press Release** title line.

18. Click the second icon on the Clipboard to paste the **Flexico,® Inc.** heading.
    As you can see, the Clipboard toolbar can be useful if you are collecting items from several places in a document. Keep in mind, however, that Cut, Copy, and Paste can be used in the traditional manner without change, and without using the Clipboard toolbar.

19. Click the Clear Clipboard 🗙 button to clear the Clipboard contents.

20. Close the Clipboard toolbar by clicking its Close ✖ button.

Drag and Drop

Drag and drop produces the same result as Cut, Copy, and Paste. However, Drag and Drop is usually more efficient if you are moving or copying text a short distance within the same document. If the original location and destination are both visible in the current window, then it is usually easier to use Drag and Drop. With Drag and Drop, you select the text you wish to move or copy and release the mouse button. Then you drag the text to the desired destination. If you press the (CTRL) key while releasing the mouse button, the text is copied to the destination.

Right Dragging

Right dragging is a variation of the drag-and-drop technique. Many beginners find Drag and Drop difficult to use because they have difficulty controlling the mouse. This difficulty is compounded if they are trying to copy text using Drag and Drop. This is because copying requires the (CTRL) key to be held while dragging the text. With the Right-Drag method, the right mouse button is used when dragging. When the right mouse button is released at the destination, a pop-up menu appears. The pop-up menu lets you choose

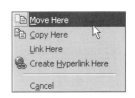

Right-Drag Pop-Up Menu

Move, Copy, or Cancel. This provides more control because there is no need to use the (CTRL) key when copying, and you have the option of canceling the move or copy. The Right-Drag pop-up menu is shown in the illustration to the right.

 ## Hands-On 2.10 Use Drag and Drop and Right Drag

In this exercise, you will use Drag and Drop and the Right-Drag method to rearrange paragraphs.

Use Drag and Drop

1. If necessary, scroll down until the paragraphs with the headings About Flexico, FlexMax Styles, and Delivery and Availability are all visible on the screen.
   Drag and Drop is most effective for moving or copying a short distance on the screen.

2. Follow these steps to move the **Delivery and Availability** paragraph and heading.

Ⓐ *Select from the empty paragraph above the* Delivery and Availability *heading to the end of the paragraph as shown in the illustration.*

Ⓑ *Release the mouse button.*

Ⓒ *Position the mouse pointer on the selected text, and drag the text up until the move pointer is just above the* About Flexico *heading, as shown here.*

Ⓓ *Release the mouse button to drop the text above the* About Flexico *heading.*

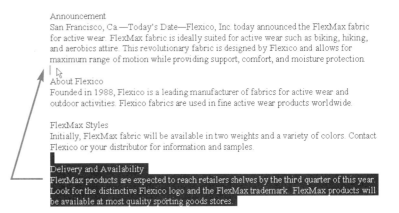

If you selected the empty paragraph above the text as shown and dropped the text in the empty space above the About Flexico *heading, then your paragraphs should be properly spaced.*

Use Right Drag

3. Follow these steps to move the FlexMax Styles paragraph and heading.

Ⓐ *Select from the empty paragraph above the FlexMax Styles heading to the end of the paragraph as shown here; then release the mouse button.*

Ⓑ *Position the mouse pointer on the selected text, and press and hold the right mouse button.*

Ⓒ *Drag the mouse up while holding the right button until the move pointer is positioned just above the* About Flexico *heading, as shown here.*

Delivery and Availability
FlexMax products are expected to reach retailers shelves by the thi
Look for the distinctive Flexico logo and the FlexMax trademark. I
be available at most quality sporting goods stores.

About Flexico
Founded in 1988, Flexico is a leading manufacturer of fabrics for a
outdoor activities. Flexico fabrics are used in fine active wear prod

Ⓓ *Release the mouse button, and choose* **Move Here** *from the pop-up menu that appears. Notice that the pop-up menu would have allowed you to cancel the move if desired.*

Move a Sentence

4. Use any of the move techniques you have learned thus far to move the last sentence in the Announcement paragraph as shown in the following illustration. You can use Cut and Paste, Drag and Drop, or Right Drag.

Move the selected sentence to this location in front of the previous sentence. You will probably need to insert a space after moving the sentence.

Announcement
San Francisco, Ca.—Today's Date—Flexico, Inc. today announced the FlexMax fabric for active wear. FlexMax fabric is ideally suited for active wear such as biking, hiking, and aerobics attire. This revolutionary fabric is designed by Flexico and allows for maximum range of motion while providing support, comfort, and moisture protection.

The Spike

The Spike is another tool that allows you to gather text from various parts of Word documents. The primary benefit of the Spike is that there is no limit to the number of text items you can place on it. However, you can only place text on the Spike, not graphics, tables, or other Word objects. Also, text formatting is not saved when text is cut to the Spike. When you have finished gathering text with the Spike, you paste all text items at one location. The Spike's contents are pasted in the order in which they were placed on the Spike. The following Quick Reference table shows you how to use the Spike. You will use the Spike in a Skill Builder exercise later in this lesson.

USING THE SPIKE

- Select text you would like to place on the Spike.
- Press (CTRL)+(F3) to cut the text to the Spike.
- Continue to cut as many text items as desired.
- Position the insertion point at the location where you want to paste the Spike's contents.
- Press (CTRL)+(SHIFT)+(F3) to paste the Spike's contents and clear the Spike.

Document Scraps

Document Scraps are a useful way to copy text to or from a Word document. To create a document scrap, you drag text from a Word document onto the Windows Desktop. Likewise, you can drag a document scrap from the Desktop and drop it in any Word document. A document scrap is a self-contained document residing on the Windows Desktop. Document scraps are useful if you have a frequently used block of text that you would easily like to add to documents.

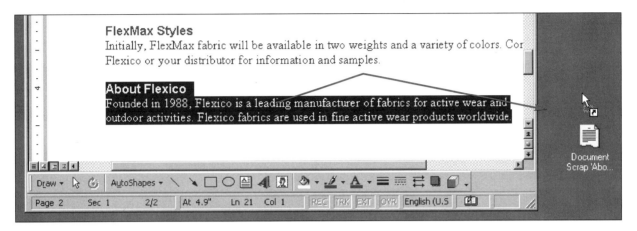

Creating a Document Scrap

The Format Painter

The Format Painter lets you copy text formats from one location to another. This is convenient if you want the same format(s) applied to text in different locations. The Format Painter copies all text formats, including the font, font size, color, and character effects. The Format Painter saves time and helps create consistent formatting throughout a document. The Format Painter can also be used to copy paragraph formats, such as alignment settings.

> **COPYING TEXT FORMATS WITH THE FORMAT PAINTER**
>
> ■ Click on the text with the format(s) you wish to copy.
>
> ■ Click the Format Painter once if you want to copy formats to one other location, or double-click if you want to copy to multiple locations.
>
> ■ Select the text at the new location(s) that you want to format. If you double-clicked in the previous step, the Format Painter will remain active, allowing you to select text at multiple locations. You can even scroll through the document to reach the desired location(s).
>
> ■ If you double-clicked in the first step, then click the Format Painter button when you have finished. This will turn off the Format Painter.

Format Text

1. Click on the **Announcement** heading (just above the first large paragraph of text).

2. Choose **Format→Font** to display the Font dialog box.

Ⓐ *Scroll through the list of fonts, and choose Arial.*

Ⓑ *Set the font size to 14.*

Ⓒ *Click the Font color button, and choose the same color you choose for the title lines.*

Ⓓ *Notice the Effects section. You can apply one or more character effects to text (but don't do it now).*

Ⓔ *Click OK to apply the formatting to the Announcement heading.*

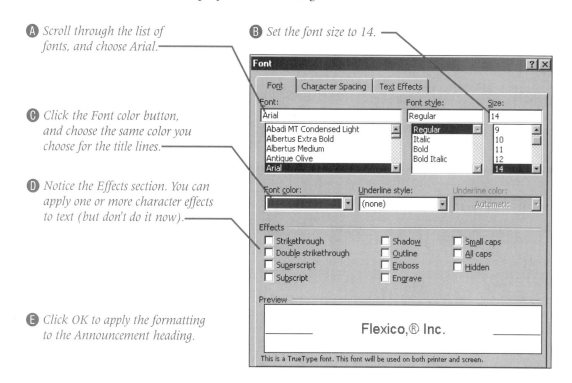

Notice that you were able to format the word Announcement without actually selecting it. You can format a single word by clicking on the word and applying the desired formats.

Copy Formats to One Location

3. Make sure the insertion point is on the Announcement heading.

4. Click the Format Painter 🖌 button on the Standard toolbar.
   An animated paintbrush icon will be added to the I-beam pointer.

5. Drag the mouse pointer across the Delivery and Availability heading.
   The Arial, 14pt, bold, colored formats should be copied to the heading. The animated paintbrush icon also vanished because you clicked the Format Painter button just once in the previous step. If you want to copy formats to multiple locations, you must double-click the Format Painter. Actually, the 14pt heading is too large for these paragraphs. In the next few steps, you will change the size to 12pt for the Announcement heading and then copy the formats to the other headings in the press release.

Copy Formats to Several Locations

6. Click anywhere on the Announcement heading.

7. Click the Font Size [14 ▾] drop-down button on the Formatting toolbar, and choose 12.
   Once again, you can format an individual word by just clicking on the word and applying the desired formats.

8. Double-click the Format Painter .

9. Select the heading **Delivery and Availability** by either dragging the mouse over the heading or by clicking in front of the heading in the margin.

10. Select the **FlexMax Styles** heading to copy the formats to that heading.

11. If necessary, scroll down, and then select the **About Flexico** heading.

12. Click the Format Painter to turn it off.

13. Scroll through your document, and take a moment to appreciate your work.

14. Feel free to experiment with any of the techniques you have learned in this lesson.

15. When you have finished, save the changes to your document; then close the document. *Continue with the end-of-lesson questions and exercises.*

Concepts Review

True/False Questions

1. The zoom control changes the size of printed text. TRUE FALSE

2. The Formatting toolbar can be used to set all text formats and character effects. TRUE FALSE

3. Normal view is the default view in Word 2000. TRUE FALSE

4. The Format Painter is used to copy and paste text. TRUE FALSE

5. Manual page breaks remain in place until the user removes them. TRUE FALSE

6. The Right-Drag method displays a pop-up menu when the mouse button is released. TRUE FALSE

7. The Office Clipboard can hold up to 12 cut or copied items. TRUE FALSE

8. Items must be pasted from the Office Clipboard in the same order that they were placed on the Clipboard. TRUE FALSE

Multiple-Choice Questions

1. In order to copy text formats to several locations in a document, you must
   a. click the Format Painter button and then select the desired text.
   b. double-click the Format Painter button and then select the desired text.
   c. use the Copy button.
   d. This cannot be done in Word.

2. Which of the following statements can be used to describe manual page breaks?
   a. Manual page breaks remain in place until they are deleted.
   b. Manual page breaks are inserted by the user.
   c. Manual page breaks can be inserted by pressing (CTRL)+(ENTER).
   d. All of the above

3. What is the percentage range of the zoom control?
   a. 25%–200%
   b. 10%–500%
   c. 25%–500%
   d. None of the above

4. Which key should you press if you want to copy while using drag-and-drop?
   a. (SHIFT)
   b. (CTRL)
   c. (ALT)
   d. (HOME)

Skill Builders

Skill Builder 2.1 Alignment and Formatting Practice

1. Click New ▢ to start a new document.

2. Click the Center ▤ button.

3. Tap (ENTER) several times to space down to 2″.

4. Set the font to Arial, the point size to 18, and turn on bold.

5. Click the drop-down button on the Font Color 🅰▾ button (on the right end of the Formatting toolbar), and choose your favorite color.

6. Type **The Wilson Family**, and tap (ENTER) *twice.*
   Notice you can apply text formats prior to typing text. The formats remain in effect until you change them or move the insertion point to a location with different formats.

7. Set the font size to 14.

8. Type **Is Having a**, and tap (ENTER) *twice.*

9. Set the font size to 18.

10. Type **Big Yard Sale**, tap (ENTER) twice, and set the alignment to Left ▤.

11. Set the font to Times New Roman, the size to 14, turn off bold, and set the color to black.

12. Complete the document as shown below. You will need to apply bold formatting to the date and time as shown.

13. Save the document as **Skill Builder 2.1**, then close the document.

The Wilson Family

Is Having a

Big Yard Sale

Stop by our home at 22 Maple Street in Walnut Grove on July 21 for the yard sale of the summer! We'll have furniture, toys, electronics, antiques, and much more. We start at 8:00, so arrive early and be prepared to find bargains, one-of-a-kind items, and rare antiques!

Skill Builder 2.2 The Spike, Format Painter, Drag and Drop

In this exercise, you will open a document on your exercise diskette. You will use the Spike to rearrange paragraphs, the Format Painter to paint formats, and Drag and Drop to move blocks of paragraphs.

Use the Spike

1. Open the document named **Skill Builder 2.2** on your exercise diskette.
   Notice that the document contains a list of professional contacts. In the next few steps, you will use the Spike to reorganize the contacts by contact type. In other words, all of the attorneys will be grouped together, followed by the designers, then the bookkeepers.

2. Select the first attorney contact, **David Roberts, Attorney,** by clicking in front of the contact in the left margin.

3. Press (CTRL)+(F3) to cut the text and place it on the Spike.

4. Select the next attorney, **Lisa Wilson, Attorney**, and press (CTRL)+(F3) to cut the text to the Spike.

5. Cut the remaining attorney contacts to the Spike. Use Undo if you make a mistake. However, try to be extra careful because even if you use Undo, the item you cut will remain on the Spike.

6. Cut the designer contacts to the Spike.
   The bookkeeper contacts should now be grouped together in the document. The insertion point should also be at the end of the document.

7. Press (CTRL)+(SHIFT)+(F3) to paste the Spike's contents.
   The Spike pastes the contents and inserts an empty paragraph between each contact. Notice that the attorneys are now grouped together, and the designers are grouped together.

Create Headings

8. Click in the empty space between any two contacts, and tap (DELETE) to remove the empty space.
   You are actually deleting a paragraph mark when you do this.

9. Remove the remaining empty paragraphs between the contacts.

10. Click in front of the first bookkeeper contact, and tap (ENTER) to create a blank line.

11. Click on the blank line, and type **Bookkeepers**.

12. Use this technique to create an **Attorneys** heading above the first attorney contact, and a **Designers** heading above the first designer contact.

Use the Format Painter

13. Click on the **Professional Contacts** heading at the top of the document.

14. Double-click the Format Painter ⬚.

15. Click the **Bookkeepers** heading to copy the formats to that heading.

16. Click the **Attorneys** and **Designers** headings.

17. Turn off the Format Painter ⬚.

18. Select the **Professional Contacts** heading, and increase the size to 14.

Use Drag and Drop

19. Select the **Attorneys** heading and the four attorney contacts by dragging in the left margin.

20. Release the mouse button.

21. Position the mouse pointer on the selection, and drag up until the pointer is just in front of the **Bookkeepers** heading.

22. Release the mouse button to move the **Attorneys** block above the **Bookkeepers**.

23. Now move the **Designers** heading and the designer contacts above the **Bookkeepers**.

Create Space and Center the Title

24. Position the insertion point just in front of the **Attorneys** heading, and tap (ENTER) to create a blank line between the **Professional Contacts** heading and the **Attorneys** heading.

25. Insert blank lines above the **Designers** and **Bookkeepers** headings.

26. Click on the **Professional Contacts** heading, and click the Center Align button.

27. Use (ENTER) to push the entire document down to the 2″ position.

28. Save the changes, and close the document when you have finished.

Skill Builder 2.3 Create a Memorandum

1. Follow these guidelines to create the memorandum shown below.

   ■ Position the MEMO TO: line approximately 2″ down from the top of the page.

   ■ Double space between all paragraphs, and apply bold to the lead words MEMO TO:, FROM:, DATE:, and SUBJECT:.

   ■ Apply bold formatting as shown in the body paragraph.

2. Save the memo with the name **Skill Builder 2.3,** and then close the document.

MEMO TO: Jason Alexander

FROM: Tamika Jackson

DATE: Today's Date

SUBJECT: Monthly Sales Meeting

Our monthly sales meeting will be held in the conference room at **10:00 a.m.** on **Thursday, July 24.** Please bring your sales forecast for August and any important accounts that you wish to discuss. I will give you a presentation on our new products that are scheduled for release in September. I look forward to seeing you then.

xx

Skill Builder 2.4 **Formatting Skills**

1. Follow these guidelines to create the document shown below.

   ▪ Begin the document 2″ down and enter all text. Center the titles as shown. Notice the dashes between the locations and days of the week in the Hands-On Workshops list and the other lists. These are em dashes inserted using the Special Characters tab of the Symbols dialog box. An easy way to insert these dashes is to insert the first one, select it, and copy it with the Copy command. Then, paste the dash at every other location where it is needed.

   ▪ Format the first title line with an Arial, bold, 16pt font. Apply a color to the title.

   ▪ Use the Format Painter to copy the formats to the subtitle, then change the font size of the subtitle to 14pt.

   ▪ Format the Hands-On Workshops heading with an Arial, bold, 12pt font, and apply the same color you applied to the titles.

   ▪ Use the Format Painter to copy the formats from the Hands-On Workshops heading to the Seminar Series heading and the Internet Events heading.

2. Save the document with the name Skill Builder 2.4, and then close the document.

Southern California Computer Training

Summer Training Schedule

The following schedule is for hands-on workshops, seminars, and Internet events for July, August, and September. If you plan on attending an event, make your reservations early as we have limited seating. You should also pick up your training materials at least one week prior to your event.

Hands-On Workshops
Irvine—Tuesday, July 20
Los Angeles—Wednesday, July 21
San Diego—Wednesday, August 18
Riverside—Tuesday, September 21

Seminar Series
Irvine—Wednesday, July 21
Los Angeles—Thursday, August 19
Riverside—Wednesday, September 22

Internet Events
Los Angeles—Friday, August 20
Woodland Hills—Thursday, September 2

Assessments

Assessment 2.1 Create a Memorandum

1. Follow these guidelines to create the memorandum shown below.

   - Begin the document 2" down from the top of the page.

   - Boldface the lead words MEMO TO, FROM, DATE, and SUBJECT as shown.

   - Use the em dash after the department names.

   - Type your initials at the bottom of the memo.

2. Save the document to your exercise diskette with the name **Assessment 2.1.**

3. Print the document, and then close it.

MEMO TO: Mark Paxton

FROM: Tamara Niu

DATE: Today's Date

SUBJECT: Purchase Orders

The following departments have requested that purchase orders be issued for the specified products. Please conduct the necessary research and issue purchase orders as soon as possible.

Marketing—A cordless mouse that can be used at least six feet away from the base unit.

Systems—A flatbed scanner with high resolution. It should have software that allows enhancing of images even as scanning is taking place.

Research—A video camera that is supported by the Universal Serial Bus (USB) standard. The price should be lower than what we paid for the analog camera.

xx

Assessment 2.2

1. Open the document named **Assessment 2.2** on your exercise diskette.

2. Follow these guidelines to modify the memorandum.

   ■ Apply bold formatting as shown below.

   ■ Insert the *Do Not Try to Please Everyone* line and the paragraphs following it as shown below, including the initials line and the attachment line.

MEMO TO: Office Staff

FROM: Ariel Ramirez

DATE: Today's Date

SUBJECT: Multiple Supervisors

Most executive assistants at our firm have multiple supervisors. Therefore, we are offering the following suggestions to make your work easier.

Prioritize—What is important may take preference over what is urgent. Which project can be delayed? Overall, which has the greatest importance to our firm? Evaluate and schedule your time accordingly.

Refuse Assignments—If you do not have the time, ask your supervisor if someone else can do the assignment. It's better to say no than to not meet the deadline.

Enjoy Multiple Projects—Learn to enjoy the challenge of switching from one project to another. You may not be able to finish them all, but realize the contribution you have made to each one.

Do Not Try to Please Everyone—There is no way you will please all of your supervisors all of the time. Set your own approval rating and go with it.

Listed on the attached sheet are some related workshops you may want to attend. Contact Human Resources for registration forms.

xx
Attachment

(Continued on the next page)

3. Tap (ENTER) once after the Attachment line; then insert a page break.

4. Follow these guidelines to create the following page.

- Start the title line 2″ down.

- Center and bold the title as shown.

- Apply the color of your choice to the title.

- Double-space between all paragraphs.

RECOMMENDED WORKSHOPS

How to Manage Your Boss, April 23, Holiday Inn, Fremont, Phoenix Extension

The Perfect Support Person, April 30, Hyatt at the Airport, ProPeople Associates

Prioritizing Made Easy, May 5, Sheraton at the Wharf, CareerTech

Office Procedures for the Executive Assistant, May 7, SF Marriott, Phoenix Extension

---

5. Save the changes, print the document, and then close it.

Assessment 2.3

1. Open the document named **Assessment 2.3.**

2. Follow these guidelines to modify the document until it matches the following document.

   - Rearrange the paragraphs into groups as shown, using Cut and Paste, drag-and-drop, or the Spike. Use whichever method you prefer. The rearranged paragraphs should match the following example.

   - Insert a title, headings, and empty paragraphs as shown in the example.

   - Format the title and headings with an Arial bold font and a sea-green color. The title should have a font size of 16.

   - Use (ENTER) to push the entire completed document down to the 2″ position.

3. Save the document, print the document, and then close it.

Bay Area Environmental Groups

Marin County
Marin Wetlands Conservation Corps, Marin County
Mt. Tamalpais Hiking Club, Marin County
John Muir Society, Marin County
Redwood Preservation Group, Marin County

East Bay
East Bay Conservation Corps, East Bay
El Cerrito Wetlands Restoration, East Bay
San Pablo Reservoir Water Reclamation, East Bay
Citizens for Environmental Restoration, East Bay

South Bay
South Bay Water Restoration, South Bay
San Jose Environmental Corps, South Bay
Gilroy Preservation Society, South Bay
Bay Wildlife Foundation, South Bay

Critical Thinking

Critical Thinking 2.1 On Your Own

Tanisha Johnson is the Director of Human Resources for Big Time Video Distributors. Tanisha works hard to provide Big Time employees with a variety of attractive fringe benefits. She realizes this is necessary in today's competitive job market. Recently, Tanisha set up the Big Time Discounts program with other local businesses. Through this program, Big Time employees are issued a Big Time discount card. The card gives Big Time employees a 10% discount on the products or services they purchase from participating businesses.

Set up a memorandum from Tanisha Johnson to the Big Time employees announcing the program. Let the employees know that the effective date will be the beginning of next month and that all employees are eligible to participate. Let them know that a 10% discount will be given to them on all purchases. Mention that the participating businesses list will be issued within a few days. Save your completed memorandum as **Critical Thinking 2.1,** and then close it.

Critical Thinking 2.2 On Your Own

Tanisha Johnson has prepared the memorandum that was set up in Critical Thinking 2.1 but she changes her mind and decides not to send the memo until the participating businesses list is completed. Open the Critical Thinking 2.1 memorandum and save it as **Critical Thinking 2.2.** Add a second page to the memorandum that includes the following participating businesses list. You can use the (TAB) key to line up the list entries. Also, bold the headings as shown.

Discount Provider	Contact	Number
West Side Chiropractic	Dave Smith	223-1345
The Panda Restaurant	Sam Chin	223-0909
Spiffy Cleaners	Carol Caruso	222-9090
Southside Cinemas	Ken Turner	221-2121
Dave's Auto Repair	Dave Adams	221-4545

Include a centered title at the top of the second page. Edit the memorandum text on the first page to indicate that the participating businesses list is attached. Your memorandum should also have an attachment notation. Save the changes to the document, and then close it.

Critical Thinking 2.3 **Web Research**

Veronica Smith was recently promoted to Vice President of Operations for Veritime Systems. Veritime develops transaction processing systems and employs more than 1,500 people. One of Veronica's primary goals is to streamline the procurement process. She realizes that Veritime's procurement processes are outdated and too centralized. Veronica wants to push decision making down to the departmental level and use the Internet to streamline processes and ultimately save money.

The first directive that Veronica issues is to push purchasing decisions for office supplies down to the various department managers. Set up a memorandum from Veronica to all departmental managers. The memo should state that office supply purchases can now be made at the department level. Use Internet Explorer and a search engine of your choice to locate three office supply companies that allow purchases to made from their Web sites. Add a second page to your memorandum listing the approved Web-based office supply stores. Include the URLs and 800 numbers of the stores. Save your completed memorandum as **Critical Thinking 2.3.**

Critical Thinking 2.4 **With a Group**

In this exercise, you will work with the same classmate that you worked with to set up Health-e-Meals.com in Critical Thinking 1.5. Health-e-Meals.com has been in business for over two years, and you have tremendous success. The credit line that was secured through Citizen's Bank has allowed Health-e-Meals to surpass even your most optimistic projections. During this time, you have hired 16 employees to do everything from delivery to office management. To celebrate your success, you and your classmate have decided to organize a company Christmas party.

Set up a memorandum to all employees announcing the Christmas party. Praise your employees for their hard work and the success of the company. Let them know how optimistic the future looks and how you look forward to the coming year. Have your classmate write an attachment page outlining the details of the Christmas party. The date, time, location, and agenda should be included. Have your classmate save the attachment page in a separate file from your memorandum. Open your classmate's attachment page, and copy and paste the information onto a new page (second page) of your memorandum. Save the completed memorandum as **Critical Thinking 2.4.**

Professional Writing and Editing Tools

In this lesson, you will use the Office Assistant, online Help, and professional writing and editing tools. The Office Assistant and online Help allow you to get assistance at any time. Word 2000 provides spell checking, grammar checking, and a powerful thesaurus. Word 2000 even has automatic spell checking and grammar checking that check your work as you write. Another powerful tool in Word 2000 is Find and Replace. Find and Replace is especially useful for finding and replacing text in large documents. Once you master the writing tools in Word 2000, you'll be able to write business documents, research papers, and reports with confidence.

In This Lesson

Case Study

Sarah Thomas is a Health Science major at Upper State University. In order to fulfill the requirements of her Nutritional Studies class, Sarah has chosen to write a research paper on diabetes. Sarah is enthusiastic about this topic since one of her family members was recently afflicted with diabetes. Sarah takes full advantage of the powerful writing and editing tools in Word 2000. She uses the spelling and grammar checkers to proof her paper prior to submission. She uses the thesaurus to find the best words to express her ideas. Finally, Sarah uses the find and replace feature to make changes and ensure consistency throughout her paper.

DEFEATING DIABETES

A low-fat diet can be an important tool in preventing or managing diabetes, a metabolic disorder that affects over 13 million Americans. In people with diabetes, the pancreas doesn't produce enough insulin, a hormone that's needed to control blood sugar levels in your body and to convert food to energy.

While Type I (insulin-dependent) diabetes is fairly common, most people with diabetes develop it after age 40. This is known as Type II, or non-insulin-dependent, diabetes. Without proper treatment, Type II diabetes can lead to serious complications,

---

A polished paper, thanks to Word 2000's writing tools.

The Office Assistant

The Office Assistant is an interactive Help tool available in all Office 2000 applications. The Assistant monitors your activities and provides tips, suggestions, and alert messages whenever it assumes you need assistance. For example, the Assistant recognizes certain phrases such as salutations beginning with the word *Dear*. The Assistant displays a **speech balloon** when it recognizes such a phrase. The speech balloon contains the suggestion or alert message. The Assistant can also be configured to display a tip of the day when Word is started.

Assistant offering assistance

Using the Assistant to Get Help

The Assistant's speech balloon contains a search box where you can enter phrases and questions. When you click the Search button, the Assistant interprets the phrase or question in the search box and displays a list of topics relating to the search box text. When you click a topic, Word displays a Help window providing you with detailed help information.

Controlling the Assistant

You can control all aspects of the Assistant. For example, you may not want the Assistant to display a tip of the day, or you may want to turn the Assistant off. You can set options for the Assistant in the Office Assistant dialog box. The following Quick Reference table outlines various methods of controlling the Assistant.

CONTROLLING THE OFFICE ASSISTANT

Task	Procedure
Display the Assistant's speech balloon (four different methods).	■ Click anywhere on the Assistant. ■ Press F1. ■ Click the Help button on the Standard toolbar. ■ Choose Microsoft Word Help from the Help menu.
Close the speech balloon.	Click anywhere in the document, or tap ESC.
Display Office Assistant dialog box.	Display the speech balloon, and click the Options button.
Change animated character.	Display the Office Assistant dialog box, click the Gallery tab, use the Next button to browse the available characters, choose a character, and click OK.
Temporarily hide the Assistant.	Choose Help→Hide the Office Assistant, or right-click the Assistant, and choose Hide from the pop-up menu.
Turn Assistant off completely.	Display the Office Assistant dialog box, and uncheck the Use the Office Assistant box.
Unhide the Assistant or turn on the Assistant.	Choose Help→Show the Office Assistant.

In this and the following exercise, you will use the Assistant to learn more about inserting dates. You learned about inserting dates in the previous lesson.

Display the Speech Balloon

1. Start Word, and the Assistant should appear.

2. If the Assistant is not visible on your screen, choose Help→Show the Office Assistant.
   This text shows the default Assistant character known as "Clippit." The Assistant on your machine may be different.

3. Click the Assistant and the speech balloon will pop up.

4. Click anywhere in the document window to close the speech balloon.

5. Position the mouse pointer on the Assistant, and drag the Assistant to a new screen location.
   You can always reposition the Assistant even if the speech balloon is displayed.

Get Help

6. Click the Assistant to display the speech balloon.

7. Follow these steps to get help on inserting the date in documents.

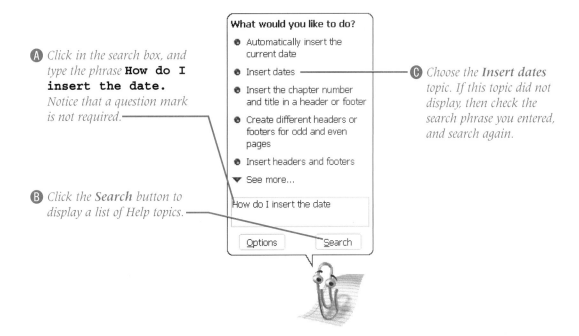

Ⓐ *Click in the search box, and type the phrase* **How do I insert the date.** *Notice that a question mark is not required.*

What would you like to do?
- Automatically insert the current date
- Insert dates
- Insert the chapter number and title in a header or footer
- Create different headers or footers for odd and even pages
- Insert headers and footers
- ▼ See more...

How do I insert the date

Options   Search

Ⓒ *Choose the* **Insert dates** *topic. If this topic did not display, then check the search phrase you entered, and search again.*

Ⓑ *Click the* **Search** *button to display a list of Help topics.*

Word will display a Help window relating to Inserting the date and time. The Help window will most likely appear beside the Word document window. As you can see, the Assistant can be used to display Help windows. You will learn more about inserting the date and time and online Help in a moment.

(Continued on the next page)

8. For now, click the Close ☒ button at the top–right corner of the Help window.
   The Help window should close, and the Word window will return to its original size.

9. Type the word **date** in the Assistant's search box.

10. Click the Search button, and a list of topics will appear.
    Notice that Insert dates is one of the topics. This is the same topic you searched for previously when you entered the search phrase "How do I insert the date." This example shows that it isn't always necessary to type long phrases in the search box. Often, a single word is enough to locate a desired topic.

Check Out the Options

11. Click the Options button on the speech balloon.

12. If necessary, click the Options tab in the dialog box that appears.

13. Click the Question Mark ⃞ button at the top-right corner of the dialog box, and then click on any option check box.
    Word will provide a ScreenTip describing the purpose of the option.

14. Tap the (ESC) key to close the ScreenTip.

15. Feel free to get help on the various Office Assistant options. You may also want to click the Gallery tab in the dialog box to check out the other Assistant characters. If you are studying in a computer lab, it is recommended that you not change any options.

16. Close the Office Assistant dialog box when you have finished.

Online Help

Word's online Help puts a complete reference book at your fingertips. Help is available for just about any topic you can imagine. Online Help is important because Microsoft does not provide reference manuals with Office 2000. The reference manuals are now integrated into online Help.

Locating Help Topics

Your goal when using online Help is to locate Help topics. There are several different search methods you can use to locate topics. All Help topics have key words that identify them. For example, a Help topic that discusses printing documents can probably be located by including the key word *printing* in your search method. Regardless of which search method you use, the goal is to locate a topic. Once you locate the desired topic, you can display it and follow the instructions in the topic.

When Help Is Available

In Word 2000, you can display the Help window directly only when the Office Assistant is turned off. You learned how to turn off the Office Assistant in the previous topic. When the Office Assistant is turned off, the Help window can be displayed using any of the following methods:

■ Click the Help ⃞ button on the Standard toolbar.

■ Press (F1).

■ Choose Help→Microsoft Word Help from the menu bar.

The following Quick Reference table explains the various methods for locating Help topics.

LOCATING HELP TOPICS	
Search Method	**Procedure**
Contents	The Contents method is useful if you are trying to locate a topic but you aren't really sure how to describe it. The Contents method lets you navigate through a series of categories until the desired topic is located.
Answer Wizard	The Answer Wizard lets you find topics the same way that you find them with the Office Assistant. You type a phrase into a search box and execute a search.
Index	The Index method lets you locate a topic by typing key words. An alphabetically indexed list of topics is displayed from which you can choose the desired topic. This method is most useful if you know the name of the topic or feature for which you need assistance.

The Help Window Toolbar

The Help window contains a toolbar to assist you with online Help. The following illustration defines the buttons on the Help toolbar.

The Show/Hide button is used to show or hide the tabbed area of the Help window. The tabbed area is used to locate Help topics.

Move back one topic.

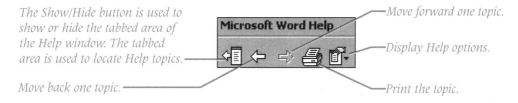

Move forward one topic.

Display Help options.

Print the topic.

 Hands-On 3.2 Use Online Help

Turn Off the Office Assistant

1. Click the Office Assistant, and then click the Options button.

2. Make sure the Options tab is active, and remove the check from the Use the Office Assistant box.

3. Click **OK,** and the Office Assistant will vanish.
   Once the Office Assistant is turned off, commands that would normally display the Office Assistant display the Help window instead.

Use an Index Search

4. Choose **Help→Microsoft Word Help** from the menu bar.
   The Help window will be displayed beside the Word window. If the Office Assistant had been active, this command would have popped up the Assistant's speech balloon.

5. If the tabbed area of the Help window is not displayed, then click the Show ⊞ button on the Help toolbar.

(Continued on the next page)

6. Click the Index tab.

7. Type the word **date** in the Type keywords box, and click the **Search** button.
The topic Insert the current date and time *should appear in the right side of the Help window.*

8. Click the **Insert the current date and time** topic.
The Help information for that topic will appear in the right side of the Help window.

9. Take a moment to read the help information; then click the **Show Me** hyperlink that appears in Step 2.
The Show Me hyperlink will displays the actual dialog box that is used for setting the date and time.

10. Click the Cancel button on the Date and Time dialog box.

Experiment with Help

11. Click in the Help window to redisplay the entire window.

12. Feel free to experiment with Help. Try using the Contents method to locate Help topics, and try using the Index method to locate additional topics.

13. When you have finished, click the Close ☒ button on the Help window.

14. Finally, turn the Office Assistant back on with the **Help→Show the Office Assistant** command. If necessary, close the Assistant's speech balloon.

Spell Checking

Word checks a document for spelling errors by comparing each word to the contents of a main dictionary. The main dictionary is a standard, college-level dictionary. The spell checker also looks for double words such as *the the,* words with numbers such as *99budget,* and a variety of capitalization errors.

Custom Dictionaries

Word actually compares your document with two (or more) dictionaries: the main dictionary and one or more custom dictionaries. Custom dictionaries contain words such as last names or company names that may not be in the main dictionary. You can add words to a custom dictionary during a spell check. For example, you may want to add last names or company names you frequently use in your work. The spell checker will ignore those words during future spell checks. Word also lets you use dictionaries for languages other than English. You can even purchase dictionaries with specific terminology, such as medical or legal terminology.

Automatic Spell Checking

Word can automatically check your spelling as you type. Word flags spelling errors by underlining them with wavy red lines. You can correct a flagged error by right-clicking the error and choosing a suggested replacement word or other option from the pop-up menu that appears.

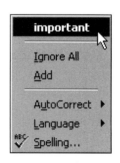

Spell Check Pop-Up Menu

Correct Spelling Errors

1. Open the document named **Hands-On Lesson 3** on your exercise diskette.
   This document has plenty of spelling errors for you to correct.

2. Notice the word *iportant* in the first sentence has a wavy red underline.
   Misspelled words are identified by wavy red underlines.

3. **Right-click** the word *iportant,* and the following pop-up menu will appear.
   Take a few moments to study the following illustration.

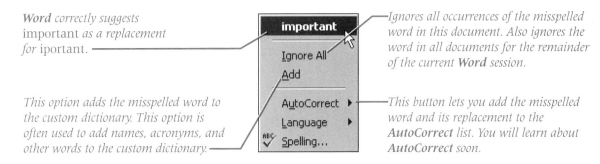

Word correctly suggests important *as a replacement for* iportant.

This option adds the misspelled word to the custom dictionary. This option is often used to add names, acronyms, and other words to the custom dictionary.

Ignores all occurrences of the misspelled word in this document. Also ignores the word in all documents for the remainder of the current Word session.

This button lets you add the misspelled word and its replacement to the AutoCorrect list. You will learn about AutoCorrect soon.

4. Choose **important** from the top of the list as shown in the preceding illustration.
   Important will replace iportant.

5. Right-click the word *millionAmericans* on the second line of the first paragraph, and choose **million Americans** from the pop-up menu.

Double Word and Capitalization Errors

6. Notice the double word *with with* on the second line.
   Word reports these types of errors as well.

7. **Right-click** the second occurrence of *with,* and choose **Delete Repeated Word** from the pop-up menu.

8. **Right-click** the word *WHile* at the start of the second paragraph.

9. Choose **While** from the pop-up menu.
   As you can see, the spell checker looks for spelling, double words, and capitalization errors. You can always correct spelling as you type by right-clicking words with a wavy red underline and choosing an option from the pop-up menu.

Grammar Checking

Word has a sophisticated grammar checker that can help improve your writing skills. Like the spell checker, the grammar checker can check grammar as you type. The grammar checker "flags" grammar errors by underlining them with wavy green lines. You can correct a flagged error by right-clicking the error and choosing a replacement phrase or other option from the pop up menu. Be careful when using the grammar checker, however, because it isn't perfect. There is no substitute for careful proofreading.

The Spelling and Grammar Dialog Box

 The Spelling and Grammar dialog box is useful when you are spell checking and/or grammar checking a large document. It also provides access to customization options. For example, you use the Spelling and Grammar dialog box to choose a customized dictionary for the spell checker and to choose the writing style for the grammar checker. The available writing styles are casual, standard, formal, technical, and custom. The Spelling and Grammar dialog box is displayed with the **Tools→Spelling and Grammar** command or by clicking the Spelling and Grammar button on the Standard toolbar.

From the Keyboard

Press F7 to start Spelling and Grammar checker

Hands-On 3.4 Use the Spelling and Grammar Dialog Box

1. Click the Spelling and Grammar button on the Standard toolbar.
    The spell check will begin, and the speller should stop on the misspelled word famil in the third paragraph.

2. Take a few moments to study the following illustration.

You can choose a suggestion from this list and click the ***Change*** *button.*

You can change the custom dictionary, writing style, turn on grammar checking as you type, and set other options.

This box turns on grammar checking when using this dialog box; however, it does not activate grammar checking as you type.

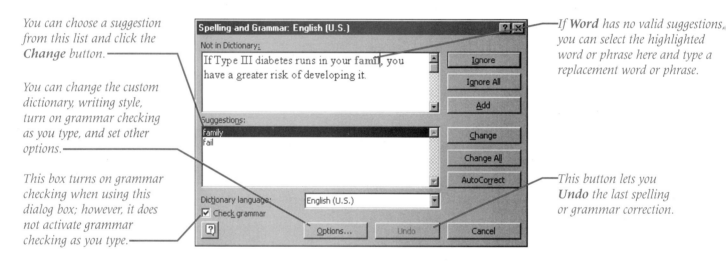

If **Word** *has no valid suggestions, you can select the highlighted word or phrase here and type a replacement word or phrase.*

This button lets you ***Undo*** *the last spelling or grammar correction.*

3. Choose **family** from the suggestions list, and click the **Change** button.

4. Use the following guidelines to spell check and grammar check the remainder of this document.

    ■ Use your best judgment to determine the correct spelling of all misspelled words.

    ■ Use your best judgment to determine the correct grammar if Word reports grammar errors.

    ■ From time-to-time, messages may pop up helping you with reported spelling and grammar errors. The messages will vanish as soon as you take any kind of action.

5. When the spell check is complete, the Office Assistant will display a message. Click anywhere in the document to close the message.

6. Click the Save button to update the changes.
    Leave the document open; you will continue to use it.

Thesaurus

The thesaurus can help improve your vocabulary and writing skills by providing synonyms (words with the same meaning) for words or phrases. The thesaurus can help you choose just the right words or phrases to accurately express your ideas. You can easily display of list of synonyms by right-clicking a selected word or phrase and choosing Synonyms from the pop up menu that appears. The thesaurus dialog box can also be used to display synonyms and antonyms (words or phrases with the opposite meaning). You display the Thesaurus dialog box with the **Tools→Language→Thesaurus** command.

From the Keyboard

(SHIFT)+(F7) to display the Thesaurus dialog box

Hands-On 3.5 Use the Thesaurus

1. Scroll up and **right-click** the word *manufacture* in the third line of the first paragraph.

2. Choose **Synonyms** from the bottom of the pop-up menu.

3. Choose **produce** from the synonym list.

4. Use the preceding steps to replace the word **manage** with **control** also on the third line of the first paragraph.

5. Click anywhere on the word **control**, and choose **Tools→Language→Thesaurus** from the menu bar.

6. Follow these steps to explore the thesaurus dialog box.

Ⓐ *Notice that* control *is the word that is currently being looked up.*

Ⓑ *A list of suggested synonyms is displayed here.* **Word** *may also display antonyms at the bottom of this list.*

Ⓒ *The* **Meanings** *list shows various meanings for the word.* **Word** *displays a different synonym list if you choose a different meaning.*

Ⓓ *Click the* **Replace** *button now to replace* control *with* manage.

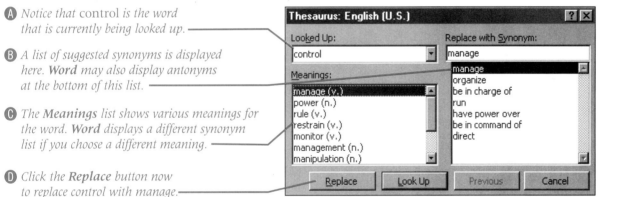

7. **Right-click** the word *manage,* and choose **control** from the Synonyms list on the pop-up menu.

8. Feel free to experiment with the thesaurus.

9. Save 🖫 your document when you have finished experimenting.

Find and Replace

From the Keyboard

Press CTRL+F for Find
Press CTRL+H for Replace

Word's Find command lets you search a document for a particular word or phrase. You can also search for text formats, page breaks, and a variety of other items. Find is often the quickest way to locate a phrase, format, or item in a document. The Replace option lets you replace the found phrase, format, or item with a replacement phrase, format, or item. The Find and Replace dialog box is displayed with either the **Edit→Find** command or the **Edit→Replace** command.

 ## Hands-On 3.6 Use Find

Find a Word

1. Position the insertion point at the top of the document, and make sure that no text is selected.

2. Choose **Edit→Find** from the menu bar.

3. Follow these steps to search for the word *pancreas*.

Ⓐ *Type* **pancreas** *in the Find what box. Notice the drop-down button. The drop-down button displays a list of previous words for which you have searched.*

Ⓑ *Click this button if it is labeled More. The Search and Find options will appear as shown here.*

Ⓒ *Make sure this option is set to All. You can search up or down from the insertion point or through the entire document.*

Ⓓ *Notice these check boxes. You will use these boxes later in this exercise.*

Ⓔ *These options let you search for formats and other types of elements.*

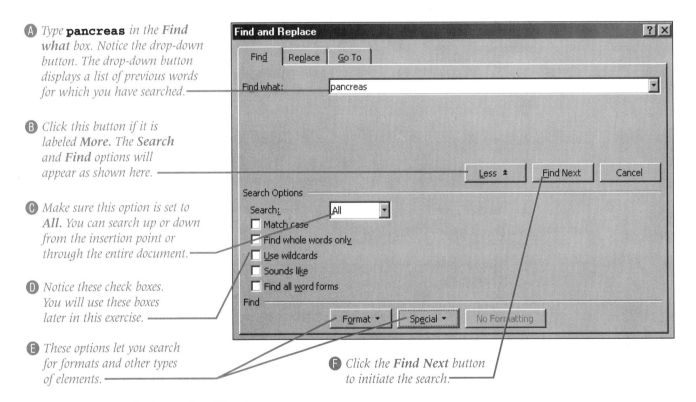

Ⓕ *Click the Find Next button to initiate the search.*

Find Another Word

4. Click in the **Find what** box, delete *pancreas* and type **With** (with a capital *W*) in its place.

5. Click the **Find Next** button, and *With* should be located in the second paragraph.

6. Click **Find Next** again, and the word *Without* should be located in the second paragraph. *Notice that* With *was found even though it is part of the word* Without. *By default,* **Find** *is not case-sensitive, and it doesn't recognize the difference between a whole word or part of the word. You will change this, however, in the next few steps.*

Use Match Case

7. Click the **Match case** check box under the search options.
   This box instructs Word to find only occurrences of the search string with the same matching case.

8. Click the **Find Next** button, and Word will locate the capitalized word *With* further down in the document.

9. Click **Find Next** again, and the Office Assistant will indicate the entire document has been searched.
   Word skipped over several occurrences of with in lowercase.

10. Uncheck the **Match case** check box.

Search for a Whole Word

11. Scroll to the top of the document, and click the insertion point anywhere on the document title. Notice you can scroll while the Find and Replace box is open, although you may need to move the box out of your way.

12. Check the **Find whole words only** check box.

13. Click **Find Next** several times until the Office Assistant indicates that the entire document has been searched.
    Notice that the word without was not located this time.

14. Uncheck the **Find whole words only** check box.

Search for Text Formats and Tab Characters

   Notice the Format and Special buttons at the bottom of the dialog box.

15. Click the **Special** button, and a list of items will appear.
    You can search a document for the presence of any item.

16. Choose **Tab Character** (the second item on the list).
    Word will place a ^t character in the Find what box. This character tells Word to search for a tab.

17. Click **Find Next.**
    Word will select the space at the front of the credit line at the end of the document. A tab created this space.

18. Click the **Format** button at the bottom of the dialog box.
    The Format button lets you search for specific fonts, paragraph formats, and other formats.

19. Choose **Font** from the list.

20. Choose **Bold** from the Font Style list, and click **OK.**
    The words Format: Font: Bold *should appear below the Find what box.*

21. Remove the ^t character from the Find what box; then **click** the **Find Next** button.
    Word should select the title because it is in bold.

22. **Click** the **Cancel** button to close the Find and Replace dialog box.

23. Click anywhere on the title to remove the selection.

(Continued on the next page)

Use Replace

24. Press (CTRL)+H to display the Find and Replace dialog box.

    Notice that the Replace tab is active in the dialog box. The shortcut keystroke you use determines which tab displays when the dialog box appears. Notice that there are tabs for Find, Replace, and Go To. Go To is covered later in this lesson.

25. Click the **No Formatting** button at the bottom of the dialog box.

    This turns off the bold setting that you searched for in the previous exercise. In the next step, you will begin replacing the Roman numeral III with II.

26. Type the Roman numeral **III** (3 capital I's) in the **Find wha**t box and **II** in the **Replace** box.

27. Click the **Find Next** button.

    Word will locate and select the first occurrence of III.

28. Click the **Replace** button.

    Word replaces III with II and selects the next occurrence of III in the document.

29. Now click **Replace All**, and Word will replace all occurrences of III with II.

    The Office Assistant will display a pop-up message indicating the number of replacements that were made.

30. Click anywhere in the dialog box to close the pop-up message.

    Be careful with Replace All because you may make accidental replacements. For example, if you replace cat *with* dog, *then words like* catapult *may become* dogapult. *You should use the Find Whole Words Only option if the word you are replacing might be part of a larger word (like* cat *and* catapult).

31. Use Replace to replace all occurrences of the word *Boulder* with *Denver*. Make sure you type the word *Denver* with an uppercase D in the replace box. This way, it will be capitalized in the document.

32. Feel free to experiment with find and replace.

33. Close the Find and Replace dialog box when you have finished, but leave the document open.

Word Count

The word count feature counts the number of words, sentences, paragraphs, and pages in a document. Word count can be useful if you need to adjust your document to a specific length. For example, students who are creating reports or research papers often have length limitations. Word count is particularly useful to word processing professionals who bill clients by the word or page. You initiate word count with the **Tools→Word Count** command.

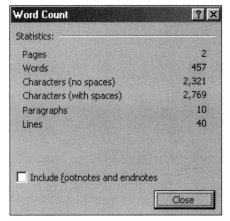

Word Count Statistics

Hands-On 3.7 Use Word Count

1. Click anywhere in the document to make sure no words are selected.

2. Choose **Tools→Word Count** from the menu bar.
   Word will analyze the document and display the statistics.

3. Take a few moments to study the results; then click the **Close** button.

4. Save the changes to the document; then close the document.

Recently Used File List

Word and other Office applications list up to nine of the most recently used files at the bottom of the File menu. You can open any of these documents by choosing them from the list. This is often the most efficient way to open a recently used document. The following Quick Reference steps explain how to adjust the number of files displayed on the recently used file. list

> **MODIFYING THE RECENTLY USED FILE LIST**
> ■ Choose Tools→Options from the menu bar.
> ■ Click the General tab.
> ■ Adjust the number of entries in the *Recently used file list* box.

Hands-On 3.8 Use the Recently Used Files List

1. Choose **File** from the menu bar.
   You will notice up to nine recently used documents are listed at the bottom of the menu. The Hands-On Lesson 3 document should be at the top of the list because you used it in the previous exercise.

2. Choose **Hands-On Lesson 3** from the list, and the document will open.
   Leave the document open; you will continue to use it in the next exercise.

The Go To Command

The Go To command lets you rapidly locate a specific page in a document. Go To can also be used to locate objects (which you have not learned about) such as bookmarks, tables, footnotes, and endnotes. You choose the object you wish to go to in the Go To tab of the Find and Replace dialog box. You can display the Go To tab of the Find and Replace dialog box by choosing **Edit→Go To** from the menu bar. You can also display the Go To tab by double-clicking the page number section of the status bar.

From the Keyboard

(CTRL)+G to display Go To dialog box

Hands-On 3.9 Go to a Page

Use the Keyboard

1. Press (CTRL)+G, and the Go To tab of the Find and Replace dialog box will appear.

2. Type **2** into the Enter page number box, and click the **Go To** button.
   The insertion point should move to the top of page 2.

3. Click the **Close** button on the dialog box.

Use the Status Bar

4. Double-click anywhere on the page number section of the status bar to display the Go To tab of the Find and Replace dialog box.
   Notice that you can go to other locations, such as Sections, Lines, etc.

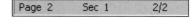

| Page 2 | Sec 1 | | 2/2 |

5. Type **1** into the Enter Page Number box, and then click the **Go To** button.

6. Close the Find and Replace dialog box.

Hyphenation

Word lets you hyphenate text automatically or manually. With **automatic** hyphenation, Word hyphenates words whenever it determines that hyphenation is necessary. With **manual** hyphenation, Word searches the document for words to hyphenate. When a word requiring hyphenation is located, Word prompts you to confirm the hyphen location within the word. Hyphenation is most useful in documents with short line lengths, such as documents containing newspaper style columns.

Quick Reference

HYPHENATING TEXT

To Hyphenate a Document Automatically:

- Choose Tools→Language→Hyphenation from the menu bar.

- Check the *Automatically hyphenate document box,* and click OK.

To Hyphenate a Document Manually:

- Choose Tools→Language→Hyphenation from the menu bar.

- Click the Manual button.

- If Word identifies a word to hyphenate and you want the hyphen positioned at the location Word proposes, click Yes. If you want the hyphen positioned at a different location in the word, then use the arrow keys on the keyboard to adjust the position, and then click Yes.

The Hyphenation Zone

The Hyphenation dialog box contains a Hyphenation Zone setting. The hyphenation zone lets you adjust the sensitivity of the hyphenation. You can widen the hyphenation zone by entering a larger number in the Hyphenation Zone box. This will reduce the number of words that are hyphenated. Likewise, you can increase the number of words that are hyphenated by entering a smaller number for the hyphenation zone.

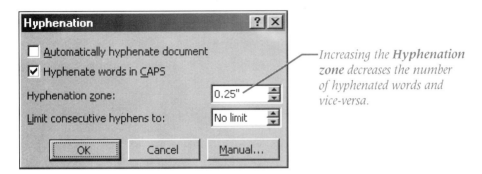

*Increasing the **Hyphenation zone** decreases the number of hyphenated words and vice-versa.*

Nonbreaking Hyphens Nonbreaking Spaces

Some phrases (such as *easy-to-use*) require hyphens between the words in the phrase. You can use nonbreaking hyphens to ensure that all words in the phrase stay together on the same line. If you use nonbreaking hyphens and there is not enough space on a line for the entire phrase, then Word will move the entire phrase to the beginning of the next line. You insert nonbreaking hyphens with the (CTRL)+(SHIFT)+Hyphen keystroke combination. Likewise, you can insert nonbreaking spaces with the (CTRL)+(SHIFT)+(SPACE BAR) keystroke combination.

 Hands-On 3.10 Use Hyphenation

___

1. Browse through the document and notice that there is only one hyphenated word at the end of the lines.
   This is because automatic hyphenation is turned off. Any words currently hyphenated in the document had the hyphens inserted when the document was created.

2. Scroll to the top of the document, and click on the title.

3. Choose **Tools→Language→Hyphenation** from the menu bar.

4. Make sure the hyphenation zone setting is set to .25", and click the **Automatically hyphenate document** check box.

5. Click **OK**, and browse through the document counting the number of end-of-line hyphens.
   You will increase the hyphenation zone setting in the next few steps and notice how this affects the number of hyphens.

6. Choose **Tools→Language→Hyphenation** from the menu bar.

7. Set the hyphenation zone to .5" and click **OK.**

8. Browse through the document, count the number of hyphens.
   The number of hyphens should have been reduced.

(Continued on the next page)

9. Choose **Tools→Language→Hyphenation** from the menu bar.

10. Uncheck the **Automatically hyphenate document** box, and click **OK.**

11. Browse through the document and notice that all automatic hyphens have been removed. *The only hyphens that remain are for words that were manually hyphenated when the document was created.*

12. Save the document, close it, and continue with the end-of-lesson questions and exercises.

CONCEPTS REVIEW

True/False Questions

1. The Office Assistant cannot be turned off in Word 2000. TRUE FALSE

2. Word marks misspelled words with wavy red underlines. TRUE FALSE

3. You can correct a misspelled word by clicking it with the left mouse button and choosing a suggested replacement from the pop-up menu. TRUE FALSE

4. The Ignore All command on the Spelling and Grammar dialog box ignores a misspelled word for the current spell check only. TRUE FALSE

5. The spell checker can identify certain types of capitalization errors. TRUE FALSE

6. The Go To command can be initiated by pressing (ALT)+G. TRUE FALSE

7. The thesaurus lets you find and replace misspelled words. TRUE FALSE

8. Increasing the hyphenation zone measurement increases the number of hyphenated words. TRUE FALSE

Multiple-Choice Questions

1. Which of the following statements is true?
   a. The spell checker uses only a main dictionary.
   b. The only time a custom dictionary is used is with legal documents.
   c. The spell checker uses a main and custom dictionary for all spell checks.
   d. None of the above

2. Which command initiates Word Count?
   a. Tools→Word Count
   b. Edit→Word Count
   c. Format→Word Count
   d. None of the above

3. What will happen if the Office Assistant is turned off and you click the Help button on the Standard toolbar?
   a. The Office Assistant will appear.
   b. You will receive an error message.
   c. The online Help window will appear.
   d. The Save dialog box will appear.

4. On which menu is a list of the most recently used documents displayed?
   a. File
   b. Edit
   c. Insert
   d. Format

Skill Builders

Skill Builder 3.1 Use the Office Assistant and Online Help

1. Make sure the Office Assistant is displayed. If it isn't displayed, use the **Help→Show the Office Assistant** command.

2. Click the Assistant to display the speech balloon.

3. Type the phrase **Office Clipboard** in the search box, and click the Search button.

4. Click the **View the contents of the Office Clipboard** topic that appears.

5. Take a moment to read the topic, and notice the word *docked* is displayed in color.

6. Clicked the word *docked* and take a moment to read the definition that pops up.

7. Close the definition by clicking in the Help window.

8. If necessary, click the Office Assistant to display the speech balloon.

9. Use the Assistant to locate the Help topic **Create and use custom dictionaries.**

10. Click the **Create and use custom dictionaries** topic, then click the **Creating and using custom dictionaries** hyperlink in the Help window.

11. Take a moment to read the topic, then click the Back ⬅ button on the Help toolbar to return to the previous topic screen.
    You can always use the Back and Forward buttons to revisit topics.

12. Click the Show ⬅▤ button to display the tabs in the Help window.

13. Click the Contents tab.
    The Contents tab contains a list of books that you can expand or collapse to locate a Help topic. This method is most useful if you have a general idea of the topic you are trying to locate but don't know the name of the topic.

14. Click the plus + sign to the left of the **What's New?** book at the top of the window.
    The book will open, displaying a single topic.

15. Click the **What's new in Microsoft Word 2000?** topic to display a list of topics in the right pane of the Help window.

16. Feel free to click any topic to find out about the new features in Word 2000. When you have finished reading a topic, use the Back button to return to the list of new features in Word 2000.

17. Feel free to experiment with Online Help and the Office Assistant.

18. When you have finished, close the Help window, and continue with the next exercise.

1. Start a new document, and type the business letter shown below. Use Word's automatic spell checking and grammar checking as you type the letter. Format the text with bold and italics as shown.

Today's date

Mr. Juan Lopez
Editor-in-Chief
Western Wildlife Publications
1450 Parker Lane
Ventura, CA 93003

Dear Mr. Lopez:

A short time ago, I subscribed to *Birds of Prey* magazine and I am enjoying it immensely. Your monthly tips have been especially useful. I have spotted more than twenty new species in my local area since I first subscribed to *Birds of Prey*. **Keep up the good work!**

One thing that I would like to see more of in *Birds of Prey* is recommendations on bird watching sites in the Western United States. I am especially interested in bald eagles and golden eagles. I would appreciate any suggestions you may have.

Sincerely,

Jason Torval
450 Lighthouse Lane
Manhattan Beach, CA 90266

---

2. Press (CTRL)+H to open the Find and Replace dialog box.

3. Replace all occurrences of *Birds of Prey* with *Bird Watcher.*
   Word should automatically italicize the phrase Bird Watcher *because* Birds of Prey *was italicized.*

4. Make sure there are no spelling errors in the document.

5. Save the document with the name **Skill Builder 3.2,** then close the document.

Skill Builder 3.3 Using the Thesaurus

In this exercise, you will modify the letter you created in the previous exercise.

1. Choose **File** from the menu bar, and then choose **Skill Builder 3.2** from the list of recently used files.
   Suppose you want to use a word other than especially *in the second paragraph.*

2. **Right-click** anywhere on the word *especially* in the second paragraph.

3. Choose **Synonyms** from the pop-up menu, and then choose **particularly**.

4. Use the thesaurus to find replacements for the word **useful** in the first paragraph and **appreciate** in the second paragraph.

5. Select the phrase **A short time ago** at the beginning of the first paragraph.

6. **Right-click** the selected phrase.

7. Choose the replacement phrase *not long ago,* from the Synonym list.
   Notice that Word replaces the phrase but does not capitalize the first word of the sentence.

8. Click Undo ⤺ to restore the original phrase.

9. Choose **Tools→Language→Thesaurus** from the menu bar.

10. Choose the replacement phrase *not long ago,* and click **Replace.**
    In this case, Word should have replaced the phrase and capitalized the first word of the sentence. This is one minor advantage to using the dialog box over the right-click method.

11. Choose **File→Save As** from the menu bar.
    This command can be used to save a document under a new name.

12. Change the name **Skill Builder 3.2** in the filename box to **Skill Builder 3.3,** and click the Save button.
    The Skill Builder 3.2 file remains unchanged, and Skill Builder 3.3 now also resides on your diskette.

13. Close the document, and continue with the next exercise.

Skill Builder 3.4 Editing a Business Letter

1. Open the document on your exercise diskette named Skill Builder 3.4.

2. Use Find and Replace to replace all occurrences of the word *bill* with *account*.

3. Use Find and Replace to replace all occurrences of the word *payment* with *check*.

4. Spell check the entire document.

5. Select the entire document, and change the font size to 12.

6. Use (ENTER) to start the date line at approximately the 2″ position.

7. Replace the phrase Today's Date with the current date.

8. Move the address block from the bottom of the letter to the space between the last body paragraph and the complimentary close (Sincerely). If necessary, insert or remove hard returns until there is a double space between the address block and the last body paragraph, and between the address block and the complimentary close (sincerely).

9. Center the three address block lines horizontally on the page.

10. Insert your typist's initials and the document name below the signature block.

11. Save the changes; then close the document.

Assessments

1. Open the document on your exercise diskette named Assessment 3.1.

2. Spell check the document. Use your best judgment to determine which replacement words to use for incorrectly spelled words. Assume all proper names are spelled correctly.

3. Use Find and Replace to make the following replacements. Also, write the number of replacements in the third column of the table.

Word	Replace With	Number of Replacements
Mary	Chitra	1
arthritis	cancer	4

4. Print the document when you have finished.

5. Save the changes; then close the document.

Assessment 3.2

1. Open the document on your exercise diskette named Assessment 3.2.

2. Replace the phrase Today's Date with the current date, using the Date and Time feature. Insert the date as a field so that it updates automatically.

3. Spell check the document. Use your best judgment to determine which replacement words to use for incorrectly spelled words. Assume all proper names are spelled correctly.

4. Use Find and Replace to make the following replacements. Make sure the case (lowercase or uppercase) remains the same for all replacements. Also, write the number of replacements in the third column of the table.

Word or phrase	Replace With	Number of Replacements
Dan	Mr. Heywood	4
Do not replace Dan in the inside address		
families	people	3
special consideration	something special	3

5. Print the document when you have finished.

6. Save the changes; then close the document.

Critical Thinking

Critical Thinking 3.1 On Your Own

Amanda Jackson is the owner of Amanda's Bookstore. Amanda's Bookstore is located in a small community and specializes in fiction and poetry books. For the past 15 years, Amanda has held weekly poetry readings by local and nationally recognized poets and poets. Write a personal business letter to Amanda thanking her for the poetry readings. Let Amanda know that you enjoy the readings very much and that you would like her to hold monthly book signings. Try to sell her on the idea of holding book signings by convincing her that the events will complement the poetry readings by encouraging fiction enthusiasts to visit the store. The address of Amanda's Bookstore is

Amanda Jackson
Amanda's Bookstore
3420 Colonial Lane
Atlanta, GA 30308

Use Word's spell checker and grammar checker to spell check and grammar check the letter. Use the thesaurus to find replacement words for at least five words in the letter. Save the completed letter as **Critical Thinking 3.1.**

Critical Thinking 3.2 On Your Own

Open the letter that you created in Critical Thinking 1.1. Use Word's spell checker and grammar checker to spell check and grammar check the letter. Use the thesaurus where necessary to replace words in the letter. Save the changes to the completed letter, and close it.

Spell check, grammar check, and use the thesaurus on Critical Thinking exercises 1.3, 1.4, 2.1, 2.2, and 2.3. Save the changes to each document, and then close it.

Critical Thinking 3.3 On Your Own

Bill Patterson is the Executive Director of the Southside Coalition for the Homeless. Bill wants to open a new housing center that will provide shelter, meals, counseling, and job training for needy single mothers and their children. Bill has found the perfect building for the new shelter, but he needs to raise $250,000 to renovate and furnish the building. In addition, he needs $185,000 per year for food, medical supplies, staff salaries, and other expenses. Bill has decided to solicit large corporations in the area for donations. He believes this could be a profitable venture for the corporations because they will receive the following benefits:

Tax deductions
Positive publicity in the community
A pool of trained job candidates

Write a letter for Bill requesting donations from the corporations. The letter should specify the total amount of money needed, how it will be spent, and the benefits realized by the corporations. In addition, ask for specific donation amounts. The recommended donation amounts for the building renovation are $10,000, $15,000, and $25,000. The recommended donation amounts for the annual expenditures are $2,500, $5,000, and $10,000.

Spell check and grammar check your letter, and use the thesaurus to choose the right words. In an important letter such as this, choosing the right words can be very important. Save your completed letter as **Critical Thinking 3.3.**

Critical Thinking 3.4 Web Research

Use Internet Explorer and a search engine of your choice to find information on dictionaries that can be used with Word 2000. There are many third-party dictionaries available with legal, medical, and scientific terminology. Try to locate Web sites of companies that offer such products. Create a Word document that documents your findings. Include the company names, Web site URLs, and any other relevant information that you find. Save your document as **Critical Thinking 3.4.**

Critical Thinking 3.5 With a Group

Open the document you created in Critical Thinking 1.5. Work with your classmate to spell check and grammar check the document. Together, use the thesaurus to choose replacement words for several words in the letter. Choose words that enhance the letter and make your sentences stronger. Discuss the various choices with your partner, and try to choose the right word for each occasion. Save the changes to the letter when you have finished.

Open the memorandum you created in Critical Thinking 2.4. Work with your partner to spell check and grammar check the letter. Together, use the thesaurus to choose replacement words for several words. Save the changes to the memorandum when you have finished.

Creating a Simple Report

In this lesson, you will create a simple report. Reports are important documents often used in business and education. You will format your report using various paragraph formatting techniques. Paragraphs are a fundamental part of any Word document. You will learn how to use Word 2000's new Click and Type feature and change line spacing. In addition, you will master indenting techniques using the ruler and the indent buttons on the Formatting toolbar. This lesson will prepare you for more advanced report techniques discussed in the next lesson.

In This Lesson

Case Study

Bill Nelson is a freshman at West Side Junior College. Bill has enrolled in an information systems course in which Office 2000 is an important component. Bill has been assigned the task of preparing a report on the importance of computer technology in the twenty-first century. Professor Williams has instructed Bill to use Word 2000. After conducting the necessary research, Bill uses the paragraph formatting techniques in Word 2000 to prepare a report that is easy to read, properly formatted, and has a professional appearance.

COMPUTER TECHNOLOGY IN THE TWENTY-FIRST CENTURY

Our society has changed from a manufacturing-oriented society to an information society. Those with access to capital had power in the early 1900s. In the twenty-first century, however, power will come from access to information. The amount of worldwide information is growing at a rapid pace. Computer technology is responsible for much of this growth, but it can also help us manage the information.

Information management is an important use of computer technology. Daryl Richardson of Harmond Technology describes four other reasons why the average person may want to acquire thorough knowledge of computers.

Computer skills are becoming more important in the business world. Many companies need employees with excellent computer skills.

The Internet and other information resources provide access to a global database of information.

Computer skills can often simplify ones personal life. Computers can be used to entertain, to manage finances, and to provide stimulating learning exercises for children.

Using computers can provide a sense of accomplishment. Many people suffer from "computerphobia." Learning to use computers often creates a feeling of connection with the information age.

Report Formats

Overview

There are a variety of acceptable report formats. The example below shows a traditional business report in unbound format. Other report formats can be used for research papers and other types of documents.

Traditional Unbound Business Report Format

Double-spacing is typically set before beginning the report. Three double-spaced returns are used to space the title down to approximately the 2" position.

The title is typed in uppercase, centered, and bold face. You can also apply a distinctive font to the title.

The body of the report is double-spaced. The first line of each body paragraph is indented to 0.5".

Quotations and other text you wish to emphasize are single-spaced and indented 0.5" to 1" on the left and right. You should double-space (by tapping (ENTER) *twice) between quotes.*

COMPUTER TECHNOLOGY IN THE TWENTY-FIRST CENTURY

Our society has changed from a manufacturing-oriented society to an information society. Those with access to capital had power in the early 1900s. In the twenty-first century, however, power will come from access to information. The amount of worldwide information is growing at a rapid pace. Computer technology is responsible for much of this growth, but it can also help us manage the information.

Information management is an important use of computer technology. Daryl Richardson of Harmond Technology describes four other reasons why the average person may want to acquire thorough knowledge of computers.

Computer skills are becoming more important in the business world. Many companies need employees with excellent computer skills.

The Internet and other information resources provide access to a global database of information.

Computer skills can often simplify ones personal life. Computers can be used to entertain, to manage finances, and to provide stimulating learning exercises for children.

Using computers can provide a sense of accomplishment. Many people suffer from "computerphobia." Learning to use computers often creates a feeling of connection with the information age.

Click and Type

Click and Type is a new feature in Word 2000 that lets you automatically apply formatting in blank areas of a document. Click and Type lets you set paragraph alignments (Align Left, Center, and Align Right), customize tab stops, insert tables, and apply other formats. To use Click and Type, position the mouse pointer in a blank area of a document and double-click. Click and Type inserts hard returns and adjusts the paragraph alignment as necessary to achieve the formatting you desire. Click and Type is only available in Print Layout and Web Layout views. The following illustrations demonstrate the use of Click and Type.

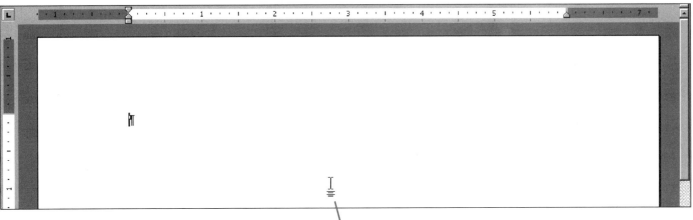

With Click and Type, the mouse pointer changes shape to reflect the formatting that will be applied when you double-click. In this example, the mouse pointer shows that center alignment will be applied.

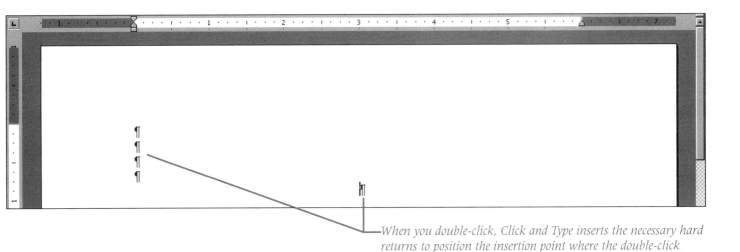

When you double-click, Click and Type inserts the necessary hard returns to position the insertion point where the double-click occurred. In this example, center alignment is also applied.

1. Start Word, and a blank document window will appear.

2. Make sure you are in Print Layout view. If necessary, use the View→Print Layout command to switch to Print Layout view.

3. Slide the mouse pointer to various locations in the blank document, and notice how the mouse pointer changes shape.
   The align left or align right shapes reflect the formatting that would be applied if you were to double-click.

4. Click the Show All ¶ button to display the symbols.

5. Make sure the ruler is displayed at the top of the document window. If necessary, use the View→Ruler command to display the ruler.

6. Follow these steps to use Click and Type to format the title line of the report.

Ⓐ *Position the mouse pointer approximately 2" down and centered on the line. You can tell you are two inches down by looking at the vertical ruler. The 1" position on the white section of the vertical ruler means you are 2" down on the page. This is because the ruler's white section begins at the top margin, which is already 1" down from the top of the page.*

Ⓑ *Double-click when the mouse pointer has the center alignment shape, as shown here.*

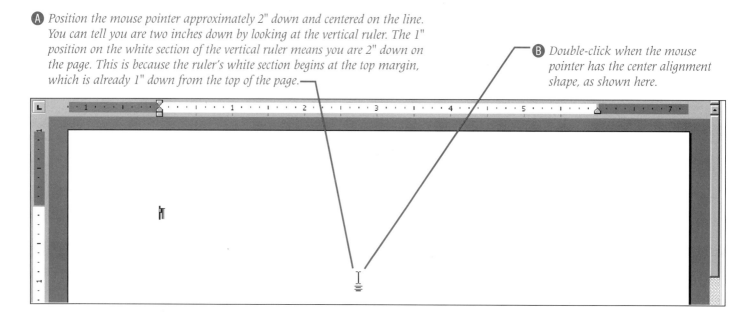

Word inserts paragraph marks as necessary and applies center alignment. Check the Status bar at the bottom of the window to ensure the insertion point is at approximately the 2" position. As you can see, Click and Type can be useful for rapidly applying formats. However, it does lack the precision that may be required for formatting some types of documents.

7. If the insertion point is not at the 2" position, use (ENTER) to insert hard returns as necessary to force it to the 2" position.

8. Turn on (CAPS LOCK), and click the Bold **B** button.

9. Type the report title **COMPUTER TECHNOLOGY IN THE TWENTY-FIRST CENTURY**.

10. Turn off Bold, and tap (ENTER) twice.

11. Slide the mouse pointer to the left end of the current line.

12. Double-click when the mouse pointer has this shape $I^{\equiv}$.
The alignment should change to left, and the insertion point should be positioned two lines below the title. Use Undo and try again if the alignment is not set to left.

13. Save the document to your exercise diskette with the name **Hands-On Lesson 4.**

Line Spacing

From the Keyboard

(CTRL)+1 for single spacing
(CTRL)+5 for 1.5 spacing
(CTRL)+2 for double spacing

Line spacing determines the amount of vertical space between lines in a paragraph. The default line spacing is single. Word makes a single-spaced line slightly higher than the largest character in the line. For example, if you are using a 12-point font, then single line spacing is slightly larger than 12 points. You apply line spacing by selecting the desired paragraph(s) and choosing the desired line spacing from the Paragraph dialog box. The following table describes Word's line spacing options.

Line Spacing	Description
Single	Default spacing in Word
1.5 Lines	1.5 times single-spacing
Double	Twice single-spacing
At Least	Specifies the minimum line spacing. The spacing may increase if the font size increases. However, the line spacing will never be smaller than the number of points specified in the At Least setting.
Exactly	Fixes the line spacing at the number of points specified. The line spacing remains fixed even if the font size of characters within the line changes.
Multiple	Lets you precisely control the line spacing by setting multiples such as 1.3 or 2.4.

 Hands-On 4.2 Set Line Spacing

1. Make sure the insertion point is on the second blank line below the title.

2. Choose **Format→Paragraph** from the menu bar.

3. Click the Line spacing drop-down ▪ button, and notice the various options.

4. Choose **Double** from the list, and click **OK.**

5. Tap the (TAB) key once to create a 0.5″ indent at the start of the paragraph.

(Continued on the next page)

6. Now type the following paragraph, but only tap (ENTER) after the last line in the paragraph. *The lines will be double-spaced as you type them.*

> Our society has changed from a manufacturing-oriented society to an information society. Those with access to capital had power in the early 1900s. In the twenty-first century, however, power will come from access to information. The amount of worldwide information is growing at a rapid pace. Computer technology is responsible for much of this growth, but it can also help us manage the information.

7. Make sure you tap (ENTER) after the last line. Then (TAB) once, and type the following paragraph.
   Notice the double-spacing has been carried to the new paragraph.

> Information management is an important use of computer technology. Daryl Richardson of Harmond Technology describes four other reasons why the average person may want to acquire thorough knowledge of computers.

8. Tap (ENTER) to complete the paragraph, then press (CTRL)+1 to set single-spacing.
   The shortcut keystrokes can be quite useful for setting line spacing.

9. Now type the following paragraphs, tapping (ENTER) twice between paragraphs. There is no need to tab at the beginning of these paragraphs.

> Computer skills are becoming more important in the business world. Many companies need employees with excellent computer skills.
>
> The Internet and other information resources provide access to a global database of information.
>
> Computer skills can often simplify one's personal life. Computers can be used to entertain, to manage finances, and to provide stimulating learning exercises for children.
>
> Using computers can provide a sense of accomplishment. Many people suffer from "computerphobia." Learning to use computers often creates a feeling of connection with the information age.

10. Save ▣ the changes, and continue with the next topic.

Indenting Text

Indenting offsets text from the margins. The **left indent** is the most widely used indent. The left indent sets off all lines in a paragraph from the left margin. Likewise, the **right indent** sets off all lines from the right margin. The **first line indent** sets off just the first line of paragraphs. This is similar to using (TAB) at the start of a paragraph. The **hanging indent** sets off all lines except for the first line.

From the Keyboard

(CTRL)+M for left indent
(CTRL)+(SHIFT)+M to remove left indent
(CTRL)+T for hanging indent
(CTRL)+(SHIFT)+T to remove hanging indent

The Increase Indent 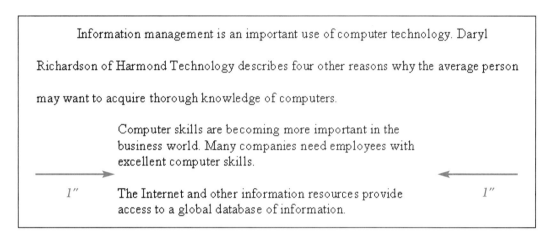 button and Decrease Indent button on the Formatting toolbar let you adjust the **left** indent. These buttons increase or decrease the left indent to the nearest tab stop. The default tab stops are set every 0.5″, so the left indent changes 0.5″ each time you click the buttons. You can also set indents using keystrokes, the Paragraph dialog box, and by dragging indent markers on the horizontal ruler.

Information management is an important use of computer technology. Daryl Richardson of Harmond Technology describes four other reasons why the average person may want to acquire thorough knowledge of computers.

> Computer skills are becoming more important in the business world. Many companies need employees with excellent computer skills.
>
> 1″ ⟶ The Internet and other information resources provide access to a global database of information. ⟵ 1″

These paragraphs are indented 1″ from the left and right margins.

Hands-On 4.3 Experiment with Left Indents

Indent One Paragraph

1. Click on one of the single-spaced paragraphs you just typed.

2. Click the Increase Indent button near the right end of the Formatting toolbar.
   The paragraph should be indented 0.5″ on the left.

3. Click the Decrease Indent button to remove the indent.

Indent Several Paragraphs

4. Use the mouse to select any part of two or more paragraphs.
   You only need to select part of a paragraph when indenting or applying other paragraph formats.

5. Click Increase Indent **twice** to create a 1″ left indent on each of the selected **paragraphs**.

6. Now click Decrease Indent **twice** to remove the indents.
   You will continue to work with indents in the next Hands-On exercise.

The Horizontal Ruler

You can set indents, margins, and tab stops by dragging markers on the horizontal ruler. When you use the ruler, you can see formatting changes as they are applied. The horizontal ruler is positioned just above the document in the document window. You can display or hide the ruler with the **View→Ruler** command. The following illustration shows the ruler, the margin boundaries, and the various indent markers.

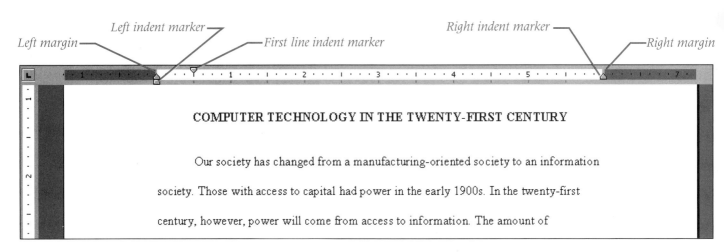

INDENT MARKERS

Indent Type		How to Set It
First line		Drag this marker.
Hanging		Drag the top triangle.
Left		Drag the bottom square.
Right		Drag this marker on the right end of the ruler.

Hands-On 4.4 Use the Ruler to Indent Paragraphs

Set Left and Right Indents

1. If necessary, scroll down until the four single-spaced paragraphs at the bottom of your document are visible.

2. Select all four paragraphs by dragging the mouse pointer in the left margin.

3. Use the following steps to adjust the left and right indents.

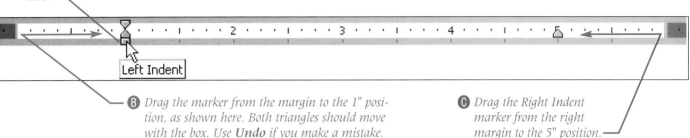

Convert Tab Stops to First Line Indents

4. Scroll to the top of the document.

5. Make sure the nonprinting characters are displayed in your document. If necessary, use the Show All button to display the nonprinting characters.
   In the next step, you are instructed to remove the tab → symbol from the start of the first paragraph. You should have inserted the tab when you created the paragraph. It is possible that your paragraph will not have a tab symbol (even if it is indented). Skip the following step if there is no tab symbol.

6. Follow these steps to remove the tab symbol at the start of the first body paragraph.

   Ⓐ *Click to the left of the tab symbol.*————| → Our·society·has·changed·

   Ⓑ *Tap the* (DELETE) *key.* society.·Those·with·access·to·ca|

   The space created by the tab should be removed from the first line.

7. Make sure the insertion point is at the start of the paragraph and tap the (TAB) key.
   The first line will be indented 0.5" although you won't see a tab → symbol in the document. The First Line Indent marker should have moved to the 0.5" position on the ruler. Word 2000 automatically creates a first line indent when you tap the (TAB) key at the start of an existing paragraph. This has the same effect as inserting a tab symbol. This feature is known as AutoIndent.

8. Use the technique in Step 6 to remove the tab → symbol from the beginning of the second double-spaced paragraph.

9. Now drag the First Line Indent ▽ marker to the 0.5" position on the ruler.
   The paragraph should have the same 0.5" indent as the first paragraph. As you can see, there are several ways to indent the first line of a paragraph.

(Continued on the next page)

Experiment with the Indent Markers

10. Select both of the double-spaced paragraphs.

11. Drag the First Line Indent ▽ marker to the left or right.
    The first line indent of both paragraphs will be adjusted.

12. Make sure the paragraphs are still selected, and drag the Left Indent ⬒ marker (bottom square).
    The left indent affects all lines in the paragraph because it moves both the First Line Indent marker and the Hanging Indent marker.

13. Feel free to experiment with indents, but restore the 0.5″ first line indents when you have finished.

14. Save the changes to your document, and then close the document.

■

Concepts Review

True/False Questions

1. The Increase Indent button changes the right indent. TRUE FALSE

2. The Decrease Indent button changes the right indent. TRUE FALSE

3. The ruler can be used to indent paragraphs. TRUE FALSE

4. The (CTRL)+D keystroke combination is used to set double-spacing. TRUE FALSE

5. The (CTRL)+1 keystroke combination is used to set single-spacing. TRUE FALSE

6. The Ruler is displayed with the Edit→Ruler command. TRUE FALSE

7. First Line indents only affect the first line of each selected paragraph. TRUE FALSE

8. The title begins 2" from the top of the page in a traditional business report. TRUE FALSE

Multiple-Choice Questions

1. In which of the following view modes is Click and Type available?
   a. Print Layout
   b. Web Layout
   c. Outline
   d. Both a and b

2. What will happen if you tap the (TAB) key at the beginning of an existing paragraph?
   a. The Left indent will increase.
   b. The First Line indent will increase.
   c. A tab symbol will be inserted.
   d. None of the above

3. Which of the following actions should you take ito adjust the right indent of three paragraphs?
   a. Drag the Right Indent marker.
   b. Select the paragraphs, and then drag the Right Indent marker.
   c. Select the paragraphs, and tap the Tab key.
   d. All of the above

4. Which command is used to display the horizontal ruler?
   a. View→Ruler
   b. Edit→Display Ruler
   c. Insert→Ruler
   d. File→Ruler

Skill Builders

Skill Builder 4.1 Indents and Line Spacing

1. Start a new document, and choose **Format→Paragraph** from the menu bar.

2. Set the line spacing to double, and click **OK.**

3. Click the Center ▤ button, and tap (ENTER) three times to double-space down to the 2" position.

4. Set the font to Arial, bold, 12pt, and type the title shown below.

5. Tap (ENTER), and set the alignment to left.

6. Turn off bold and set the font size to 11.

7. Type the first paragraph shown below, tapping (ENTER) once at the end of the paragraph.

8. Choose **Format→Paragraph** from the menu bar, and set the line spacing to single and the left and right indents to 1".
   The Paragraph dialog box is useful when setting several options, or when you want to precisely set line spacing, indents, or other options.

9. Click Italics *I* and type the quotations shown below. Use the Em Dash symbol from the Symbols dialog box between the end of paragraph periods and the author's names. Do not use italics on the author's names.

FAMOUS AMERICAN QUOTATIONS

Quotations have the power to inspire and define moments in our history. They are windows into the minds and lives of great people. Famous Americans certainly have contributed their share of famous quotations.

There was never yet an uninteresting life. Such a thing is an impossibility. Inside of the dullest exterior, there is a drama, a comedy, and a tragedy.—Mark Twain

We hold these truths to be sacred and undeniable; that all men are created equal and independent, that from that equal creation they derive rights inherent and inalienable, among which are the preservation of life, and liberty, and the pursuit of happiness.—Thomas Jefferson

I think, at a child's birth, if a mother could ask a fairy godmother to endow it with the most useful gift, that gift would be curiosity.—Eleanor Roosevelt

---

10. Save the document with the name **Skill Builder 4.1.**
    You will continue to use the document in the next exercise.

Skill Builder 4.2 Add Another Quotation

In this exercise, you will add a new quotation, and a paragraph to the Skill Builder 4.1 document. The document should be open from the previous exercise.

1. Position the insertion point in front of the word *We* at the beginning of the second quote.

2. Tap (ENTER) twice to push the last two quotations down.

3. Tap ↑ twice to move the insertion point into the blank space between the paragraphs.

4. Now type the following quotation.

> *No one has been barred on account of his race from fighting or dying for America—There are no "white" or "colored" signs on the foxholes or graveyards of battle.— John F. Kennedy*

5. Now add the paragraph shown below to the bottom of the document. Make sure you double-space with (ENTER) between the last quote and the new paragraph. For the new paragraph, set the left and right indents to zero, the first line indent to 0.5″, and the line spacing to double. You will also need to turn off italics.

> Famous quotations help us express those hard-to-find words and feelings that
>
> are in all of our hearts. They become a part of our national conscience and memory.

6. Choose **File→Save As** from the menu bar.

7. Change the name of the document to **Skill Builder 4.2,** save it, and close it.

Skill Builder 4.3 Format an Existing Document

In this exercise, you will open a report on your exercise diskette. You will adjust the line spacing and indents and spell check the document.

Adjust the First Line Indent and Line Spacing

1. Open the document named Skill Builder 4.3.

2. Use the Zoom Control to switch to a Whole Page zoom.

3. Select the entire document by triple-clicking in the left margin, or choose **Edit**→*Select All* from the menu bar.

4. Drag the First Line Indent ▽ marker to the 0.5″ position on the ruler.
   This will indent the first line of all paragraphs by 0.5″ (including the title).

5. Set the line spacing to double.

6. Use the Zoom Control to switch to a Page Width zoom.

Format the Title and Credit Line

7. Use (ENTER) to push the title down to approximately the 2″ position.

8. Center ▤ the title.
   Look at the ruler, and notice that the First Line Indent marker is at the 0.5″ position. This will cause the title to be slightly off center.

9. Set the First Line Indent ▽ for the title paragraph to zero.

10. Format the title as Arial Bold, 14pt.

11. Click on the credit line at the bottom of the report.

12. Set the First Line Indent ▽ to zero, and right-align ▤ the paragraph.
    The paragraph should be flush with the right margin.

13. Format the title *The Forest People* in the credit line with italics.

14. Spell check the entire document. Assume that the names of all people and places are correct.

15. Save the changes, and close the document.

Skill Builder 4.4 Create an Announcement

1. Use the following guidelines to create the announcement shown below.

   - Begin the announcement 2″ down. Use double-spacing between all title lines and for the first body paragraph. Use ⒺⓃⓉⒺⓇ to double-space between the cast member paragraphs. Use single-spacing within the cast member paragraphs.

   - Use an Arial font for the entire document. Use a font size of 12 for the body paragraphs. All title lines are centered, 14pt, and bold.

   - Use Em Dash symbols after the names of the cast members. Indent the cast member paragraphs 0.5″ on both the left and right.

2. Save the announcement with the name **Skill Builder 4.4,** and close the document.

The West Coast Playhouse

Presents

An Evening with Mabel

This fabulous play has been entertaining audiences since its opening night on

March 1, 1998. The cast is first-class, and the ambience is magical. You will find

this play delightfully humorous and deeply moving.

The Cast

> **Rebecca Thomas**—Rebecca is a graduate of the Smithton School of Dramatic Arts. Rebecca has played lead roles in 17 theatrical productions. She has also appeared on *Saturday Night Live* and other television productions.

> **Jim Oliver**—Jim is a recent graduate with a major in drama. Jim was voted the best overall actor in his graduating class, and he has won numerous other awards. We are confident that you will find Jim's performance truly memorable.

> **Clara Boyd**—Clara recently moved here from London, England, where she specialized in Shakespearean theatrical performances. Clara is also a world-class pianist.

Assessments

Assessment 4.1 Format an Existing Document

1. Open the document named Assessment 4.1 on your exercise diskette.

2. Apply double-spacing to the entire document.

3. Center the title, and apply bold formatting to the title.

4. Apply bold formatting to the two capitalized headings.

5. Apply a 0.5" First Line indent to all body paragraphs except for the headings.

6. Print the document, save the changes, and close the document.

Assessment 4.2 Create a Report Using Indents

1. Use the skills and report formatting knowledge you have acquired to create the report shown below. The single-spaced paragraphs are indented 1" on both the left and right.

2. Print the report, save it as **Assessment 4.2,** but leave it open, as you will continue to use it.

CLASSIFICATIONS OF EMPLOYMENT

CFEB Associates—Company Handbook

It is important that you understand how CFEB Associates classifies its employees.

We have established the following classifications for purposes of salary administration

and eligibility for overtime payment and benefits.

Full-Time Regular Employees. These are staff members hired to work CFEB's normal, full-time workweek on a regular basis.

Part-Time Regular Employees. These are staff members hired to work at CFEB fewer than thirty-five hours per week on a regular basis.

Exempt Employees. These are staff members of CFEB Associates who are not required to be paid overtime, in accordance with applicable federal wage and hour laws, for work performed beyond forty hours in a workweek.

Nonexempt Employees. These are staff members of CFEB Associates who are required to be paid overtime at the rate of time and one-half their regular rate of pay for all hours worked beyond forty hours in a workweek.

Assessment 4.3 **Add Paragraphs to a Document**

1. Use the **File→Save As** command to save Assessment 4.2 with the name Assessment 4.3.

2. Add the following two paragraphs to the end of the Assessment 4.3 document. Notice that the first paragraph is indented and single-spaced, and the second paragraph is not indented and double-spaced.

3. If your report wraps to a second page after inserting the text, then remove hard returns from the top of the document until it fits on one page. If necessary, use a Whole Page zoom setting so that you can see the entire document. You should remove enough hard returns to center the document vertically on the page.

4. Print the report, save the changes, and close the document.

Temporary Employees. These are staff members of CFEB Associates who are engaged to work full-time or part-time on the firm's payroll with the understanding that their employment will be terminated no later than upon completion of a specific assignment.

You will be informed of your initial employment classification and of your exempt or nonexempt status during your orientation session. Please direct any questions regarding your employment classification or exemption status to the Director of Human Resources.

Critical Thinking

Critical Thinking 4.1 On Your Own

Alexis Winston is a sophomore at Big State University majoring in computer science. Alexis has completed her freshman courses and is finally taking her first computer science courses. Computer Science 101 provides an introduction to computing theory and requires each student to submit several reports. The topic of the first report assigned by Professor Carpenter is to research trends in computer science and technology. Each student must write a one-page report on the four most relevant computing trends of the twenty-first century. Alexis conducts the necessary research and decides upon the four trends that she considers to be the most relevant. She writes the following report text describing these trends.

The Internet—Use of the Internet has grown exponentially since 1995. The Internet has affected nearly every aspect of the computer world. Use of the Internet for business, education, communication, and other functions will continue to expand exponentially in the near future.

Open source—The move towards open source software (particularly operating systems) appears to be gathering momentum. The driving force behind the open source movement is the emergence of the Linux operating system. Linux has become the operating system of choice for many server systems and applications. Linux is also gaining recognition as a potential operating system for personal computers.

Internet appliances—Computing in the twenty-first century will no longer be restricted to personal computers and larger servers. The emergence of smart appliances and Internet-enabled consumer devices is a major trend. It is estimated that sales of Internet appliances in the United States will reach $15.3 billion by 2002.

Computers on a chip—The semiconductor industry has made remarkable advances in miniaturization and specialization. Soon, the functions of a motherboard will be condensed into a single chip. Single-chip computers will play a major role in a variety of devices from personal computers to cell phones, Internet appliances, and consumer electronics.

Write a one-page report on computing trends of the twenty-first century. Include a title, at least one main body paragraph, and the four trends discussed above. You can retype the trends exactly as they appear above. Format the report using the traditional unbound business report format. Indent the four trends 0.5″ on both the left and right.

Spell check and grammar check your report. Use the thesaurus to find replacement words for at least four words in the trends shown above. Save your completed report as **Critical Thinking 4.1.**

Critical Thinking 4.2 Web Research With a Group

Alexis Winston's CS 101 class incorporates a business component that addresses the impact of computing trends on business. Professor Carpenter has assigned a second report that requires each student to discuss the business implications of one of the trends mentioned in the previous report (the report written in Critical Thinking 4.1). Alexis decides to write her report on companies that will benefit from the emergence of Internet appliances.

Work with your classmate to write a brief, one-page report on four companies that will benefit from the use of Internet appliances. Together, use Internet Explorer and a search engine of your choice to get information about the companies. You can choose any four companies. Some examples of companies that may benefit from this trend include Wind River Systems, Network Appliance, Cisco Systems, and Intel. Write a brief description of how each company may benefit from the use of Internet appliances. You can visit the Web sites of the companies or search for relevant articles on the Web. Position the information on the four companies below the main body paragraph, and indent them 1" on both the left and right. Use the unbound business report format with a title, at least one body paragraph, and the four indented paragraphs on the companies. Save your completed report as **Critical Thinking 4.2.**

LESSON 5

Margins and Lists

In this lesson, you will expand upon the formatting techniques you learned in the previous lesson and you will use margins, bulleted lists, and hanging indents to create a more sophisticated document. You will also learn how to customize bulleted and numbered lists, and you will work with outline-style numbered lists.

In This Lesson

Case Study

Lisa Madison has found the summer job that most students dream about: she is a whitewater-rafting guide for Outdoor Adventures. Outdoor Adventures has been wooing thrill seekers for 25 years with rafting trips, helicopter skiing, wilderness trekking, and other high-octane adventures. Recently, Lisa realized that many guests have been forgetting to bring items, while others have been getting lost on the way to the starting points. Lisa decides to take charge of this situation using the power of Word 2000 designing a pre-trip checklist that includes a list of recommendations, a bulleted list of items to bring, and directions to the starting points. With her take-charge attitude and her Office 2000 skills, Lisa should have no problem navigating the turbulent waters awaiting her in today's rough-and-tumble business world.

OUTDOOR ADVENTURES

Pre-Trip Checklist

The following checklist and directions will help you prepare for your trip. Also, remember to keep three important things in mind:

1. Pack light—We have limited space on our rafts, and you must carry all of your belongings with you. You will make more friends if you pack light.

2. Bring waterproof bags—One thing you can count on is that you bag(s) will get wet. Make sure they are waterproof and they float.

3. No valuables please—Leave valuables such as camcorders and cameras at home. Inexpensive 35mm cameras are the safest bet.

Checklist:
- ❑ Sunglasses
- ❑ Sunscreen
- ❑ Insect repellant
- ❑ Three sets of dry clothing
- ❑ Tennis shoes
- ❑ A warm, waterproof jacket

Directions:

Upper Granite Canyon—Take Highway 240 to the Forest Lake exit. Take Forest Lake Drive to Creekside Lane, and look for the starting point.

Middle Granite Canyon—Take Highway 240 to the Pine Meadows turnoff. Go right for two miles until you see a fork in the road. Go right for one mile to the starting point.

Margins

Margins determine the overall size of the text area on a page. In Word, the default top and bottom margins are 1", and the left and right margins are 1.25". You can set margins by dragging the margin boundaries on the rulers. You can also use the **File→Page Setup** command and set the margins in the Margins tab of the Page Setup dialog box. Margin settings are applied to the entire document or to an entire section (if the document has multiple sections). Sections are not discussed in this lesson.

Differences Between Margins and Indents

The margins determine the space between the text and the edge of the page. Indents are used to offset text from the margins. For example, imagine a document has a 1" left margin, and one of the paragraphs in that document has a 0.5" indent. The margin plus the indent will position the paragraph 1.5" from the edge of the page. If the margin were changed to 2", then the indented paragraph would be positioned 2.5 " from the edge of the page (the 2" margin plus the 0.5" indent).

 ## Hands-On 5.1 Set Margins

1. Start Word, and choose **File→Page Setup** from the menu bar.
   The Page Setup dialog box lets you adjust a number of important settings that affect pages; for example, margins, paper size, page orientation, and headers and footers.

2. Make sure the Margins tab is selected, and notice the default settings for the margins.

3. Change the top margin to 1.5" and the left and right margins to 1".

4. Click **OK** to apply the changes.
   The top of the vertical ruler will have a 1.5" dark gray area representing the top margin. Also, the Status bar will indicate that the insertion point is at the 1.5" position.

5. Set the font size to 14, and type the following text. Use (ENTER) to double-space between the title and subtitle and to triple-space between the subtitle and body paragraph. Also, use (ENTER) to double-space after the body paragraph.

OUTDOORS ADVENTURES

Pre-Trip Checklist

The following checklist and directions will help you prepare for your trip. Also, remember to keep three important things in mind:

---

6. Format the title with an Arial 18 pt bold font, and the subtitle with an Arial 16 pt bold font.

7. Save the document with the name **Hands-On Lesson 5.**
   You will continue to enhance this document throughout the lesson.

Setting Margins with the Rulers

You can set all four margins by dragging the margin boundaries on the rulers. The benefit of this technique is that you can see the effect immediately in the document. If you press the (ALT) key when dragging a margin boundary, Word displays the precise margin measurement; on the rulers however, you must press (ALT) after you have begun dragging the margin boundary.

Hands-On 5.2 Change Margins with the Ruler

1. Follow these steps to adjust the margins.

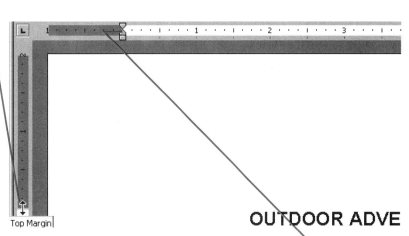

Ⓐ *Position the mouse pointer here on the top margin boundary so that a double-headed arrow will appear.*

Ⓑ *Drag the margin boundary down until the numeral 2 appears at the top of the ruler. This indicates that the margin is set to 2".*

Ⓒ *Try adjusting the top margin again but press and hold the (ALT) key after you begin dragging. Word will display the margin measurements on the ruler.*

Ⓓ *Set the top margin to 2".*

Ⓔ *Try changing the left margin by dragging this margin boundary. However, be patient because the indent markers may prevent the double-headed arrow from appearing. When you have finished, make sure the left margin is set to 1".*

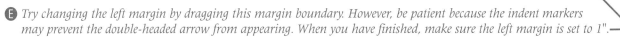

Bulleted and Numbered Lists

You can create bulleted and numbered lists with the Bullets 📇 and Numbering 📇 buttons on the Formatting toolbar. In Word, a list is a series of two or more paragraphs. You can apply bullets and numbers to paragraphs by selecting the paragraphs and clicking the desired button. For a new list, you can turn on bullets or numbers when you begin typing the list. Word will format the first paragraph with a bullet or number. When you complete the paragraph and tap (ENTER), Word formats the next paragraph with a bullet or number. In a numbered list, Word numbers the paragraphs sequentially. Paragraphs in a numbered list are automatically renumbered if paragraphs are inserted or deleted.

AutoFormat as You Type

You can also start a bulleted list by typing an asterisk * followed by a space or a tab at the beginning of a new paragraph. When you complete the paragraph and tap (ENTER), Word converts the asterisk to a bullet character. Likewise, you can begin a numbered list by typing 1 followed by a space or tab and tapping (ENTER). This feature is known as **AutoFormat as You Type.**

Turning Bullets and Numbering Off

You can remove bullets or numbers from paragraphs by selecting the paragraphs(s) and clicking the Bullets button or the Numbering button. If you are typing a list, you should complete the list by tapping (ENTER) after the last paragraph in the list. You can then turn off bullets or numbering for the first paragraph following the list by clicking the Bullets button or the Numbering button.

Create a Numbered List

1. Position the insertion point at the bottom of the document.
   The insertion point should be on the second blank line below the body paragraph.

2. Click the Numbering 📋 button on the Formatting toolbar.
   The indented numeral 1 appears followed by a period.

3. Type the following text, inserting the Em Dash symbol as shown.

   > 1. Pack light—We have limited space on our rafts, and you must carry all of your belongings with you. You will make more friends if you pack light.

4. Tap (ENTER) once after typing the text.
   Notice that Word begins the next paragraph with the numeral 2. Paragraphs are numbered sequentially unless you tell Word otherwise. You will learn how to change the starting number later in this lesson.

5. Tap (ENTER) again, and numbering will be turned off for the new paragraph.
   Word assumes you want to turn off numbering when you tap (ENTER) without typing any text.

6. Click the Numbering 📋 button again.
   Word will number the new blank paragraph with the numeral 2. Word continues the numbering from the previous list.

7. Type the following text.

   > 2. Bring waterproof bags—One thing you can count on is that your bag(s) will get wet. Make sure they are waterproof and they float.

8. Tap (ENTER) and notice that Word creates a double-space and starts the numbering at 3.
   Word now understands that you want a double-space between each paragraph in the list.

9. Type the following text.

   > 3. No valuables please—Leave valuables such as camcorders and cameras at home. Inexpensive 35 mm cameras are the safest bet.

10. Tap (ENTER) and another double-space will be inserted.

11. Click the Numbering 📋 button to turn off numbering for the new paragraph.

12. Type **Checklist**: and tap (ENTER) once.

13. Click the Bullets ▦ button on the Formatting toolbar.
    Word will most likely insert a round • bullet (although another bullet style may appear). Also, the bullet may be indented further than the numbers in the numbered list.

14. Type **Sunglasses**, and tap (ENTER).
    Word formats the new paragraph with the bullet style.

15. Complete the following checklist.

> Checklist:
> - Sunglasses
> - Sunscreen
> - Insect repellant
> - Three sets of dry clothing
> - Tennis shoes
> - A warm, waterproof jacket

16. Tap (ENTER) twice after the last list item to turn off bullets.

The Bullets and Numbering Dialog Box

The **Format→Bullets and Numbering** command displays the Bullets and Numbering dialog box. The Bullets and Numbering dialog box lets you choose a style for your bulleted or numbered list, customize lists, and create outline numbered lists.

Built-in Bullet and Numbering Styles

Word provides seven built-in styles for bulleted and numbered lists. The styles are displayed in **style galleries** in the Bullets and Numbering dialog box. You can easily change the appearance of a bulleted or numbered list by choosing a style from the style galleries. The following illustration shows the built-in bullet and number styles available.

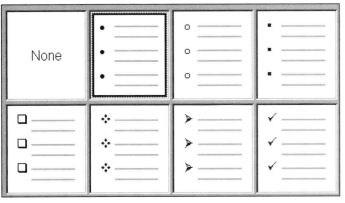

Bullet style gallery

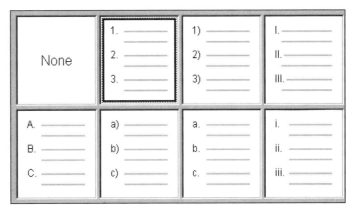

Number style gallery

1. Select the bulleted list as shown below.

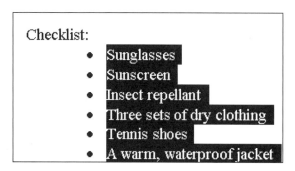

Checklist:
- Sunglasses
- Sunscreen
- Insect repellant
- Three sets of dry clothing
- Tennis shoes
- A warm, waterproof jacket

2. Choose **Format→Bullets and Numbering** from the menu bar.

3. Choose the Checkbox style from the bullets gallery, and click **OK.**

Customizing Bullet and Number Styles

You can customize the built-in bullet and number styles in several ways. For example, you may want to use a bullet character other than the built-in bullet characters, or you may want to change the default indentation of a particular built-in bullet or number style. These and other customization options are available in the Customization dialog box. To display the Customization dialog box first display the Bullets and Numbering dialog box, and then choose a bullet or number style from the style galleries, and click the Customize button.

Resetting Customized Bullet and Number Styles

Once you customize a built-in bullet or number style, the new customized style replaces the built-in style in the style gallery from that point onward. Fortunately, the Bullets and Numbering dialog box contains a Reset button that restores a style in the gallery to its original built-in format. To reset a style, you choose the style from the style galleries and click the Reset button.

Modifying List Numbering

Many documents have more than one numbered list. In some documents, you may want the numbering to continue sequentially from one list to the next. For example, if one list ends with the numeral 4 you may want the next list to begin with the numeral 5. Then again, you may want the numbering in each new list to begin with 1. Fortunately, Word has two options on the Numbered tab of the Bullets and Numbering dialog box that let you control the list numbering:

- **Restart numbering option**—This option forces a list to begin with the number 1.

- **Continue previous list option**—This option forces the numbering to continue from the previous list.

1. Scroll up, and click anywhere on the first numbered paragraph.

2. Choose **Format→Bullets and Numbering** from the menu bar.
   Notice the seven different number styles in the gallery. As with bullets, you can apply a style by choosing it from the gallery and clicking OK. When you use the Numbering button on the Formatting toolbar, it always applies the most recently used number style.

3. Notice the **Restart numbering** and **Continue previous list** options below the number styles.
   These options are used to adjust the starting number of a numbered list. These options will not be available for the paragraph numbered 1 because it is the first numbered paragraph in the document.

4. Click the **Customize** button.

5. Follow these steps to explore the Custom Numbered List dialog box.

Ⓐ *Notice that you can change the font for the numbers and the number format. The **Number format** can be customized by adding text in front of the shaded number. For example, you could type the word Step in front of the shaded number to begin each item in a numbered list with the word Step (e.g. Step 1, Step 2).*

Ⓑ *This option lets you start a list with any number.*

Ⓒ *You can adjust the number position and the indent of the text from the number with these options.*

Ⓓ *Now, change the **Indent at** setting to 0.75" and click OK.*

Customize Numbered List | ? | X

Number format
```
1.
```
Font...

Number style: `1, 2, 3, ...`   **Start at:** `1`

Number position
Left   **Aligned at:** `0.25"`

Text position
Indent at: `0.5"`

OK
Cancel

Preview
1.
2.
3.

The new number style should be applied to all numbered paragraphs. This will move the text following the number to the 0.75" position.

6. Make sure the insertion point is somewhere on the first paragraph in the numbered list.

7. Choose **Format→Bullets and Numbering** from the menu bar.
   The current number style should be highlighted in the gallery.

8. Locate the **Reset** button at the bottom of the dialog box.
   The Reset button will be available because the current number style has been customized.

9. Click the **Reset** button.

(Continued on the next page)

10. Click **Yes** on the message box that appears.

Word asks if you want to restore the gallery position to the default style. Each style has a position in the gallery. When you reset a style, you are resetting a particular gallery position to the default formats for that position. Notice that the Reset button is no longer available. The Reset button is only available if the high-lighted gallery style has been customized.

11. Click **OK,** and the numbered paragraphs will be restored to their original format.

Keep in mind that you can customize bullet styles in a similar manner to number styles.

Adjusting Bullet and Number Alignment with the Ruler

You can easily adjust the indents of bulleted and numbered lists and the text following the bullets and numbers by dragging markers on the ruler. This technique is useful because it can be applied to specific paragraphs without changing the built-in styles in the style galleries. Drag the First Line Indent ▽ marker to adjust the bullet position and a Left Tab **L** marker to adjust the text position.

Hands-On 5.6 Adjust Bullet Position and the Text Indent

1. Scroll to the bottom of the document, and select all of the bulleted paragraphs.

2. Follow this step to adjust the **First Line Indent** ▽ marker.

Ⓐ *Drag the **First Line Indent** marker to the 0.25" position on the ruler as shown here. The bullets will move over to the 0.25" position. As you can see, the **First Line Indent** marker determines the bullet position.*

3. Follow these steps to adjust the **Left Tab L** marker.

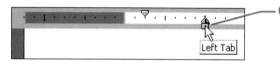

Ⓐ *Position the mouse pointer on the **Left Indent** marker (the bottom square) and a **Left Tab** ScreenTip will appear. Notice a **Left Tab** marker is superimposed on the indent marker. The **Left Tab** marker appears whenever a paragraph has bullets or numbers. You will learn more about tab markers soon.*

Ⓑ *Drag the **Left Tab** marker until it is positioned at the 0.5" position as shown here. The bullet text should now be aligned at the 0.5" position.*

4. Follow these steps to adjust the **Hanging Indent** marker.

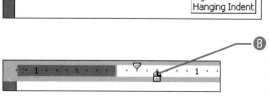

Ⓐ *Position the mouse pointer on the **Hanging Indent** marker (the upward pointing triangle) and a **Hanging Indent** ScreenTip will appear.*

Ⓑ *Drag the **Hanging Indent** marker until it is positioned at the 0.5" position as shown here. You won't notice any change in the alignment at this point. You will learn about hanging indents in the next topic.*

The bulleted checklist should have the appearance and alignment shown below.

> 3. No valuables please—Leave valuables such as camcorders and cameras at home. Inexpensive 35 mm cameras are the safest bet.
>
> Checklist:
> - Sunglasses
> - Sunscreen
> - Insect repellant
> - Three sets of dry clothing
> - Tennis shoes
> - A warm, waterproof jacket

5. Save the changes, and continue with the next topic.

Hanging Indents

The Hanging Indent ⬆ marker (upward-pointing triangle) offsets all lines of a paragraph except for the first line. Hanging indents are often used in bibliographic entries, glossary terms, and bulleted and numbered lists. You create hanging indents by dragging the Hanging Indent marker on the ruler or with the Paragraph dialog box.

> Middle Granite Canyon—Take Highway 240 to the Pine Meadows turnoff. Go right for two miles until you see a fork in the road. Go right for one mile to the starting point.

Hands-On 5.7 Create Hanging Indents

1. Position the insertion point on the second blank line below the checklist.

2. Type **Directions:** and tap (ENTER).

3. Type the following text:

> Upper Granite Canyon—Take Highway 240 to the Forest Lake exit. Take Forest Lake Drive to Creekside Lane and look for the starting point.

(Continued on the next page)

4. Click anywhere on the paragraph you just typed.

5. Follow these steps to create a hanging indent.

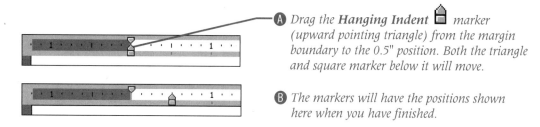

Ⓐ Drag the **Hanging Indent** ⌂ marker (upward pointing triangle) from the margin boundary to the 0.5" position. Both the triangle and square marker below it will move.

Ⓑ The markers will have the positions shown here when you have finished.

The formatted paragraph should match the following example. Notice how the second line is indented, but the first line remains at the margin.

> Upper Granite Canyon—Take Highway 240 to the Forest Lake exit. Take Forest Lake Drive to Creekside Lane and look for the starting point.

6. Now click the Increase Indent ⊞ button to increase both the First Line indent and the Hanging indent.

7. Position the insertion point at the end of the paragraph (to the right of the period).

8. Tap (ENTER) twice, then type the following text.

> Middle Granite Canyon—Take Highway 240 to the Pine Meadows turnoff. Go right for two miles until you see a fork in the road. Go right for one mile to the starting point.

9. Tap (ENTER) twice, and drag the First Line Indent marker and the Hanging Indent marker to the 0" position on the ruler.

10. Save the changes, and continue with the next topic.

Outline-Style Numbered Lists

An outline-style numbered list can have up to nine levels of numbers or bullet characters. Outline-style lists are often used in the legal profession where multiple numbering levels are required. You format paragraphs as an outline-style numbered list by displaying the Bullets and Numbering dialog box and choosing the desired style from the style gallery on the Outline Numbered tab.

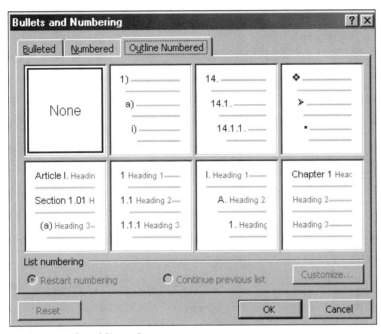

Outline numbered list styles

Promoting and Demoting List Items

From the Keyboard

 to demote

(SHIFT)+(TAB) to promote

The Increase Indent ![] button and the Decrease Indent ![] button are used to promote or demote paragraphs in an outline-style numbered list. The Increase Indent button indents selected paragraphs one level, thus demoting them one level. The Decrease Indent button reduces the indentation level and thus promotes the paragraph one level.

Hands-On 5.8 Create a Policies and Procedures Page

In this exercise, you will use outline-style numbered lists to create a policies and procedures page at the end of the document.

Set Up the New Page

1. Make sure the insertion point is at the end of the document and that the paragraph has no preset indents set.

2. Press (CTRL)+(ENTER) to insert a page break.
   Notice that the top margin is still set to 2".

3. Click the Center ![] button.

4. Type **OUTDOOR ADVENTURES**, and tap (ENTER) twice.

5. Type **Policies and Procedures**, and tap (ENTER) three times.

6. Click the Align Left ![] button.

(Continued on the next page)

7. Choose **Format→Bullets and Numbering** from the menu.

8. Click the Outline Numbered tab.

9. Click the first style in the gallery. If the Reset button is available at the bottom of the dialog box, click it to restore the style to the default setting. The style should match the example shown to the right.

10. Click **OK** to apply the style.

11. Type **Medical and Injury**, and tap (ENTER).
    The heading Medical and Injury should be preceded by the number 1 followed by a closing parenthesis, and the number 2) should be applied to the new paragraph.

12. Click the Increase Indent ![] button to demote the new paragraph.
    The number 2) should now become the letter a).

13. Type **All guests must have medical insurance**, and tap (ENTER).
    The new paragraph will be preceded by the letter b).

14. Complete items b) and c) as shown below, tapping (ENTER) once after each paragraph. The insertion point should be on the new paragraph d) when you have finished.

> 1) Medical and Injury
>   a) All guests must have medical insurance
>   b) All guests must sign an injury waiver
>   c) All guests agree to pay out-of-pocket medical expenses including:
>   d)

15. Click the Increase Indent ![] indent to demote the new paragraph.
    The new paragraph will be preceded by the letter i).

16. Type **Injuries resulting from on-trip accidents**, and tap (ENTER).

17. Complete the document as shown on the following page. You should double-space between the three list headings as shown. When you do this, the outline numbering will be turned off for the new heading paragraph. Turn the numbering on again using the Numbering button on the Formatting toolbar. Finally, format the title with an Arial 18 pt bold font and the subtitle with an Arial 16 pt bold font.

18. Save the changes, and close the document.

OUTDOOR ADVENTURES

Policies and Procedures

1) Medical and Injury
   a) All guests must have medical insurance
   b) All guests must sign an injury waiver
   c) All guests agree to pay out-of-pocket medical expenses including:
      i) Injuries resulting from on-trip accidents
      ii) Aero medical evacuation
      iii) Rehabilitation costs

2) Cancellations and Refunds
   a) A full refund will be given for cancellations with 60 days notice
   b) A 50% refund will be given for cancellations with 30 days notice
   c) No refund for cancellations with less than 30 days notice

3) Alternate Trip Destinations and Cancellations
   a) Your trip may be cancelled for any of the following reasons:
      i) Inclement weather
      ii) Poor water flow
      iii) Insufficient number of guests
      iv) Unavailability of a guide
   b) Your trip destination may be changed for any of the following reasons:
      i) Inclement weather
      ii) Poor water flow
      iii) Insufficient guest turnout requiring reorganization of trips

Concepts Review

True/False Questions

1. Margins can be set with the ruler.   TRUE   FALSE

2. The File→Page Setup command displays a dialog box that can be used to adjust margins.   TRUE   FALSE

3. Bullets can be offset from the margins.   TRUE   FALSE

4. Numbering always continues sequentially from one list to the next in documents with multiple lists.   TRUE   FALSE

5. Bullet formats are carried to the next paragraph when (ENTER) is tapped.   TRUE   FALSE

6. Bullet formats cannot be changed once (ENTER) is tapped.   TRUE   FALSE

7. Only the first line of a paragraph is indented when a hanging indent is applied.   TRUE   FALSE

8. Outline-style numbered lists can have up to seven numbering levels.   TRUE   FALSE

Multiple-Choice Questions

1. Which of the following keys is used to display measurements on the ruler while the margin boundary is dragged?
   a. (ALT)
   b. (SHIFT)
   c. (CTRL)
   d. None of the above

2. Which command displays the Bullets and Numbering dialog box?
   a. Format→Bullets and Numbering
   b. Edit→Bullets and Numbering
   c. Format→Paragraph
   d. None of the above

3. Which technique indents the *bullets* in a bulleted list?
   a. Select the desired paragraphs, and drag the First Line Indent marker.
   b. Select the desired paragraphs, and drag the Left Tab symbol on the indent marker.
   c. Use the (TAB) key.
   d. None of the above

4. Which technique should you use to indent the **text** in a bulleted list?
   a. Select the desired paragraphs, and drag the First Line Indent marker.
   b. Select the desired paragraphs, and drag the Left Tab symbol on the indent marker.
   c. Use the (TAB) key.
   d. None of the above

Skill Builders

Skill Builder 5.1 Create a Personal Business Letter

In this exercise, you will create the document shown on the following page.

Set-Up the Letter

1. Start a new document, and Choose **File→Page Setup** from the menu bar.

2. Set the left and right margins to 1″ and click **OK.**

3. Type the date, address, salutation, and first paragraph as shown on the following page.

Create the Numbered List

4. Tap (ENTER) twice after the first main paragraph, and then click the Numbering button.
   It's OK if the number style and indentation are different than shown on the following. You will adjust the style and indentation soon.

5. Type the three numbered paragraphs, tapping (ENTER) once after each paragraph.

6. Tap (ENTER) twice after the third numbered paragraph.
   This will turn off numbering.

7. Now complete the document as shown on the following. Turn bullets on and off as necessary, and tap (ENTER) either once or twice between paragraphs as shown. Don't be concerned with text formats or bullet alignments at this point. You will be instructed to make those changes in the following steps.

(Continued on the next page)

Today's Date

Mr. Dave Olson, President
Financial Freedom Network
300 South Meyers Fork Road
San Jose, CA 95136

Dear Mr. Olson:

I recently attended your quick start seminar on tax planning for retirement, and I was impressed with both the speaker and content of the presentation. I spoke with Mr. Barry after the presentation, and he asked me to provide you with three types of feedback:

1. Topics that I feel should be included in next year's presentation
2. Ways to improve the presentation
3. Comments on the facilities

I have organized my comments into the three lists that follow.

Topics to Include Next Year
✓ Information on 401K plans
✓ Method for calculating projected net worth
✓ Planning for children's college expenses

How to Improve the Presentation
✓ Make it longer (8 hours).
✓ Include more visuals.
✓ Have multiple speakers.

About the Facilities
✓ The food was excellent.
✓ The chairs were a little uncomfortable.
✓ The employees were very friendly and helpful.

Mr. Olson, I hope my feedback helps you plan for and improve next year's presentation. Please feel free to contact me if you need additional information.

Sincerely,

Richard Ellison, Seminar Participant
2400 Fairview Lane
Richmond, CA 94803

Format the Lists and Headings

8. Select the three paragraphs in the numbered list.

9. Drag the First Line Indent ▽ marker to the 0″ position on the ruler to align the numbers with the left margin.

10. Drag the Left Tab ∟ marker and the Hanging Indent ⌂ marker to the 0.5″ position on the ruler. This will indent the text 0.5″ from the numbers.

11. Now align the bulleted paragraphs the same way.

12. Format the headings with bold as shown on the preceding page.

13. If necessary, use the **Format→Bullets and Numbering** command to choose the numbering style and bullet style shown on the preceding page.

14. Save the document with the name **Skill Builder 5.1,** then close the document.

Skill Builder 5.2

1. Start a new document.

2. Set the top margin to 2″ and the left and right margins to 1.5″.

3. Follow these guidelines to create the document shown below.

   ■ Use a Times New Roman 16 pt font for all text except for the title and subtitle. Use an Arial Bold 18 pt font for the title and an Arial Bold 16 pt font for the subtitle.

   ■ Use (ENTER) to create the single-, double-, and triple-spacing shown below.

   ■ Use the bullet style shown below.

4. Save the document as **Skill Builder 5.2,** and close the document.

Baron's Model Train Supply

Going Out of Business Sale

Baron's Model Train Supply has provided the widest selection of model train accessories for over 43 years, but our lease has run out. We have decided to close up shop and liquidate our inventory. Please stop by before the end of June to take advantage of rock-bottom prices and a wide selection of accessories and collectibles. Here is just a sample of what you will find.

Accessories
   ❖ Scenery
   ❖ Tracks and switches
   ❖ Buildings

Collectibles
   ❖ Antique locomotives
   ❖ Antique cabooses
   ❖ Figures: Switchmen, engineers, animals, and more

Skill Builder 5.3

In this exercise, you will open a document on your exercise diskette. You will format the document until it matches the document on the following page.

1. Open the document named Skill Builder 5.3.

2. Set the left and right margins to 1".

3. Look at the document below, and notice the title shown at the top of the document. Insert the title, separating it from the first body paragraph with three hard returns (tap (ENTER) three times). Format the title with an Arial 14 pt bold font.

4. Select the first four body paragraphs, and apply double-spacing to them. Adjust the first line indent of the first four body paragraphs to 0.5".

5. Apply the bullet style shown on the following page to the next three paragraphs. Use (ENTER) to double-space between the paragraphs.

6. Indent the last paragraph 1" on both the left and right as shown. You will also need to insert hard returns above and below the paragraph with the phrase "Levy concludes that".

7. Your completed document should match the document on the following page.

8. Save the changes to the document, and close it.

(Continued on the next page)

LEFT BRAIN/RIGHT BRAIN

In recent years it has become popular to speak of people as being either "left-brained" or "right-brained." The notion is that the hemispheres of the brain are involved in very different kinds of intellectual and emotional functions and responses.

Like other popular ideas, the "left brain / right brain" notion is exaggerated. Research does suggest that the dominant hemisphere is somewhat more involved in intellectual undertakings that require logic and problem solving, whereas the non-dominant hemisphere is more concerned with decoding visual information, aesthetic and emotional responses, imagination, understanding metaphors, and creative mathematical reasoning.

Despite these differences, it would be erroneous to think that the hemispheres of the brain act independently, or that some people are "left-brained" and others are "right-brained." The functions of the left and right hemispheres tend to respond simultaneously as we focus our attention on one thing or another.

Biological psychologist Jerre Levy summarized left-brain and right-brain similarities and differences as follows:

- The hemispheres are similar enough so that each can function quite well independently, but not as well as they function in normal combined usage.

- The left hemisphere seems to play a special role in understanding and producing language, while the right hemisphere seems to play a special role in emotional response.

- Creativity is not confined to the right hemisphere.

Levy concludes that:

> There are significant differences between the right and left brains; however, these differences may not be as significant as we have been led to believe.

Assessments

1. Follow these guidelines to create the document shown below.

   ▪ Set the top margin to 2″.

   ▪ Insert the date as a field using the Insert→Date and Time command.

   ▪ Use the bullet style shown for the bulleted list.

2. Print the document, save it with the name Assessment 5.1, and close the document.

Current Date

Mr. John Upshaw
1204 Wilkins Drive
Sacramento, CA 90518

Dear Mr. Upshaw:

I am pleased to inform you that you have won the grand prize in our sweepstakes contest. Please contact me as soon as possible to verify receipt of this letter. You may contact me in any of the following ways.

   ➢ Stop by our office at 2400 Gerber Road.
   ➢ Call 1-916-682-9090 between the hours of 9:00 a.m. and 5:00 p.m.
   ➢ Write to me at the address listed on this letterhead.

I look forward to hearing from you soon. Please be prepared to present us with your verification number. Your verification number is JB101.

Sincerely,

Jerry Williams
Prize Notification Manager

Assessment 5.2

1. Follow these guidelines to create the document shown below.

   ■ Set the top margin to 2″ and the left and right margins to 1″.

   ■ Use an Arial Bold 16 pt font for the title and a Times New Roman 14 pt font for all other text.

   ■ Center the title, and use three hard returns after the title.

   ■ Use single-spacing and double-spacing as necessary to format the document as shown.

   ■ Set the First Line indent of the two body paragraphs to 0.5″ as shown. Adjust the indents of the numbered paragraphs and the quotation as shown.

2. Print the document, save it with the name **Assessment 5.2,** and close the document.

SUCCESS

The quest for success is a driving force in the lives of many Americans.

This force drives the business world and often results in huge personal fortunes.

However, success can come in many forms, some of which are listed below.

1. Many people in America view success monetarily.

2. Our society also views public figures such as movie stars, athletes, and other celebrities as being successful.

3. Educational achievement such as earning an advanced degree is often perceived as successful.

It is easy to see that success means many things to many people. The poet

Ralph Waldo Emerson provides this elegant definition of success:

To laugh often and much; to win the respect of intelligent people and the affection of children; to earn the appreciation of honest critics and endure the betrayal of false friends; to appreciate beauty, to find the best in others; to leave the world a bit better, whether by a healthy child, a garden patch or a redeemed social condition; to know even one life has breathed easier because you have lived. This is to have succeeded.

Assessment 5.3

1. Follow these guidelines to create the document shown below.

   ▪ Set the top margin to 2″.

   ▪ Center the title, and use three hard returns after the title.

   ▪ Use an Arial Bold 16 pt font for the title and a Times New Roman 14 pt font for all other text. Apply bold to the list headings as shown.

   ▪ Apply line spacing, indents, and bullets as shown.

2. Print the document, save it with the name **Assessment 5.3,** and close the document.

THE GOLDEN STATE

With more than thirty million people, California has become the most populous state in America. From the beaches of Southern California to the great redwood forests of Northern California, the Golden State is home to a diverse population and a vibrant economy.

A recent poll asked Californians to list the five things they liked best about life in California. The same poll also asked them to list the five biggest drawbacks to life in the Golden State. The poll results appear below.

Five Best Things
- Climate
- Cultural attractions
- Economic opportunities
- Educational opportunities
- Recreational activities

Five Biggest Drawbacks
- Air pollution
- Cost of living
- Crime
- Taxes
- Traffic and congestion

Critical Thinking

Critical Thinking 5.1 On Your Own

Jessica Owens is a student at Mid Town High School. Jessica has always dreamed of working in the film industry. Jessica chose to attend Mid Town High primarily because they offer college prep classes for film majors. Jessica's just started her first film class, Film 101. Her instructor, Ms. Watkins, has asked students to prepare brief reports on their favorite films. Each report must include a report title and a brief paragraph describing the purpose of the report. In addition, Jessica must include brief paragraphs on her favorite comedy, drama, action, and love story films. The paragraphs should describe why she likes each film and why she believes the film is the best of its category.

Prepare a report using the criteria described above. Include a paragraph describing your favorite film in each category. Use a bullet list for the category paragraphs. Save the completed report as **Critical Thinking 5.1.**

Critical Thinking 5.2 On Your Own

Jack Dennings loves to cook! He finds that the best way to relieve a little tension is to cook up a storm for friends and family. Recently, Jack started a monthly gourmet meal event at his home. Each month, he invites a group of friends and/or family to enjoy his feast. While preparing this month's menu, Jack was perusing his grandmother's recipes when he came across his childhood favorite—Glazed Garlic Prawns.

One of Jack's pet peeves is organization. He has computerized all of his menus by scanning or retyping them into Word documents. His grandmother's Glazed Garlic Prawns recipe was scribbled on a piece of paper as shown below:

Ingredients
1 pound of peeled prawns
1 tablespoon olive oil
1/4 cup coarse sea salt
3/4 cup chicken broth
2 tablespoons finely minced garlic
3 tablespoons fresh lemon juice
1/4 cup finely chopped parsley

Directions: 1. Rinse the prawns, pat dry, and brush with olive oil. 2. Spread the salt on a large plate and roll the prawns in the salt. Preheat the broiler. 3. Place the prawns directly on a rack and broil 4 inches from the heat 2 minutes per side. 4. Meanwhile, heat the chicken broth in a small saucepan over medium heat. Add the garlic, and cook for 2 minutes, stirring constantly. Add the lemon juice and parsley, and cook for 1 minute. Transfer the sauce to a serving bowl. Serve the prawns and dipping sauce immediately.

Enter the recipe above into a Word document. Use a descriptive title, put the ingredients in a bulleted list with the heading "Ingredients," and put the directions in a numbered list with the heading "Directions." If necessary, adjust the indents of the numbered list to allow the numbers to align with the bullets and the bullet text to align with the numbered text. Also, make sure you give Grandma credit for the recipe. Save the completed document as **Critical Thinking 5.2.**

Critical Thinking 5.3 Web Research

Bud Richardson works as an Administrative Assistant for Fremont Investment Group. Each month, Jerry Wilkins, Fremont's Chief Investment Advisor, sends a letter to his clients with his top stock picks of the month. Bud has been asked to prepare this month's letter and an attached stock pick page. Jerry's top technology recommendations for this month are 1. Oracle (ORCL), 2. Sun Microsystems (SUNW), 3. Cisco Systems (CSCO), 4. BMC Software (BMCS), and 5. Microsoft (MSFT). His top Dow Jones Industrial Average picks are 1. Citigroup (C), 2. Boeing Aircraft (BA), 3. Microsoft (MSFT), 4. Gillette (G), and 5. IBM (IBM).

Prepare a business letter to Fremont's clients from Jerry informing them that Jerry's top technology and Dow picks are attached. Use Internet Explorer to navigate to the Web site of a company that offers free stock quotations. Get the current stock price for each of the stocks listed above. Include an attachment page with a heading for each group of stocks, a brief paragraph describing some rationale for choosing the stocks, and a numbered list. The numbered lists should be numbered from 1 to 5 with each numbered item including the company name, stock symbol, and current price. Make sure the numbering starts over at 1 for the second list. Thus, each list will be numbered from 1 to 5. Save the completed document as **Critical Thinking 5.3.**

Critical Thinking 5.4 With a Group

Health-e-Meals.com has been in business for over three years now and employees 42 people. Your classmate and you have done a remarkable job building the business. However, you realize that you cannot continue to grow at this rate without having a formal business plan and goals in place. You and your classmate have decided to develop a business plan to help you with strategic planning and to help secure additional credit lines and financing. Part of the business plan is a list of the top five financial goals and the top five customer service goals for the next year.

Create a Word document that lists the top five financial goals and the top five customer service goals of Health-e-Meals.com in the current fiscal year. Have your classmate determine the top five financial goals, and you determine the top five customer service goals. Use numbered lists to format the goals. Include a title and headings in the document. Save the completed document as **Critical Thinking 5.4**.

LESSON 6

Internet Integration: Online Collaboration

Team projects are a key business activity. As email becomes a routine tool in business, project teams can now be composed of people from various parts of the country. By attaching documents and other types of files to email messages, team members located across the country can exchange feedback and revisions as if they were working in the same building. In this lesson, you will learn how to participate in an online collaboration. You will set up folders for project files, receive an attachment from email, and place comments into a working document.

In This Lesson

Case Study

Grace works at a property tax accounting firm. She's played a key role supporting one of their most important clients for the past year. When she was called into a meeting with her manager, Grace figured that it had to do with this client, but she was wrong. Instead, they talked about a potential client whose business the company wants to secure. Grace was asked to help develop a sales proposal to the prospective client. The "meeting" turned out to be a conference call over the phone with people in other states. Grace's manager introduced her to Terry Sanchez, a sales representative in San Antonio and Robert Smith, a writer in their New York Headquarters. Grace, Robert, and Terry will work to develop the sales proposal and presentation. Grace was asked to participate because of her in-depth knowledge of her company's day-to-day services to a key client. To start the project, Terry will send a draft proposal document for Grace and Robert Smith to review. They must have a final version of the proposal ready by the end of the week.

Terry attached a Word document to his message. Grace can open the document with a double-click and read it like any other Word document. Later, Grace can attach the document to an email message to send it back to Terry.

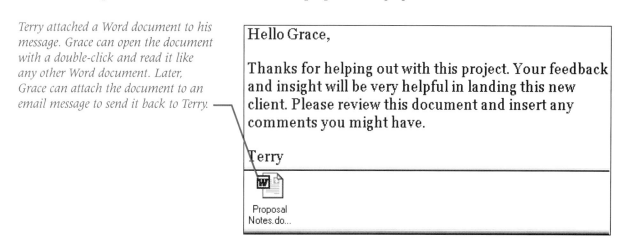

Hello Grace,

Thanks for helping out with this project. Your feedback and insight will be very helpful in landing this new client. Please review this document and insert any comments you might have.

Terry

Proposal
Notes.do...

The shaded area of this message indicates there is a comment embedded in the document.

When Grace points at the shaded highlight, she sees a question from Terry about a statement in the draft document.

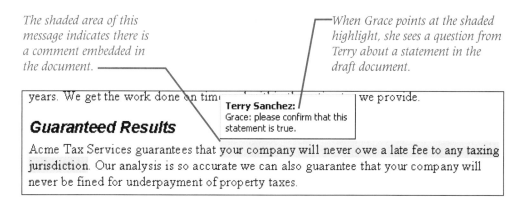

years. We get the work done on tim...   we provide.

Terry Sanchez:
Grace: please confirm that this statement is true.

Guaranteed Results

Acme Tax Services guarantees that your company will never owe a late fee to any taxing jurisdiction. Our analysis is so accurate we can also guarantee that your company will never be fined for underpayment of property taxes.

Organizing a Project

When you work on a project, it is usually a good idea to create one or more folders on the computer to store the documents and other types of files with which you will work. This topic will give you practice creating folders and teach you techniques to access these new folders quickly.

Project Folders

Depending on the size of the project and the number of files you must organize, you may need to create more than one folder. Windows lets you create folders inside of other folders. Thus you can have one main folder for the project, and create subfolders inside it for major types of documents or major sections of the project. The following diagram displays an example of project folders.

*This My Computer window is displaying the **Sales Proposal** folder that Grace created for this online team project.*

*Grace will use these folders to store additional files, leaving the **Sales Proposal** folder clear to store just the proposal files.*

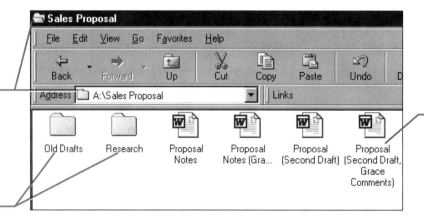

As Grace works on the project she saves files with her comments under different names. This leaves the original files intact for future reference.

Grace sets up a special project folder in the *My Documents* folder on her hard drive. She also creates a subfolder for old drafts (in case something that was deleted earlier might be useful) and for research documents. This will keep the list of files in any given folder from becoming long and confusing.

 Hands-On 6.1 Create Project Folders

In this exercise, you will create Grace's three folders for the project on your floppy disk. Two of these folders will be subfolders.

1. *Double-click* the My Computer icon near the top-left corner of the Desktop. If necessary, Maximize the window.

2. Follow the instructions on the next page for your version of windows.
Some computers may be set to display a new window for each new drive or folder that you browse. You will set the My Computer window to display just a single window as you browse—to avoid cluttering the Desktop with too many windows.

Windows 98

- Choose **View→Folder Options** from the menu bar.

- Click the **Settings** button.

- Make sure that the Browse folders option is set to *same window* as shown at right.

- Click **OK;** then click the **Close** button to close the dialog box.

Windows 95 and Windows NT

- Click **View** on the menu bar. Follow the instructions in the *Windows 98* section above if the last item in the view menu reads: *Folder Options*. Otherwise, click **Options** in the View menu.

- Make sure that the Folders option is set to *single window* as shown at right.

- Click **OK** to close the dialog box.

Windows 2000

- Choose **Tools→Folder Options** from the menu bar.

- Make sure that the Browse folders option is set to *same window* as shown at right.

- Click **OK** to close the dialog box.

3. Make sure your *exercise diskette* is in the floppy drive.

4. *Double-click* the 3½ Floppy (A:) icon to view the exercise diskette.

5. Choose **View→Large Icons** from the menu bar.

6. Follow these steps to create a new folder on your floppy disk.

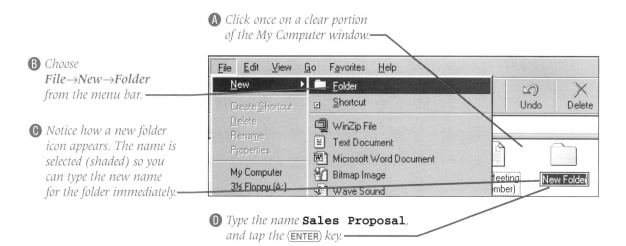

Ⓐ *Click once on a clear portion of the My Computer window.*

Ⓑ *Choose File→New→Folder from the menu bar.*

Ⓒ *Notice how a new folder icon appears. The name is selected (shaded) so you can type the new name for the folder immediately.*

Ⓓ *Type the name* **Sales Proposal**, *and tap the* (ENTER) *key.*

7. Double-click the **Sales Proposal** folder icon to navigate to your new folder.
   Notice that the name of the folder is displayed in the Address bar near the top of the My Computer window and also in the Title bar.

(Continued on the next page)

Create SubFolders

Now that you have created a new project folder, you can add the two subfolders to it. Any new folders you create will be added inside *the Sales Proposal folder, since this is the currently displayed folder.*

8. Choose **File→New→Folder** from the menu bar. Type **Old Drafts** as the name for the new folder, and tap the (ENTER) key.

9. Choose **File→New→Folder** from the menu bar. The **New** command may appear further down the menu than it did previously. Type **Research** as the name for the new folder, and tap the (ENTER) key.
   There should now be two folders displayed in the Sales Proposal folder.

10. Minimize ▬ the *My Computer* window.

Placing a Shortcut on the Desktop

A shortcut is a type of file that points to some other file, folder, drive, or device on your system. You can recognize a shortcut by the small arrow in the lower left corner of its icon.

When to Use a Shortcut

You should use a shortcut if you want to access a file, folder, or drive from more than one location. For example, you might keep a file named *Sales Proposal First Draft* in a folder named *Sales Proposal,* but you also want to access the file from another folder named *Current Work.* You could place a shortcut to Staff Assignments inside *Current Work,* and leave the actual file in the *Sales Proposal* folder.

The Benefits of Shortcuts

A shortcut occupies less storage space (about one kilobyte) than another complete copy of the same file. You could make copies of a file or folder and place them at different locations on your system. However, this would have two disadvantages:

■ Each copy of the file would occupy additional storage space on a drive. Since shortcuts are just one kilobyte in size, they take up very little space compared to the file they point to.

■ If you wanted to change the file, you would have to change *each* copy of the file individually. This could become very confusing and time-consuming. When you use shortcuts to the file or folder, only one file needs to be modified.

TIP!

Avoid placing folders on the Desktop. Place shortcuts to folders on the Desktop instead.

Placing Shortcuts to Folders on the Desktop

You can easily open a folder by placing a shortcut to it on the Desktop. It is a bad idea to place the actual folder on the Desktop. If you move a folder to the Desktop, it loses its place in the hierarchy on your floppy or hard drive. Shortcuts help you work around this problem. The actual folder can be in its proper spot in the disk drive/folder hierarchy while the shortcut sits on the Desktop ready for quick access.

HOW TO CREATE A FOLDER SHORTCUT ON THE DESKTOP

Task	Procedure
Create a shortcut to a folder on the Desktop.	■ Open a *My Computer* or *Exploring* window, and *restore* the window so part of the Desktop is visible. ■ Navigate to the item for which you are creating a shortcut. ■ Drag the folder with the *right* mouse button (right-drag) from the My Computer window to a spot over the Desktop; then release the mouse button. ■ Choose *Create Shortcut(s) here* from the pop-up menu.

Since she will be working with files on this project a great deal during the coming week, Grace places a shortcut to the folder on the Desktop. This makes it easy to open the folder quickly, while keeping it in its proper location on her hard drive (or on your floppy disk).

Using Favorites for Folders

A Favorite works like a command that points to a specific folder or file on a disk drive. There may be some folders on your system that you will want to jump to frequently. Although you could create shortcuts to these folders, a Favorite may be a better choice. You can access Favorites from the Favorites menu in a My Computer or Exploring window or in the Open and Save dialog boxes in Office 2000 application programs, such as Word. Because you access Favorites from a menu, they are often more convenient than shortcuts, which must always reside on the Desktop or in a specific location on a hard drive or floppy disk.

Uses for Favorites

You can use Favorites to quickly navigate to three different types of locations:

■ Folders on the computer system or on a network

■ Disk drives on your computer or on a network

■ Web pages

Creating Favorites

You can create a new favorite whenever you need one. You create favorites in My Computer and Exploring windows, in Internet Explorer, or in the *Open* and *Save* dialog boxes of Office 2000 applications, such as Word, Excel, and Outlook.

WORKING WITH FAVORITES TO FOLDERS AND FILES

Task	Procedure
Create a Favorite to a folder from a My Computer or Exploring window.	■ Navigate to display the folder for the Favorite. ■ Choose **Favorites→Add to Favorites** from the menu bar. ■ Revise the name for the Favorite if necessary; then click **OK**. *Note: Some versions of Windows 95 and NT 4.0 do not support this method.*
Create a Favorite to a folder from an Open or Save dialog box.	■ Use **File→Save As** or **File→Open** to view a dialog box. ■ Click to select the disk drive, folder, or file for which to create a Favorite. ■ Click the Tools button in the dialog box; then choose **Add to Favorites** from the drop-down menu.
Access a Favorite from an Office 2000 Open or Save dialog box.	■ Use **File→Save As** or **File→Open** to view a dialog box. ■ Click the **Favorites** button to view all of your Favorites.
Access a Favorite from a My Computer or Exploring Window.	■ Open a *My Computer, Exploring,* or *Internet Explorer* window. ■ Click **Favorites** on the menu bar, and choose the Favorite to which you wish to navigate. *Note: Some versions of Windows 95 and NT 4.0 do not support this method.*

 Hands-On 6.2 Create a Shortcut and a Favorite

In this exercise, you will create a Favorite that opens the Sales Proposal folder on your floppy disk. You will also create a shortcut the on the Desktop to the Sales Proposal folder.

Create a Favorite

1. Start Microsoft Word; then click the Open ⏏ button on the toolbar.

2. Follow these steps to create the Favorite.

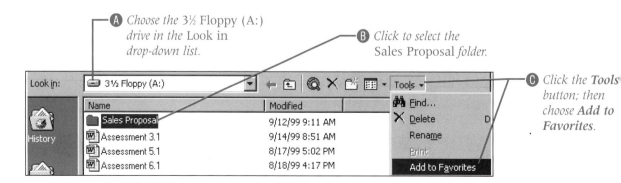

Ⓐ *Choose the 3½ Floppy (A:) drive in the* Look in *drop-down list.*

Ⓑ *Click to select the* Sales Proposal *folder.*

Ⓒ *Click the* **Tools** *button; then choose* **Add to Favorites***.*

3. Click the **Favorites** button on the left side of the dialog box.
The dialog box will display a list of all of the Favorites defined for your log-on name. Each log-on name can maintain a custom list of Favorites.

4. Click the drop-down portion of the Views ⊞⋅ button on the dialog box toolbar; then choose **List** from the drop-down menu. Tap the letter **S** on the keyboard until you see a Favorite named *Sales Proposal* or *Sales Proposal Folder.*

5. If you see a Favorite named **Sales Proposal folder,** click the **icon** (not the name) to select the Favorite; then tap the (DELETE) key. Click **Yes** if you are asked to confirm the deletion.
Another student may have created this Favorite previously. There is no need to have more than one Favorite to this folder.

 Ⓐ *Right-click on the* Sales Proposal *Favorite; then choose* **Rename** *from the pop-up window.*

 Ⓑ *Tap the* (END) *key, tap the* (SPACE BAR) *and type* **folder** *at the end of the Favorite name; then tap the* (ENTER) *key.*

6. Follow these steps to rename the Favorite.
You can use this technique to rename any file or folder that you view in an Open *or* Save As *dialog box.*

7. Click the **Cancel** button to close the dialog box, and then minimize ▬ the Word window.
The Cancel *button cancels the* Open File *command, not the creation of the Favorite. The Favorite you created in this dialog box will remain after you give the Cancel command.*

Create a Shortcut to the Folder

8. If you see a shortcut on the Desktop named **Shortcut to Sales Proposal,** drag it to the **Recycle Bin.** Click **Yes** if you are asked to confirm the deletion.

9. Click the **Sales Proposal** button on the Windows Taskbar to make the window active.

10. Click the Restore ⊡ button at the top-right corner of the My Computer window. If necessary, *drag* on the borders of the window to make a portion of the Desktop visible.

11. Click the Up ⬆ button to return to the first (root) level of the floppy drive.
Now the 3½ Floppy (A:) drive is displayed in the Address bar. Looking at the Address bar as you navigate in folders helps you keep track of where you are.

(Continued on the next page)

12. Follow these steps to create the shortcut.

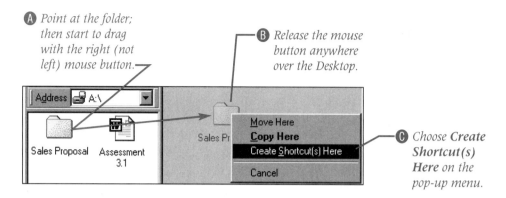

A Point at the folder; then start to drag with the right (not left) mouse button.

B Release the mouse button anywhere over the Desktop.

C Choose **Create Shortcut(s) Here** on the pop-up menu.

Now a shortcut to the folder will appear on the Desktop. Notice the small arrow on the icon that identifies it as a shortcut.

13. Close ☒ the *My Computer* window.

Navigate with the Shortcut and Favorite

14. Double-click on the **Sales Proposal** folder shortcut.
    A new My Computer window will open to display the folder.

15. Close ☒ the *My Computer* window.

16. Double-click the **My Computer** icon to open a new *My Computer* window.

17. Choose **Favorites→Sales Proposal folder** from the menu bar. If you do not see **Favorites** on the menu bar, skip to Step 18—your version of Windows does not support this menu command in the My Computer window.
    The contents of the Sales Proposal folder are displayed immediately. You can access this folder from any window that features the Favorites command. You will see a Favorites command in Word's Open dialog box later in this lesson; which even works with versions of Windows that do not have a Favorites command on the My Computer window menu bar.

18. Close ☒ the My Computer window.

Sending an Email Message

Outlook is a program for managing email, your calendar, names and addresses of contacts, and task lists. The Outlook program has a flexible interface that lets you shift among these various functions. This topic will only cover the basic knowledge required to send and receive email messages with Outlook. For a more complete treatment of this program, see Labyrinth Publications Office 2000 Essentials Course and Outlook 2000 Essentials Course in the Off to Work series.

Hands-On 6.3 Start Outlook

In this exercise, you will start the Outlook program and browse views of some program features.

1. Choose **Start→Programs→Microsoft Outlook** from the Start menu.

2. Make sure that the Outlook window is Maximized ▣.

3. Follow these steps to open the Inbox view in Outlook.
   This view displays incoming email messages.

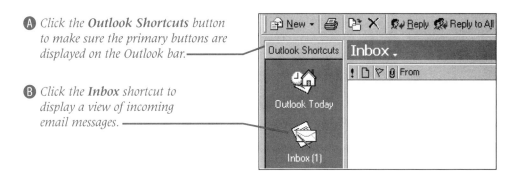

Ⓐ *Click the **Outlook Shortcuts** button to make sure the primary buttons are displayed on the Outlook bar.*

Ⓑ *Click the **Inbox** shortcut to display a view of incoming email messages.*

About Electronic Mail

Along with the Web, *electronic mail (email)* is the most popular of all Internet services. Email is simply the capability to send a message to a specific individual's email address anywhere in the world. An email message can also have one or more computer files (*attachments*) sent along with it. With email you can send and receive messages, send one message to more than one recipient, and exchange documents and images.

Sending an Email Message

Sending an email message is easy. If you know how to use a word processor, you know more than enough to create and send an email message. This topic will take you through the steps of sending an email message with Outlook 2000. To start an email message, you simply choose **File→New→Mail Message,** or you can click the *New Message* button on the toolbar while the Inbox view is displayed.

Email Addresses

You send and receive email with email addresses. An email address uniquely identifies your email account and where the mail server system that serves your account is located on the Internet. An email address looks similar to, and functions much like, the URL for a Web page. The diagram below shows the parts of a typical email address.

rsmith@offtowork.com

Account name   *Separator*   *Domain name*

RULES FOR EMAIL ADDRESSES

- Email addresses *always* contain the @ symbol to separate the account name from the domain name.

- An email address *cannot* contain space characters.

- An email address *can* contain certain punctuation characters, such as a dash and periods.

Hands-On 6.4 **Create and Send an Email Message**

In this exercise, you will create a new email message and send it to an email address at offtowork.com. This email address will automatically send a message back to you.

Before you begin: *If you do not have access to email in your computer lab, skip this exercise, continue with the next topic, and then start with* Step 5 *in* Hands-On Exercise 6.5.

Compose an Email Message

1. Click the New Mail Message ![New] button at the left side of the Outlook toolbar.
   A new email message window will appear on the screen. Outlook always gives you a separate window to compose email messages.

2. Follow these steps to start composing the first email message.

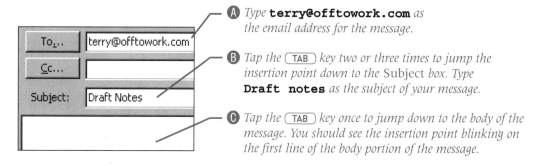

Ⓐ *Type* **terry@offtowork.com** *as the email address for the message.*

Ⓑ *Tap the* (TAB) *key two or three times to jump the insertion point down to the* Subject *box. Type* **Draft notes** *as the subject of your message.*

Ⓒ *Tap the* (TAB) *key once to jump down to the body of the message. You should see the insertion point blinking on the first line of the body portion of the message.*

3. Follow these guidelines as you type the message that appears below:

   - Don't worry about the message lines wrapping around exactly as they appear below. When you type to the end of the message box, a new line will be started for you automatically.

   - You only need to tap (ENTER) when you want to start a new line at the end of a paragraph or insert a blank line in the message.

   - If you tap (ENTER) at the end of each line, your message will be difficult for the addressee to read.

```
Hello Terry:

Please send me your current notes on the proposal
draft as we discussed in this morning's phone call.
I will look them over and give you my input.

Regards,

Grace
```

4. Look over the message and fix any typographic errors you may have made. If you see an error, click just to the right of the error, then tap the (BACKSPACE) key to delete the error. You can then retype the word and it will be inserted into the message. After you've made any necessary corrections, go on to the next step.

TIP!

Many users make typos in their email messages. It's a good idea to scan your messages for typos before you send them off. You should use the same level of care with business correspondence via email as you would use in a standard business letter.

5. Click the [Send] button on the message toolbar to send your message.
Depending on how Outlook is configured, this command may not actually send the message over the Internet just yet. The message may be held in Outlook's Outbox, ready to transmit when you give the Send/Receive command in the next step.

6. Click the [Send/Receive] button on the Outlook toolbar.

7. Follow these steps if you are asked to enter a password.

Ⓐ *Click in the* Password *box; then type your password. Notice how the password is displayed as a series of asterisks. This helps protect the confidentiality of your password from passers-by.*

Ⓑ *Make sure that the* Remember Password *box is not checked. If you tell Outlook to remember your password, anyone can send and receive email on your account.*

Ⓒ *Click OK.*

Outlook will usually display a window that shows the progress of sending and receiving messages. Since your message is very short, this window may only appear for a few seconds. A portion of the window is displayed below.

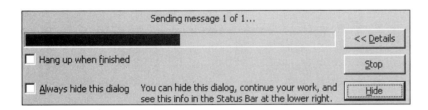

If the progress window is not visible, you should see a display at the bottom-right *corner of the Outlook window in the* Status *bar. The Status bar can display information about making a connection to the mail server and the delivery of email messages.*

Email Attachments

An *attachment* is a file you include with an email message. Some types of information are not as easy to work with in the form of an email message. For example, if you needed to submit a multi-page report for review by others, you could lose some of the document formatting (such as pagination) if you converted the report from a word processor file to an email message. It would be much simpler to send the report document as an attachment. An attachment can be any type of file.

Project Budget   Project Plan   Project Status
           Presentation   Report

A single email message may have several files attached to it.

Here are some examples of attachments:

- A Word document, Excel worksheet, or PowerPoint presentation.

- A photograph (converted to an image file).

Receiving and Opening Attachments

When you receive a message, Outlook will indicate if the message has an attachment by displaying a small paper clip next to the message name. As you view the message in the Outlook window, you will also see a paper clip at the top-right corner of the Preview pane. Clicking on the paper clip will display the names of all the attachments. If you double-click to open an email message, any attachments are displayed as icons at the bottom of the message window.

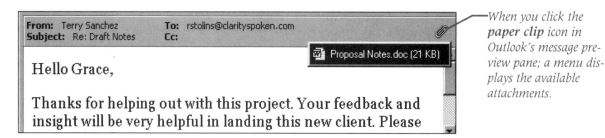

*When you click the **paper clip** icon in Outlook's message preview pane; a menu displays the available attachments.*

File Compatibility

In order to open an attachment, you must have installed an application program that is capable of opening the attachment file. For example, if the file is an Access database file, you must have Access (or another program capable of opening Access database files) installed on your computer. If Windows cannot find a program that can open the file, it will ask you to select an application program. Fortunately, most attachments you receive will probably be word processing and workbook files, so file compatibility will rarely be an issue.

OPENING ATTACHMENTS	
Task	**Procedure**
Open an attachment from the *Inbox* view.	■ Click to select the message with the attachment. ■ Click the **paper clip icon** on the right corner of the Preview pane; then select the attachment you wish to open.
Open an attachment from a *message* window.	■ Double-click to **open** the message in a message window. ■ *Double-click* the *icon* for the attachment, or *right-click* on the icon; then choose **Open** from the pop-up menu.

Saving Attachments

After you receive an attachment, you may wish to store it somewhere else on the hard drive or a floppy disk. Outlook stores attachments as a part of the email message. In order to work with the attachment apart from the email message it was attached to, you must save the attachment file(s). One way to save an attachment is to open it in an application program, then use the programs' *Save As* command. You can also right-click on an attachment in a message window, and then give the *Save As* command.

TIP!

When you delete a message that has attachments, the attachment files are deleted as well—unless you have already saved the attachments.

When Grace gets the email message from Terry with the draft proposal, she saves it into the project folder she set up earlier. Otherwise, it would be difficult to locate the document later unless she looked up the email message it was attached to.

Attachments and Computer Viruses

Remember that an attachment may contain a computer virus. This will probably be rare, but you should always be cautious when handling attachments from users you do not know well. Even coworkers can unknowingly transmit a virus through a *macro virus* in a document file.

Quick
Reference

SAVING ATTACHMENTS

Task	Procedure
Save an attachment in a message window.	■ Double-click to open the message with the attachment. ■ *Right-click* on the attachment file icon at the bottom of the message window; then choose *File→Save As* from the pop-up menu.

Hands-On 6.5 Save an Attachment

In this exercise, you will save an attachment to an email message in one of the project folders.

Before you begin: If you do not have access to email in the computer lab, you should skip directly to the *Move the Attachment file* section (Step 5) later in this exercise.

1. Click the [Send/Receive] button on the Outlook toolbar and look at the top of the Inbox message list for a reply to the message you sent in the previous exercise. The reply will have an attachment. If you do not receive a reply, keep clicking the **Send/Receive** button on the toolbar about twice a minute until a reply arrives.
   Notice the small paper clip for the message in the message list. This indicates that the message contains an attachment.

   > ✉ 📎 Terry Sanchez   Re: Draft Notes

2. Double-click to open the *Re: Draft Notes* message in its own message window.
   The attachment will appear at the bottom of the message.

(Continued on the next page)

3. Follow these steps to save the attachment to your floppy disk.

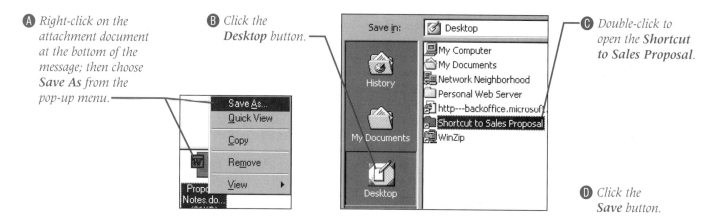

Ⓐ *Right-click on the attachment document at the bottom of the message; then choose Save As from the pop-up menu.*

Ⓑ *Click the Desktop button.*

Ⓒ *Double-click to open the Shortcut to Sales Proposal.*

Ⓓ *Click the Save button.*

4. Close ⊠ the **message** window; then minimize ▬ the **Outlook** window.
   You should skip the next section of this exercise, and continue with Step 14 *near the end of this exercise.*

Move the Attachment File into the First Quarter Report Folder

If you do not have access to email in the computer lab, you should move the attachment file on your exercise diskette to the First Quarter Report folder.

5. Minimize ▬ the Outlook window, then double-click the My Computer 🖳 icon near the top-left corner of the Desktop. If necessary, maximize ☐ the My Computer window.

6. Double-click the **3½ Floppy (A:)** 🖫 icon to view the exercise diskette.
   In the next step, you will hold down the (CTRL) *key as you click to select files. This lets you select more than one file at a time for your next command.*

7. Hold down the (CTRL) key; then click to select the *Hands-on Lesson 6a* and *Hands-on Lesson 6b* files. Release the (CTRL) key.

8. *Right-click* on the *Hands-on Lesson 6a* file on the exercise diskette; then choose **Cut** from the pop-up menu.

9. Double-click to open the *Sales Proposal* folder.

10. Use (CTRL)+V to paste the two document files into the *Sales Proposal* folder.

11. *Right-click* on the *Hands-on Lesson 6a* document; then choose **Rename** from the pop-up menu. Change the name of the file to **Proposal Notes** and tap the (ENTER) key.

12. *Right-click* on the *Hands-on Lesson 6b* document; then choose **Rename** from the pop-up menu. Change the name of the file to **Proposal Second Draft** and tap the (ENTER) key.

13. Use the command **Start→Programs→Microsoft Outlook** to start the *Outlook 2000* application; then minimize ▬ the Outlook window.
    This step ensures that your Windows Taskbar matches the instructions later in this exercise.

14. Double-click the **Shortcut to Sales Proposal** shortcut on the Desktop.

15. Double-click to open the **Proposal Notes** document in Word.

Sending Attachments

Sending one or more attachments with an email message is easy to do. You simply create an email message in Outlook and then give the command to attach one or more files to the message. The files you select to attach can be anywhere on the computer's hard drive or on your floppy disk. You can use either of two methods to send one or more files as attachments:

- **From My Computer and Exploring windows**—You can attach any file by dragging and dropping it from a My Computer or Exploring window into the desired email message.

- **From the Message window**—While you are composing a message, you always have the option to attach one or more files to the message with the **Insert→File Attachment** command, or the *Insert File* button.

SENDING ATTACHMENTS

Task	Procedure
Attach one or more files to a message you are composing.	■ Start composing the new message. ■ Click the **Insert File** button on the message toolbar. ■ Navigate to the file you wish to attach; then double-click to select it, or click the **Insert** button. ■ To select more than one file in a folder, press the (CTRL) key as you click to select each file. ■ If you need to attach additional file(s) from another folder or drive on your computer, click the **Insert File** button again, and repeat the previous two steps.

TIP! *You will send an attachment later in this lesson.*

Working with Comments

Word's Comment feature is a great tool for online collaboration. A *comment* is a text note that you can embed inside a Word document without cluttering the actual text of the document page. When someone inserts a comment, Word places a yellow highlight over the text associated with the comment. When you point over the highlight, Word will display the name of the author and the text of the comment. You can also display a list of comments in a document, and even print them out. The illustration on the next page shows highlighted text and an associated comment.

years. We get the work done on tim[...]   we provide.

Terry Sanchez:
Grace: please confirm that this statement is true.

Guaranteed Results

Acme Tax Services guarantees that your company will never owe a late fee to any taxing jurisdiction. Our analysis is so accurate we can also guarantee that your company will never be fined for underpayment of property taxes.

When Grace points at the shaded highlight, she sees a question from Terry about a statement in the draft document.

When to Use a Comment

Comments are an excellent way to handle situations such as the following:

- When you want to document a piece of writing or record what you had in mind as you wrote the text.

- To record a question about the writing, such as a fact you are not quite sure of.

- To ask a question of an online collaborator without placing it into the normally printed page of the document.

Viewing Comments

To read comments, simply point over the yellow comment highlight. You can also view comments with the **View→Comments** command to open the Comments panel. The Comments panel lets you view comments by a specific author, or by all authors. It is also possible to print out comments by setting an option in Word's *Print Options* dialog box.

Navigating Comments

You can jump from one comment to the next in the Comments panel. When you click on a comment in the panel while in *Normal* or *Print Layout* view, Word displays the highlighted text associated with the comment on the top line of the document window. This makes it easy to move from comment to comment without the need for a page-by-page search through the document.

*A click on a comment in the **Comments** panel lets you view the associated text in the document window. In this example, Comment has just been clicked in the comments panel.*

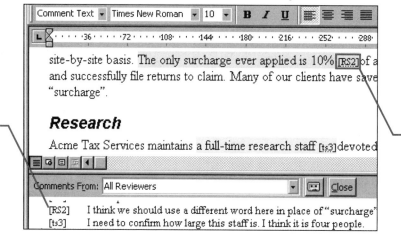

Comment Text | Times New Roman | 10 | **B** *I* <u>U</u>

site-by-site basis. The only surcharge ever applied is 10% [RS2] of a and successfully file returns to claim. Many of our clients have save "surcharge".

Research

Acme Tax Services maintains a full-time research staff [ts3] devoted

Comments From: All Reviewers | Close

[RS2]   I think we should use a different word here in place of "surcharge"
[ts3]   I need to confirm how large this staff is. I think it is four people.

The author's initials and comment number are visible when the Comments panel is open. When the Comments panel is closed, only the yellow highlight remains visible.

Hands-On 6.6 Review Comments

In this exercise, you will review comments inserted into the document previously by Robert Smith and Terry Sanchez.

1. Point at the yellow highlighted text in the *Guaranteed Results* paragraph. Leave the pointer on the highlighted text until you see a small pop-up window.
   This window contains the text of a comment from Terry Sanchez. Later, you will edit this comment to insert Grace's answer to the question.

2. Point at the yellow highlighted text in the *Fee Structure* paragraph.
   This comment is from Robert Smith. Word makes it easy to identify the author of any comment.

3. Scroll down the page, and point to read the remaining two comments.

4. Choose **View→Comments** from the menu bar.
   The Comments panel will appear at the bottom of the Word window to display all of the comments for this document.

5. Follow these steps to begin working with the Comments panel.

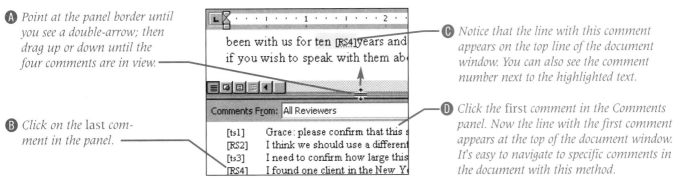

Ⓐ *Point at the panel border until you see a double-arrow; then drag up or down until the four comments are in view.*

Ⓑ *Click on the last comment in the panel.*

Ⓒ *Notice that the line with this comment appears on the top line of the document window. You can also see the comment number next to the highlighted text.*

Ⓓ *Click the first comment in the Comments panel. Now the line with the first comment appears at the top of the document window. It's easy to navigate to specific comments in the document with this method.*

6. Click the *second* and *third* comments in the Comments panel.

7. Click the **Comments From** drop-down list; then choose *Terry Sanchez*.
   Now only comments from this author are displayed.

8. Click the **Comments From** drop-down list; then choose *All Reviewers*.
   Now all of the comments are displayed again.

9. Click the Close button on the comments panel.
   The comments panel is closed. You can reopen it at any time with the **View→Comments** *command.*

Inserting Comments

You can insert comments into any part of a Word document or Excel worksheet. You can select the text that the comment applies to before you give the **Insert→Comment** command. After you insert the comment, any text you had selected is automatically highlighted in a light yellow. This yellow is dimmer than the color created by the yellow *highlighter* tool that you will learn about later in this lesson. The author's initials and a comment number identify each comment.

Setting the Author's Initials

Before you insert comments, you should make sure that Word has your name and initials. You make this setting in Word's **Tools→Options** window, under the *User Information* tab. Once you set the author name and initials, Word will keep this setting until someone else changes it again.

Grace shares her computer with a co-worker who comes into the office part-time. Before she starts working on the draft proposal, Grace checks to make sure her own name and initials are set in Word's User Information tab.

Editing Comments

You can edit a comment at any time. You can even edit or add to comments made by other authors. When you edit a comment made by another author, that author's initials remain with the comment ID number. You edit comments in the Comments window.

As she reads comments inserted by one of the team members, Grace notices one that requests her opinion. Rather than insert a new comment, Grace decides to add her answer by editing the existing comment. Grace also applies a different text color to this edit, so that the other readers can readily distinguish her addition from the original comment.

Task	Procedure
WORKING WITH COMMENTS IN WORD	
Insert a comment.	■ Select the text to which your comment applies; then choose **Insert→Comment** from the menu bar.
	■ Type the text of your comment.
	■ Click the **Close** button to close the Comments panel, or continue your work with the Comments panel left open.
Associate your initials with comments.	■ Choose **Tools→Options** from the menu bar.
	■ Click the **User Information** tab.
	■ Enter your name and initials; then click **OK**.
View a comment in a document window.	■ *Point* on the comment highlight for about 2 seconds.
View all of the comments for a document.	■ Choose **View→Comments** from the menu bar.
	■ Click on a comment in the Comments panel to view its associated text at the top of the document window.
Edit a comment.	■ *Point* on the comment highlight; then *right-click* on the comment highlight, and choose **Edit Comment** from the pop-up menu.
	■ Edit the comment text normally.
	■ Click **Close** to close the Comments panel.
Delete a comment.	■ *Point* on the comment highlight.
	■ *Right-click* on the comment highlight; then choose **Delete Comment** from the pop-up menu.

In this exercise, you will insert one of Grace's comments into the document and edit an existing comment with her answer to a question.

Set the Author's Initials

1. Choose **Tools→Options** from the menu bar; then click the **User Information** Tab.

2. Enter your first and last name in the *Name* box; then tap the TAB key, and enter two or three initials. The initials can be in upper- or lowercase letters.

3. Click **OK** to save the change.

Insert a Comment

4. Use CTRL+END to jump to the bottom of the document. Tap ENTER to add another line; then type the following text.

> Computer Automation
> Acme analysts use a state-of-the-art information system to track property tax data.

5. *Drag* to select the *Computer Automation* line that you just typed; then choose **Insert→Comment** from the menu bar.
   The Comments panel will open with the insertion point on a new line for your comment. Notice that your initials are placed as a prefix to the new comment number.

6. Type the following comment: TAB **You should include information on the computer system I use to serve clients.**

7. Click the Close button on the **Comments** panel.

8. *Point* (don't click) on the yellow highlighted text in the *Computer Automation* line to display your comment.
   Notice that your name is spelled out as you entered it under the User Information *tab.*

Edit a Comment

9. Use CTRL+HOME to jump to the top of the document.

10. *Point* to display the first comment in the document under *Guaranteed Results*.

11. *Right-click* on the comment; then choose **Edit Comment** from the pop-up menu.
    The comments panel will open to display the text of the comment you selected to edit.

(Continued on the next page)

12. Follow these steps to edit the comment.

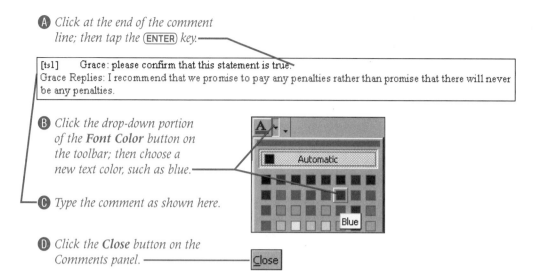

Ⓐ *Click at the end of the comment line; then tap the* (ENTER) *key.*

[ts1]   Grace: please confirm that this statement is true.
Grace Replies: I recommend that we promise to pay any penalties rather than promise that there will never be any penalties.

Ⓑ *Click the drop-down portion of the* **Font Color** *button on the toolbar; then choose a new text color, such as blue.*

Ⓒ *Type the comment as shown here.*

Ⓓ *Click the* **Close** *button on the Comments panel.*

13. Point at the yellow highlight for the comment to view your editing.
Notice that none of the formatting you used in the comment is visible in the pop-up comment. You may want to remind readers that they may need to read your comments in the Comments view rather than just the pop-up window.

14. Choose **File→Save As** from the menu bar. Save the document with a new name: **Proposal Notes (Grace Comments)**.
By saving the file with a new name, you preserve the original version for future reference. The new name will also let you and the other team members know that it contains your comments.

Printing Comments

Word does not normally print comments. To print the comments in a document, you must select this option in Word's *Print Options* dialog box. When you choose to print comments, Word will automatically print the author's initials and the comment number beside each comment in the document. Word also prints one or more sheets with the text of all comments.

PRINTING COMMENTS IN WORD	
Task	**Procedure**
Print comments.	■ Choose **File→Print** from the menu bar.
	■ Click the **Options** button.
	■ Click the check box by **Comments**; then click **OK**.

To stop printing comments reverse the above procedure.

1. Choose **File→Print** from the menu bar.

2. Click the **Options** button.

3. Make sure the **Comments** check box is checked.

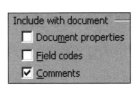

4. Click **OK;** then click **OK** again to print the document with comments, and retrieve the printout from the printer.

   Notice that the printout includes the initials and comment number of each comment. A separate sheet was printed that contains the text of the comments themselves.

Emailing the Document

When you send someone a Word document, you have two choices. You can send the document as an attachment similar to the one you received earlier in this lesson, or you can send the document itself as the message. Each method has its uses. Sending the document as a message may cause some formatting to be lost. However, if it is a short document, sending it as an email message may be more convenient for the recipient to open and print.

TIP! *Documents of several pages or more are best sent as attachments rather than as messages.*

The Send To Command

Word's **Send To** command lets you choose whether the document should be sent as an email message or as an attachment. You simply choose **File→Send To** from the menu bar; then choose the method of transmission. If you want to send the document as an email message, Word offers an even faster way to give this command.

The E-mail Button

The Word 2000 toolbar contains a button that makes it easy to send any document as an email message. When you click the **E-mail** button on the toolbar, Word immediately displays boxes for you to fill in, the To: and Cc: addresses, the subject, and a **Send a Copy** button to send the message.

TIP! *If you click the E-mail button by mistake, just click it again to dismiss the command.*

SENDING A DOCUMENT VIA EMAIL

Task	Procedure
Send a document as an email message.	■ Open or create the document to be sent. ■ Click the **E-mail** button on the Word toolbar. ■ *Address* the message, and accept or revise the default *subject* for the message (the document name). ■ Click the **Send a Copy** button on the Word toolbar.
Send a document as an attachment to an email message.	■ Open or create the document to be sent. ■ Choose **File→Send To→Mail Recipient as Attachment** from the menu bar. A new message will be created in a normal Outlook (Or Outlook Express) message window. ■ *Address* the message, and accept or revise the default *subject* for the message (the document name). ■ Click the **Send** button on the message toolbar.

Hands-On 6.9 **Send a Document**

In this exercise, you will send the Proposal Notes document twice: once with the E-mail button and once as an attachment.

Use the Email Message Command

1. Click the E-mail 🖃 button on the Word toolbar.
   A new toolbar will appear at the top of the Word window. It has boxes that let you address the message and enter a subject, just like the Outlook message window. Your Word document has become the "body" of the message.

2. Click once on any email address that may already be in the To: box and tap (DELETE). Take care to place a semicolon between the two addresses, and address the message as shown here: **terry@offtowork.com; rsmith@offtowork.com**.

3. Change the subject line to read: **Grace's feedback**.
   Although you could type the body of the message, in this case it is unnecessary. Both correspondents will recognize the document immediately and see the highlighting for your comments.

4. Click the 🖃 Send a Copy button on the Word toolbar.
   The message is placed into Outlook's Outbox view for delivery. It will be sent the next time Outlook checks your email account.

Send the Document as an Attachment

5. Choose **File→Send To→Mail Recipient (as Attachment)** from the Word menu bar.
   A new message will be created in a normal Outlook message window.

6. Address the message to **terry@offtowork.com**.

7. Change the message subject to: **Comments Attached**

8. Type the body of the message as shown below:

```
Hello Terry:

Here are my comments on the Proposal Notes document.
Please let me know how else I may assist you.

Regards,

Grace
```

9. Click the **Send** button on the message window toolbar.
   The message is sent to the Outlook outbox for delivery.

10. Follow these steps to close the document.

Notice that there are two close window quick-sizing buttons at the top-right corner of the Word window. *Click the lower close button to close the document without closing the Word window. Click **Yes** if you are asked to save the document.*

Open an Attachment from the Preview Pane

11. Click the **Outlook** button on the Windows Taskbar to activate the window.

12. Click the **Send/Receive** button to send the outgoing messages and receive incoming messages. Continue to check for new messages until you have received *two* replies from Terry Sanchez and *one* from Robert Smith. Read the replies

13. Click to select the **Latest Draft** message from Terry Sanchez in the **Inbox** view.

14. Click on the paper clip at the right side of the Preview pane; then choose the **Proposal Second Draft** attachment.
    The attachment will open in the Word window.

15. Choose **File→Save As** from the menu bar.
    Notice that Temp *is listed as the* Save in *folder at the top of the dialog box. This means that the document is currently stored in that folder. You will now save the document to the* Sales Proposal folder *instead.*

16. Click the **Favorites** button in the Open dialog box; then **double-click** to open the *Sales Proposal folder* favorite. You may need to scroll through the list to find this Favorite.
    The contents of the folder will be displayed. This Favorite saves you time navigating through the system to the folder.

17. Click the **Save** button to save the document in the Sales Proposal folder.

Other Composition Tools

Word includes additional composition tools that may be useful in a collaborative project. This topic covers three of these tools: the highlighter, hyperlinks, and cross-references.

Adding Cross-References

A *cross-reference* is special item you can insert into a Word document that points to another element somewhere else in the document. For example, you can add a cross-reference that points to a heading on another page. When you place a cross-reference in a document, you must also choose the type of information it displays. For example, a cross-reference might contain the text of a heading in the document or the page number where the heading appears.

Example

In the example below, both cross-references refer to the same heading, but the first appears as the text of the heading, and the second appears as the page number.

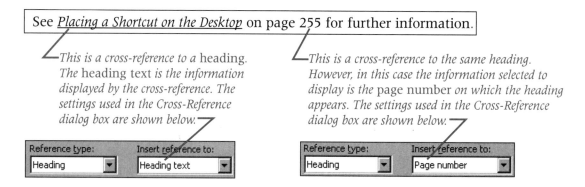

See *Placing a Shortcut on the Desktop* on page 255 for further information.

This is a cross-reference to a heading. The heading text *is the information displayed by the cross-reference. The settings used in the Cross-Reference dialog box are shown below.*

This is a cross-reference to the same heading. However, in this case the information selected to display is the page number *on which the heading appears. The settings used in the Cross-Reference dialog box are shown below.*

Reference type: Heading
Insert reference to: Heading text

Reference type: Heading
Insert reference to: Page number

Cross-References as Hyperlinks

Any cross-reference you insert can also act as a hyperlink. When you click on the cross-reference, Word will immediately jump the view to the location of the cross-reference item. For example, if you place a cross-reference to a heading in the document, clicking that cross-reference will immediately jump the view to the page containing the cross-referenced heading.

As Grace writes, she sees where two different topics are closely related. Grace places a cross-reference to the other topic so it will be easy to jump between the topics to make comparisons.

Using the Highlighter

Word's *highlighter* tool works just like its real-life counterpart (except that you can easily erase this highlighter). The highlighter tool applies a transparent color to the background of text. You can apply the highlighter by selecting a highlight color and then dragging, or you can select the text first and then click to apply the highlight color.

As Grace makes additions to the draft document, she highlights each change in blue. This will make it easy for the other team members to quickly identify and review her additions.

In this exercise, you will insert a cross-reference to a heading in the document. You will also highlight new text that you will type and remove a highlight applied by another user.

1. The **Proposal (Second Draft)** document should now be open in the Word window. If you did not receive the attachment in the previous exercise because you do not have an email account, make *Word* the active window and use the **File→Open** command to open the document from the **Sales Proposal folder.**
   Now you will type an addition to one of the points in the proposal. You will stop mid-sentence in the addition to add a cross-reference.

2. Click to the right of the period after the word *provide* at the very end of the paragraph beneath the *Reliability* heading.

3. Type the following text at the end of the paragraph.

```
One reason we are able to provide such a high level of
reliability is due to Acme's proprietary ATTACK system. See
```

4. Make sure that there is a space after the word *See;* then choose **Insert→Cross-reference** from the menu bar.

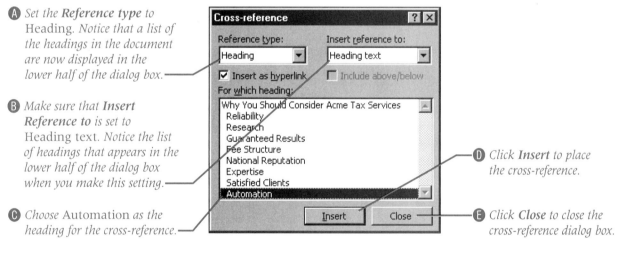

Ⓐ *Set the **Reference type** to Heading. Notice that a list of the headings in the document are now displayed in the lower half of the dialog box.*

Ⓑ *Make sure that **Insert Reference to** is set to Heading text. Notice the list of headings that appears in the lower half of the dialog box when you make this setting.*

Ⓒ *Choose Automation as the heading for the cross-reference.*

Ⓓ *Click **Insert** to place the cross-reference.*

Ⓔ *Click **Close** to close the cross-reference dialog box.*

5. Follow these steps to insert the cross-reference.

6. Hold down the (SHIFT) key; then tap the ← key to select the new hyperlink.

7. Click the Underline 🅄 button on the toolbar.
   Most hyperlinks on Web pages are underlined. An underline makes it easier for readers of this document to identify the hyperlink.

(Continued on the next page)

8. *Point* (don't click) on the Automation cross-reference. Notice that the pointer changes to a hand, which indicates that this text is a hyperlink.

9. Click on the *Automation* cross-reference.
   Your pointer jumps to the Automation heading on page 2. Notice that the Style box at the top-left corner of the Word toolbar reads Heading 2. *Automation was listed as a heading earlier because this heading style had been applied to the paragraph.*

   Notice also that a new toolbar has appeared in the Word window. This is the Web *toolbar. Its controls are similar to those you used in Internet Explorer.*

10. Click the Back button on Word's Web toolbar.
    This navigates you back to the hyperlink you clicked in Step 9.

Highlight and Unhighlight Text

11. Tap the (END) key to jump to the end of the current line. If the Underline 【U】 button appears to be "pressed," click the button to *switch off* the text underline.

12. Type the following text to complete the addition to this paragraph: **on the following page.**

13. Follow these steps to highlight the new text you typed in this exercise.

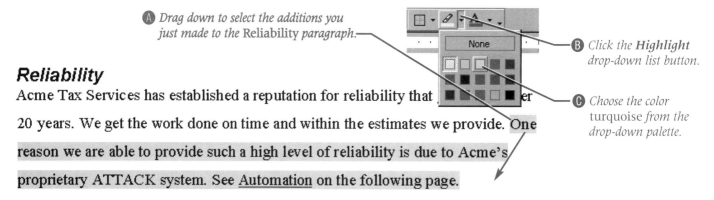

Ⓐ *Drag down to select the additions you just made to the* Reliability *paragraph.*

Ⓑ *Click the* **Highlight** *drop-down list button.*

Ⓒ *Choose the color* turquoise *from the drop-down palette.*

Reliability

Acme Tax Services has established a reputation for reliability that [...] er 20 years. We get the work done on time and within the estimates we provide. One reason we are able to provide such a high level of reliability is due to Acme's proprietary ATTACK system. See Automation on the following page.

   The highlight color is applied immediately to the selected text.

14. Scroll down the page to the **Guaranteed Results** topic. Read the comment on this heading.

15. *Right-click* on the comment; then choose **Delete Comment** from the pop-up menu.
    The comment and its highlight are removed. You cannot delete a comment by deleting the text in the comment inside the Comments panel. You must delete the comment in the Document window.

16. Drag to select the text with the green highlight; then click the **drop-down** portion of the **Highlight** button on the toolbar and choose **None.**
    The highlight is removed from the selected text.

17. Use (CTRL)+(HOME) to jump to the top of the page; then click the Automation hyperlink to navigate to that section of the following page.

18. Type the following text at the *end* of the last paragraph: **This allows us to serve our clients with unexcelled reliability.**

19. Follow these steps to highlight the sentence you just typed.

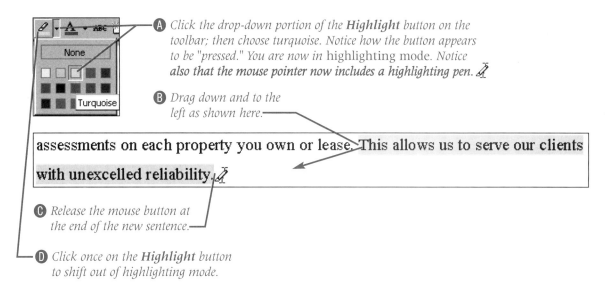

Ⓐ Click the drop-down portion of the **Highlight** button on the toolbar; then choose turquoise. Notice how the button appears to be "pressed." You are now in highlighting mode. *Notice also that the mouse pointer now includes a highlighting pen.*

Ⓑ Drag down and to the left as shown here.

Ⓒ Release the mouse button at the end of the new sentence.

Ⓓ Click once on the **Highlight** button to shift out of highlighting mode.

20. Save the document.

Adding Hyperlinks

Word makes it easy to insert hyperlinks to Web pages and other types of documents. For example, if a Web site contains information that would be useful in writing a document, you can embed a hyperlink to that Web site directly into your text. When another user clicks on the hyperlink, Word will transform its window into an Internet Explorer window and open up the linked Web site.

HOW TO INSERT A HYPERLINK

Task	Procedure
Insert a hyperlink to a Web page.	■ Click where you wish to insert the hyperlink.
	■ Choose **Insert→Hyperlink** from the menu bar, or click the **Insert Hyperlink** button on the toolbar, or use (CTRL)+K from the keyboard.
	■ Click the **Web Page** button; then navigate in Internet Explorer to the desired page, or type the URL into the dialog box.
	■ Make Word the active program window; then click **OK** to insert the hyperlink.

During her research, Grace looks at a competitor's Web site. She notices a few services and benefits on one page that her company might address in its own proposal. Grace decides to place a hyperlink directly into her input on the draft proposal document.

In this exercise, you will add a hyperlink to a Web page. When Terry and Robert click on this hyperlink, it will navigate them directly to that Web page.

1. Tap (ENTER) twice to add blank lines to the bottom of the document.

2. Type the following text: **Terry: Check this competitor's Web site for some interesting information about their tax data system.**

3. Tap the (SPACE BAR) twice to add space after the period.

4. Click the Insert Hyperlink [icon] button on the toolbar.
   Word will display the Insert Hyperlink dialog box. This dialog box offers several different methods to insert hyperlinks. In this exercise, you will use the method that lets you navigate to the Web page with Internet Explorer.

5. Click the **Web Page** button on the right side of the dialog box.
   Word will launch the Internet Explorer browser and display the Home page.

6. Click on the Internet Explorer Address bar; then type **www.offtowork.com/word** as shown here and tap (ENTER).

7. Click the **Lesson 6** button; then click the **Competition** hyperlink.
   A simulated competitor's Web page will appear. Now that you are displaying the Web page to be linked, you will return to Word and insert the hyperlink.

8. Click the **Proposal (Second Draft)** button on the Windows Taskbar to make Word the active program.

9. Follow these steps to complete the Insert Hyperlink command.

Ⓐ *Select the current name here, then type*
A Competitor's Web site.

Ⓑ *Notice that the URL for the page here matches the page displayed in the Internet Explorer window.*

Ⓒ *Click the ScreenTip button; then type* **Coyote Tax Services** *in the dialog box and click* **OK**.

Ⓓ *Click* **OK** *to insert the hyperlink.*

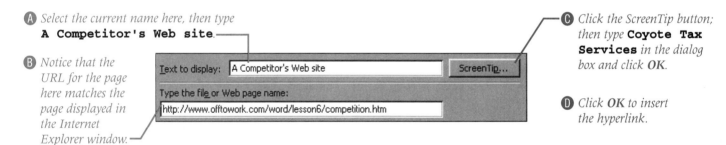

A new hyperlink is inserted on the page. Notice that it is underlined.

10. *Point* (don't click) over the new hyperlink.
    A pointer hand appears on the hyperlink. Notice that your ScreenTip appears as well.

    (Continued on the next page)

11. **Click** once on the hyperlink to test it.

    The Word window will temporarily transform into an Internet Explorer window to display the Web page. Notice that all of the toolbar buttons have changed. You can navigate in the Web site from this window just as you would with Internet Explorer.

12. Click the Back ⬅ button on the Internet Explorer toolbar to return to the Word document.

    The normal Word toolbars will return to the window.

Pasting Data from Other Sources

In previous lessons, you have used the copy and paste command to paste information from one place to another within the same document. However, it is also possible to copy and paste information from *one application program* to another. For example, you can copy and paste text from a Web page displayed in *Internet Explorer* into a *Word* document.

Pasting Various Formats

The information you work with in various applications can be pasted in a variety of formats. Each format has features that may make it well- or ill-suited for pasting into a document. For example, some formats may include additional codes that you would not want to appear in the Word document. The following table lists three examples of commonly used formats.

Format Name	Description
Formatted Text (RTF)	This format transfers any font or paragraph-level formatting such as bold, italics, and indents, and table formatting.
Unformatted Text	This format will lose any font or paragraph-level formatting in the original text. The pasted text will be formatted according to the current settings in the paragraph where you give the Paste command.
HTML format	This format will retain any types of formatting of text that you copy from a Web page. For example, if the text appears in a table on the Web page, the Paste command will paste the table into your document as well.

Paste Special Command

Word's *Paste Special* command lets you select the format for the content you paste into a document. When you give the Paste Special command, Word will list all of the available formats you can choose. Depending on the type of content you are pasting, there may be several formats in the list, or just one.

As she searches Acme's Web site, Grace notices some details that will be useful in preparing the sales proposal. Since the Web page contains other information that is not of interest, Grace decides to copy and paste the useful content on the Web page directly into the Word document. To ensure that the content is formatted clearly, and to save the time of manually formatting it herself, Grace uses the *Paste Special* command to paste the content into the Word document.

Hands-On 6.12 Navigate to a Web Page and Copy Text From It

1. Click [Competition - Microsoft I...] on the Windows Taskbar to activate the *Internet Explorer* window.

2. Click the Back [←] button on the Internet Explorer toolbar to return to the *Lesson 6* Web page.

3. Click the **Acme Tax Services** button.

4. Make sure that the Internet Explorer window is *maximized*.

5. Follow these steps to copy the table from this Web page.

Ⓐ *Point here; then drag down and to the right.*

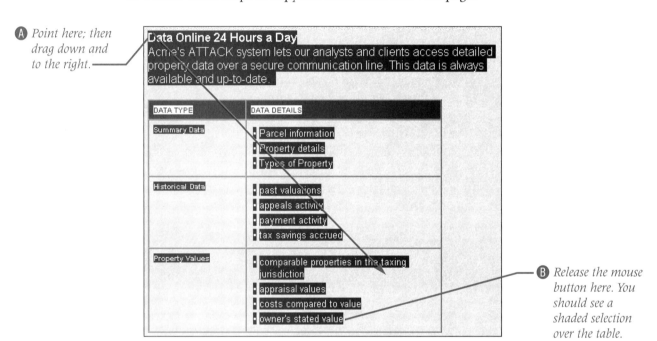

Ⓑ *Release the mouse button here. You should see a shaded selection over the table.*

6. Choose **Edit→Copy** from the menu bar.

7. Minimize [_] the Internet Explorer window.
The Word window should now be displayed as the active program.

Paste the Web Page Information

8. Use the *Zoom* box on the Word toolbar to set the magnification to [75% ▼].
This will let you see more of the pasted text when you use the paste command later.

9. Use (CTRL)+(END) to jump to the bottom of the document. Tap (ENTER) twice to add space below the last line of the document.

10. Use (CTRL)+(ENTER) to create a page break in the document; then type the following note:
Terry: let's also include this information about our data system.

11. Tap (ENTER) to add a new line after the text you just typed.

12. Choose **Edit→Paste Special** from the menu bar.

13. Choose **Unformatted Text** from the paste special dialog box; then click **OK.**

As:

Formatted Text (RTF)
Unformatted Text
HTML Format
Unformatted Unicode Text

14. Scroll back up the page to review the text that you just pasted.
Notice that the pasted text does not appear as it did on the Web page. All of the formatting (including the table) has been stripped away from the text. Only the words were pasted.

15. Click the Undo 🔙 button on the toolbar.

16. Choose **Edit→Paste Special** from the menu bar; then choose **Formatted Text (RTF)** from the option list, and click **OK.** Scroll if necessary to review the pasted text.
Now the table looks pretty good, and the text is still formatted as well. The Paste Special command lets you choose a paste format that gives the most useful results.

Send the Message

17. Choose **File→Save As** from the menu bar. Save the message to the Sales Proposal folder as:
Proposal (Second Draft, Grace Comments).

18. Choose **File→Send To→Mail Recipient (as Attachment)** from the menu bar.
This will transmit the document as a normal Word file rather than inside an email message. Working with a normal document should make it easier for Terry to complete the final version of the proposal.

19. Compose the following message.

To:	[yourself]
Subject:	Additions
Body:	Hello Terry and Robert:
	Attached are my additions to the second proposal draft. All additions are highlighted in blue. Let me know if there is anything else you need for me to contribute. Good luck with the proposal.
	Regards,
	Grace

20. **Send** the message.

21. Close ☒ any open Word, Internet Explorer, and My Computer windows.

22. Activate the *Outlook* window; then use *Send/Receive* to check for new messages.

23. Click the message you just sent yourself in the **Inbox** view. Click on the **paper clip** icon in the Preview pane, and choose the attachment document.
This is how Terry and Robert would receive the attachment Grace sent to them.

24. Close ☒ the Word and Outlook windows.

Concepts Review

True/False Questions

1. Windows lets you create folders inside of other folders.   TRUE   FALSE

2. A shortcut lets you access a folder from the Desktop.   TRUE   FALSE

3. An attachment is a file that is sent along with an email message.   TRUE   FALSE

4. Word always automatically prints the comments in any document.   TRUE   FALSE

5. A cross-reference can also work like a hyperlink.   TRUE   FALSE

6. A hyperlink in a Word document to a Web page works just like a   TRUE   FALSE
   hyperlink on a typical Web page.

7. It doesn't matter which format you select when you use the Paste Special command.   TRUE   FALSE

8. Word's E-mail button on the toolbar sends the document as an attachment.   TRUE   FALSE

9. Word's highlighter tool lets you insert comments into a document.   TRUE   FALSE

10. A Favorite can help you navigate quickly to a folder or disk drive.   TRUE   FALSE

Multiple-Choice Questions

1. Which statement about email message attachments is true?
   a. An attachment can be any type of file.
   b. An attachment must be a Word document file.
   c. An attachment is a second email message attached to the first one.
   d. None of the above

2. What controls the initials and name that identify a comment?
   a. The initials are set up in the Comments window.
   b. You must reinstall Word in order to change the initials.
   c. The initials are set in the Options window.
   d. Word sets the initials according to your log-on name.

3. Which description of a cross-reference in Word is true?
   a. A cross-reference can also act as a hyperlink.
   b. A cross-reference can be the text of a heading or a page number.
   c. A cross-reference is created with the Insert→Cross-Reference command.
   d. All of the above

4. Which statement best describes how the Paste Special command differs from an ordinary Paste command?
   a. Paste Special can only be used to paste particular types of data.
   b. Paste Special lets you select the format of the data you paste.
   c. Paste Special works exactly like the Paste command.
   d. Paste Special never pastes text formatting.

LESSON 7

Creating Personalized Letterhead and Envelopes

In this lesson, you will use Word 2000 to create a personalized letterhead. You will use custom tab stops to align text, and you will use paragraph borders and shading to enhance the appearance of the letterhead. The completed letterhead will be saved as a template so that it can be used repeatedly as the basis for new documents. In addition, you will create an envelope for mailing the letter. Finally, you will use Word 2000's powerful AutoCorrect feature to automatically insert text.

In This Lesson

Case Study

Rebecca Thomas is an Office Support Specialist with Fremont Medical Supplies. Prior to joining Fremont, Rebecca received extensive training in Office 2000 while attending Wilson Technical College. After completing her training, Rebecca was able to pass all Microsoft Office User Specialist exams, and she became a certified Microsoft Office specialist. Rebecca has decided to capitalize on her knowledge of Office 2000 by applying for part-time positions as a computer instructor. To automate the job search process, Rebecca uses Word 2000 to set up a personalized letterhead template for cover letters. Rebecca also uses the powerful formatting capabilities of Word to make her cover letters shine like diamonds.

Rebecca Thomas
1645 Bird Lane, Ojai, CA 93023   (510) 426-4566   Email: rthomas@aol.com

July 2, 1999

Ms. Mary Prichard
Director of Career Education
Wilkins Adult Education
345 Fremont Lane
San Jose, CA 95134

Dear Ms. Prichard:

I enjoyed meeting you last night and learning more about the variety of programs offered through your school. I was especially excited to learn that you are looking for a new Word 2000 instructor.

Pursuant to our conversation, I have listed my availability for the Fall 1999 semester. As I mentioned, I may be able to adjust my schedule to meet your needs.

> - Monday—Not available
> - Tuesday—6:00 p.m.–9:30 p.m.
> - Wednesday—6:00 p.m.–9:30 p.m.
> - Thursday—Not available
> - Friday—9:00 a.m.–4:30 p.m.
> - Saturday—Not available
> - Sunday—Not available

Ms. Prichard, thank you once again for taking the time to meet with me. I look forward to hearing from you soon.

Sincerely,

Rebecca Thomas
Computer Instructor

Tab Stops

The (TAB) key moves the insertion point to the nearest tab stop. In Word, default tab stops are set every 0.5". This is the reason why the insertion point moves 0.5" whenever you tap the (TAB) key.

Changing the Default Tab Stops

You can change the default tab stops if you want the insertion point to move a smaller or larger distance when the (TAB) key is tapped. For example, you may want the insertion point to move 0.25" instead of 0.5". The default tab stops are used in all paragraphs except paragraphs that have custom tab stops. You change the default tab stops by issuing the **Format→Tabs** command and setting the Default tab stops measurement.

Custom Tab Stops

TIP!

Use tab stops or tables to line up columns of text.

You can set custom tab stops for selected paragraphs. Custom tab stops are useful for mixing alignments within a line. For example, you will use custom tab stops in Rebecca Thomas's letterhead to center the telephone number and right-align the email address. You should always avoid using the (SPACE BAR) to line up columns of text. Columns may go out of alignment if you decide to change fonts or edit the text. Always use tab stops or tables to line up columns of text. Custom tab stops are also useful for creating *leaders*. Leaders are lines that extend across a page to a custom leader tab stop.

Setting Custom Tab Stops with the Ruler

Word provides four types of custom tab stops: left, right, center, and decimal. You can set custom tab stops using the horizontal ruler. You set tab stops by choosing the desired tab type from the Tab box at the left end of the ruler. Then you click at the desired location on the ruler to set the tab stop The tab stop is set for the paragraph with the insertion point or for all selected paragraphs. You can move a custom tab stop by dragging it to a different location on the ruler.

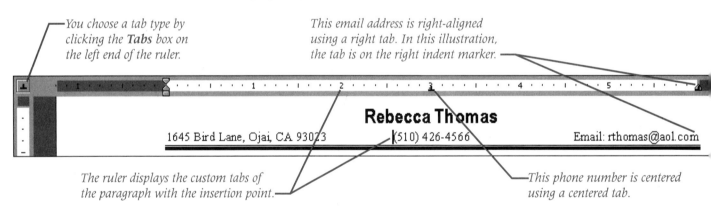

You choose a tab type by clicking the **Tabs** box on the left end of the ruler.

This email address is right-aligned using a right tab. In this illustration, the tab is on the right indent marker.

Rebecca Thomas

1645 Bird Lane, Ojai, CA 93023   (510) 426-4566   Email: rthomas@aol.com

The ruler displays the custom tabs of the paragraph with the insertion point.

This phone number is centered using a centered tab.

In this exercise, you will use custom tabs to set up the letterhead.

Set Up the Letterhead

1. Start Word, or start a new document if Word is already running.

2. Choose **File→Page Setup** and set the top margin to 0.5″.
   Your letterhead will begin 0.5″ down from the top of the page.

3. Click the Center Align ▤ button, and type **Rebecca Thomas**.

4. Tap (ENTER), and click the Align Left ▤ button.

5. Set the font size to 10, and type **1645 Bird Lane, Ojai, CA 93023**.
   It is OK to use a small font size, such as 10pt in letterhead.

Set Custom Tabs

6. Follow these steps to set and use a center tab.

Ⓐ *Click this box until the* ***Center Tab*** *symbol appears, as shown here.*

Ⓑ *Click just under the 3″ position on the ruler to set a center tab; 3″ is the center of the line.*

Ⓒ *Tap the* (TAB) *key, and the insertion point will move to the 3″ position.*

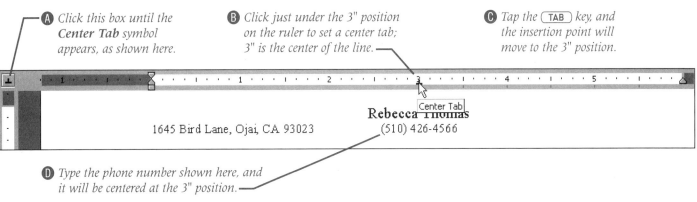

Ⓓ *Type the phone number shown here, and it will be centered at the 3″ position.*

7. Follow these steps to set and use a Right Tab.

Ⓐ *Click this box until the* ***Right Tab*** *symbol appears, as shown here.*

Ⓑ *Click here to place a* ***Right Tab*** *just to the left of the* ***Right Indent*** *marker.*

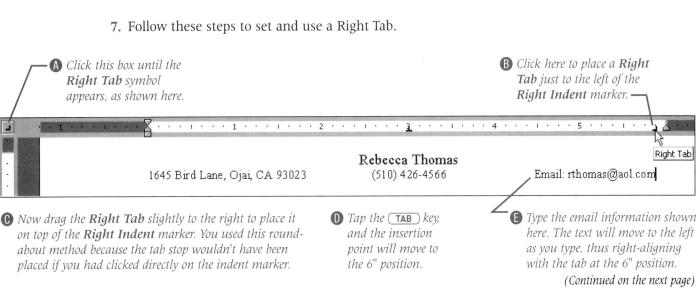

Ⓒ *Now drag the* ***Right Tab*** *slightly to the right to place it on top of the* ***Right Indent*** *marker. You used this roundabout method because the tab stop wouldn't have been placed if you had clicked directly on the indent marker.*

Ⓓ *Tap the* (TAB) *key, and the insertion point will move to the 6″ position.*

Ⓔ *Type the email information shown here. The text will move to the left as you type, thus right-aligning with the tab at the 6″ position.*

(Continued on the next page)

8. Tap (ENTER), and Word will most likely convert the email address rthomas@aol.com to a blue underlined hyperlink.

   Word 2000 automatically converts email addresses and Web site URLs (addresses) to hyperlinks. Word opens Outlook or Internet Explorer when a hyperlink is clicked.

9. Click Undo 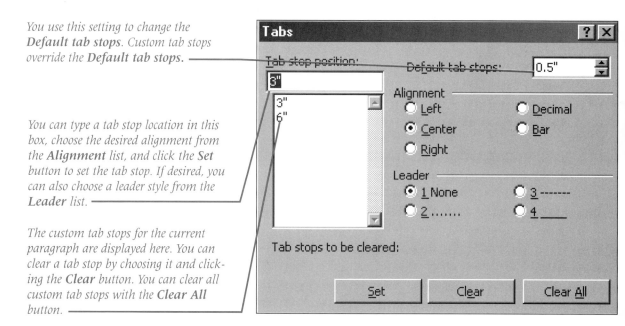 to override the conversion and remove the hyperlink.

   You can always use Undo to override automatic conversions such as this.

10. Look at the ruler, and notice that the custom tab stops for the new paragraph are visible.

    Custom tab stops are paragraph formats, so they are carried to new paragraphs when (ENTER) is tapped. In the next exercise, you will remove them from the new paragraph. Keep in mind that you could leave the custom tab stops in the new paragraph even though you will not use them. You will remove them to help keep your document clean.

The Tabs Dialog Box

You can also set custom tab stops by issuing the **Format→Tabs** command and using the Tabs dialog box. The Tabs dialog box lets you specify precise positions for custom tab stops, clear custom tab stops, and set leader tabs.

You use this setting to change the **Default tab stops**. *Custom tab stops override the* **Default tab stops**.

You can type a tab stop location in this box, choose the desired alignment from the **Alignment** *list, and click the* **Set** *button to set the tab stop. If desired, you can also choose a leader style from the* **Leader** *list.*

The custom tab stops for the current paragraph are displayed here. You can clear a tab stop by choosing it and clicking the **Clear** *button. You can clear all custom tab stops with the* **Clear All** *button.*

Clear Tab Stops

1. Make sure the insertion point is on the line below the address line, and choose **Format→Tabs.**

2. Click the **Clear All** button to remove the tab stops from the tab stop list.

3. Click **OK,** and the tab symbols will be removed from the ruler.

4. Tap ↑ once to position the insertion point on the address line.
   *Notice that the tab stops are visible on the ruler. When you issued the **Format→Tabs** command, the tab stops were only removed from the paragraph with the insertion point.*

5. Tap ↓ to position the insertion point below the address line.

6. Set the font size to 12, and tap (ENTER) six times to position the insertion point at the 2″ position.

Set a Left Tab

7. Choose **Format→Tabs** from the menu bar.

8. Follow these steps to set a left tab at the 3″ position. This tab will be used to align the date in modified block style business letters.

Ⓐ *Type **3** in the Tab stop position box.*

Ⓑ *Make sure the alignment is set to left.*

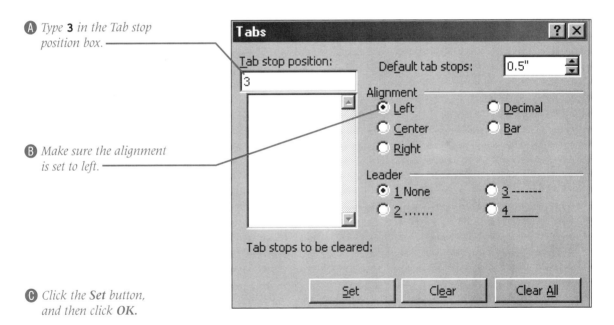

Ⓒ *Click the **Set** button, and then click **OK.***

Notice that a Left Tab symbol appears on the ruler at the 3″ position.

9. Tap the (TAB) key, and type the date **July 2, 1999**.
   Notice that using a custom tab stop to align the date is cleaner and easier than tapping the (TAB) key six or seven times. Once you get used to custom tab stops, it is quick and easy to insert a tab by clicking on the ruler.

(Continued on the next page)

10. Tap (ENTER) to move to the next line.

   Notice that the insertion point moves to the left end of the line. Even though the tab stop has been carried to the new paragraph, you would need to tap the (TAB) key to actually use the tab stop.

11. Use the **Format→Tabs** command to display the Tabs dialog box and clear all tabs from the new paragraph.

   Now continue with the next topic, where you will learn how to apply borders and shading.

Borders and Shading

You can apply borders and shading to selected text, paragraphs, and pages. In this lesson, you will apply borders to paragraphs. Borders can be applied to the top, bottom, left, and right edges of paragraphs. You can choose the style, color, and thickness of borders. You can also choose various shading patterns and colors.

The Tables and Borders ⊞ button displays the Tables and Borders toolbar. You can use the Tables and Borders toolbar to apply borders and shading to text and paragraphs. You can also use the **Format→Borders and Shading** command to display the Borders and Shading dialog box.

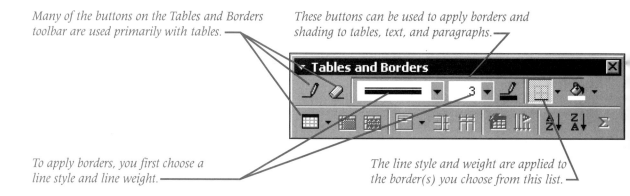

Many of the buttons on the Tables and Borders toolbar are used primarily with tables.

These buttons can be used to apply borders and shading to tables, text, and paragraphs.

To apply borders, you first choose a line style and line weight.

The line style and weight are applied to the border(s) you choose from this list.

1. Click anywhere on the address line in the letterhead.
   Borders and shading are applied to the paragraph with the insertion point, or to selected paragraphs.

2. Click the Tables and Borders ⊞ button on the Standard toolbar to display the Tables and Borders toolbar.

3. Follow these steps to apply a border to the bottom of the paragraph.

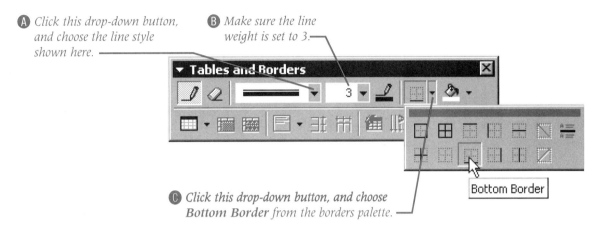

Ⓐ *Click this drop-down button, and choose the line style shown here.*

Ⓑ *Make sure the line weight is set to 3.*

Ⓒ *Click this drop-down button, and choose* **Bottom Border** *from the borders palette.*

Notice that the border extends between the margins. Paragraph borders fill the space between the margins unless the paragraph(s) are indented. You will get extensive practice working with borders and shading as you progress through this lesson.

4. Click the Tables and Borders ⊞ button to close the Tables and Borders toolbar.

Templates

All Word documents are based upon templates. Templates can include text, formatting, graphics, and any other objects or formats available in Word. The benefit of templates is they do not change when documents that are based upon them change. This lets you use templates repeatedly as the basis for new documents. Word provides a variety of ready-to-use templates that can be used for new documents. If necessary, you can modify the ready-to-use templates to suit your needs. You can also create custom templates with the text, objects, and formats you desire. For example, you will save Rebecca's letterhead as a template. You will then use the letterhead as the basis for new letters.

Using Templates

You use the **File→New** command to display the New dialog box. You base a new document upon a template by choosing the desired template from the New dialog box and clicking OK. You then develop the document and eventually save it as any other Word document. The underlying template remains unchanged.

You can also base a document upon a template by navigating to the location where the template is stored, and double-clicking the template. This is the technique you will use in the hands-on exercises in this lesson.

Templates are organized into categories such as Letters & Faxes.

The General category is the default category where custom templates are stored.

You base a new document upon a template by double-clicking the template or choosing it and clicking the OK button.

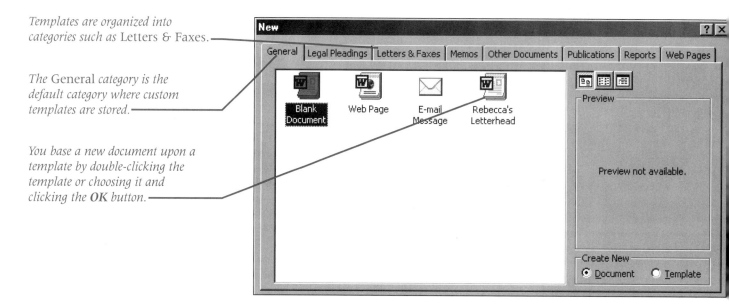

The Normal Template

When you click the New 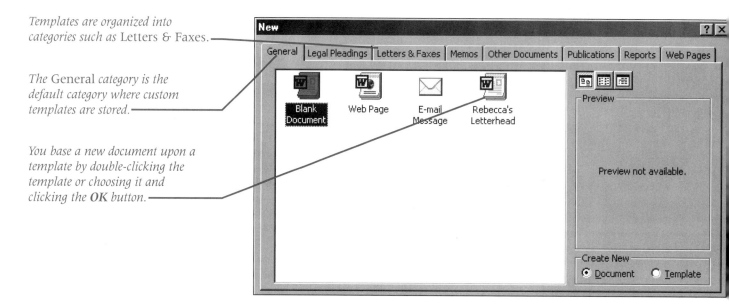 button on the Standard toolbar, Word creates a new document that is based upon the Normal template. The Normal template is one of the built-in templates in Word. In the preceding illustration, the Normal template appears as the Blank Document option in the General tab. Choosing the Blank Document option has the same effect as clicking the New button on the Standard toolbar. The Normal template contains 1.25" left and right margins, a Times New Roman 12pt font, and other format settings. This is why your new documents have a default font size of 12, and 1.25" left and right margins.

Template Organization

Templates are used with all Office 2000 applications. The built-in templates that are part of Office 2000 are stored in the C:\Program Files\Microsoft Office\Templates\1033 folder. The Normal.dot template is stored in the C:\Windows\Application Data\Microsoft\Templates folder. This also happens to be the default location for storing your custom templates.

Creating Your Own Templates

The easiest way to create a template is to first create a document with the text, formatting, graphics, and other settings you desire. Then, save the document as a template. The following Quick Reference table highlights three methods you can use to turn your documents into templates.

CREATING TEMPLATES

Save to the Default Template Location

- Create the document and choose **File→Save As.**

- Choose Document Template from the Save as Type box.

- Type a filename, and click the **Save** button. The template will appear in the General tab of the New dialog box whenever you issue the **File→New** command.

Save the Template to a Diskette or Other Location

- Create the document and choose **File→Save As.**

- Choose Document Template from the Save as Type box.

- Choose a storage location from the Save in box, type a file name, and click the **Save** button.

- To use the template, use My Computer or Windows Explorer to navigate to the diskette or other storage location where the template is located.

- Double-click the template, and a new document will appear that is based upon the template.

Create Another Tab in the New Dialog Box and Save to That Tab

- Create the document, and choose **File→Save As.**

- Choose Document Template from the Save as Type box.

- Click the New Folder ⬚ button on the Save As dialog box.

- Type a name for the new folder, and click **OK.**

- Type a name for the template and click the **Save** button. The next time you issue the **File→New** command, a new tab will appear in the New box with the same name you assigned to the folder. Your template will appear in the new tab.

Hands-On 7.4 Create and Use a Template

*In this exercise, you will be instructed to save your template to your exercise diskette. You won't save templates to the C: drive in this course. This is because many computer labs prevent students from accessing the C: drive. If you need to save templates to the default template folder and access them using the **File→New** command, then use the first method discussed in the Quick Reference table on the previous page.*

Create the Template

1. Click the Save ![save icon] button, and follow these steps to save the letterhead as a template.

Ⓐ *Choose Document Template from the Save as type list at the bottom of the dialog box.*

Ⓑ *Choose 3½ Floppy (A:) from the Save in list at the top of the dialog box.*

Save As

Save in:	3½ Floppy (A:)

History
My Documents
Desktop
Favorites
Web Folders

File name: Rebecca's Letterhead

Save as type: Document Template

Save

Cancel

Ⓒ *Type* **Rebecca's Letterhead** *in the File name box.*

Ⓓ *Click the Save button.*

2. Choose **File→Close** from the menu bar to close the template.

Use the Template

In the next few steps, you will use Window's My Computer tool to display the contents of your exercise diskette. You will base a new document upon the Rebecca's Letterhead template.

3. Click the Show Desktop ![show desktop icon] button on the Windows Taskbar to hide all program windows. If you don't have a Show Desktop button on your Taskbar, then right-click on an open part of the Taskbar and choose *Minimize All Windows* from the pop-up menu.

NOTE! *In Steps 4 through 6, you can click once instead of double-clicking if you point to the objects and they appear as underlined hyperlinks.*

4. Double-click the My Computer icon on the Desktop.

5. Double-click the 3½ Floppy (A:) icon to display the contents of your exercise diskette.

6. Double-click the **Rebecca's Letterhead** template.
   A new document will appear with the same text and formatting as the template.

TIP! *Use the previous steps to open templates that are stored in locations (such as a diskette) that prevent them from appearing in the New dialog box. Templates that appear in the New dialog box can be used by double-clicking them in the New dialog box.*

7. Now choose **File→Close** from the menu bar.
   Notice that Word did not ask you to save the document. This is because it is a new document that has not been changed in any way.

Modifying Custom Templates

You can easily modify a custom template after it has been created. The following Quick Reference table describes the methods you can use to locate, modify, and save changes to templates.

Quick Reference

MODIFYING CUSTOM TEMPLATES

Modifying Templates That Are Not Stored in the Default Templates Folder

■ Click the Open 🗁 button, and choose Document Templates from the Files of Type list.

■ Navigate to the location where the template is stored, choose the template, and click the **Open** button.

■ Modify the template, save the changes, and then close the template.
Note: To modify a template, you must use the Open dialog box to open the template. If you use My Computer to navigate to the template and then double-click the template, you will create a new document.

Modifying Templates Stored in the Default Template Folder

■ Choose **File→New** from the menu bar.

■ Choose the template you wish to modify, click the **Template** button at the bottom of the dialog box, and click **OK.**

■ Modify the template, and choose **File→Save As** when you have finished.

■ Choose the original template in the Save As box, click the **Save** button, and click **Yes** when Word asks if you want to replace the original template.

■ Close the template when you have finished.

Since this letterhead will be used repeatedly, it makes sense to insert the date as a field. This way, the date will update automatically whenever the template is used. Also, you will add hard returns after the date so that the inside address is ready to be entered whenever the template is used.

Open the Template

1. Click the Open [icon] button on Word's Standard toolbar.

2. Choose Document Templates from the Files of Type list at the bottom of the dialog box.

3. Choose 3½ Floppy (A:) from the Look in list at the top of the dialog box.

4. Choose Rebecca's Letterhead on your diskette, and click the **Open** button.
   Look at the title bar at the top of the Word window and notice the name Rebecca's Letterhead. You are now working with the original Rebecca's Letterhead template—not a document that is based upon the template.

Modify the Template

5. Select the name Rebecca Thomas at the top of the letterhead.

6. Format the selected text with an Arial Bold 14 font.

7. Select the date by dragging the mouse over it.

8. Choose **Insert→Date and Time** from the menu bar.

9. Choose the third format on the list, and make sure the Update automatically box is checked.

10. Click **OK,** and the date field will replace the date you typed originally.

11. Click on the line below the date, and tap (ENTER) three times.
    This inserts the proper space between the date and the inside address.

12. Click the Save [icon] button to save the changes.

13. Close the template when you have finished.

Use the Modified Template

14. Click the 3½ Floppy (A:) button on the Windows Taskbar to switch to the My Computer window where your exercise diskette is displayed.

15. Double-click the Rebecca's Letterhead template to base a new document upon the modified template.
    Notice that the changes you made to the name and the date appear in the document.

16. Click the Save [icon] button, and save the new document to your exercise diskette with the name **Hands-On Lesson 7.**

17. Click the 3½ Floppy (A:) button on the Windows Taskbar, and then close the window.

18. Close any other My Computer windows that are open.

Enter Text

1. Click anywhere in the document, and press (CTRL)+(END) to move the insertion point to the location where the inside address is to begin.

2. Enter the following text. Use the em dash symbol from the Special Characters tab of the Symbols dialog box to insert the dash after the days. Use the en dash symbol between the hours.

Ms. Mary Prichard
Director of Career Education
Wilkins Adult Education
345 Fremont Lane
San Jose, CA 95134

Dear Ms. Prichard:

I enjoyed meeting you last night and learning more about the variety of programs offered through your school. I was especially excited to learn that you are looking for a new Word 2000 instructor.

Pursuant to our conversation, I have listed my availability for the Fall 1999 semester. As I mentioned, I may be able to adjust my schedule to meet your needs.

Monday—Not available
Tuesday—6:00 p.m.–9:30 p.m.
Wednesday—6:00 p.m.–9:30 p.m.
Thursday—Not available
Friday—9:00 a.m.–4:30 p.m.
Saturday—Not available
Sunday—Not available

Ms. Prichard, thank you once again for taking the time to meet with me. I look forward to hearing from you soon.

Sincerely,

Rebecca Thomas
Computer Instructor

(Continued on the next page)

Apply Borders and Shading

In the next few steps, you will add borders and shading to the "days of the week" paragraphs. You will use the Borders and Shading dialog box instead of the Tables and Borders toolbar.

3. Select the "days of the week" paragraphs as shown below.

4. Choose **Format→Borders and Shading** from the menu bar.

5. Follow these steps to choose a border.

Ⓐ *Click the* ***Borders*** *tab.*

Ⓑ *Choose a 1½ pt line width.*

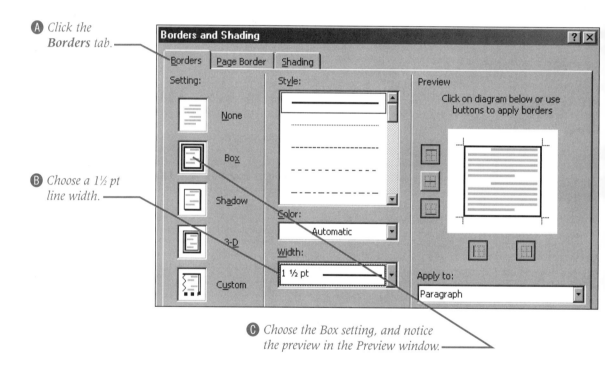

Ⓒ *Choose the Box setting, and notice the preview in the Preview window.*

6. Follow these steps to set shading.

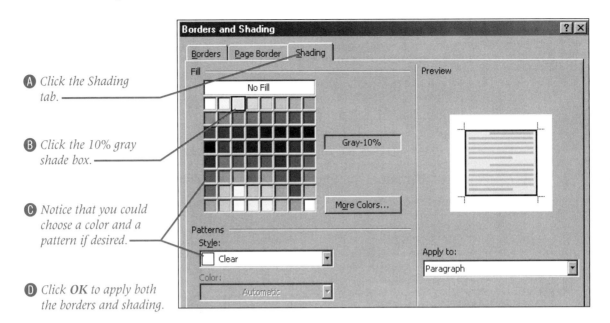

Ⓐ *Click the Shading tab.*

Ⓑ *Click the 10% gray shade box.*

Ⓒ *Notice that you could choose a color and a pattern if desired.*

Ⓓ *Click OK to apply both the borders and shading.*

Notice that the border was applied to the outside of the selected group of paragraphs. Also notice that the horizontal borders and the shading extend all the way to the right margin. In a moment, you will adjust the width of the borders and shading by changing the indents.

Add Bullets and Adjust Indents

7. Make sure that the paragraphs you just formatted are still selected.

8. Set both the left and right indents to 1½".
   The paragraphs should still be selected, and the shaded box will appear to be centered on the line.

9. Choose **Format→Bullets and Numbering** from the menu bar.

10. Choose the third ➤ bullet style in the second row, and click **OK.**
    The formatted paragraphs should match the example shown below.

> ➤ Monday—Not available
> ➤ Tuesday—6:00 p.m.–9:30 p.m.
> ➤ Wednesday—6:00 p.m.–9:30 p.m.
> ➤ Thursday—Not available
> ➤ Friday—9:00 a.m.–4:30 p.m.
> ➤ Saturday—Not available
> ➤ Sunday—Not available

(Continued on the next page)

11. Select from the complimentary close *Sincerely* to the end of the document. Your selection should include the complimentary close, the signature block, and the blank lines in between.

12. Choose **Format→Tabs** from the menu bar.

13. Type **3** in the Tab stop position box.

14. Make sure the Left alignment option is chosen, and click **OK.**
    Look at the horizontal ruler, and you will notice that a Left Tab symbol is now positioned at the 3" mark. Notice also that the tab stops have no effect on the document unless you tap the `TAB` *key.*

15. Click in front of the complimentary close Sincerely, and tap the `TAB` key.
    The complimentary close should move to the 3" position.

16. Use the `TAB` key to move the name and title in the signature block to the 3" position.

17. Save the changes to your document and continue with the next topic.

AutoCorrect

Word's AutoCorrect feature lets you automatically enter text and graphics. AutoCorrect is most useful for replacing abbreviations with full phrases. For example, you could set up AutoCorrect to insert the phrase *as soon as possible* whenever you type *asap.* AutoCorrect is also used for automatically correcting common spelling errors. For example, the word *the* is often misspelled as *teh,* and the word *and* is often misspelled as *adn.* Common spelling mistakes such as *adn* and their replacement words are built-in AutoCorrect entries. This way, the word *and* will automatically replace *adn* whenever you type the latter. You may have noticed AutoCorrect changing the spelling or format of certain words as you have worked through this course.

Expanding AutoCorrect Entries

AutoCorrect is activated each time you type a word and tap the `SPACE BAR`. Each word you type is compared to all entries in an AutoCorrect table. If a word matches an entry in the AutoCorrect table, then a word or phrase from the AutoCorrect table replaces the word. This is known as expanding the AutoCorrect entry.

Replacement Text and Graphics

AutoCorrect is very powerful. You can use any text and graphics as replacements for an AutoCorrect entry. This gives AutoCorrect great flexibility and makes it very useful. In this lesson, you will use AutoCorrect to insert formatted text and formatted paragraphs.

Creating New AutoCorrect Entries

You create new AutoCorrect entries by selecting the desired text in your document and choosing **Tools→AutoCorrect.** You then type the desired abbreviation in the AutoCorrect dialog box.

In this exercise, you will use the complimentary close and signature block to create an AutoCorrect entry. Once the AutoCorrect entry is set up, you will be able to use it to insert the complimentary close and signature block.

Create the Entry

1. Follow this step to select the necessary text for the AutoCorrect entry.

Ⓐ *Position the mouse pointer in the left margin and drag down until the selection looks like this.*

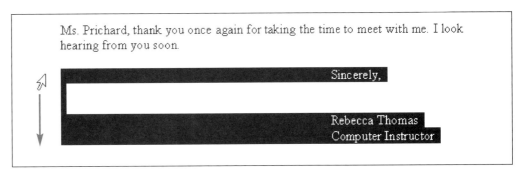

Ms. Prichard, thank you once again for taking the time to meet with me. I look hearing from you soon.

It is important that you select the text in this manner so that the tab that precedes the complimentary close (Sincerely) is included in the selection.

2. Choose **Tools→AutoCorrect** from the menu bar.

3. Follow these steps to create the AutoCorrect entry.

Ⓐ *Notice these check boxes. These boxes instruct AutoCorrect to automatically make the specified corrections in your documents.*

Ⓑ *Type* **rt** *(the initials of Rebecca Thomas) in the Replace box.*

Ⓒ *Make sure the* Formatted text *option is chosen. This option instructs AutoCorrect to insert the selected text exactly as it is formatted, including the hard returns, fonts, and graphics. Notice that the selected text is not visible in the With box. This is because the tab that precedes "Sincerely" was included in the selection. The With box is displaying the blank space created by the tab.*

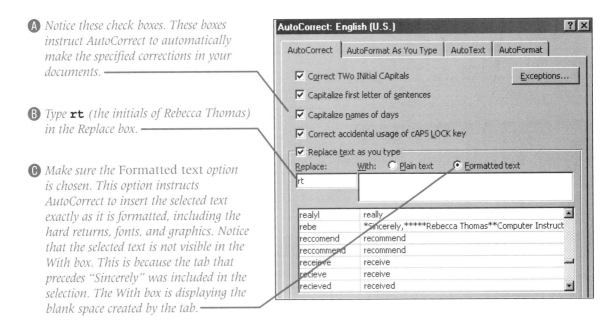

Ⓓ *Click either the* **Add** *button or the* **Replace** *button (depending on which button is available). If the entry already exists, then click* **Yes** *to replace it.*

Ⓔ *Click* **OK**.

(Continued on the next page)

Use the Entry

4. Delete the selected complimentary close and signature block text.

5. Type **rt**, and tap the (SPACE BAR) once.

AutoCorrect expands the entry inserting the complimentary close and signature block. Notice that the tab indentation is included in the expanded entry. This AutoCorrect entry is now available for use in all Word documents.

6. Click Undo ⟲ to reverse the AutoCorrect expansion.

You can always use Undo to reverse an AutoCorrect expansion. You may need to do this from time to time to eliminate an unwanted expansion. Notice that you could continue typing at this point, and the abbreviation rt would remain in the document as text.

7. Click Redo ↻ to restore the expansion.

Delete the Entry

8. Choose **Tools→AutoCorrect,** and follow these steps to delete the rt entry.

Ⓐ *Scroll through the list and notice the large number of entries. Most of the entries are designed to correct common spelling errors.*

Ⓑ *Click in the Replace box and type* **rt**. *Word will rapidly scroll the list and the* rt *entry will appear.*

Ⓒ *Click the* rt ***entry*** *to select it.*

Ⓓ *Click the* **Delete** *button to remove the entry.*

Replace:	With:	○ Plain text	◉ Formatted text
rt			

rt	*Sincerely,*****Rebecca Thomas**Computer Instruct
rumers	rumors
rwite	write
rythm	rhythm
saidhe	said he
saidit	said it
saidt he	said the

Replace   Delete

9. Click the **OK** button to close the dialog box.

10. Save the changes, and continue with the next topic.

Creating Envelopes

Word makes setting up and printing envelopes a breeze. In fact, Word is so efficient that it can automatically capture the delivery address in a letter and insert it in an envelope for you. You use the Envelopes and Labels dialog box to choose an envelope size, type return and delivery addresses, and choose formatting options, such as the font and font size. You can even print postal service bar codes on your envelopes to help speed up mail delivery. In this topic, you will learn how to create an envelope for a single letter. You can also use Word's mail merge feature to generate envelopes for each address in a mailing list.

CREATING ENVELOPES

■ Create a letter or open a letter containing the delivery address you want in the envelope. If you don't have an existing letter, you can skip this step.

■ Choose **Tools→Envelopes and Labels** from the menu bar.

■ Type the desired delivery address and return address. You won't need to type the delivery address if you displayed the dialog box from an existing letter. You won't need the return address if your envelopes have a preprinted return address.

■ If necessary, use the Options button to change the envelope size, insert a bar code, change fonts and font sizes, and set margins.

■ Use the Print button to print the envelope, or click **Add to Document** to make the envelope a separate page in the document.

Hands-On 7.8 Create an Envelope

1. Choose **Tools→Envelopes and Labels** from the menu bar and click the Envelopes tab.
   Word should capture the delivery address from your letter and place it in the Delivery address section of the dialog box. You should type the delivery address in the dialog box if Word did not capture it for you.

2. Follow these steps to enter a return address, and explore the dialog box.

Ⓐ *Notice the address book buttons. These buttons let you choose addresses from an Outlook address book.*

Ⓑ *Type the return address shown here. You could print the envelope at this point; however, you will explore the dialog box options first.*

Ⓒ *Click the **Options** button. Notice that you can change the envelope size, insert a bar code, set margins, and change the font and font size for both the delivery and return addresses.*

Ⓓ *Click the **Cancel** button on the Envelope Options dialog box.*

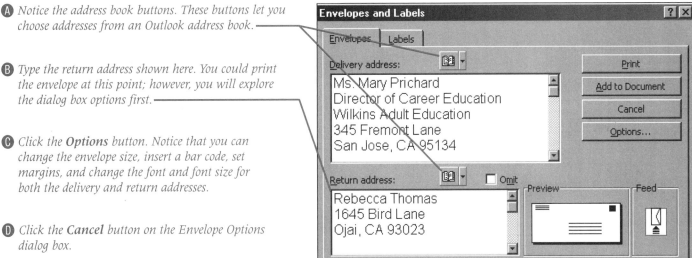

Ⓔ *If you have an envelope, feel free to print it by clicking the **Print** button in the Envelopes and Labels dialog box. The dialog box will close automatically after you print the envelope. If you do not have an envelope, click the **Cancel** button to close the dialog box.*

3. Save the changes to your letter, and then close the document.

4. Continue with the end-of-lesson questions and exercises.

Concepts Review

True/False Questions

1. Borders cannot be applied to the bottom edges of paragraphs.   TRUE   FALSE

2. A template is updated whenever you save a document that is based upon the template.   TRUE   FALSE

3. A template can only be used once as the basis for a new document.   TRUE   FALSE

4. Templates can contain text and graphics, but they cannot contain formatting.   TRUE   FALSE

5. AutoCorrect is useful for inserting frequently used text in a document.   TRUE   FALSE

6. AutoCorrect entries are expanded when the spacebar is tapped.   TRUE   FALSE

7. The Envelopes dialog box is displayed with the Tools→Envelopes and Labels command.   TRUE   FALSE

8. Word lets you choose from a variety of envelope sizes.   TRUE   FALSE

Multiple-Choice Questions

1. Which command is used to base a new document upon a template?
   a. Format→Template
   b. File→New
   c. Insert→Template
   d. None of the above

2. Which command displays the Borders and Shading dialog box?
   a. Insert→Borders and Shading
   b. Format→Borders and Shading
   c. Tools→Borders and Shading
   d. None of the above

3. Which of the following sequences of steps saves a document as a template?
   a. Choose File→Save As, choose Document Template from the Save as type list, type a name for the template, and click OK.
   b. Save the document as you normally would. Templates are created the first time you use the File→New command after saving the document.
   c. You cannot save a document as a template.
   d. None of the above

4. Which template is used as the basis for new documents when the New button is clicked?
   a. Letters & Faxes
   b. Normal
   c. General
   d. Rebecca's Letterhead

Skill Builders

Skill Builder 7.1 Set Up a Personal Letterhead Template

In this exercise, you will create your own personalized stationary. You will also create an AutoCorrect entry to automatically insert the complimentary close in cover letters.

Set Up the Letterhead

1. Start a new document, and set the top margin to 0.5".

2. Type your name, address information, and telephone number as shown below. Make sure you use your actual name, address information, and telephone number—not the generic text shown below.

```
Your Name
Street address
City, State Zip
Phone
```

3. Tap (ENTER) until the insertion point is 2" down.

4. Insert the date as a field, choosing the third date format in the Date and Time dialog box. Make sure the Update automatically option is turned on.

5. Tap (ENTER) four times after the date.

6. Select your name, and format it as Arial 14 Bold.

7. Select the address lines and telephone number, and format them as Arial 8 (no bold).

8. Click anywhere on the telephone number line.

9. Choose **Format→Borders and Shading,** and click the **Borders** tab.

10. If necessary, choose the single-line style, and choose a line width of 1pt.

11. Click the Bottom Edge ▦ button, and click **OK.**

12. At this point, your letterhead should look similar to the following example.

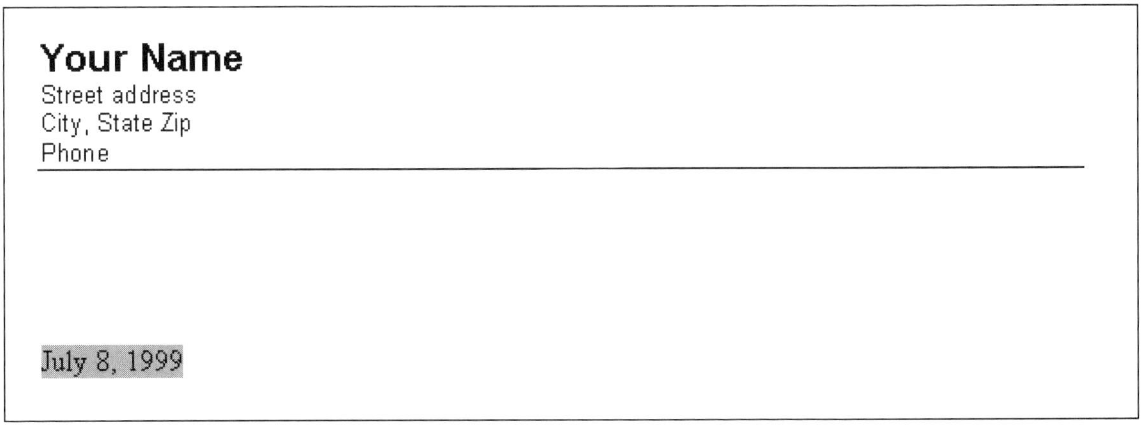

Your Name
Street address
City, State Zip
Phone

July 8, 1999

(Continued on the next page)

Save the Letterhead As a Template

In the next few steps, you will save the letterhead to your exercise diskette as a template so that you can use the letterhead whenever you compose a letter.

13. Click the Save [icon] button.

14. Choose Document Template from the Save as type list at the bottom of the dialog box.

15. Choose 3½ Floppy (A:) from the Save in list at the top of the dialog box.

16. Type **My Letterhead** in the File name box, and click the **Save** button.

17. Choose **File→Close** to close the template.
    You will use your template in the next two exercises.

Create an AutoCorrect Entry

18. Click the New [icon] button to start a new document.

19. Type the text shown below. Make sure you tap (ENTER) four times after the complimentary close and twice after your name. Also, use your name instead of the generic *Your name* shown below. You will use this closing with letters when a resumé is enclosed.

```
Sincerely yours,



Your name

Enclosure
```

20. Select all of the text you just typed, including the blank lines.

21. Choose **Tools→AutoCorrect** from the menu bar.

22. Type **myclose** in the Replace box, and make sure the Formatted text option is chosen.

23. Add the entry to the list, or replace the entry if it already exists.

24. Click **OK** to exit from the dialog box.

25. Close the document without saving the changes.
    In the next exercise, you will use your letterhead.

Skill Builder 7.2 **Create a Generic Cover Letter Template**

In this exercise, you will use your letterhead template as the basis for a cover letter. Cover letters are important business documents. You should always use a cover letter when sending a resume to a prospective employer. The cover letter that you will create in this exercise will be useful when you are applying to a company but are unsure what positions the company has available. When you are finished, you will save your cover letter as a template. You will have a ready-to-use template whenever you need this type of cover letter.

1. Click the Show Desktop ⬜ button on the Windows Taskbar to hide all program windows. If you don't have a Show Desktop button, then right-click on an open part of the Taskbar, and choose Minimize All Windows from the pop-up menu.

2. Double-click the My Computer ⬜ icon on the Desktop.

3. Double-click the 3½ Floppy (A:) icon to display the contents of your exercise diskette.

4. Double-click the My Letterhead template.
   A new document will open in Word with your letterhead displayed.

5. Position the insertion point on the fourth blank line below the date, and complete the letter as shown below.

Mr. Milton Jones
Director of Human Resources
HiTech Computing Solutions
1400 Hillsdale Avenue, Suite 120
San Jose, CA 95136

Dear Mr. Jones:

I will graduate soon from a business and technology training program, and I am anxious to use my skills in a permanent or temporary position with HiTech Computing Solutions. I will be available for employment as of December 1, 1999.

As you can see from my enclosed resume, I have the necessary skills and technical expertise to be a first-rate word processor. I would like to have the opportunity to prove to you what a valuable employee I would be. HiTech Computing Solutions has a reputation for being an innovative firm with high growth potential. I have the skills, desire, and ability to make a valuable contribution to such an organization.

I will contact you early next week to see whether I can provide you with any further information in an interview. I appreciate your time and consideration.

(Continued on the next page)

6. Tap (ENTER) twice after the last paragraph.

7. Type **myclose**, and tap the (SPACE BAR).
   AutoCorrect will insert the complimentary close, signature line, and enclosure notation.

Save the Cover Letter As a Template

8. Click the Save ⊞ button, and set the Save as type to Document Template.

9. Choose 3½ Floppy (A:) from the Save in list.

10. Type **Generic Position** in the File name box, and click the **Save** button.

11. Choose **File→Close** to close the template.

12. Click the 3½ Floppy (A:) button on the Windows Taskbar to switch to the My Computer window.

13. Double-click the Generic Position template, and Word will create a new document that is based upon the template.
    With this template, you can rapidly create cover letters by opening the template and changing the company-specific information. If necessary, you can then save the letter as a regular Word document. The template remains unchanged, and is ready for the next employment opportunity.

14. Now close the document.

Skill Builder 7.3 Create a Specific Cover Letter Template

In this exercise, you will use the template and AutoCorrect entry that you created in Skill Builder 7.1 as the basis for another cover letter. The cover letter you will create in this exercise will be useful when you are applying for a specific position. You will save the cover letter to your exercise diskette as a template.

1. Click the 3½ Floppy (A:) button on the Windows Taskbar to switch to the My Computer window.

2. Double-click the My Letterhead template.

3. Position the insertion point on the fourth blank line below the date, and type the following text.

Mr. Milton Jones
Director of Human Resources
HiTech Computing Solutions
1400 Hillsdale Avenue, Suite 120
San Jose, CA 95136

Dear Mr. Jones:

It is with interest and enthusiasm that I am applying for employment as a Word Processing Specialist with HiTech Computing Solutions.

I have acquired excellent word processing skills through an intensive vocational training course at the Central City Regional Occupational Program and through prior work experience. I have extensive hands-on experience in word processing programs, and I believe that my experience and ability to learn rapidly will make me an asset to your organization.

It is my sincere hope that HiTech Computing Solutions can use my skills and abilities. I will telephone your secretary next week and arrange for a personal interview.

Thank you in advance for your time and consideration.

4. Tap (ENTER) twice after the last paragraph.

5. Type **myclose**, and tap the (SPACE BAR).

6. Click the Save 🖫 button, and set the Save as type to Document Template.

7. Choose 3½ Floppy (A:) from the Save in list.

(Continued on the next page)

8. Type **Specific Position** in the File name box and click the **Save** button.

9. Choose **File→Close** to close the template.

10. Click the 3½ Floppy (A:) button on the Windows Taskbar to switch to the My Computer window.

11. Double-click the Specific Position template, and Word will create a new document that is based upon the template.
You can use this template in the future to create cover letters for specific employment opportunities.

12. Now close the document.

13. Close all My Computer windows.

Skill Builder 7.4 Use AutoCorrect

In this exercise, you will use AutoCorrect to automatically insert formatted text and paragraphs.

1. Start a New ☐ document, and type the text shown below. Center the title line and format it with an Arial 14 Bold font. Format the body paragraph with a Times New Roman 14 font. Also, you will notice that AutoCorrect will automatically apply the accent character to the word Café.

Carl's Café—Serving the Best Brew Since 1955!

Carl's Café has been a Bay Area tradition since 1955. Carl Burns opened Carl's Café on June 12, 1955, and he's been making the best cup of coffee ever since. From drip coffee to café latte, Carl's Café has a brew for you. So stop by Carl's Café the next time you're in our neighborhood. We're located at 14520 Union Street.

---

2. Tap (ENTER) twice after the last paragraph.

3. Select the title, body paragraph, and blank line between them. **Do not** include the two blank lines below the body paragraph in the selection.

4. Choose **Format→Borders and Shading** from the menu bar.

5. Click the **Borders** tab, set the border width to 2¼ pt, and choose the Box setting.
The preview area will show the paragraphs with a thick border surrounding them.

6. Click the **Shading** tab, and choose any color or style you desire.

7. Click **OK** to apply the formats. The formatted paragraphs should match the following example.

> ### Carl's Café—Serving the Best Brew Since 1955!
>
> Carl's Café has been a Bay Area tradition since 1955. Carl Burns opened Carl's Café on June 12, 1955, and he's been making the best cup of coffee ever since. From drip coffee to café latte, Carl's Café has a brew for you. So stop by Carl's Café the next time you're in our neighborhood. We're located at 14520 Union Street.

Create the AutoCorrect Entry

8. Make sure the formatted paragraphs are selected (they already should be).

9. Choose **Tools→AutoCorrect** from the menu bar.

10. Follow these steps to create the AutoCorrect entry and explore the dialog box.

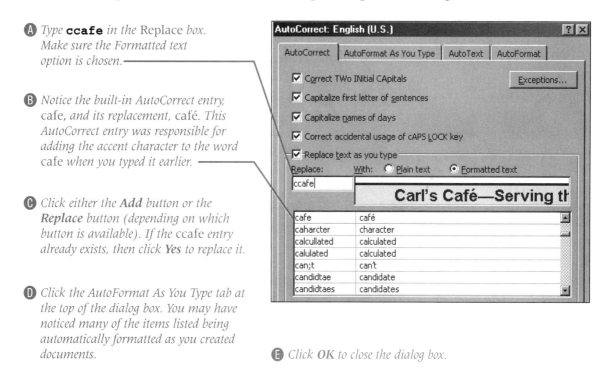

Ⓐ *Type* **ccafe** *in the* Replace *box. Make sure the Formatted text option is chosen.*

Ⓑ *Notice the built-in AutoCorrect entry,* cafe, *and its replacement,* café. *This AutoCorrect entry was responsible for adding the accent character to the word* cafe *when you typed it earlier.*

Ⓒ *Click either the* **Add** *button or the* **Replace** *button (depending on which button is available). If the ccafe entry already exists, then click* **Yes** *to replace it.*

Ⓓ *Click the AutoFormat As You Type tab at the top of the dialog box. You may have noticed many of the items listed being automatically formatted as you created documents.*

Ⓔ *Click OK to close the dialog box.*

11. Close the document without saving it, and then start a new ▢ document.

12. Type **ccafe**, and tap the (SPACE BAR).
    The formatted paragraphs should be inserted. This example demonstrates that you can create AutoCorrect entries using almost any text, graphics, and formats.

13. Now close the document without saving the changes.

Skill Builder 7.5 Delete AutoCorrect Entries

In this exercise, you will experiment with AutoFormat as you type, and you will delete AutoCorrect entries that you created in previous Skill Builder exercises.

Delete AutoCorrect Entries

1. Click the New button to start a new document.

2. Choose **Tools→AutoCorrect** from the menu bar.

3. Type **ccafe** in the Replace box.
   Word will scroll the list, and the ccafe entry will appear.

4. Choose the entry on the list, and click the **Delete** button to remove the entry.

5. Now delete the **myclose** entry.

6. Click the **AutoFormat As You Type** tab in the dialog box.

7. Make sure the **Fractions (½) with fraction character** option is checked in the Replace as you type list.

8. Click **OK** to close the AutoCorrect dialog box.

9. Type **1/2** and tap the (SPACE BAR).
   AutoFormat as you type will reformat the fraction. Like AutoCorrect, AutoFormat as you type will reformat many things that you type. You can always use Undo to reverse automatic formatting.

10. Click Undo to restore the original fraction format.

11. Feel free to experiment with AutoFormat as you type.

12. Close the document without saving it.

Skill Builder 7.6 Use Tabs with Leaders

In this exercise, you will use right tabs with leaders to create the document shown at the end of this exercise.

1. Start a new document.

2. Set the font to Arial 12, and click the Center button.

3. Tap (ENTER) until the insertion point is at approximately the 2" position.

4. Type the following four lines of text, tapping (ENTER) twice between each line.

West Coast Playhouse

Presents

An Evening with Mabel

Starring

5. Make sure you tap (ENTER) twice after the last line.

6. Set the alignment to left ▤, and choose **Format→Tabs** from the menu bar.

7. Follow these steps to set a right leader tab at the 6″ position.

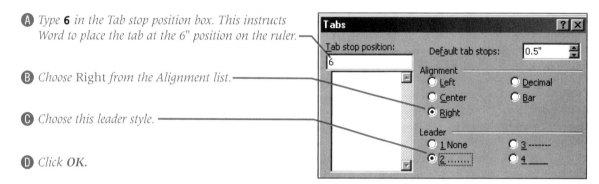

Ⓐ Type **6** *in the Tab stop position box. This instructs Word to place the tab at the 6″ position on the ruler.*

Ⓑ *Choose* Right *from the Alignment list.*

Ⓒ *Choose this leader style.*

Ⓓ *Click **OK**.*

Notice that the Right Tab symbol is positioned on top of the Right Indent marker at the 6″ position on the ruler. You could have set the Right Tab using the ruler. However, you must use the Tabs dialog box to set leader tabs.

8. Type **Mabel**, and tap the (TAB) key.
   A leader should extend to the right margin.

9. Type **Tisha Franklin**, and tap (ENTER).
   Notice that the name moved to the left as you typed it. This is because you set a right tab.

10. Type **Jonathan**, and tap the (TAB) key.

(Continued on the next page)

11. Type **Brian Jones** and tap (ENTER).

12. Complete the document as shown below.
You will need to type text and use the Tab key to create the leaders.

West Coast Playhouse

Presents

An Evening with Mabel

Starring

Mabel .... Tisha Franklin
Jonathan .... Brian Jones
Burt.. Sidney Stone
Cynthia .... Jessica Frenz

Other Credits

Written By... Mary Markowitz
Director.. Stanley Whitefield
Choreography .... Alex Fairweld
Costumes .... Dave Donaldson

13. Save the document as **Skill Builder 7.6,** and then close the document.

Assessments

Assessment 7.1 Format a Memorandum

In this assessment, you will open a memorandum from your exercise diskette, and then format the memorandum. The memorandum uses a slightly different style than the memorandum format you learned earlier in this course.

1. Click the Open button, set the Files of type setting to Word Documents, and open the document named **Assessment 7.1.**

2. Apply 10% gray shading to the Interoffice Correspondence paragraph.

3. Apply a ½ pt single-line border to the bottom edge of the Subject paragraph.

4. Use drag-and-drop to rearrange the bulleted paragraphs in alphabetical order.
   Your completed document should match the document shown below.

5. Print the document, save the changes, and close the document.

Interoffice Correspondence

To: George Jamison

From: Linda Evans

Date: October 23, 1999

Subject: Action items

I have prepared a list of items for you to take care of prior to next month's meeting. Please follow up on these items as soon as possible.

- Contact a catering service to have lunch catered.
- Create the PowerPoint presentation.
- Invite the attendees.
- Prepare the revenue report for the past two years.
- Prepare the sales forecast for 2000.
- Reserve the conference room.
- Send the attendee packages to the copy shop for duplication.
- Send the revenue and sales forecast reports to Juan Martinez.

Thank you for your assistance.

Assessment 7.2 Use AutoCorrect

1. Open the document named **AutoCorrect Text.**

2. Select the entire document.

3. Use the selected text to create an AutoCorrect entry named **bplate.** Make sure you choose **Formatted text** for the With option. Also, replace the bplate AutoCorrect entry if it already exists.

4. Close the AutoCorrect Text document.

5. Open the document named **Assessment 7.2.**

6. Position the insertion point at the bottom of the document. The insertion point should be on the second blank line below the last paragraph.

7. Use the bplate AutoCorrect entry to insert the boilerplate text. Your completed document should match the example shown below.

8. Print the document, save the changes, and then close the document.

Interoffice Correspondence

To: Allan Simpson

From: Bill Watson

Date: October 23, 1999

Subject: Boilerplate text

I have included the boilerplate text for the notice to shareholders. Please contact me if you require further information.

Notice of any meeting of shareholders shall be given either personally or by first class mail or telegraphic or other written communication. Charges are to be prepaid and addressed to each shareholder at the address of such shareholder appearing on the books of the corporation. If no such address appears on the corporation's books or has been so given, notice shall be deemed to have been properly given to such shareholder if sent by first class mail. Notice may also be given by telegram or other means of written communication.

Assessment 7.3 **Set Tabs with Leaders**

1. Follow these guidelines to create the document shown below.

   ■ Start a new document, and use (ENTER) to space down to approximately the 2″ position.

   ■ Center and type the two title lines shown below.

   ■ Tap (ENTER) after typing the second title line, and set the alignment to left on the line immediately following the second title line.

   ■ Tap (ENTER) again to create a double space between the second title line and the first line of the personnel list.

   ■ Use the Tabs dialog box to set a Right Tab at the 6″ position with leader style number 2.

   ■ Type text, and use the (TAB) key to create the remainder of the document shown below.

2. Print the document, save it as **Assessment 7.3,** and close the document.

Personnel Directory
Fiscal Services Department

Linda Johnson ....Director of Fiscal Services
Thuy Nguyen .... Assistant to Director
Betty Cox ....Purchasing Manager
Tina Lowe .... Accounts Receivable Manager
Gregg Chin..Accounts Payable Manager
Jack Johnson ....Receptionist

Critical Thinking

Critical Thinking 7.1 On Your Own

Sarah Richardson has decided to leave her current job and search for opportunities elsewhere. As part of the job search process, Sarah wants to set up her own letterhead and envelope. Set up letterhead and an accompanying envelope for Sarah. Sarah's address, telephone, and email information are

Sarah Richardson
1422 North Main Street
Round Rock, TX 78682
Phone: (512) 218-4433
Email: srichardson@aol.com

Save the completed letterhead as a template with the name **Critical Thinking 7.1—Letterhead.** Save the completed envelope as a template with the name **Critical Thinking 7.1—Envelope.**

Critical Thinking 7.2 Web Research with a Group

You and your classmate have decided to revamp the menu at Health-e-Meals.com. Although your company has been very successful, you have decided to reinvent the business before your competition has a chance to catch up to you. Use Internet Explorer and a search engine of your choice to locate several health-oriented menus for restaurants that display their menus on the Web. Work with your classmate to find one or more menus that you think would be appropriate for Heath-e-Meals.com. Print the menus and continue with the next exercise.

Critical Thinking 7.3 As a Group

In the previous exercise, your classmate and you printed several menus from the Web. Use Word to set up your own menu for Health-e-Meals.com. Include at least five menu items from the menus you printed from the Web. In addition, include five items of your own on the menu, with a brief description of each item. Set the left and right margins to 1". Set up the menu so that the price of each item is right-aligned at the right margin. Use custom tab stops with leaders to create a dotted line between the end of each menu item description and the right-aligned price. Save your completed menu as **Critical Thinking 7.3.**

Critical Thinking 7.4 As a Group

You and your classmate have decided to create stationary for Health-e-Meals.com. Follow these guidelines to create the stationary.

Letterhead—Include the company name, address, 800 number, and URL (www.Health-e-Meals.com) on the letterhead. Use whatever address and 800 number you desire. Make sure the URL is prominently displayed on the letterhead. Begin the letterhead 0.5″ below the top of the page. Include a border at the base of the letterhead. Save the completed letterhead as a template with the name **Critical Thinking 7.4—Letterhead.** Base a new document upon the template to ensure that it functions properly, and then close the document without saving it.

Envelopes—Use a standard size 10 envelope. Include the company name, address, and Web site URL on the return address. Add the envelope to the document. Format the Web site URL so that it is prominently displayed on the envelope. Save the completed envelope as a template with the name **Critical Thinking 7.4—Envelope.** Base a new document upon the template to ensure that it functions properly, and then close the document without saving it.

Memorandum—Set up your own memorandum template. Include a shaded bar at the top of the memorandum with the word "Memorandum" displayed in the shaded bar. Save the completed memorandum as a template with the name **Critical Thinking 7.4—Memo.** Base a new document upon the template to ensure that it functions properly, and then close the document without saving it.

Critical Thinking 7.5 As a Group

Your classmate and you have decided to set up AutoCorrect entries for commonly used phrases at Health-e-Meals.com. Work together to choose five or more words or phrases that you think would be used often at Health-e-Meals.com. Create AutoCorrect entries for these words or phrases. Write the words or phrases and their AutoCorrect abbreviations in the space below.

AutoCorrect Entry	AutoCorrect Abbreviation

LESSON 8

Desktop Publishing

In this lesson, you will use desktop publishing techniques in Word 2000. Word 2000 makes desktop publishing fun and easy. Everyone from beginners to advanced users will find something exciting in Word 2000. As you progress through this lesson, you will work with a variety of graphic objects, including WordArt, clip art, and drawing objects. You will also visit Microsoft's ClipGallery Live Web page, where thousands of high-quality clip art images are available for download. In addition, you will enhance the appearance of paragraphs with drop caps.

In This Lesson

Case Study

Jane Thompson is the owner of West Side Bakery. West Side Bakery is located on the fringes of a major university and caters to the large student population on campus. Jane has decided to produce an inexpensive flyer to be handed out around campus. The flyer is designed to entice students to visit the store for the first time. Jane uses the desktop publishing features of Word 2000 to produce the flyer on her office computer. Once the flyer is produced, Jane will take it to the nearest copy shop to have it duplicated.

Drawing Object Concepts

Office 2000 has an excellent set of drawing tools that let you draw lines, arrows, rectangles, callouts, WordArt, and many other objects. Drawing objects are easy to work with and a lot of fun! Drawing objects are particularly useful for creating flyers and other types of graphically-rich documents. You insert a drawing object by choosing the desired object from the Drawing toolbar and then dragging the mouse in the document.

The Drawing ⏺ button on the Standard toolbar is used to display and hide the Drawing toolbar. The Drawing toolbar is usually located at the bottom of the document window just above the status bar. You can also display or hide the drawing toolbar with the **View→Toolbars→Drawing** command. The following illustration explains the buttons on the Drawing toolbar.

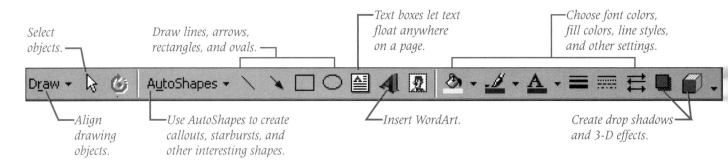

Select objects.

Draw lines, arrows, rectangles, and ovals.

Text boxes let text float anywhere on a page.

Choose font colors, fill colors, line styles, and other settings.

Align drawing objects.

Use AutoShapes to create callouts, starbursts, and other interesting shapes.

Insert WordArt.

Create drop shadows and 3-D effects.

Object Layers

Drawing objects reside on invisible layers in the document that are independent of the text layer. For this reason, drawing objects can be placed behind the text layer or in front of the text layer. This allows you to superimpose drawing objects over text or hide objects behind text. You can also place drawing objects in front of or behind other drawing objects.

The Grid

In Word, a hidden grid is used to align drawing objects. When you move or size an object, it will snap to a grid point. The grid makes it easy to align objects along horizontal or vertical lines. You can display the grid by choosing the *Display gridlines on screen* option in the Grid dialog box. You display the Grid dialog box by clicking the Draw button on the Drawing toolbar and choosing Grid.

Drawing objects snap to grid points.

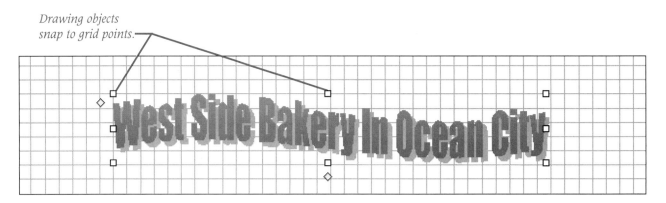

1. Start Word, and locate the Drawing toolbar at the bottom of the Word window. If the Drawing toolbar isn't displayed, use the **View→Toolbars→Drawing** command to display the toolbar.

2. Click the **Draw** button on the left end of the Drawing toolbar, and choose Grid from the menu. *Notice the* Snap objects to grid *option is checked at the top of the dialog box. This option is set by default.*

3. Check the **Display gridlines on screen** box, and click **OK**.
    The grid will be displayed. As you work with objects in the following exercises, they will snap to points on the grid.

4. Display the Grid dialog box, and turn off the gridline display.
    Objects will still snap to the gridlines even though the grid is not displayed.

WordArt

The **WordArt**  button on the Drawing toolbar displays the WordArt Gallery. You can add special effects to text by choosing a style from the gallery. Once you choose a style, Word displays a dialog box where you enter the text, and choose the font and font size for your stylized WordArt text. The WordArt gallery is shown below.

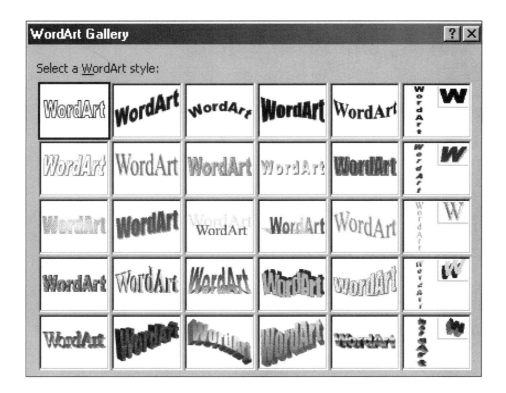

1. Click the **WordArt**  button on the Drawing toolbar.
   The WordArt Gallery appears.

2. Choose the style in the third row and fifth column, and click **OK**.
   The Edit WordArt Text box appears. This is where you enter your WordArt text.

3. Type the phrase **West Side Bakery in Ocean City**.

4. Choose Impact from the font list, and set the font size to 28. Choose Arial as the font if Impact is not available.

5. Click **OK** to insert the *WordArt* object in your new document.
   The WordArt toolbar should have appeared. The WordArt toolbar lets you edit the text in the WordArt object and format the object.

6. Click the **Edit Text** button on the WordArt toolbar.

7. Select the first two words (West Side), and replace them with the words **The Best**.

8. Click at the end of the phrase, and type an exclamation point.
   The phrase in the Edit WordArt Text box should now be The Best Bakery in Ocean City!.

9. Change the font size to 32, and click **OK**.

Selecting, Moving, and Sizing Objects

You must select objects before you can move or size them. The easiest way to select an object is to click anywhere on the object. Small squares called sizing handles appear on the corners and four sides of a selected object. The following Quick Reference table explains the techniques you can use to select, move, and size objects. The methods apply to both drawing objects and pictures. You will work with pictures later in this lesson.

SELECTING, MOVING, AND SIZING OBJECTS

Task	Method
Select a single object.	Click the object
Select multiple objects.	Click the Select Objects 🔲 button on the Drawing toolbar, and drag to enclose the desired objects in the selection box. You can also press (SHIFT) while you click the desired objects.
Move an object with the mouse.	Drag the object (not the sizing handles) to a new location. You can also press and hold (ALT) while dragging an object to prevent the object from snapping to the grid.
Move an object with the keyboard.	Tap ← → ↑ or ↓ to nudge the object to the next grid point. You can also press (CTRL) while tapping the arrow keys to nudge the object a tiny amount.
Size an object.	Drag any sizing handle. Dragging a corner sizing handle lets you change both the width and height at the same time.
Size an object while maintaining the original shape and proportions.	Press (SHIFT) while dragging a corner sizing handle to maintain the original shape and proportions of the object.

Hands-On 8.3 Move and Size the WordArt Object

1. Follow these steps to move and size the WordArt object.

A *Drag any sizing handle to increase the size.*

B *Click **Undo** to restore the original size.*

C *Position the mouse pointer on the object and drag it towards the top of the document. You will notice the object snaps to grid points as it moves. Position the object about 1" from the top, and center it horizontally. Use the horizontal ruler to help you align the object horizontally.*

2. Click anywhere outside of the object, and it will become deselected.

3. Now click the object, and it will become selected (sizing handles will appear).

4. Feel free to experiment with the buttons on the WordArt toolbar.
   The object must be selected (with sizing handles) in order to edit it. Use Undo if you make a mistake or wish to reverse an action.

5. Save 💾 the document as **Hands-On Lesson 8.**

Object Anchors

All objects are anchored to paragraphs when they are inserted into a document. As a document changes, an object moves with the paragraph to which it is anchored, thus maintaining the same position relative to the paragraph. When you move an object, its anchor will change to a paragraph in close proximity to the object's new location. You can determine the paragraph to which an object is anchored by selecting the object and using the Show All button to display the nonprinting characters.

An anchor symbol appears next to the paragraph to which an object is anchored.

1. Click anywhere outside of the WordArt object to deselect the object.
   The insertion point will be positioned at the top of the document.

2. Tap (ENTER) *four* times.
   The object should move down each time you tap (ENTER) because it was anchored to the first paragraph mark, which has now been pushed down four lines.

3. Click the Show All ¶ button on the Standard toolbar.

4. Click the object to select it, and an anchor ⚓ symbol will appear to the left of the last paragraph mark.
   The object is anchored to that paragraph.

5. Drag the WordArt object up until the anchor is positioned to the left of the first paragraph mark.
   Now the object will move only when the first paragraph mark moves. In a moment, you will add additional paragraphs to the bottom of the document, and the WordArt object will remain stationary. The purpose of this exercise is to help you understand what is going on "behind the scenes." Normally, you can move an object without being concerned about the anchor position.

6. Now click the insertion point in front of the last paragraph mark.

7. Tap (ENTER) *twice*, then click Show All ¶ to hide the nonprinting characters.

Drop Caps

Word's Drop Caps feature lets you easily create large drop-down capitals at the beginning of paragraphs. To create a drop cap, click anywhere in the desired paragraph and issue the **Format→Drop Cap** command. The dialog box options are quite simple, as described below.

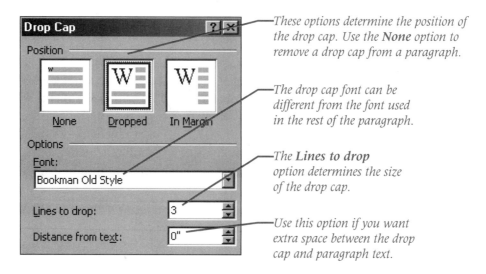

*These options determine the position of the drop cap. Use the **None** option to remove a drop cap from a paragraph.*

The drop cap font can be different from the font used in the rest of the paragraph.

*The **Lines to drop** option determines the size of the drop cap.*

Use this option if you want extra space between the drop cap and paragraph text.

Hands-On 8.5 Drop Caps

Create the Drop Cap

1. Change the font size to 18, and type the following paragraph.

> Stop by the West Side Bakery before June 30, and get a free loaf of sourdough bread when you buy a dozen muffins. Our award-winning muffins will please your palette and satisfy your hunger. All of our breads and muffins are made with the finest ingredients. We are located at 1450 Market Street in Ocean City.

2. Make sure the insertion point is positioned somewhere in the paragraph you just typed.
   The insertion point can be positioned anywhere in the paragraph when creating a drop cap.

3. Choose **Format→Drop Cap** from the menu bar.

4. Choose the Dropped position (the middle position), and click **OK.**
   Notice that the drop cap is surrounded by a border and its sizing handles. The drop cap is also a type of object.

5. Click anywhere in the paragraph, and the drop cap border will disappear.

Remove and Restore the Drop Cap

6. Choose **Format→Drop Cap** from the menu bar.

7. Choose the None option, and click **OK.**
   As you can see, removing a drop cap is just as easy as creating one.

8. Click **Undo** to restore the drop cap, and continue with the next topic.

Clip Art and Pictures

You can dress up your documents using the professionally designed clip art provided with Office 2000. The clip art that is built into Office 2000 is in a Windows metafile format. The metafile format lets you size and scale the clip art while preserving the image quality. You can also use your own clip art or digitized pictures. Digitized pictures are usually created using a scanner or a digital camera. Digitized pictures have a bit-mapped format, which may cause images to look grainy or decrease in quality as they are enlarged and scaled.

The Office 2000 Clip Gallery

The Insert Clip Art button on the Drawing toolbar displays the Clip Gallery. The Clip Gallery has been redesigned in Office 2000 to make it easier to locate and manage clip art and pictures. The Clip Gallery organizes clip art into categories such as Business, Animals, and Academic. The Clip Gallery can also be displayed with the **Insert→Picture→Clip Art** command.

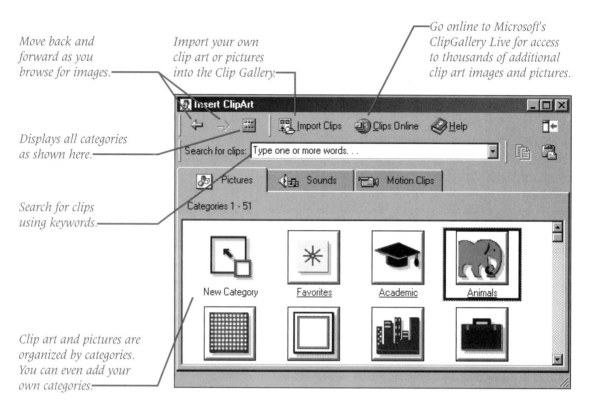

Move back and forward as you browse for images.

Import your own clip art or pictures into the Clip Gallery.

Go online to Microsoft's ClipGallery Live for access to thousands of additional clip art images and pictures.

Displays all categories as shown here.

Search for clips using keywords.

Clip art and pictures are organized by categories. You can even add your own categories.

Hands-On 8.6 Use the Clip Gallery

In this exercise, you will explore the Clip Gallery and insert a picture. You will also explore Microsoft's ClipGallery Live Web page.

Explore the Clip Gallery and Insert a Clip

1. Click in the middle of the large paragraph with the drop cap.

2. Click the Insert Clip Art button on the Drawing toolbar.

3. Click the Academic category to display clips related to academia.

4. Follow these steps to preview a clip.

A *Click the books clip.*

B *Point (but don't click) at each button on the pop-up menu, and the button's function will appear in a ScreenTip.*

C *Click the **Preview clip** option to display an enlarged preview of the clip.*

D *Click the **Close** ☒ button on the Preview window.*

5. Follow these steps to navigate in the Clip Gallery and to search for a clip.

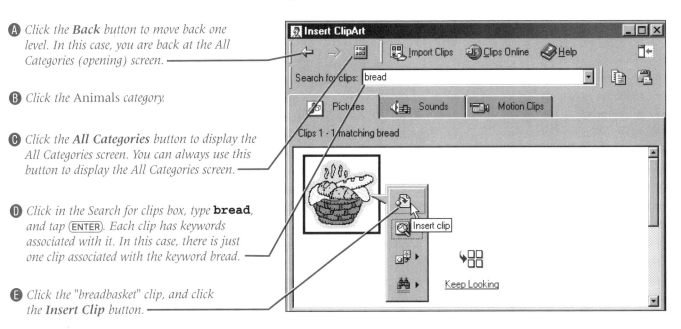

A *Click the **Back** button to move back one level. In this case, you are back at the All Categories (opening) screen.*

B *Click the Animals category.*

C *Click the **All Categories** button to display the All Categories screen. You can always use this button to display the All Categories screen.*

D *Click in the Search for clips box, type **bread**, and tap (ENTER). Each clip has keywords associated with it. In this case, there is just one clip associated with the keyword bread.*

E *Click the "breadbasket" clip, and click the **Insert Clip** button.*

6. Click the **Close** ☒ button on the Clip Gallery.
   As you can see, the bread basket picture is quite large, and it has been inserted in the middle of the paragraph. By default, pictures are inserted in line with the text. They do not "float" on the page as do drawing objects and WordArt. In the next exercise, you will size the picture and change it's text wrapping settings to allow it to float on the page.

7. Use the Zoom Control to switch the zoom to Whole Page.
   This will allow you to see the layout of the entire page.

(Continued on the next page)

Explore Microsoft's ClipGallery Live Web Page

In order to complete the remainder of this exercise, you will need an Internet connection and a Web browser. This exercise will assume you are using Microsoft's Internet Explorer 5.0 Web browser.

8. Click the Insert Clip Art 🖼 button on the Drawing toolbar.

9. Click the Clips Online 🖾 Clips Online button on the Clip Gallery toolbar.
   The Internet Explorer Web browser will start, and a Connect to Web dialog box may appear.

10. If the Connect to Web dialog box appears, click **OK** to continue to Microsoft's Web page.

11. Read the licensing terms page, then click **OK.**

12. Follow these steps to explore the ClipGallery Live page.

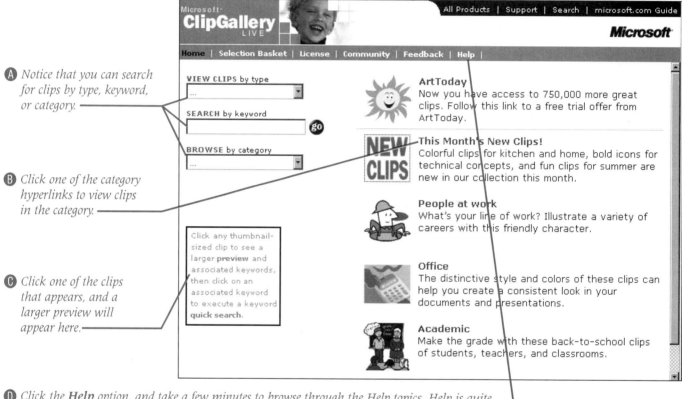

(A) *Notice that you can search for clips by type, keyword, or category.*

(B) *Click one of the category hyperlinks to view clips in the category.*

(C) *Click one of the clips that appears, and a larger preview will appear here.*

(D) *Click the **Help** option, and take a few minutes to browse through the Help topics. Help is quite thorough, and you should be able to learn everything you need to about choosing and downloading clips. However, don't download any clips if you are working in a computer lab, because the clips are automatically added to the ClipGallery. When you have finished using Help, you can click the **Home** link on the left end of the ClipGallery Live menu bar to return to the opening screen.*

13. When you have finished browsing the ClipGallery Live site, click the Close ☒ button on the Internet Explorer window.

14. Continue with the next topic, where you will learn how to position the breadbasket clip.

Formatting Objects

You can format drawing objects, clip art, and pictures using the Format dialog box that is associated with each object type. The easiest way to display the dialog box is to right-click the object and choose Format (Object Type) from the pop-up menu. You can also click the object, choose Format from the menu bar, then choose the object type from the drop-down menu. The following illustration explains the Format Picture dialog box.

The Colors and Lines, Size, Layout, and Web tabs are available for all object types.

The Picture tab is only available with pictures. The Text Box tab is only available with text boxes (a type of drawing object).

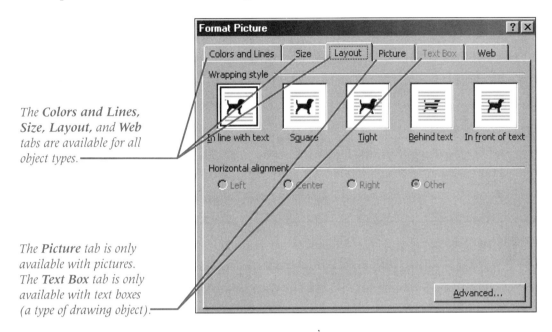

The Size Tab

Earlier in this lesson, you learned how to change the size of objects by dragging sizing handles. You can use the Size tab on the Format Object dialog box to size an object with precision. You can specify the width and height in inches or you can scale the original width and height by a percentage. The Size tab also has a Lock aspect ratio check box. If this box is checked, you can adjust either the width or height, and Word will determine the other measurement (width or height) to ensure that the object has the original proportions. For example, in the following exercise, you will specify the height for the picture in your document. Word will adjust the width as necessary to maintain the current proportions.

Hands-On 8.7 Size the Picture

1. Make sure that the picture is selected in your document and that the zoom control is set to *Whole Page.*

2. Right-click the picture (click the right mouse button), and choose **Format→Picture** from the pop up menu.

3. Click the Size tab in the Format Picture dialog box.

4. Set the first height measurement to 1, make sure the *Lock aspect ratio* box is checked, and click in the first Width box.
   Word should adjust the width to 1.06", thus maintaining the original proportions. Notice that the width and height in the scaling section have been set to 27%. The height you chose is 27% of the original height.

5. Click **OK,** and the picture size should be reduced in your document.
   The paragraph text may be positioned above and below the picture. You will adjust the layout options in the next exercise.

6. Save the changes to your document, and continue with the next topic.

The Layout Tab

Currently, your picture is in line with the text. In other words, the picture behaves like a text character. If you add or remove text in the paragraph, the picture will remain in the same position relative to the text within the paragraph. Earlier in this lesson, you moved the WordArt object by dragging it with the mouse. You were able to position the WordArt object anywhere on the page because it uses a different Wrapping style than your picture. The Wrapping style is chosen in the Layout tab of the Format Object dialog box. You can change the Wrapping style of a picture so that it behaves like a drawing object. In the following exercise, you will do this, so that the picture floats near the bottom of the page.

 ## Hands-On 8.8 Work with Layout Options

1. Try dragging the picture down to the bottom edge of the page.
   Notice that the furthest you can drag the picture is into the last line of text within the paragraph. At this point, the picture is like any other character in the paragraph. You can't drag it beyond the paragraph unless you use the (ENTER) *key to create space below the paragraph.*

2. Drag the picture up, and place it in the middle of the paragraph.

3. Right-click the picture, and choose **Format→Picture** from the pop-up menu.

4. Click the Layout tab, and notice that the Wrapping style is currently set to *In line with text*. *This Wrapping style is always used when a picture is first inserted. Notice the other available wrapping styles. In particular, notice the way the text flows around the sample picture in the various Wrapping styles.*

5. Choose the Tight wrapping style, and notice that the horizontal alignment options are now available.
The horizontal alignment options are not available if the Wrapping style is set to In line with text. The alignment options are used to align a floating object horizontally on the page.

6. Click **OK,** and the picture should now have text wrapping around it within the paragraph.

7. Drag the picture to another location within the paragraph.
The text will adjust to wrap around the picture.

8. Drag the picture down until it is around 2″ from the bottom of the page.
Now the picture is floating on the page, so it behaves like a drawing object. You can position it anywhere on the page.

9. Right-click the picture, and choose Format Picture from the pop-up menu.

10. Click the Layout tab and notice the *Behind text* and *In front of text* Wrapping styles.
These styles let you place the picture on a layer behind or in front of the text layer. Currently, the picture is on the same layer as the text. This is why the text wrapped around the picture when it was in the large body text paragraph.

11. Click the Size tab.

12. Set the Height to 3″, and make sure the *Lock aspect ratio* box is checked.

13. Click the Layout tab and continue with the next topic.

Advanced Text-Wrapping Options

The Advanced button on the Layout tab of the Format Object dialog box displays the Advanced Layout options. The Advanced Layout options give you two additional text-wrapping options and more control over the positioning of objects on the page.

In this exercise, you will use advanced options to precisely position the picture on the page.

1. Click the Advanced button on the dialog box.

2. If necessary, click the Text Wrapping tab.
   Notice that the Advanced Layout box gives you access to two additional wrapping options: Through, and Top and Bottom. Also, you can specify the sides you want text to wrap on and the distance of the object from the text.

3. Click the Picture Position tab, and follow these steps to position the picture on the page.

Ⓐ *Set the **Horizontal Alignment** to Centered relative to Page. This will center the picture horizontally.*

Ⓑ *Set the **Vertical Alignment** to Bottom relative to Margin. This will place the bottom edge of the picture at the bottom margin. The bottom margin is 1", so the picture will be placed 1" from the bottom edge of the page.*

Ⓒ *Uncheck the Move object with text box. When this box is checked, it causes the picture to move with the paragraph to which it is anchored. You unchecked the box to force the picture to remain stationary. This box is checked when objects are first inserted.*

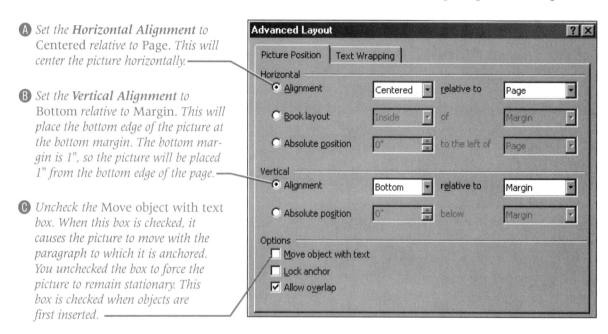

4. Click **OK** to close the Advanced Layout box, and click **OK** again to apply the settings.
   Your picture should now be centered horizontally and positioned 1" from the bottom edge of the page.

5. Right-click the WordArt object at the top of the page, and choose Format WordArt from the pop-up menu.

6. If necessary, click the Layout tab.

7. Set the horizontal alignment to Center, and click **OK.**
   Notice that there is no need to use the advanced alignment options when setting the horizontal alignment.

Remaining Tabs

The four remaining tabs in the Format Object box are defined in the following table. You will receive hands-on experience with some of these options later in this lesson.

Tab	Purpose
Colors and Lines	This tab lets you apply fill colors and borders to objects. The Arrows options are used to change the arrowhead styles on lines.
Pictures	The Pictures tab has several options that are only used with pictures. For example, you can crop the picture (chop off a portion of the picture) and change the image brightness and contrast.
Text Box	The Text Box tab lets you set internal margins for text boxes. Text boxes let you float text anywhere on a page.
Web	The Web tab is useful if you intend to post your document on the Web. You can type alternative text in the box on the Web tab. The alternative text is displayed on a Web page as the picture is loading or if the picture is missing.

AutoShapes and Other Shapes

You can use AutoShapes to add a variety of fun shapes to your documents. AutoShapes are predefined shapes organized by categories, such as stars and banners, callouts, and flowchart symbols. You choose AutoShapes with the AutoShapes button on the Drawing toolbar. You can also draw lines, arrows, rectangles, and ovals in your documents. To draw a shape, click the desired button on the Drawing toolbar, then either click or drag in the document.

AutoShapes are organized by categories. You choose a shape from a category and drag in the document to draw the shape.

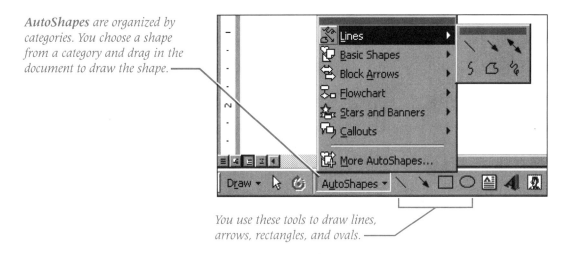

You use these tools to draw lines, arrows, rectangles, and ovals.

Constraining Objects

You can constrain objects to specific shapes or angles as you draw. These techniques are explained in the following Quick Reference table.

CONSTRAINING OBJECTS	
Task	**Procedure**
Draw or insert squares.	Choose the Rectangle ▫ tool, and click in the document. You can also press the (SHIFT) key while drawing a new rectangle. If you press (SHIFT) while sizing an existing rectangle, then the original shape of the rectangle is maintained.
Draw or insert circles.	Choose the Oval ▢ tool, and click in the document. You can also press the (SHIFT) key while drawing a new oval. If you press (SHIFT) while sizing an existing oval, then the original shape of the oval is maintained.
Draw lines at 15-degree increments.	Press the (SHIFT) key while drawing a line or arrow.

Deleting Objects

You can delete pictures and drawing objects by selecting the objects and tapping the (DELETE) key. If you accidentally delete an object, you can always use Undo to restore it.

 ## Hands-On 8.10 Draw AutoShapes

In this exercise, you will draw a starburst and cloud AutoShape. The Zoom Control should still be set to Whole Page.

Draw a Starburst

1. Click the insertion point at the end of the large paragraph. The insertion point should be just to the right of the period in the last sentence.

2. Tap (ENTER) to insert a blank line below the paragraph.
   Notice that the picture remains at the same location on the page. The picture remains stationary because you unchecked the Move object with text box in the previous exercise.

3. Click the AutoShapes ▾ button on the Drawing toolbar.

4. Follow these steps to choose a starburst shape.

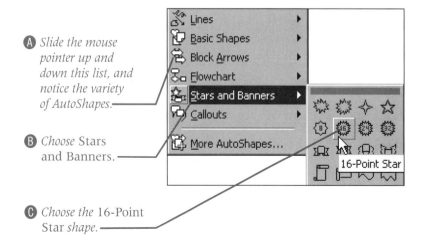

A *Slide the mouse pointer up and down this list, and notice the variety of AutoShapes.*

B *Choose* Stars and Banners.

C *Choose the* 16-Point Star *shape.*

5. Follow these steps to draw the starburst.

Ⓐ *Position the mouse pointer here, and drag up to the right until the starburst has approximately this shape and size.*

Ⓑ *Release the mouse button to complete the starburst. You will add text to the starburst later.*

The Best Bakery in Ocean City!

Stop by the West Side Bakery before June 30, and get a free loaf of sourdough bread when you buy a dozen muffins. Our award-winning muffins will please your palette and satisfy your hunger. All of our breads and muffins are made with the finest ingredients. We are located at 1450 Market Street in Ocean City.

6. Tap the (DELETE) key to delete the selected starburst.
   You can always delete an object by selecting it and tapping (DELETE).

7. Click Undo 🔄 to restore the starburst.

(Continued on the next page)

Draw a Callout

8. Click the AutoShapes button, and choose Callouts.

9. Choose the **Cloud Callout** 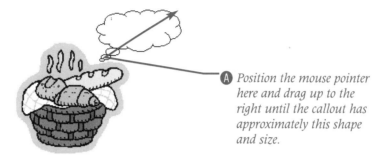 shape (fourth button on the top row).

10. Follow this step to draw the callout.
    If you make a mistake, delete the callout and start over.

Ⓐ *Position the mouse pointer here and drag up to the right until the callout has approximately this shape and size.*

Formatting Buttons on the Drawing Toolbar

 TIP!

Use the Format Object dialog box for size, layout, and position formatting.

The Drawing toolbar has several buttons that let you format drawing objects. You can use the Drawing toolbar to format AutoShapes, rectangles, ovals, lines, text boxes, and other drawing objects. To format an object, you must select the object first and then apply the desired format(s). You can also select several objects and format them as a group. The following Quick Reference table discusses the formatting buttons on the Drawing toolbar.

FORMATTING BUTTONS ON THE DRAWING TOOLBAR

Button	Function
Fill Color	Fills an object with a solid color, pattern, or gradient
Line Color	Changes the color of lines, or applies a line pattern
Font Color	Changes the font color of text in a text box or other object
Line Style	Changes thickness and style of lines and object borders
Dash Style	Formats lines and borders with various dash styles
Arrow Style	Applies arrowheads to lines, or changes the arrowhead style of lines
Shadow	Applies a shadow effect to objects
3-D	Applies a 3-D effect to objects

Add Text to the Callout, and Format the Text

One of the benefits of a callout is that you can type text directly into it. Other AutoShapes, such as the starburst you drew earlier, lack this capability.

1. Set the Zoom Control to Page Width.

2. If necessary, scroll up or down until the callout is visible.

3. Click inside the callout cloud and type the phrase **We're fresh from the oven.**
   The phrase will wrap within the callout

4. Select the entire phrase within the callout. If a portion of the text is not visible within the callout, then click on the callout and drag a sizing handle to enlarge the callout.

5. Set the font size to 18.

6. Add color to the text with the **Font Color** ![Font Color button] button on the Drawing toolbar or the Standard toolbar.

7. Click the **Center Align** ![Center Align button] button to center the text.

8. Click anywhere outside the callout. It should closely match the following example.

Format the Callout

9. Follow these steps to format the callout using buttons on the Drawing toolbar.

Ⓐ *Click anywhere on the callout, and a thick border will appear.*

Ⓑ *Click the border, and the pattern will change to indicate the callout is selected. (You must click the border before you can size, move, and format callouts.)*

Ⓒ *Use the **Fill Color** ![Fill Color button] button on the Drawing toolbar to fill the callout with a light color.*

Ⓓ *Use the Line Color ![Line Color button] button on the Drawing toolbar to format the cloud border with the same color you used for the text inside the callout.*

Ⓔ *Feel free to adjust the callout size by dragging any sizing handle.*

Ⓕ *Feel free to move the callout by dragging the border.*

Ⓖ *Feel free to change the anchor position by dragging the yellow anchor point.*

10. Save the changes, and continue with the next topic.

Text Boxes

You use the Text Box tool to draw text boxes. Text boxes are one of the most useful drawing objects. They look like rectangles when they are inserted; however, unlike rectangles, you can type text inside a text box. Text boxes let you position text anywhere on a page. You can use text boxes to superimpose text on other text, pictures, and other graphics. For example, in the following exercise, you will use a text box to superimpose text on the starburst you inserted in the previous exercise.

Layering Objects

Drawing objects reside on different layers than the text in your document. Drawing objects can be placed in front of or in back of the text layer. You can also layer drawing objects on top of one another. For example, the text box that you will draw in the following exercise will be on a layer in front of the starburst. Thus, the text box text will appear to float on top of the starburst. You can change the layering of drawing objects by clicking the Draw button on the Drawing toolbar and choosing layering options from the Order menu.

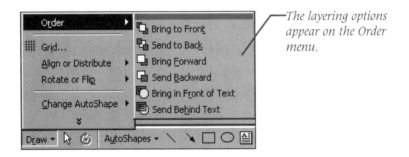

The layering options appear on the Order menu.

Hands-On 8.12 Draw a Text Box, and Layer Objects

Draw the Text Box

1. If necessary, scroll up or down until the starburst is visible.

2. Click the **Text Box** button on the Drawing toolbar.

3. Follow this step to draw the text box.

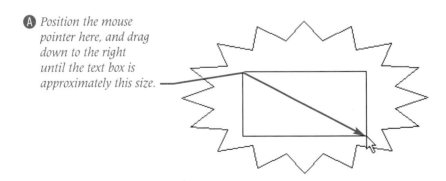

Ⓐ *Position the mouse pointer here, and drag down to the right until the text box is approximately this size.*

4. Type the word **Huge** in the text box, and then tap ⒺⓃⓉⒺⓇ.

5. Type the word **Muffins**.

Format Text Within the Text Box

6. Select both of the paragraphs you just typed, and set the font size to 18.

7. If necessary, adjust the width and/or height of the text box and starburst.
   The text should fit in the box without wrapping, and the text box should fit inside of the starburst.

8. Select the text in the text box, and use the Font Color  button on the Drawing toolbar to apply the same font color that was used in the callout.

9. Now Center Align the paragraphs within the text box.

10. Click anywhere outside the textbox.
    The text box and starburst should closely match the example shown to the right.

Experiment with Layering

11. Follow this step to select the text box.

Ⓐ *Click any edge of the text box, and a border with sizing handles will appear.*

12. Click the Draw ▼ button on the Drawing toolbar.

13. Choose Order from the Draw menu, and then choose Send to Back.
    The text box text should vanish as it is sent behind the starburst.

14. Click the Draw ▼ button, choose Order, and then choose Bring to Front.
    The text should reappear, since it is now in front of the starburst. You can also use the Send Backward and Bring Forward commands to move objects backward and forward one layer at a time. This is useful with complex graphics where you have several drawing layers. The Bring in front of text and Send behind text options are useful for placing drawing objects in front of and behind the text layer.

Remove the Text Box Border, and Nudge the Text Box

15. Make sure the text box is still selected.

16. Click the Line Color drop-down button on the Drawing toolbar.
    A color palette will be displayed.

17. Choose No Line from the top of the color palette.

18. Now fine tune the position of the text box within the starburst by pressing the (CTRL) key while you tap any of these ← → ↑ ↓ keys. Adjust the position until you are satisfied with its placement.
    You can always nudge a selected object by using this keystroke technique.

(Continued on the next page)

Format the Starburst

19. Click anywhere on the starburst, and sizing handles will appear.

20. Click the Line Style ▤ button on the Drawing toolbar.

21. Choose a 1½ pt line style.
    The starburst should now have a much thicker line.

22. Use the Line Color 🖊▾ drop-down button to apply the same line color to the starburst as you used for the border of the cloud callout.

23. Select the cloud callout by clicking it once.

24. Use the Line Style ▤ button to apply a 1½ pt line style to the cloud callout.

25. Save the changes, and continue with the next topic.

Paragraph Spacing

The amount of space inserted between paragraphs by the (ENTER) key is dependent upon the font size in effect when (ENTER) is tapped. Up until now, you have been limited to single spacing or double-spacing between paragraphs. You can add additional space before and after paragraphs with the Spacing Before and Spacing After options on the Paragraph dialog box. These options are quite useful in desktop publishing where spatial arrangements are important.

Paragraph Spacing vs. Line Spacing

Line spacing affects the spacing within and after a paragraph. Paragraph spacing has no impact on spacing within a paragraph. Paragraph spacing only changes the spacing before or after a paragraph. For example, in the following exercise, you will change the spacing before the paragraph in the cloud callout. This will allow you to precisely control the vertical position of the text within the callout without changing the spacing between the two lines of text. The following illustration shows the text in the cloud callout before and after Spacing Before has been applied. Notice that the text has been pushed down slightly in the second cloud.

Spacing Before 0   *Spacing Before 4 pt*

 Hands-On 8.13 Increase Paragraph Spacing

1. Click anywhere on the text inside the cloud.

2. Choose **Format→Paragraph** from the menu bar.

3. Set the paragraph Spacing Before to 4 pt, as shown on the right.

4. Click **OK** to push the callout text down slightly.

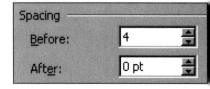

5. If necessary, continue to adjust the paragraph Spacing Before until you are satisfied with the text position within the callout.
Now continue with the last topic in this lesson.

Page Borders

Word 2000 lets you apply borders to pages. Page borders are applied to all pages in a document unless the document is organized into sections. If a document is organized in sections, you can apply page borders to individual sections. You use the **Format→Borders and Shading** command to display the Borders and Shading dialog box. You use the options on the Page Border tab to apply page borders.

 Hands-On 8.14 Apply a Page Border

1. Click anywhere on the main paragraph in your flyer.
You must make sure no objects are selected before issuing the Borders and Shading command. Otherwise, a different dialog box will be displayed.

2. Choose **Format→Borders and Shading** from the menu bar.

3. Follow these steps to apply a page border.

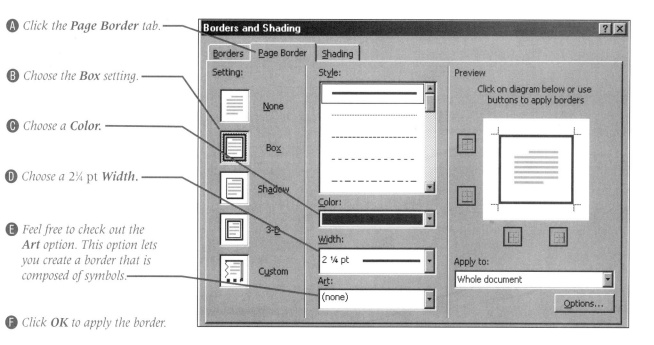

Ⓐ *Click the **Page Border** tab.*

Ⓑ *Choose the **Box** setting.*

Ⓒ *Choose a **Color**.*

Ⓓ *Choose a 2¼ pt **Width**.*

Ⓔ *Feel free to check out the **Art** option. This option lets you create a border that is composed of symbols.*

Ⓕ *Click **OK** to apply the border.*

4. Click the Print Preview 🔍 button to view your completed flyer.
You should now have a border around the entire page. Word places the border approximately 0.5" from the edges of the page. Keep in mind that you can always remove a border by issuing the Format→Borders and Shading command, and choosing the None option. Your flyer should closely match the flyer shown in the case study at the start of this lesson.

5. Click the Close button to exit from Print Preview.

6. Save the changes, close the document, and continue with the questions and exercises.

Concepts Review

True/False Questions

1. You can change the size of pictures after they have been inserted.　　　TRUE　　FALSE

2. The Drawing 🔲 button displays and hides the Drawing toolbar.　　　TRUE　　FALSE

3. Clicking the Select Objects 🔲 tool displays the Format Object dialog box.　　TRUE　　FALSE

4. The paragraph Spacing Before and After settings are used to create additional space between the lines within a paragraph.　　TRUE　　FALSE

5. Text boxes can be used to superimpose text on other text or objects.　　　TRUE　　FALSE

6. Drop Caps are inserted with the **Insert→Drop Cap** command.　　　TRUE　　FALSE

7. WordArt objects cannot be moved once they have been inserted.　　　TRUE　　FALSE

8. Pictures are always positioned in line with text.　　　TRUE　　FALSE

Multiple-Choice Questions

1. Which technique can be used to display an object's anchor?
   a. Use the Show All button to display the nonprinting characters, then select the desired object.
   b. Select the desired object. There is no need to display the nonprinting characters.
   c. Display the nonprinting characters. There is no need to select the object.
   d. None of the above

2. Which of the following statements most accurately describes the paragraph Spacing Before command?
   a. The Spacing Before command only adds space before each selected paragraph.
   b. The Spacing Before command adds space before each selected paragraph and to each line within the selected paragraphs.
   c. The Spacing Before command adds space before and after each selected paragraph.
   d. None of the above

3. Which command displays the Borders and Shading dialog box?
   a. Format→Paragraph
   b. Edit→Borders and Shading
   c. Format→Borders and Shading
   d. None of the above

4. Which keyboard key is used to select multiple drawing objects?
   a. (SHIFT)
   b. (ALT)
   c. (CTRL)
   d. None of the above

Skill Builders

Skill Builder 8.1 **Create a Flyer with Guidance**

In this exercise, you will open a document on your exercise diskette. You will use WordArt and Clip Art to liven up the document.

Insert and Format WordArt

1. Open the document named **Skill Builder 8.1.**

2. Tap (ENTER) until the text is pushed down to approximately the 3″ position.

3. Tap ↑ until the insertion point is positioned on the first blank line at the top of the document.
   In the next few steps, you will insert a WordArt object. Positioning the insertion point on the first blank line will ensure that the WordArt object is anchored to that line.

4. Click the WordArt ▣ button on the Drawing toolbar.

5. Choose the third WordArt style in the second row, and click **OK.**

6. Type **Everything Is On Sale!** as the WordArt text, set the font size to 28, and click **OK.**

7. If necessary, drag the WordArt object up until it is approximately 2″ from the top of the page.

8. Right click the WordArt object, and choose **Format→WordArt** from the pop-up menu.

9. Click the Layout tab, set the horizontal alignment to Center, and click **OK.**
   This will ensure that the object is centered between the margins.

Insert Drop Caps

10. Click anywhere in the first body paragraph, and choose **Format→Drop Cap.**

11. Choose the Dropped position option, leave the Lines to drop setting at 3, and click **OK.**

12. Insert a drop cap in the second body paragraph using the same settings.

Insert and Format Clip Art

13. Click anywhere in the first body paragraph.

14. Click the Insert Clip Art ▣ button on the Drawing toolbar.

15. Insert the Presentations clip located in the Business category, as shown on the following page.

16. Close the Clip Gallery, and then click the clip to select it.

17. Now right-click the clip, and choose **Format→Picture** from the pop up menu.

18. Click the Layout tab, and set the wrapping style to Square.

(Continued on the next page)

19. Click the Size tab, set the height to 1″, make sure the Lock aspect ratio box is checked, and click **OK.**

20. Drag the picture to the bottom right corner of the paragraph as shown below.

21. Now insert the clip shown below into the second paragraph. The clip is located in the Office category in the Clip Gallery. Set the layout option to Tight, and set the size exactly as you did for the clip in the first body paragraph.

22. Click Print Preview . Your document should match the example shown below.

23. Close Print Preview, save the changes, and then close the document.

Everything Is On Sale!

Stop what you are doing! Zen Electronics is having a sale. We are growing rapidly and cannot keep up with customer demand. Our sales keep climbing upward, and we must move to a larger store where we can stock more merchandise. We are selling everything in our store at rock-bottom prices to reduce our moving costs. This incredible sale will last for two weeks beginning this Saturday. We must sell everything! Zip over to Zen if you are in the market for electronics.

Computers have always been our hottest products, and right now the prices are so hot that we're afraid the cabinets might melt. Computers can be difficult to transport because of the delicate components inside, so we are practically giving them away. All name-brand PCs printers, modems, software and other accessories are priced below our cost. This is no joke. We are actually selling PCs below our cost! So Zip into Zen as soon as possible and speak with one of our excellent customer service representatives. At Zen, we are known for our blue ribbon support.

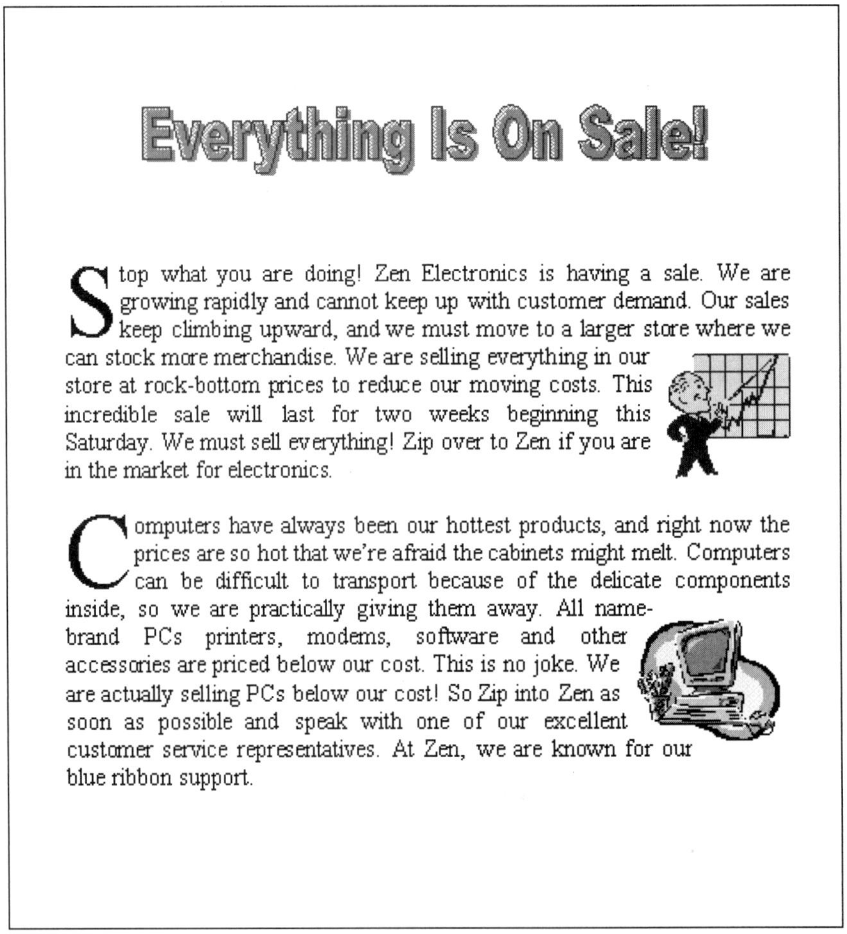

Skill Builder 8.2 Create a Flyer on Your Own

1. Create the flyer shown below. Use WordArt to insert the "Protected Wetlands" title. The clip art can be found in the Animals category of the Clip Gallery. You can leave the layout of the clip art set to **In line with text** and use the Center Align button on the Formatting toolbar to center align the clip. Use any page border thickness and style that you desire. Insert the drop cap as shown. Use a Times New Roman font for the body paragraph and an Arial font for all other text. Use bold and italics as necessary, and choose font sizes to give the document the appearance shown below.

2. Save the document as **Skill Builder 8.2,** then close the document.

Protected Wetlands

Keep Out!

This land is owned and protected by the East Bay Preservation Society. Only qualified members of the Preservation Society are allowed to enter. Please do not litter or disturb wildlife in any way.

For More Information
Call 1-510-237-3233

Skill Builder 8.3 Practice with Drawing Objects

In this exercise, you will use WordArt, text boxes, and lines to create the family tree shown at the end of this Skill Builder.

Insert WordArt, and Draw and Format the First Text Box

1. Start a new document, and insert the WordArt object shown in the completed document at the end of this exercise. Position the object approximately 2″ down from the top of the page centered horizontally.

2. Click the **Text Box** button on the Drawing toolbar.

3. Draw a box approximately 0.5″ high by 1.5″ wide that is centered horizontally about 1″ below the WordArt object. Don't be too concerned about the size and position of the box. You can always adjust the size and position later.

4. Type the name **Wayne Westover** in the box.

5. Select the text within the box and format it as Arial 11 Bold.

6. **Center align** the text within the box.

7. If necessary, adjust the size of the box until it has the approximate dimensions shown in Diedre's Family Tree.

8. Use the **Format→Paragraph** command and the Spacing Before option to insert a small amount of space above the text. Your objective is to center the text vertically within the box. You will need to insert between 1 and 10 points.

Draw the First Connector Line

Take a moment to study Diedre's Family Tree. Notice the position of the vertical line under the first text box. The line is centered horizontally on the box and intersects the bottom edge of the box. When you draw the line, it will connect to the bottom of the box because it will snap to a grid point on the box. The Snap to Grid feature makes it easy to connect objects.

9. Click the **Line** button on the Drawing toolbar.

10. Position the mouse pointer on the bottom center edge of the text box, and drag down about 0.5″.

11. Release the mouse button to complete the line. If you aren't satisfied with your line, you can click Undo and start over.

Make Copies of the Box and Line

12. Follow this step to copy the box and line using right drag.

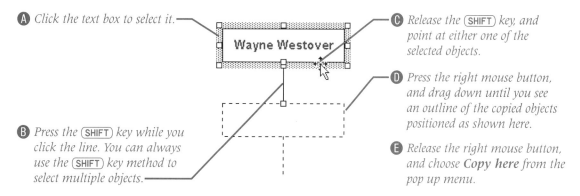

A *Click the text box to select it.*

B *Press the (SHIFT) key while you click the line. You can always use the (SHIFT) key method to select multiple objects.*

C *Release the (SHIFT) key, and point at either one of the selected objects.*

D *Press the right mouse button, and drag down until you see an outline of the copied objects positioned as shown here.*

E *Release the right mouse button, and choose **Copy here** from the pop up menu.*

TIP!

You can also press the (CTRL) key and drag with the left mouse button.

13. If you made a mistake, click Undo, and try again.

14. Change the text in the copied box to Miah Healy.

15. Repeat the procedure once more to create the Jean Healy box and the line below it.

16. Now copy just the Jean Healy box (not the line) three times to create the Yvonne Healy, Deidre Westover, and Joan Westover boxes. You will need to position the copied boxes in the approximate locations shown on the following page. Also, type the correct names in the boxes.

17. Add a light fill color to the Deidre Westover and Joan Westover boxes.

Draw, Copy, and Flip Arrows

18. Use the **Arrow** ⬛ tool to draw an arrow from the Yvonne Healy box to the Deidre Westover box.

19. Use the **Copy** ⬛ and **Paste** ⬛ buttons to make a copy of the arrow.

20. Make sure the copied arrow is selected, and click the ⬛ Draw ▾ button on the Drawing toolbar.

21. Choose Rotate or Flip from the Draw menu, and then choose Flip Horizontal.
    The arrow will now point in the opposite direction.

22. Now drag the flipped arrow to the proper position as shown on the following page.

23. Set the zoom control to Whole Page.

24. Click the **Select Objects** ⬛ button on the Drawing toolbar.

25. Drag the mouse in the document to enclose all of the objects (except the WordArt object) in a box. This will select all of the objects.

(Continued on the next page)

26. Use the **Line Color** 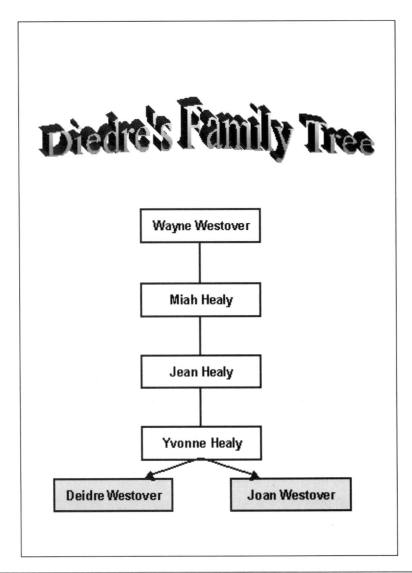 button and the **Line Style** button on the Drawing toolbar to apply a blue 1pt line to the selected objects. If necessary, use the arrow keys or the mouse to move the selected objects to the desired location below the WordArt object. Your completed document should closely match the document shown below.

27. Save the document as **Skill Builder 8.3,** then close the document.

Skill Builder 8.4 Draw an Organizational Chart

1. Use the techniques you used in Skill Builder 8.3 to create the organizational chart shown below. This project is actually quite easy if you use right drag to copy objects. The names shown below the boxes are created with text boxes that have had the lines removed. Make sure you set up the first few objects correctly, then use the right-drag method to duplicate the objects. Once you create the Dale Jones branch of the chart, you can copy the entire branch to the Paula Williams and Allen Smith branches. Then change the text in the new branches.

2. Save the document as **Skill Builder 8.4,** then close the document.

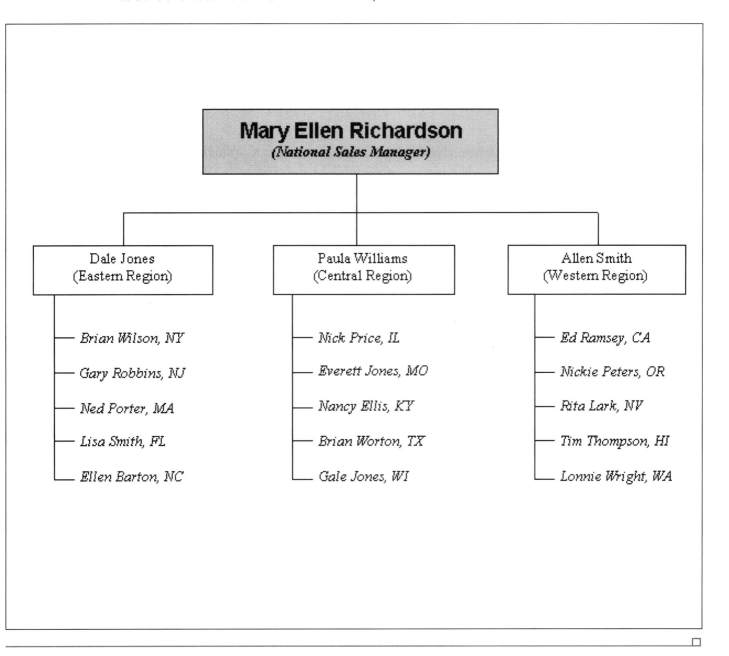

Assessments

Assessment 8.1 Format a Document

In this assessment, you will modify a document until it matches the document below.

1. Open the document named **Assessment 8.1.**

2. Follow these instructions to modify the document.

   ▪ Insert the title 2″ down from the top of the page. Format the title with an Arial 20 Bold font, and center it on the line.

   ▪ Begin the first body paragraph two lines below the title, as shown before.

   ▪ Add drop caps to the two body paragraphs as shown. Notice the drop caps only drop down two lines.

   ▪ Insert a picture in the second paragraph. The picture shown below is available in the Special Occasions category in the Clip Gallery. Set the height of your picture to 1.25″, and align it in the paragraph as shown.

3. Print the document when you have finished.

4. Save the document as **Assessment 8.1,** then close the document.

Everything Must Go Sale!

Bay Area Bicycles is closing its original store at 1600 Fairview Drive in San Francisco. This is a result of overwhelming demand for our fine bicycles and other products. We will be moving to our new location at 11240 Wesley Avenue in San Francisco. Everything must go in order to reduce our moving costs. Bicycles are expensive to transport because time and money are required to protect them from damage. For this reason, we must sell everything!

There has never been a better time to buy a bicycle, skateboard, or surfboard from Bay Area Bicycles. Many of our prices are actually below the manufacturers' retail price. You simply will not believe the quality products that you can buy at incredibly low prices. So reward yourself today with a new bicycle from Bay Area Bicycles.

Assessment 8.2 **Create a Flyer**

In this assessment, you will create the flyer shown below.

1. Follow these instructions to create the flyer.

   ▪ Set all four margins to 1.5″.

   ▪ Set the font to Times New Roman 24.

   ▪ Position the first body paragraph approximately 3.5″ down from the top of the page.

   ▪ Add drop caps to the two main paragraphs as shown.

   ▪ Add the WordArt object to the top of the document as shown. Use the fourth WordArt style in the top row of the WordArt Gallery. Position the WordArt object in the blank space at the top of the document.

   ▪ Insert the clip art shown at the bottom of the document. The clip is available in the Places category. Adjust the size and position of the clip art as shown.

   ▪ Add a 3 pt, blue, page border with a Box style.

2. Print the document when you have finished.

Congratulations Vickie

Vickie Johnson is retiring after 25 years at Velcor, and it's about time she had a party. The theme of this celebration is New Destinations.

We need volunteers and fresh ideas to help make this the celebration of a lifetime for Vickie. Please call June Roberts at 234-9900 if you are interested in volunteering your time.

3. Save the document as **Assessment 8.2,** then close the document.

Critical Thinking

Critical Thinking 8.1 On Your Own

Jason Alexander is a Technology Support Specialist for Farmington Medical Supplies. Jason is responsible for supporting over 250 personal computers and for training Farmington employees. Part of his training responsibilities is to train employees on Microsoft Office 2000 applications. Initially, Jason trained Farmington employees on an individual basis. However, his responsibilities have grown with the company, and he can no longer do this. He decides to hold larger training classes with up to eight students per class.

Design a flyer for Jason that promotes an upcoming training class on Word 2000. Include WordArt, pictures, fonts, colors, borders, and any other formats or features that will enhance the appearance of the flyer. Also, include a description of three or four Word 2000 features that you have learned that may also be attractive to the prospective students. Save your completed flyer as **Critical Thinking 8.1.**

Critical Thinking 8.2 On Your Own

Lisa Thomas works in the Human Resources department of Farmington Medical Supplies. Lisa has been asked to create an organization chart for Farmington's top officers and directors. The chart will be used for a presentation to an investment group. Lisa knows Word very well, so she uses Word to create the chart. She could use a program specifically designed to create organization charts; however, the amount of time required to learn such a program would be prohibitive.

Set up an organization chart in Word using the information below. The chart will have three levels except for the Cindy Thomas branch, which will have just two levels.

Name	Title	Level
Wilma Boyd	President and CEO	1
Ted Jones	Vice President of Sales	2
Cindy Thomas	Vice President of Marketing	2
Ned Chambers	Vice President of Operations	2
Carol Perkins	Western Sales Manager	3 (under Ted Jones)
Bill Baskin	Easter Sales Manager	3 (under Ted Jones)
Tom Chambers	Data Center Manager	3 (under Ned Chambers)
Lisa Evans	Fulfillment Director	3 (under Ned Chambers)

Add a 10% gray shade to each text box in the chart. Save the completed organization chart as **Critical Thinking 8.2.**

Critical Thinking 8.3 **Web Research**

Jay Smith works for Quality Kennels. Quality Kennels provides the best boarding and training for dogs. In addition, Bill Simms, the owner of Quality Kennels, has decided to hold a dog show for his customers. Bill has asked Jay to create a flyer to promote the dog show. The flyer will be mailed to all Quality customers. You have been assigned the task of visiting Microsoft's Web site and downloading three clip art images of dogs to be used in the flyer.

Visit Microsoft's Clip Gallery Live, and download three clip art images of dogs. Add the images to the Animals category in the Clip Gallery. Insert the pictures side by side in a Word document, and size each image to a height of 1.5 inches. Save the document as **Critical Thinking 8.3.**

Critical Thinking 8.4 **Web Research with a Group**

Open the Health-e-Meals.com letterhead template that you created in Critical Thinking 7.4. Work with your classmate, and navigate to Microsoft's Clip Gallery Live Web site. Locate a clip art image that you think would be an appropriate logo for Health-e-Meals.com. Download the image into the category of your choice in the Clip Gallery. Insert the image somewhere in your letterhead to create a logo in the letterhead. You will need to size the image and possibly change the location and wrapping options. Use the **Save As** command to save the completed letterhead as a template named **Critical Thinking 8.4—Letterhead.**

Open the envelope template that you created in Critical Thinking 7.4. Insert your Health-e-Meals.com logo into the envelope. Size and position the logo as necessary. Save your completed envelope as a template named **Critical Thinking 8.4—Envelope.**

Mail Merge, Envelopes, and Labels

Word is an excellent tool for managing mailings. Word's Mail Merge feature can help you set up form letters and other documents that you wish to mail. In addition, it helps you set up data source files where contact information is entered and stored. Mail Merge lets you conduct mailings by merging a form letter with a data source to produce personalized letters. You can also use Mail Merge to generate envelopes, labels, and other documents using the contact information in a data source. In this lesson, you will generate personalized letters, envelopes, and mailing labels using the same data source. In addition, you will generate mailing labels from an alternate data source stored in an Excel workbook.

In This Lesson

Case Study

Linda Adams is the Chief Executive Officer of Robinson Financial Services. Robinson provides a variety of financial services ranging from financial advice to estate planning and 401K plan administration. Recently, Robinson began selling a package of financial planning tools that includes books, planning documents, and a video. This package was marketed and sold through Robinson's online store. The customer service staff at Robinson has been unable to contact several of the customers who purchased the package. Linda Adams has decided to send personalized letters to all customers thanking them for their purchases, and requesting that they provide Robinson with valid phone numbers.

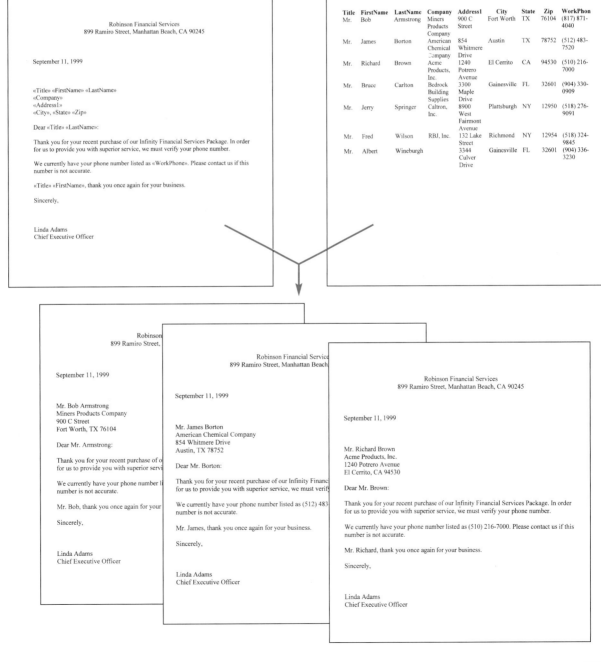

Mail Merge Concepts

Word's mail merge feature is most often used for generating personalized form letters, mailing labels, and envelopes. However, mail merge is a versatile tool that can be used with any type of document. Mail merge can be a big time saver and is invaluable for managing large mailings.

How It Works

Merging creates a **merge document** by combining information from two or more source documents. The source documents are known as the **data source** and the **main document.** The main document controls the merge. It is usually a form letter or another type of document that is sent to many people. The data source is usually a mailing list of names and addresses.

Benefits of Using Mail Merge

Mail merge will save you a lot of time and can help reduce errors in large mailings. You will really appreciate mail merge when you have already produced a merge document and then wish to make changes. Using mail merge, you can edit the main document once and then remerge it with the data source to produce a new merge document. Without mail merge, you would need to edit each personalized letter individually.

The illustration on the following page shows a form letter being merged with a data source containing address information for three people. The resulting merge document contains the three personalized letters shown at the bottom of the page.

A form letter with text and merge fields. The merge fields (surrounded by angle brackets « ») are replaced with data from the data source during the merge. All other text is inserted into each merged letter.

A data source file that contains seven records and a header row. Each record (row) contains all of the address data for one contact. The address data is inserted into the form letter merge fields during the merge.

Robinson Financial Services
899 Ramiro Street, Manhattan Beach, CA 90245

September 11, 1999

«Title» «FirstName» «LastName»
«Company»
«Address1»
«City», «State» «Zip»

Dear «Title» «LastName»:

Thank you for your recent purchase of our Infinity Financial Services Package. In order for us to provide you with superior service, we must verify your phone number.

We currently have your phone number listed as «WorkPhone». Please contact us if this number is not accurate.

«Title» «FirstName», thank you once again for your business.

Sincerely,

Linda Adams
Chief Executive Officer

Title	FirstName	LastName	Company	Address1	City	State	Zip	WorkPhon
Mr.	Bob	Armstrong	Miners Products Company	900 C Street	Fort Worth	TX	76104	(817) 871-4040
Mr.	James	Borton	American Chemical Company	854 Whitmere Drive	Austin	TX	78752	(512) 483-7520
Mr.	Richard	Brown	Acme Products, Inc.	1240 Potrero Avenue	El Cerrito	CA	94530	(510) 216-7000
Mr.	Bruce	Carlton	Bedrock Building Supplies	3300 Maple Drive	Gainesville	FL	32601	(904) 330-0909
Mr.	Jerry	Springer	Caltron, Inc.	8900 West Fairmont Avenue	Plattsburgh	NY	12950	(518) 276-9091
Mr.	Fred	Wilson	RBJ, Inc.	132 Lake Street	Richmond	NY	12954	(518) 324-9845
Mr.	Albert	Wineburgh		3344 Culver Drive	Gainesville	FL	32601	(904) 336-3230

The form letter and data source are merged together to create customized letters (only three are shown here).

Robinson
899 Ramiro Street,

September 11, 1999

Mr. Bob Armstrong
Miners Products Company
900 C Street
Fort Worth, TX 76104

Dear Mr. Armstrong:

Thank you for your recent purchase of o
for us to provide you with superior servi

We currently have your phone number li
number is not accurate.

Mr. Bob, thank you once again for your

Sincerely,

Linda Adams
Chief Executive Officer

Robinson Financial Servic
899 Ramiro Street, Manhattan Beach

September 11, 1999

Mr. James Borton
American Chemical Company
854 Whitmere Drive
Austin, TX 78752

Dear Mr. Borton:

Thank you for your recent purchase of our Infinity Finan
for us to provide you with superior service, we must veri

We currently have your phone number listed as (512) 483
number is not accurate.

Mr. James, thank you once again for your business.

Sincerely,

Linda Adams
Chief Executive Officer

Robinson Financial Services
899 Ramiro Street, Manhattan Beach, CA 90245

September 11, 1999

Mr. Richard Brown
Acme Products, Inc.
1240 Potrero Avenue
El Cerrito, CA 94530

Dear Mr. Brown:

Thank you for your recent purchase of our Infinity Financial Services Package. In order for us to provide you with superior service, we must verify your phone number.

We currently have your phone number listed as (510) 216-7000. Please contact us if this number is not accurate.

Mr. Richard, thank you once again for your business.

Sincerely,

Linda Adams
Chief Executive Officer

The Mail Merge Helper

You must have a main document and a data source to conduct a merge. You can merge an existing main document with an existing data source, or you can create the main document and data source prior to merging. Word's Mail Merge Helper provides assistance with setting up the main document and data source, and helps you with the merge. You use the **Tools→Mail Merge** command to display the Mail Merge Helper dialog box. You can display the Mail Merge Helper dialog box while setting up a new mail merge in a blank document window, or you can display the dialog box from an open main document or data source.

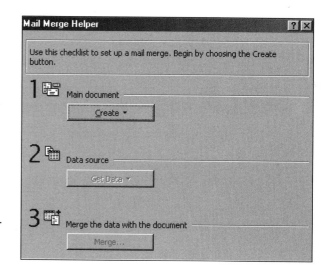

 Hands-On 9.1 Display the Mail Merge Helper

1. Start Word to display a new document window.

2. Choose **Tools→Mail Merge** from the menu bar.
   *Make sure you choose **Tools→Mail Merge**, not **Tools→Merge Documents**. The **Tools→Merge Documents** command is used for consolidating reviewer comments.*

3. Click the **Create** button.
   Word displays the types of mail merge main documents that can be created. You will learn more about these document types further on in this lesson.

4. Choose Form Letters from the menu.

5. Click the **Active Window** button to create the form letter in the current window.
   The next step is to create a new data source or to open an existing data source. You must have a data source in order to create a main document. This is because you will be inserting variable merge fields into the main document. The variable merge fields won't be available to the main document until they have been defined in the data source.

6. Click the **Get Data** button, and choose **Create Data Source.**
   Leave the Create Data Source dialog box open, and continue with the next topic. You will use the Create Data Source dialog box in a moment.

Data Sources

Data sources usually contain names, addresses, telephone numbers and other contact information. However, you can include any information in a data source. For example, you may want to include part names, part numbers, and part prices if you are using Mail Merge to create a parts catalog. You can create a data source in Word, or you can use external data sources, such as an Access database or an Excel workbook.

Word Data Sources

You can use a Word document as a data source. The Mail Merge Helper will guide you through the process of constructing the data source and entering the data. When you set up a data source in Word, the Mail Merge Helper stores the data in a Word table. Tables are composed of horizontal rows and vertical columns. The table structure is also used to store data in an Access database or an Excel worksheet. Each table row stores all of the data for one record. Each table column is a field. The following illustration shows a Word data source table with three records. Take a few moments to study the illustration before continuing.

This is the header row. The header row contains the field names for the various columns. The field names are used in the main document to determine where information from the data source is to be inserted.

Each row contains the data for one contact. The rows are known as records.

Title	FirstName	LastName	Company	Address1	City	State	Zip	WorkPhone
Mr.	Jerry	Springer	Caltron, Inc.	8900 West Fairmont Avenue	Plattsburgh	NY	12950	(518) 276-9091
Mr.	James	Borton	American Chemical Company	854 Whitmere Drive	Austin	TX	78752	(512) 483-7520
Mr.	Fred	Wilson	RBJ, Inc.	132 Lake Street	Richmond	NY	12954	(518) 324-9845
Mr.	Bob	Armstrong	Farmers Products Company	900 C Street	Fort Worth	TX	76104	(817) 871-4040

Designing Effective Data Sources

It is very important that you design effective data sources. The most important consideration is the number of fields to use. The more fields, the more flexibility you will have in the merge. An important rule to remember is that you cannot merge a portion of a field. For example, if a name field contains both the first name and last name, then you will never be able to merge only the first name into a main document. This would be a problem if you needed to merge only a last name to create salutations such as, Dear Mr. Springer. In this example, you would need to use one field for the first name and a separate field for the last name. You would also need to use a title field for the titles Mr., Ms., and Mrs.

IMPORTANT!

You can't merge a portion of a field.

Setting Up the Data Source Structure in Word

When you click the **Get Data** button on the Mail Merge Helper and choose Create Data Source, Word displays the Create Data Source dialog box. The Create Data Source dialog box displays a list of predefined fields. You can add new fields to the list, or remove fields from the list to construct a data source with the precise fields you desire. When you have finished defining the fields, the Mail Merge Helper constructs the data source using the field names you have specified.

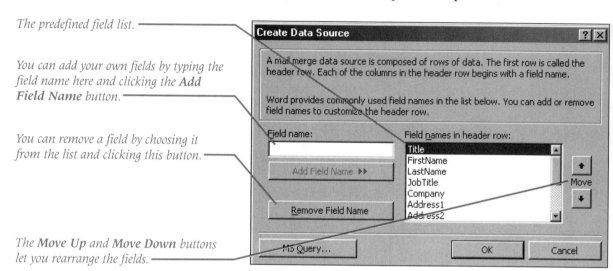

The predefined field list.

*You can add your own fields by typing the field name here and clicking the **Add Field Name** button.*

You can remove a field by choosing it from the list and clicking this button.

*The **Move Up** and **Move Down** buttons let you rearrange the fields.*

Hands-On 9.2 Set Up a Word Data Source

The Create Data Source dialog box should be open from the previous exercise.

Remove Field Names

1. The JobTitle field isn't necessary, so choose JobTitle on the fields list and click the **Remove Field Name** button.
   The JobTitle field will appear in the Field name box. It appears in the Field name box so you can quickly add it back to the list if you change your mind.

2. Click the Address2 field on the list; then click the **Remove Field Name** button.

3. Remove the PostalCode, Country, and HomePhone fields.
   You may need to scroll through the list in order to accomplish this. The HomePhone field will remain in the Field name box.

Add a Field, and Change Its Order in the List

4. Type **Zip** into the Field name box, and click the **Add Field Name** button.
   The Zip field will be added to the bottom of the list.

5. Click the Move Up button once on the right side of the dialog box to move the Zip field above the WorkPhone field.
   The field's position does not affect the merge; however, it can make it easier to enter data. For example, the company name is usually entered first, followed by the contact name, address, etc.

6. Click **OK** to complete the data source structure.
   Word will prompt you to save the data source.

7. Save the data source to your exercise diskette as **Hands-On Lesson 9—Data Source.**
   The Mail Merge Helper will display a dialog box asking if you want to edit the data source or edit the main document. Leave the dialog box displayed for the time being. You will enter data into the data source in the next exercise.

Entering Data with the Data Form

You can display a Data Form by clicking the **Edit Data Source** button after setting up a data source. The Data Form displays the data source field names and boxes that allow you to enter data into the data source. The Data Form also contains buttons that let you add new records, delete and restore records, and search for records. You move from one field to the next within the Data Form by tapping (TAB) or (ENTER).

 ## Hands-On 9.3 Enter Data Using the Data Form

1. Click the **Edit Data Source** button to display the data form.

2. Follow these steps to enter a record.

   ○A *Type* **Mr.** *in the* Title *field, and tap* (ENTER).

   ○B *Enter the remaining data for the first record as shown here. Tap* (ENTER) *after typing each field, including the* WorkPhone.

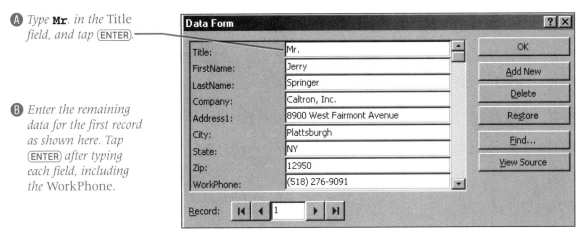

(Continued on the next page)

3. Make sure to tap (ENTER) after typing data in the WorkPhone field, and enter the following records.

Don't type the commas that follow the city names. The commas will be inserted in the main document at a later time. Also, make sure you enter the data in the correct fields. You can display a new record by tapping (ENTER) after entering data in the WorkPhone field. You can also click the Add New button to display a new record.

Mr. James Borton	Mr. Fred Wilson	Mr. Bob Armstrong
American Chemical Company	RBJ, Inc.	Farmers Products Company
854 Whitmere Drive	132 Lake Street	900 C Street
Austin, TX 78752	Richmond, NY 12954	Fort Worth, TX 76104
(512) 483-7520	(518) 324-9845	(817) 871-4040

4. Click the **OK** button when you have finished.

Word will display a new document window with the Mail Merge toolbar positioned above the ruler. This is the mail merge main document. You can always identify a main document because the Mail Merge toolbar will be displayed. You will create a form letter in this window soon. The data source has been saved to your diskette with the name Hands-On Lesson 9 - Data Source. It is also attached to this main document. You will continue to work with the data source in the next exercise. You will create the main document once the data source is complete.

From the Keyboard

(ALT)+(SHIFT)+E to display the data form from main document

Displaying the Data Form from the Main Document

Word displays a Mail Merge toolbar in mail merge main documents. The Edit Data Source button appears on the right end of the toolbar. Pressing it displays the data form. You can use this button to redisplay the data form if you need to add, edit, or delete records from the data source.

Hands-On 9.4 Redisplay the Data Form

1. Click the Edit Data Source button at the right end of the Mail Merge toolbar.

2. Click the **Add New** button on the data form to display a blank record.

3. Follow these guidelines to enter the new records shown below.

   ■ Notice that there is no company name for the third record. Just leave the Company field empty for that record.

   ■ Make sure to enter the data in the correct fields.

   ■ Tap (ENTER) after entering each record, or click the **Add New** button.

Mr. Richard Brown	Mr. Bruce Carlton	Mr. Albert Wineburgh
Acme Products, Inc.	Bedrock Building Supplies	3344 Culver Drive
1240 Potrero Avenue	3300 Maple Drive	Gainesville, FL 32601
El Cerrito, CA 94530	Gainesville, FL 32601	(904) 336-3230
(510) 216-7000	(904) 330-0909	

4. Follow these steps to use the record navigation bar at the bottom of the data form to browse through the records.

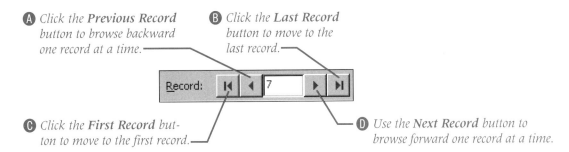

Ⓐ *Click the **Previous Record** button to browse backward one record at a time.*

Ⓑ *Click the **Last Record** button to move to the last record.*

Ⓒ *Click the **First Record** button to move to the first record.*

Ⓓ *Use the **Next Record** button to browse forward one record at a time.*

5. Use the record selection buttons to move to Record 4.

6. Click in the Company box, and change the name from Farmers Products Company to **Miners** Products Company.

7. Browse through the records, and make sure all data is entered in the correct fields.
*Notice the buttons on the right side of the dialog box. The **Delete** button deletes the current record. The **Restore** button reverses any changes that have been made to the current record (such as Farmers to Miners). The **Find** button lets you search through the records for a particular word or phrase.*

Displaying the Data Source

The **View Source** button on the Data Form dialog box displays the data source document. The data source document contains the data source table and accompanying data. You may want to display the data source for various reasons. For example, the data source table lets you view more than one record at a time. Also, it is often easier to find and replace data directly in the data source table. You can also open the data source as you would open any other document with Word's Open dialog box.

TIP!

You must enter data directly in the data source table if the entry occupies more than one line in a field. An example would be an address that requires two lines. You can't enter a multi-line entry with the Data Form.

The Data Source Toolbar

The Data Source toolbar is displayed whenever you display a data source. It contains important buttons that let you manage the data source. The following illustration defines the most important buttons on the Data Source toolbar.

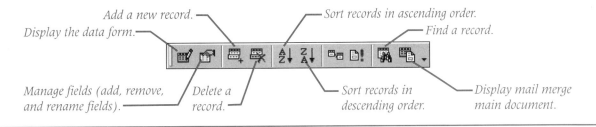

Display the data form.

Add a new record.

Sort records in ascending order.

Find a record.

Manage fields (add, remove, and rename fields).

Delete a record.

Sort records in descending order.

Display mail merge main document.

Explore the Buttons on the Data Source Toolbar

1. Click the **View Source** button, and Word will open the data source document.
   This document contains the data source table. Notice that the first row contains the field names you assigned to the fields. The first row is known as the header row. Also notice that each of the remaining rows contain data for one record.

2. Click the Data Form ⊞ button (first button on the Mail Merge toolbar).
   *This button has the same appearance as the **Edit Data Source** button you used in the previous exercise. The **Edit Data Source** button is located on the right end of the main document Mail Merge toolbar.*

3. Click **OK** to return to the data source table.

4. Click the Manage Fields ⊞ button (second button).
   The Manage Fields dialog box lets you add, remove, and rename fields.

5. Click the **Cancel** button.

6. Click the Add New Record ⊞ button (third button).
   Word adds a blank row to the bottom of the table. You could add one or more records by typing the data directly into the table (but don't do it).

7. Click Undo ⊞ to remove the record.

8. Click the Delete Record ⊞ button (fourth button), and Word will delete a row.

9. Click Undo ⊞ to restore the row.

Sort the Rows

10. Click anywhere in the LastName column.

11. Click the Sort Ascending ⊞ button.
    The rows will now be sorted alphabetically based upon the last names. The records will be merged into the main document in this order when the merge occurs.

12. Click the Mail Merge Main Document ⊞ button (last button) to switch to the main document.
    *Notice that the **Hands-On Lesson 9** button is still visible on the Windows Taskbar at the bottom of your screen. Once the data source is open, you can switch between it and the main document using the Taskbar buttons.*

13. Continue with the next topic, where you will learn more about main documents.

Main Documents

Every merge requires a main document to control the merge. You can create a new main document while setting up a mail merge, or you can use the Mail Merge Helper to choose an existing Word document. A Mail Merge toolbar appears in the document window of any document that has been identified as a mail merge main document. The Mail Merge toolbar lets you insert merge fields and control the merge.

Merge Fields

From the Keyboard

(ALT)+(SHIFT)+F to display Insert Merge Field box

Main documents often consist of a body, such as a form letter, and merge fields. Merge fields are positioned in the variable part of the document. For example, in a form letter, merge fields are positioned in the inside address block and salutation. The merge fields are replaced with data from the data source when the two files are merged. The following illustration shows the form letter you will set up with several merge fields.

*The **Insert Merge Field** button displays a list of the field names used in the data source. You use this button to insert fields.*

These merge fields will be replaced with data from the data source when the documents are merged.

Any document can be used as a main document. Main documents can contain text, graphics, tables, formatting, and any other settings you desire.

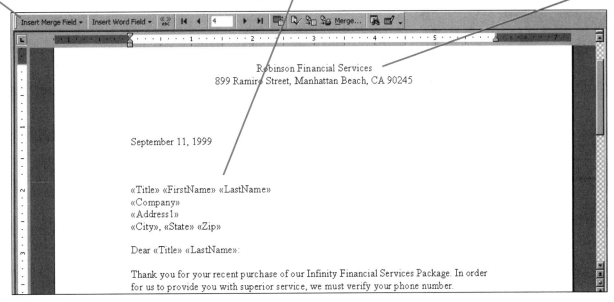

Opening Main Documents

You can use the Mail Merge Helper to open an existing main document or to set up a new document. You can also use the Open dialog box in Word to open a main document. Once the main document is open, you can edit it, insert or remove merge fields, and use the various merge buttons on the Mail Merge toolbar. When you open a main document, Word searches for the data source that is associated with the main document. If the data source has been moved from its original location or the name has been changed, Word displays a browse dialog box allowing you to manually search for the associated data source.

Hands-On 9.6 Set Up a Form Letter

In this exercise, you will set up a form letter. The main document window should be open from the previous exercise. The document window should be empty, and the Mail Merge toolbar should be displayed.

1. Type the following text, inserting the date as a field that is updated automatically. Center-align the company name and address, and tap (ENTER) enough times to position the date approximately 2″ down.

Robinson Financial Services
899 Ramiro Street, Manhattan Beach, CA 90245

Today's Date

2. Tap (ENTER) four times after inserting the date.

3. Click the [Insert Merge Field ▾] button on the Mail Merge toolbar.
The field names from the data source are displayed. This is because the Mail Merge Helper established an association between this document and the data source.

4. Choose Title from the field list, and a <<Title>> field will appear at the insertion point.

5. The title and first name should have a space between them, so tap the (SPACE BAR) once.
During the merge, Word will insert the data exactly as it appears in the data source. For this reason, you should place spaces, commas, and other punctuation marks at the appropriate locations in the main document.

6. Click the [Insert Merge Field ▾] button, and choose FirstName.

7. Tap the (SPACE BAR), and insert the LastName field.

8. Tap (ENTER) to move the insertion point to the next line.

9. Insert the Company field, and tap (ENTER).

10. Insert the Address1 field, and tap (ENTER).

11. Insert the City field, type a comma, and tap the (SPACE BAR).

12. Insert the State field, and tap the (SPACE BAR) once.

13. Insert the Zip field, and tap (ENTER) twice.

14. Type **Dear**, and tap the (SPACE BAR) once.

15. Insert the Title field, and tap the (SPACE BAR) once.

16. Insert the LastName field, type a colon **:**, and tap (ENTER) twice.

17. Type the first and second paragraphs as shown in the following letter until you reach the location that requires the phone number.

18. Insert the WorkPhone field; then type a period. Type the remainder of the paragraph; then tap (ENTER) twice.

19. Insert the Title field, and tap the (SPACE BAR) once.

20. Insert the FirstName field, type a comma, and tap the (SPACE BAR) once.

21. Complete the remainder of the letter as shown below.

22. Take a few moments to edit your letter and make sure it matches the example. In particular, make sure you have the proper punctuation (commas and spaces) between the various fields. Any punctuation that appears in your form letter will also appear in the merged letters.

23. Save the document as **Hands-On Lesson 9 - Form Letter**.
    Leave the document open; you will continue to work with it.

Robinson Financial Services
899 Ramiro Street, Manhattan Beach, CA 90245

Today's Date

«Title» «FirstName» «LastName»
«Company»
«Address1»
«City», «State» «Zip»

Dear «Title» «LastName»:

Thank you for your recent purchase of our Infinity Financial Services Package. In order for us to provide you with superior service, we must verify your phone number.

We currently have your phone number listed as «WorkPhone». Please contact us if this number is not accurate.

«Title» «LastName», thank you once again for your business.

Sincerely,

Linda Adams
Chief Executive Officer

The Main Document Mail Merge Toolbar

The Mail Merge Main Document toolbar is displayed whenever you display a main document. This toolbar contains buttons that let you manage and control the merge. Several of the buttons let you simulate the merge before it is actually performed. These buttons are helpful for debugging a merge when problems occur.

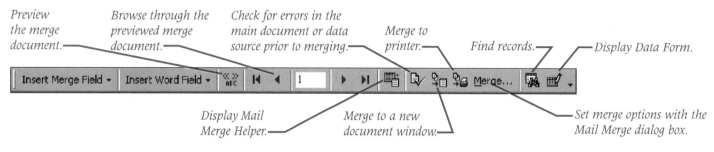

Preview the merge document. — *Browse through the previewed merge document.* — *Check for errors in the main document or data source prior to merging.* — *Merge to printer.* — *Find records.* — *Display Data Form.*

Display Mail Merge Helper. — *Merge to a new document window.* — *Set merge options with the Mail Merge dialog box.*

 ## Hands-On 9.7 Preview the Merge Document

1. Click the View Merged Data button to display a preview of the merge document.
   The first page of the merge document will be displayed. The merge hasn't occurred yet. You are simply previewing the first page of the merge document. Notice that data from the data source has replaced the merge fields.

2. Click the Next Record button on the Mail Merge toolbar to preview the next letter.

3. Use the Next Record and Previous Record buttons to browse through the letters.
   Browsing through the pages can help you spot errors in the form letter or data source prior to merging.

4. Click the View Merged Data button to redisplay the main document with the merge fields.
   You will explore the other toolbar buttons and merge the documents in the next exercise.

Conducting a Merge

Merging combines the main document with the data source to produce the merge document. If you are merging a form letter with a data source, Word creates a personalized copy of the letter for each record in the data source. The letters are separated by hard page breaks in the merge document.

Merge Techniques

The Merge to New Document button is located on the Mail Merge toolbar in the main document window. This button builds the merge document in a new document window. This is convenient because you can browse through the merge document prior to printing.

From the Keyboard

(ALT)+(SHIFT)+N to merge to new document
(ALT)+(SHIFT)+M to merge to printer

You can also merge directly to the printer using the Merge to Printer button. However, you should carefully check the main document and data source prior to using this type of merge. It is recommended that you preview the merge document with the View Merged Data button prior to conducting the merge.

To Save or Not to Save

Merge documents are rarely saved because they can easily be constructed by merging the main document with the data source. Another reason for not saving merge documents is that they often contain a large number of pages and may occupy large amounts of disk space. The merge document is usually checked for errors, printed, and then closed without saving. If the document contains errors, you can close it without saving, edit the main document or data source to fix the errors, and then conduct the merge again.

 Hands-On 9.8 Conduct the Merge

1. Click the Merge to New Document ⬚ button (fifth button from right side of toolbar).
   A new document window should appear with the merge document.

2. Scroll through the merge document.
   You should have a personalized letter for all seven records in the data source.

3. Browse through the merge document again, looking for errors.
   You will learn how to fix errors in the next topic.

4. Close the merge document without saving it.
   You will continue to work with the main document in the next exercise.

Debugging a Merge

Several common errors will cause a merge to fail or to produce incorrect results. It is important for you to be able to debug (or fix) these errors in an efficient and systematic manner. The Mail Merge toolbar in the main document window has several buttons to help you debug the merge. You already used the preview options in a previous exercise.

Fixing Errors

The merge document will usually provide clues as to why the merge failed or did not produce the intended results. Once you have identified an error in the merge document, you can switch to the main document or data source to locate the error and fix it. The merge can then be conducted again to see if the error has been fixed. This process is repeated until the merge works as intended.

Common Problems

Several common problems occur in merges. These problems and their solutions are discussed in the following Quick Reference table.

COMMON MERGE PROBLEMS AND THEIR SOLUTIONS	
Problem	**Solution**
There is a punctuation or formatting mistake in all of the merged letters.	The problem is in the main document since it occurs in all of the letters. The solution is to correct the mistake in the main document, and redo the merge.
Some of the merged letters have blank lines in the wrong locations.	This problem often occurs because some records in the data source have empty fields. Word may insert a blank line in the merged letter if there is an empty field in the data source. The following steps correct this problem. ■ Display the main document. ■ Click the Merge ⟦Merge...⟧ button on the Mail Merge toolbar. ■ Choose the *Don't print blank lines when data fields are empty* option, and redo the merge.
Some of the data is incorrect.	Switch to the data source, edit the data, and redo the merge.

 ## Hands-On 9.9 Use Merge Debugging Techniques

In this exercise, you will redo the merge several times, using various buttons on the Merge toolbar. The form letter should still be open.

Check for Errors

1. Click the Check for Errors 🗹 button on the Mail Merge toolbar.
   As you can see, the Checking and Reporting Errors dialog box provides several options to assist you in debugging a merge.

2. Make sure the middle option is chosen, and click **OK.**
   Word will merge the two documents and prompt you if errors are encountered.

3. If errors are reported, then try to resolve them using the techniques described in the preceding Quick Reference table.

4. When you have finished, close the merge document without saving it.
   The main document should be displayed.

5. Click the Merge 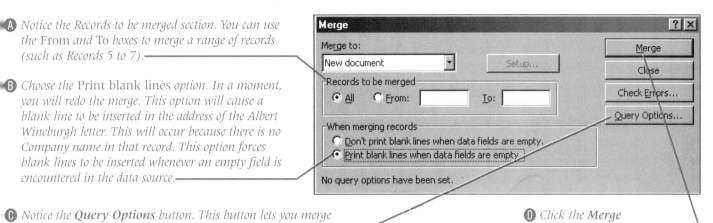 button on the Mail Merge toolbar.

6. Follow these steps to explore the Merge dialog box prior to merging.

A *Notice the Records to be merged section. You can use the* From *and* To *boxes to merge a range of records (such as Records 5 to 7).*

B *Choose the* Print blank lines *option. In a moment, you will redo the merge. This option will cause a blank line to be inserted in the address of the Albert Wineburgh letter. This will occur because there is no Company name in that record. This option forces blank lines to be inserted whenever an empty field is encountered in the data source.*

C *Notice the **Query Options** button. This button lets you merge only certain records (such as all addresses where the state is NY).*

D *Click the **Merge** button to conduct the merge.*

7. Scroll to the last letter in the merge document, and you will see a blank line between Albert Wineburgh and the address.
   The Print blank lines *option caused Word to insert the blank line.*

8. Close the merge document without saving it.

9. Click the Merge 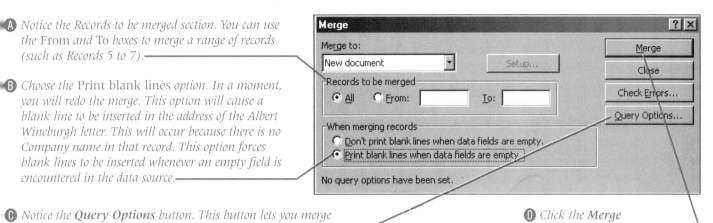 button on the Mail Merge toolbar.

10. Choose the D*on't print blank lines when data fields are empty* option, and click the **Merge** button.

11. Scroll down to the Albert Wineburgh letter, and the blank line should be removed.

12. Close the merge document without saving it.

13. Feel free to experiment with the various buttons on the Merge toolbar. After each merge is complete, close the merge document without saving it.

14. When you have finished, save the changes to the form letter and data source, and close them.

Generating Envelopes with Mail Merge

You can use mail merge to generate an envelope for each record in a data source. The Mail Merge Helper simplifies this task by helping you set up the envelope layout in the main document. The Mail Merge Helper lets you choose the envelope size and envelope formats, and displays a dialog box with an **Insert Merge Field** button. You use this button to insert merge fields in the envelope layout. When you have finished, you can save the envelope layout as you would save any other main document.

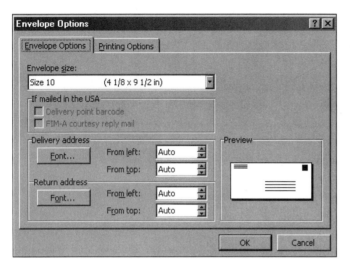
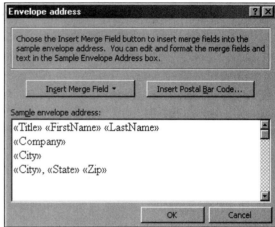

The Mail Merge Helper guides you through the setup of the envelope main document.

Hands-On 9.10 Generate Envelopes

In this exercise, you will set up an envelope main document. You will merge the main document with the Hands-On Lesson 9 - Data Source file to generate envelopes.

Set Up the Envelope Main Document

1. If necessary, click the New button to start a new document.

2. Choose **Tools→Mail Merge** from the menu bar.

3. Click the **Create** button, and choose **Envelopes.**

4. Click the **Active Window** button.

5. Click the **Get Data** button, and choose **Open Data Source.**

6. Choose Hands-On Lesson 9 - Data Source, and click **Open.**

7. Click the **Set Up Main Document** button.

8. Click **OK** to accept the default envelope size and other settings.
   The Envelope address box will appear. In the next few steps, you will enter merge fields into this box. Word will take care of the actual positioning of the merge fields on the envelope.

9. Click the **Insert Merge Field** button, and choose Title.

10. Tap the (SPACE BAR) once.

11. Click the **Insert Merge Field** button, and choose FirstName.

12. Tap the (SPACE BAR), and insert the LastName field.

13. Tap (ENTER), and insert the Company field.

14. Tap (ENTER) and insert the following fields. Make sure you insert spaces between the fields as necessary.
    Notice that no comma is shown after the City field. You will learn why a comma is not included in the next topic.

    <<Address1>>
    <<City>> <<State>> <<Zip>>

Insert a Postal Bar Code

15. Click the **Insert Postal Bar Code** button.

16. Click the drop-down ⬛ button.

17. Scroll through the list, and choose **Zip.**
    This tells Word to use the Zip field to determine the bar code to insert in each merged envelope.

18. Click **OK** on the Insert Postal Bar Code dialog box; then click **OK** on the Envelope Address box.

Conduct the Merge

19. Click the **Merge** button on the Mail Merge Helper dialog box; then click the **Merge** button on the Merge dialog box.
    Word will generate an envelope for each address in the data source.

20. Browse through the envelopes. There should be a bar code and delivery address on each envelope.

21. Close the merged envelopes without saving them.
    Word will display the merge main document, which contains an envelope page size and Merge Fields. In the next step, you will enter a return address in this main document window.

Set Up a Return Address

22. Type the following return address at the top left corner of the envelope.

    Robinson Financial Services
    899 Ramiro Boulevard
    Manhattan Beach, CA 90245

23. Redo the merge by clicking the Merge to New Document 🔲 button.

24. Close the merged envelopes without saving them.

25. Save the main document as **Hands-On Lesson 9—Envelope Main Document,** and then close it.

Labels

The **Tools→Envelopes and Labels** command displays the Envelopes and Labels dialog box. You can use the Labels tab on the dialog box to set up mailing labels, Rolodex® cards, nametags, diskette labels, and other items with a labels format. Word provides built-in label formats for Avery® labels sheets, and labels sheets from other manufacturers. The following illustration discusses the Labels tab on the Envelopes and Labels dialog box.

You can type a label in the Address *box or click the* Address *book and choose a label from Word's address book.*

The **New Document** *button uses the address in the* Address *box to create a full page of labels in a new document. If the* Address *box is empty, then a sheet of blank labels is created.*

You can choose a label format and set other options.

The Print options are used if the **Print** *button is clicked instead of the* **New Document** *button. Either a full page of labels is printed, or a single label is printed in the position (row and column) specified.*

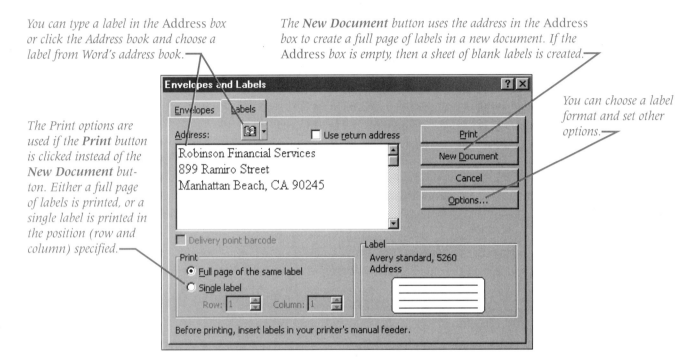

Typing Mailing Labels

The United States Postal Service recommends that labels be printed in all caps, without punctuation, and without formatting. These recommendations facilitate mail sorting and OCR (Optical Character Recognition) processing. You should use these recommendations if you are typing labels on a sheet.

Formatting Labels

You can also use the Envelopes and Labels dialog box to prepare nametags, Rolodex® cards, diskette labels and other items that may look better formatted. If you wish to format labels prior to printing, it is best to use the **New Document** button to create a blank sheet of labels. When you create a labels sheet, Word sets up a table that occupies the entire page. The easiest way to prepare formatted labels is to type the desired label text in a cell, format the text, and then copy and paste it to the other table cells. The following illustrations show the mailing label format recommended by the U.S. Postal Service and a formatted nametag label.

MR BOB BARKER
CABINET CREATIONS
6340 PALM DRIVE
ROCKRIDGE FL 32955

Robinson Financial Services

Planning for Retirement Seminar

Mailing Label

Formatted Nametag

Hands-On 9.11 **Set Up Labels**

Choose a Labels Type

1. Start a new document, and choose **Tools→Envelopes and Labels** from the menu bar.

2. Click the Labels tab, and click the **Options** button to display the Label Options box.

3. Follow these steps to choose a labels format.

Ⓐ *Choose the* Laser and ink jet *option (even if you have a dot matrix printer). Laser and inkjet labels are distributed on sheets, while dot matrix labels are on tractor-fed rolls.*

Ⓑ *Make sure Avery Standard is chosen.*

Ⓒ *Scroll through this list, and choose 5160 - Address. Notice the Label Information to the right of the list. These labels measure 1" in height by 2.63" in width.*

Ⓓ *Notice the* **New Label** *button (but don't click it). This button lets you create custom label formats. It uses the label specifications for the current label (5160) as a starting point for the custom label format.*

Label Options ? ✕

┌─ Printer information ─────────────────────┐
  ○ Dot matrix
  ● Laser and ink jet   Tray: Manual sheet feed ▼
└──┘

Label products: Avery standard ▼

Product number:
```
5096 - Diskette
5097 - Diskette
5160 - Address
5161 - Address
5162 - Address
5163 - Shipping
5164 - Shipping
```

┌─ Label information ──────┐
  Type: Address
  Height: 1"
  Width: 2.63"
  Page size: Letter (8 ½ x 11 in)
└──────────────────────────┘

[OK] [Cancel] [Details...] [New Label...] [Delete]

4. Click **OK** to choose the 5160 format.
   You could type an address in the Address box. However, you will create a sheet of blank labels instead.

Type Several Labels

5. Click the **New Document** button.
   Word will open a new document window. A table with three columns and eleven rows will occupy the page.

6. If you can't see the table, then choose **Table→Show Gridlines.**

TIP!

Use (TAB) *to move forward one cell, and* (SHIFT)+ (TAB) *to move back one cell.*

7. Click in any table cell.
   You can enter text in a table cell by clicking in the cell and then typing the desired text.

8. Click in the first table cell to position the insertion point in that cell.

9. Enter the following addresses into the first table row.
   Notice that the addresses are in all caps with no punctuation to facilitate postal service mail sorting.

```
MR BOB BARKER        MR JACKSON JOHNSON    MRS CINDY JOHNSON
CABINET CREATIONS    SDT ENTERPRISES       4220 EDWARD STREET
6340 PALM DRIVE      1250 HALCOURT WAY     NORTHLAKE IL 60164
ROCKRIDGE FL 32955   EL SOBRANTE CA 94804
```

10. Feel free to print the labels. You can print on a regular sheet of paper or use a sheet of Avery 5160 labels (if you happen to have one).

11. Save the document as **Hands-On Lesson 9—Typed Labels,** and then close the document.

(Continued on the next page)

Create Name Badges

In the remainder of this exercise, you will choose a labels format for name badges.

12. Choose **Tools→Envelopes and Labels** from the menu bar.

13. Click the **Options** button.

14. Choose the 5095 Name Badge format from the Product Number list, and click **OK.**

15. Type the following text in the Address box on the Envelopes and Labels dialog box.

    Robinson Financial Services
    Planning for Retirement Seminar

16. Click the **New Document** button to create the labels sheet.
    Notice that this format displays eight name badges in a two-column by four-row format. The text you typed in the Address box should be displayed in each cell. At this point, you could format the text by applying text and paragraph formats. If you intend to format labels, it is actually easier to create a blank sheet, type and format one label, and then copy and paste the label to the other cells.

17. Feel free to format your name badges. You have not learned how to work with tables yet; however, you can't hurt anything by attempting to format the labels sheet.

18. Save the name badge document as **Hands-On Lesson 9—Name Badges,** and then close the document.

Generating Labels with Mail Merge

You can use mail merge to generate a label for each record in a data source. The Mail Merge Helper simplifies this task by helping you set up the labels layout in the main document. The Mail Merge Helper lets you choose the label format and displays a dialog box with an **Insert Merge Field** button. You use this button to insert merge fields in the labels layout. When you have finished, you can save the labels layout as you would save any other main document.

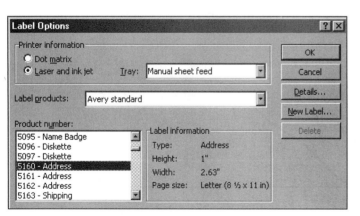
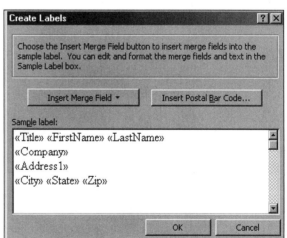

The Mail Merge Helper guides you through the setup of the labels main document.

Formatting Merged Labels

You learned in the previous topic that the U.S. Postal Service prefers label addresses to be printed in all caps. However, data sources will rarely have addresses formatted in all capital letters. You can use the following techniques to facilitate mail sorting if your labels originate from a data source.

■ Do not include punctuation marks when inserting merge fields in the Create Labels box. For example, the illustration on the preceding page shows the Create Labels box with the merge fields inserted. Notice that there is no comma after the <<City>> field.

■ Select the entire document after the labels have been merged with the **Edit→Select All** command. Then choose **Format→Change Case,** and choose the Uppercase option to change all label text to uppercase.

 ## Hands-On 9.12 Generate Mailing Labels

In this exercise, you will set up a labels main document. You will merge the main document with the Hands-On Lesson 9 - Data Source file to generate labels.

Set Up the Labels Main Document

1. A new document window should be displayed from the previous exercise. If not, then start a new document.

2. Choose **Tools→Mail Merge** from the menu bar.

3. Click the **Create** button, and choose **Mailing Labels.**

4. Click the **Active Window** button. — *N EW MAIN DOC*

5. Click the **Get Data** button, and choose **Open Data Source.**

6. Choose Hands-On Lesson 9 - Data Source, and click **Open.**

7. Click the **Set Up Main Document** button.

8. Choose the 5160 Address labels format, and click **OK.**
   The Create Labels box will appear. In the next few steps, you will enter merge fields into this box.

Insert Merge Fields

9. Click the **Insert Merge Field** button, and choose Title.

10. Tap the (SPACE BAR) once.

11. Click the **Insert Merge Field** button, and choose FirstName.

12. Tap (SPACE BAR), and insert the LastName field.

13. Tap (ENTER), and insert the Company field.

14. Tap (ENTER) and insert the following fields. Make sure you insert spaces between the City, State, and Zip fields.

    ```
    <<Address1>>
    <<City>> <<State>> <<Zip>>
    ```

15. Click **OK** when you have finished inserting the fields.

(Continued on the next page)

16. Click the **Close** button on the Mail Merge Helper box.
    You could have merged the labels prior to closing the box; however, you will examine the labels main document first.

17. Take a moment to examine the labels main document.
    Notice that the merge fields have been repeated in each cell of the labels sheet. As you can see, the Mail Merge Helper is quite useful for setting up a Labels main document.

Conduct the Merge

18. Click the Merge to New Document ⬚ button on the Mail Merge toolbar.
    Word will generate a mailing label for each address in the data source.

19. Feel free to print the labels on a blank sheet of paper or on a labels sheet if you happen to have an Avery 5160 sheet.

20. Close the merged labels document without saving it.
    Word will display the labels main document.

21. Click the Save ⬚ button, and save the main document as **Hands-On Lesson 9 - Labels Main Document.**
    Do not close the document; you will continue to use it in the next exercise.

Using Alternate Data Sources

You can use alternate data sources in a mail merge. The primary sources of external data include text files, Excel workbooks, Access databases, and Outlook address books. The Mail Merge Helper guides you through the process of choosing an alternate data source.

Accessing Excel Workbooks and Access Databases

Excel worksheets and Access tables have the same tabular structure as Word data source tables. If you use an Excel worksheet or Access table as a data source, the header row provides the field names of the data source. The remaining rows become the records. The following illustration shows the Excel worksheet you will use as a data source in the next Hands-On exercise.

The header row will be used for the field names of the data source.

Each row with data is a record.

	A	B	C	D	E	F	G	H	I	J
1	Customer ID	Title	FirstName	LastName	Company	Address1	City	State	Zip	WorkPhone
2	4543	Mr.	Bob	Barker	Cabinet Creations	6340 Palm Drive	Rockridge	FL	32955	(800) 323-4567
3	2345	Mr.	Jackson	Johnson	SDT	1250 Halcourt Way	El Sobrante	CA	94804	(510) 223-1221
4	4623	Mrs.	Cindy	Johnson		4220 Edward Street	Northlake	IL	60164	(217) 212-3232
5	4123	Mr.	Jason	Jones	Peninsula Trading Co.	2233 Crystal Street	San Mateo	CA	94403	(650) 2213243
6	2333	Mr.	Ed	Larkson	Albertsons	2300 Watson Street	Cainesville	OH	43701	(800) 901-9876
7	1353	Ms.	Tammy	Olson	Freemont Medical	1200 Big Pine Drive	Moses Lake	WA	98837	(800) 343-4546
8	3435	Mr.	Mark	Roth		760 Maple Avenue	Fremont	CA	94538	(510) 454-6789
9	4345	Mr.	Tony	Simpson	Bellmont Trading	312 York Lane	Richmond	CA	94804	(510) 223-7890
10	1234	Ms.	Alicia	Worthington	Worthington Technologies	3300 Victory Lane	San Diego	CA	90455	(619) 345-6655

Using the Mail Merge Helper with Excel Worksheets and Access Databases

The Mail Merge Helper is particularly helpful if you are accessing an Excel workbook or an Access database. If you are accessing an Excel workbook, you will be asked if you want to access the entire worksheet, a named range, or a cell range. If you are accessing an Access database, you will be asked to choose the database table that contains the data.

Using the Mail Merge Helper to access Excel workbooks or Access databases.

USING ALTERNATE DATA SOURCES

■ Use the Tools→Mail Merge command to open the Mail Merge Helper dialog box.

■ Start a new main document, or open an existing main document.

■ Click the Get Data button, and choose Open Data Source.

■ Choose the appropriate file type from the Files of Type list at the bottom of the Open Data Source dialog box. For example, choose MS Excel Worksheets if the data is in an Excel workbook.

■ Choose the data file in the Open Data Source dialog box, and click Open.

■ Follow the remaining steps presented by the Mail Merge Helper. The steps will vary slightly depending upon the type of data source you are accessing.

In this exercise, you will use an Excel workbook on your exercise diskette as a data source. You will merge the labels main document with the data source. The labels main document should still be open from the previous exercise.

Examine the Data Source

1. Click the [Start] button, and choose **Programs→Microsoft Excel** to start the Excel program.
   The Excel worksheet window will appear.

2. Click the Open [icon] button, and navigate to your exercise diskette.

3. Open the file named **Hands-On Lesson 9 - Excel Data Source.**
   Take a moment to examine the worksheet. Notice the headings in Row 1. These headings will appear as field names when you insert fields using the Mail Merge Helper. The data in rows 2–10 will be used to generate mailing labels.

4. Choose **File→Exit** from the menu bar to close the data source and Excel.

Attach the New Data Source to the Main Document

In the next few steps, you will attach the Excel data source to the labels main document. The labels main document is currently attached to the Word data source you set up earlier in this lesson. You use the Mail Merge Helper to attach new data sources to main documents.

5. Choose **Tools→Mail Merge** from the menu bar.

6. Click the **Get Data** button, and choose **Open Data Source.**

7. Choose MS Excel Worksheets from the Files of Type box at the bottom of the dialog box.
   This option must be chosen or you won't see the Excel workbook listed in the dialog box.

8. Choose the **Hands-On Lesson 9 - Excel Data Source** file, and click the **Open** button.

9. Click **OK** when the Microsoft Excel dialog box appears to choose the Entire Spreadsheet option. Choose Yes if Word asks you to save the Hands-On Lesson 9 - Data Source document.
   The Entire Spreadsheet option instructs Word to include all records in the worksheet during the merge. You will see several messages flashing on the status bar at the bottom of the screen as the link is established with the Excel workbook.

10. Click the **Close** button on the Mail Merge Helper dialog box.

11. Click the Merge to New Document [icon] button on the Mail Merge toolbar.
    Word will merge the documents and generate a merge document with nine labels.

12. Take a moment to examine the merge document, and then close the document without saving it.

13. Save the changes to the **Hands-On Lesson 9 - Labels Main Document,** and then close it.
    The document will close, and the Excel program window should close automatically.

14. Feel free to experiment with any of the merge techniques you have learned in this lesson. You can use any of the main documents or data sources you have worked with throughout the lesson.

Concepts Review

True/False Questions

1. Each row in a data source table contains one record.   TRUE   FALSE

2. You cannot merge a portion of a field into a main document.   TRUE   FALSE

3. You will have more flexibility in a merge if you use more fields in the data source.   TRUE   FALSE

4. A typical form letter contains text and fields.   TRUE   FALSE

5. The merge document is usually saved.   TRUE   FALSE

6. Mail Merge can use an Outlook address book as a data source.   TRUE   FALSE

7. Mail Merge can be used to generate mailing labels.   TRUE   FALSE

8. The U.S. Postal Service recommends that labels be printed in all caps.   TRUE   FALSE

Multiple-Choice Questions

1. Which command displays the Mail Merge Helper?
   a. Tools→Mail Merge
   b. Format→Mail Merge
   c. Insert→Mail Merge
   d. None of these

2. Which button is used to move to the next record in the Data Form dialog box?
   a.
   b.
   c.
   d. None of these

3. If the first name and last name are part of the same field, then which of the following statements describes the impact this will have on your merging flexibility?
   a. It will have little impact.
   b. You will not be able to merge just the first name into a form letter.
   c. You will not be able to merge just the last name into a form letter.
   d. Both B and C

4. Which statement most accurately describes the function of the **Insert Merge Field** button on the Mail Merge Main Document toolbar?
   a. This button displays the same field names that are in the data source.
   b. This button displays only the field names that have been inserted in the main document.
   c. This button does not appear in the main document.
   d. None of these

Skill Builders

Skill Builder 9.1 Set Up a New Mail Merge

Set Up the Data Source

1. If necessary, close all open documents, and then click the New ⬜ button to start a new document.

2. Choose **Tools**→**Mail Merge** from the menu bar.

3. Click the **Create** button, and choose **Form Letters**.

4. Click the **Active Window** button.

5. Click the **Get Data** button, and choose **Create Data Source**.

6. Use the **Remove Field Name** button to remove the following fields (you will need to select the field names on the list before clicking the button).

   JobTitle
   Address2
   Country
   HomePhone

7. Click **OK** to complete the data source design.

8. Save the data source as **Skill Builder 9.1 - Data Source**.

Enter Data

9. Click the **Edit Data Source** button.

10. Follow these guidelines to enter the six records shown below.

    ▪ If a record has no data for a field (such as no company name), then leave the field empty.

    ▪ Don't type commas after the city names. The commas will be inserted in the form letter.

    ▪ Use the Forward ▶ and Back ◀ buttons on the record navigation bar to browse through the records when you have finished. Check your data entry for accuracy.

    ▪ You can enter these records in any order. You will sort the records later in this exercise.

Mr. Sean Corn	Mr. Craig Dostie	Mr. Alex Lopez
308 Alhambra Avenue	Whole Life, Inc.	2134 Harbor Blvd.
Monterey Park, CA 91754	31200 Erwin Street	Costa Mesa, CA 92626
	Woodland Hills, CA 91367	(714) 966-9855
Mr. Winston Boey	Mr. Phil Arnold	Ms. Margaret Wong
Pasadena City College	Pasadena City College	Popcorn Video
263 East Howard Street	4745 Buffin Avenue	1308 West Ramona Blvd.
Pasadena, CA 91104	Fremont, CA 94536	Alhambra, CA 91803
	(408) 794-4950	(818) 576-8883

Sort the Records

11. Click the **View Source** button.

12. Click anywhere in the LastName column, and click the Sort Ascending [icon] button on the Mail Merge toolbar.

    This will sort the records in alphabetical order by last name.

13. Click the Mail Merge Main Document [icon] button on the right end of the Mail Merge toolbar.

    The blank main document window should be displayed.

TIP!

If the data source is open, you can switch between the main document and data source by clicking their buttons on the TaskBar.

Set Up the Form Letter

14. Set up the letterhead shown below. Use the Borders and Shading dialog box to insert the border under the telephone number as shown. Use whichever fonts you desire for the letterhead. The example below uses an Arial 10 font for the address and phone number and an Arial 12 Bold font for the organization name. However, set the font for the date and the remainder of the letter to Times New Roman 12. The date should be positioned approximately 1″ below the border of the letterhead.

West Coast Youth Services
2500 Ocean Avenue
Monterey Park, CA 91753
(310) 235-6459

Today's Date

(Continued on the next page)

15. Tap (ENTER) four times after the date, and type the remainder of the form letter shown below. Use the **Insert Merge Field** button to insert merge fields as shown in the letter. Make sure you include spaces, commas, and colons in the appropriate locations.

West Coast Youth Services
2500 Ocean Avenue
Monterey Park, CA 91753
(310) 235-6459

Today's Date

«Title» «FirstName» «LastName»
«Company»
«Address1»
«City», «State» «PostalCode»

Dear «Title» «LastName»:

We have decided to hold the annual fundraiser on July 15 in Los Angeles. As you know, last year's fundraiser was a huge success. We hope to make this year's fundraiser equally successful. This will require early planning and effective advertising.

Please RSVP as soon as possible. I must know if you can participate in the event. I would truly appreciate your support and commitment.

Also, I have your updated address, but I may need an updated telephone number. I currently have your telephone number listed as «WorkPhone». Please contact me and let me know if your number has changed.

Sincerely,

Cynthia Thompson
Fundraising Director

---

16. Spell check the document, and check it over to make sure there are no mistakes.
    The document should be ready for merging.

Conduct the Merge

17. Use the Merge to New Document ⊞ button to conduct the merge.

18. Browse through the merge document.
    Notice that the letterhead formatting has been inserted into every letter. If you locate mistakes in any of the merged letters, then close the merge document without saving it, make corrections in the main document or data source, and merge the documents again.

19. Close the merge document without saving it.

20. Save the form letter as **Skill Builder 9.1 - Form Letter**, and the close it.

21. Save the changes to the data source, and then close it.

Skill Builder 9.2 Edit a Form Letter and Data Source

In this exercise, you will open the form letter that was set up in the previous exercise. You will edit the form letter and the data source.

Edit the Form Letter

1. Open the document named **Skill Builder 9.1 - Form Letter.**

2. Change the date in the first paragraph from July 15 to **June 23**.

Edit Records in the Data Source

3. Click the Edit Data Source ⊞ button at the right end of the Merge toolbar.

4. Navigate to the Margaret Wong record.

5. Click the **Delete** button to remove the record.

6. Click the **Add New** button, and enter the following data in the new record.

   ```
   Mr. Pat Carry
   800 Ridge Road
   Monterey, CA 92340
   ```

7. Click **OK** to return to the main document.

Conduct the Merge

8. Use the Merge to New Document ⊞ button to conduct the merge.

9. Browse through the merge document, and you should see the Pat Carry letter. Also, all letters should have the new date July 15.

10. Close the merge document without saving it.
    The Skill Builder 9.1 - Form Letter document should still be open.

(Continued on the next page)

Merge the Form Letter with a Different Data Source

In the next few steps, you will use the Mail Merge Helper to attach a different data source to the main document. The new data source is located on your exercise diskette.

11. Choose **Tools→Mail Merge** to display the Mail Merge Helper.

12. Click the **Get Data** button, and choose **Open Data Source.**

13. Choose the file named **Skill Builder 9.2 - Data Source,** and click **Open.**

14. Click the **Yes** button if Word asks you if you want to save **Skill Builder 9.1 - Data Source.**
    The Skill Builder 9.2 - Data Source is now attached to the main document.

15. Click the **Merge** button, and then click the **Merge** button on the next dialog box.

16. Browse through the merge document, and you will notice that there are only two letters.
    The Skill Builder 9.2 - Data Source contains only two records.

17. Close the merge document without saving it.

18. Click the Edit Data Source [icon] button.

19. Use the scroll bar to scroll down through the field names, and notice a HomePhone field below the WorkPhone field.
    This field was not in the Skill Builder 9.1 data source. A data source can always have more fields than the main document. The main document uses only the fields it needs.

20. Click **OK** to return to the main document.

21. Save the main document, and then close it.

22. Save the changes to the data source if Word prompts you to do so.

Skill Builder 9.3 Generate Envelopes

1. Start a new document and choose **Tools→Mail Merge** from the menu bar.

2. Click the **Create** button, and choose **Envelopes.**

3. Click the **Active Window** button.

4. Click the **Get Data** button, and choose **Open Data Source.**

5. Choose **Skill Builder 9.1 - Data Source,** and click **Open.**

6. Click the **Set Up Main Document** button.

7. Click **OK** to accept the default envelope size and other settings.

8. Insert the following merge fields.
   Notice that there is no comma after the city. This helps facilitate postal service mail sorting.

   <<Title>> <<FirstName>> <<LastName>>
   <<Address1>>
   <<City>> <<State>> <<Postal Code>>

9. Click **OK,** and then merge the envelope with the data source.

10. Browse through the merge document, and make sure the merge worked correctly. If necessary, correct any mistakes, and then redo the merge.

11. When you have finished, close all open documents without saving them.

Assessments

Assessment 9.1 Set Up a Merge

1. Use the Mail Merge Helper and the following guidelines to set up a form letter and data source.

■ Create the form letter shown below. Use the three records shown below the letter to set up the data source.

■ Name the form letter **Assessment 9.1 - Form Letter** and the data source **Assessment 9.1 - Data Source**.

■ Insert the date in the form letter as a field that updates automatically.

Date Code

«Title» «FirstName» «LastName»
«Company»
«Address1»
«City», «State» «PostalCode»

Dear «Title» «LastName»:

The purpose of this letter is to inform you that your health club membership is about to expire. You have been an excellent member for some time, so we would like to offer you a low renewal rate of just $99 per year.

Please contact me as soon as possible. This offer will expire on March 31. Also, we currently have your phone number listed as «WorkPhone». Please return the enclosed change of address card and let me know if this number is still valid.

Sincerely,

Dave Nelson
Renewals Manager

Enclosure

Mr. David Roth	Mrs. Tammy Simpson	Mr. Jason Williams
760 Maple Avenue	Barkers Books	2233 Crystal Street
Fremont, CA 94538	312 Tennessee Street	San Mateo, CA 94403
(510) 234-9090	Richmond, CA 94804	(415) 312-2312
	(510) 238-2233	

2. Merge the form letter with the data source. You may want to demonstrate the merge to your instructor.

3. Close the merge document without saving it. Close the form letter, and save the changes to it and the data source if requested.

Assessment 9.2 **Generate Envelopes**

1. Use the Mail Merge Helper to set up an envelope main document using a standard Size 10 envelope. Use the **Assessment 9.1 - Data Source** file as the data source.

2. Include the following fields in the envelope main document.

   <<Title>> <<FirstName>> <<LastName>>
   <<Company>>
   <<Address1>>
   <<City>> <<State>> <<Postal Code>>

3. Use the following return address for the envelope main document.

   Global Fitness
   14460 San Pablo Avenue
   Richmond, CA 94804

4. Save the envelope main document as **Assessment 9.2 - Main Document.**

5. Merge the envelope main document with the data source. You may want to demonstrate the merge to your instructor.

6. Close the merge document without saving it.

7. Close the main document, and save the changes to it and the data source if requested to do so.

Assessment 9.3 **Generate Labels**

1. Use the Mail Merge Helper to set up a mailing labels main document using an Avery 5160 labels definition. Use the **Assessment 9.1 - Data Source** file as the data source, and use the same merge fields as in Assessment 9.2 (although a return address is not required).

2. Save the labels main document as **Assessment 9.3 - Main Document.**

3. Merge the labels main document with the data source. You may want to demonstrate the merge to your instructor.

4. Close the merge document without saving it.

5. Close the main document, and save the changes to it and the data source if requested to do so.

Critical Thinking

Critical Thinking 9.1 On Your Own

Donald Livingston, the Director of Marketing for Big Time Video Distributors, has some big ideas of his own. Until now, Big Time has operated as a local distribution company servicing small video stores in the local area. But Donald wants Big Time to become a distributor to distributors. He has identified the six key contacts shown below as prime candidates for his new marketing idea.

Tony Simpson Marketing Director Bigger Time Video Distributors 312 York Lane Richmond, CA 94804	Jason Jones Marketing Director Move It Distribution 2233 Crystal Street San Mateo, CA 94403	Debbie Thomas Marketing Director Hollywood Distribution 450 Crestwood Lane Austin, TX 78752
Wilma Boyd Marketing Director Boyd Distribution 855 State Street Richmond, NY 12954	Ted Wilkins Marketing Director Big Screen Distributors 900 C Street Fort Worth, TX 76104	Alice Simpson Marketing Director Popcorn Distribution 2450 Ridge Road Fort Worth, TX 76105

You have been assigned the task of preparing a form letter to be sent to the six contacts shown above. The form letter should be from Donald Livingston. The important points to include in the form letter are as follows:

Big Time will give smaller distributors the same access to new releases that large companies like BlockBuster receive.

Big Time will give volume discounts of up to 25%.

Big Time will provide the largest selection of DVDs in the industry.

Prepare a form letter using the information described above. Set up the data source using the contact information above. Save the form letter as **Critical Thinking 9.1—Form Letter** and the data source as **Critical Thinking 9.1—Data Source.** Close both the form letter and data source when you have finished.

Critical Thinking 9.2 On Your Own

Donald Livingston has identified the two additional contacts shown below as candidates for his new distribution program. Open the data source you created in Critical Thinking 9.1, and add the following contacts to the data source. When you have finished, save the changes to the data source, and close it.

Cynthia Adams	Gordon Johnson
Marketing Director	Marketing Director
Films At Home	Distribute It
1400 Main Lane	300 West Main Street
San Mateo, CA 94403	Austin, TX 78752

Set up an envelope main document using the Critical Thinking 9.1—Data Source document as the data source. You decide which address to use for the return address on the envelope. Save the completed main document as **Critical Thinking 9.2—Envelope.** Merge the envelope main document with the data source to determine that the merge functions correctly. Close the merged envelopes without saving them.

Critical Thinking 9.3 With a Group

You and your classmate have decided that a perfect marketing opportunity for your Health-e-Meals business is video distributors. You have decided to send a form letter to the distributor list set up in Critical Thinking 9.1 describing your plan. Your plan is as follows:

Provide video distributors with promotional literature that they can distribute to video stores. The video stores will then distribute the literature to their customers.

Each new customer that visits the Health-e-Meals.com site and uses the marketing code on the literature will receive a 20% discount.

Each time a customer purchases a meal using the marketing code, the distributor will receive a $1.00 cash payment.

Base a new document upon the letterhead **template** you created in Critical Thinking 8.4. Set up a form letter using the letterhead document and the data source created in Critical Thinking 9.1. The form letter should describe the program mentioned above. Save the completed form letter as **Critical Thinking 9.3—Form Letter.**

Base a new document upon the envelope **template** you created in Critical Thinking 8.4. Copy the return address, including the logo, to the Office clipboard. Set up an envelope main document using the data source created in Critical Thinking 9.1. Paste the copied logo and return address into the envelope main document. Save the completed envelope main document as **Critical Thinking 9.3—Envelope.**

Working with Tables

Tables are one of Word's most useful tools for organizing and formatting text, numbers, and graphics. Tables are powerful, flexible, and easy to use. Word provides a variety of tools that let you set up, modify, and format tables. In this lesson, you will use tables to create resumes and other documents. You will also learn important techniques for creating effective resumes.

In This Lesson

Case Study

Gladys Kline is employed as an Administrative Assistant at Renquist Communications. Recently, Gladys decided to search for other career opportunities. Although she enjoys working at Renquist, Gladys wants new challenges and opportunities for advancement. She begins her job search by preparing a resume. No serious job search can be conducted without one. There are a variety of resume formats from which Gladys can choose. However, she chooses the chronological format to emphasize her substantial employment history. Using Word 2000's powerful tables capabilities, Gladys produces a resume that is certain to impress any prospective employer.

Gladys Kline
845 Maple Street   El Cerrito, CA 94803   (510) 215-6902

OBJECTIVE:	To obtain an Administrative Assistant position where I can utilize my computer skills and extensive work experience.
EXPERIENCE: March 1995–Present	ADMINISTRATIVE ASSISTANT FOR DIRECTOR OF MARKETING, Renquist Communications, Fulton, CA • Compose letters, memorandums, and other business correspondence. • Maintain the Director of Marketing's schedule. • Manage multiple projects assigned by the Director of Marketing.
January 1992– February 1995	WORD PROCESSING SPECIALIST, Smart Paging Systems, Berkeley, CA • Composed documents as required by supervisor, using Microsoft Word for Windows. • Used Microsoft Excel to create worksheets.
January 1991– December 1992	STUDENT ASSISTANT, Contra Costa College, Pinole, CA • Assisted students with questions regarding financial aid. • Answered incoming telephone calls, filled out forms, and mailed literature.
EDUCATION:	Certificate of Completion, 1994, Bay Area R.O.P., Hayward, CA • Received extensive training in Office 2000 applications, office procedures, and keyboarding. A. S. Business Administration, Contra Costa College, 1992, Pinole, CA • Worked as a student intern for the Vice President of Sales at Chevron Corporation. • Extra-curricular activities included participation in student body government, athletics, and tutoring of disadvantaged youths.
COMPUTER SKILLS:	Word 2000, Excel 2000, PowerPoint 2000, Outlook 2000, Windows 98, Adobe Acrobat.

Resumes for the New Millennium

A resume is the most important tool in the job search process. When creating a resume, always keep the purpose of the resume in mind: to get an interview with a person who has the authority to hire you! Also keep in mind that a resume is just one of many tools that you will use in the job search process. The following general guidelines will help you develop effective resumes.

1. Always send a cover letter with your resume. The cover letter should provide a general overview of why you are interested in and qualified for the position.

2. Resumes should be short and to the point. In general, you should limit your resume to two pages at most. It is even better if you can condense your resume to a single page. Few employers have the time to review resumes that are longer than two pages. Once again, the purpose of the resume is to get the interview.

3. Resumes should be visually attractive and error-free. Your resume is a direct reflection of you. You should also print your resume on high-quality paper using a laser printer.

4. Hand-deliver resumes whenever possible. Personal contact is the most effective way to connect with employers. If hand-delivering a resume is impractical, then make sure you follow-up with a telephone call after the potential employer has had adequate time to review the resume.

Types of Resumes

There are three primary types of resumes that you can use depending upon your experience, skills, education, and the type of employment opportunity you are pursuing. If you are serious about finding employment, then you should develop all three types of resumes so that you have "a resume for every occasion." A brief overview of the three types follows. A more detailed discussion and examples of the various types appear on the following pages.

- **Chronological Resume**—A chronological resume is most effective when you have a history of employment and a track record of success. The chronological resume emphasizes your work experience by providing an overview of your experience in reverse chronological order.

- **Functional Resume**—A functional resume is useful when you want to de-emphasize paid work experience and emphasize skills. The functional resume emphasizes the functions or skills that you can contribute to the job.

- **Entry-level Resume or Skills Sheet**—This type of resume is useful for students who have little paid work experience or for individuals who are new to the job market. It emphasizes educational achievement and any type of skills the applicant may have.

Scannable Resumes

Technology has introduced dramatic changes in the methods employers use to screen potential applicants. Many large employers now scan resumes into an electronic database. Potential candidates are identified by querying the database for "key words" in the resumes. If you know an employer is scanning resumes, then use the following guidelines to create one that can be easily and accurately scanned.

1. Use plain white paper and print with a laser printer. Scanners may have difficulty identifying characters if you use colored paper or an ink jet printer.

2. Don't fold or bend the resume in any way.

3. Don't use bold, italics, underlining, or shading.

4. Use a 12-point font size and fonts that are easy to read. Appropriate fonts include Arial and Times New Roman.

5. Include keywords somewhere in the resume that will be picked up by the OCR (Optical Character Recognition) software. For example, employers often program OCR software to search for specific application names such as Word, Excel, and Outlook.

What to Include and Not to Include in a Resume

- Do include phrases or statements that demonstrate positive personal qualities, such as team player, excellent organizational skills, creative, and customer-oriented.

- Do not refer to your age, sex, marital status, height, weight, or other personal details unless they will help you get the job for which you are applying. Also, never list your social security number!

- Do not list references on a resume. References can be supplied on a separate reference sheet, or in person at the interview.

- Do not mention salary requirements or the amount of income you earned in previous occupations.

- Do not mention gaps in your employment history or the reasons for leaving previous positions. However, be prepared to address these issues at the interview.

Chronological Resume

Use a chronological resume when you have a significant amount of work experience that is applicable to the job for which you are applying. The most recent experience should appear first (reverse chronological order), as shown in the following example.

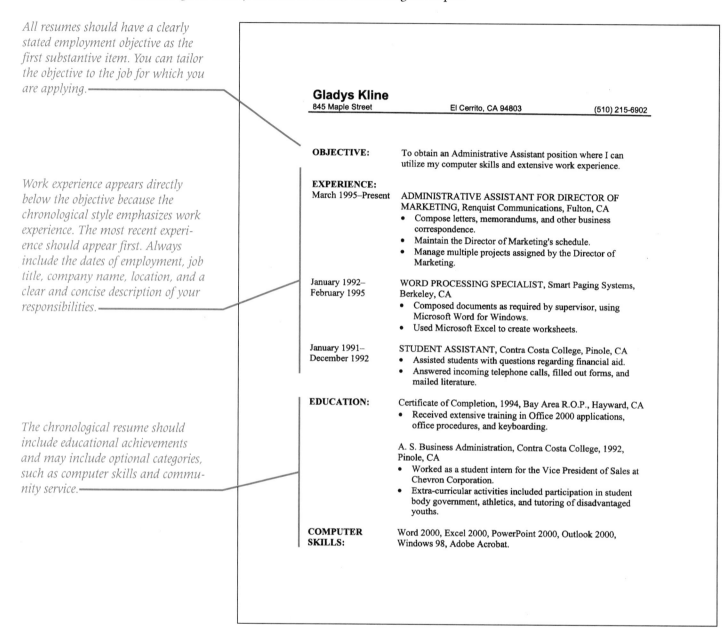

All resumes should have a clearly stated employment objective as the first substantive item. You can tailor the objective to the job for which you are applying.

Work experience appears directly below the objective because the chronological style emphasizes work experience. The most recent experience should appear first. Always include the dates of employment, job title, company name, location, and a clear and concise description of your responsibilities.

The chronological resume should include educational achievements and may include optional categories, such as computer skills and community service.

Gladys Kline
845 Maple Street   El Cerrito, CA 94803   (510) 215-6902

OBJECTIVE: To obtain an Administrative Assistant position where I can utilize my computer skills and extensive work experience.

EXPERIENCE:

March 1995–Present — ADMINISTRATIVE ASSISTANT FOR DIRECTOR OF MARKETING, Renquist Communications, Fulton, CA
- Compose letters, memorandums, and other business correspondence.
- Maintain the Director of Marketing's schedule.
- Manage multiple projects assigned by the Director of Marketing.

January 1992–February 1995 — WORD PROCESSING SPECIALIST, Smart Paging Systems, Berkeley, CA
- Composed documents as required by supervisor, using Microsoft Word for Windows.
- Used Microsoft Excel to create worksheets.

January 1991–December 1992 — STUDENT ASSISTANT, Contra Costa College, Pinole, CA
- Assisted students with questions regarding financial aid.
- Answered incoming telephone calls, filled out forms, and mailed literature.

EDUCATION: Certificate of Completion, 1994, Bay Area R.O.P., Hayward, CA
- Received extensive training in Office 2000 applications, office procedures, and keyboarding.

A. S. Business Administration, Contra Costa College, 1992, Pinole, CA
- Worked as a student intern for the Vice President of Sales at Chevron Corporation.
- Extra-curricular activities included participation in student body government, athletics, and tutoring of disadvantaged youths.

COMPUTER SKILLS: Word 2000, Excel 2000, PowerPoint 2000, Outlook 2000, Windows 98, Adobe Acrobat.

Functional Resume

Use a functional resume when you want to de-emphasize paid work experience, and emphasize skills. List skills that are applicable to the job for which you are applying.

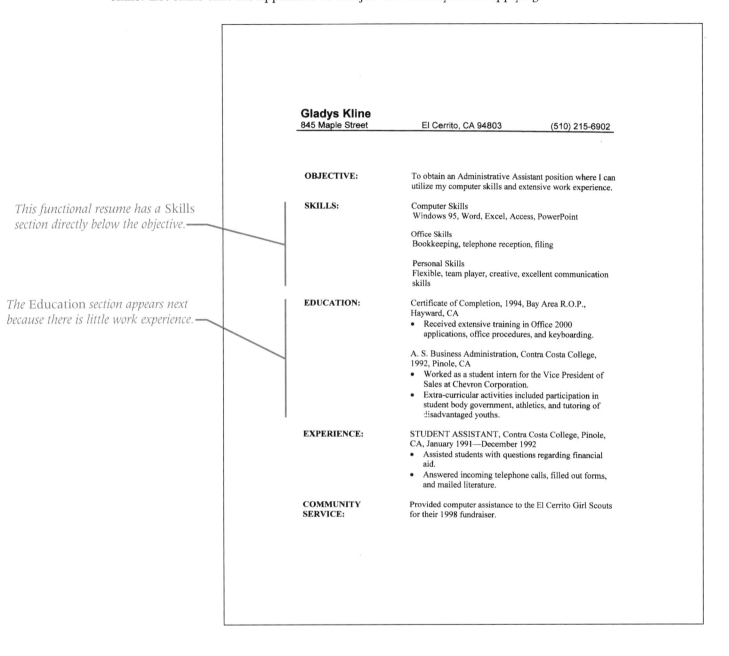

This functional resume has a Skills section directly below the objective.

The Education section appears next because there is little work experience.

Gladys Kline
845 Maple Street   El Cerrito, CA 94803   (510) 215-6902

OBJECTIVE: To obtain an Administrative Assistant position where I can utilize my computer skills and extensive work experience.

SKILLS: Computer Skills
Windows 95, Word, Excel, Access, PowerPoint

Office Skills
Bookkeeping, telephone reception, filing

Personal Skills
Flexible, team player, creative, excellent communication skills

EDUCATION: Certificate of Completion, 1994, Bay Area R.O.P., Hayward, CA
- Received extensive training in Office 2000 applications, office procedures, and keyboarding.

A. S. Business Administration, Contra Costa College, 1992, Pinole, CA
- Worked as a student intern for the Vice President of Sales at Chevron Corporation.
- Extra-curricular activities included participation in student body government, athletics, and tutoring of disadvantaged youths.

EXPERIENCE: STUDENT ASSISTANT, Contra Costa College, Pinole, CA, January 1991—December 1992
- Assisted students with questions regarding financial aid.
- Answered incoming telephone calls, filled out forms, and mailed literature.

COMMUNITY SERVICE: Provided computer assistance to the El Cerrito Girl Scouts for their 1998 fundraiser.

Working with Tables

Tables are one of Word's most useful tools for organizing text, numbers, and graphics. Tables are composed of cells organized in vertical columns and horizontal rows. Word lets you insert, edit, align, and format text within cells just as you would in a normal document. You can also change line spacing, apply bullets, and use virtually any other text or paragraph formats within cells.

Inserting Tables

You can use the Insert Table button on the Standard toolbar to insert a new table. The **Insert Table** button displays a grid. You specify the number of rows and columns for the new table by dragging in the grid. The table is inserted at the insertion point and all columns are of equal width. You can also insert a table with the **Table→Insert→Table** command. This method displays a dialog box where you can specify the number of rows and columns and several options.

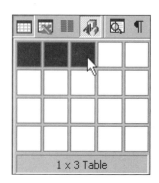

Using the Insert Table button

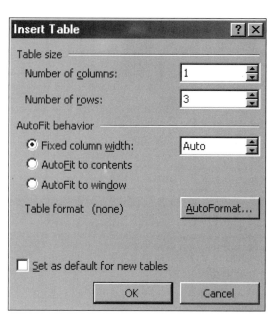

The Insert Table dialog box

Before You Insert

You should take the time to visualize your completed table prior to inserting it. You may even want to sketch it out on a piece of paper. Word lets you modify tables after they have been inserted; however, it is easier if you insert a table correctly in the first place. In particular, try to determine the correct number of rows and columns before inserting. It is very easy to adjust column widths and row heights in a table. However, inserting new columns and rows into an existing table can be cumbersome.

Hands-On 10.1 Insert a Table

*In this exercise, you will use the **Insert Table** button to insert a table with one row and three columns. The table will contain the name, address, and telephone number at the top of the resume.*

1. Start Word to display a new document window.

2. Follow these steps to insert a table.

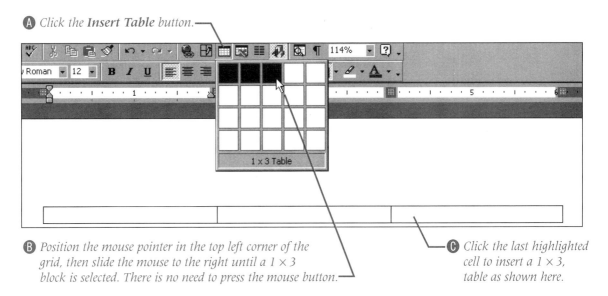

Ⓐ *Click the Insert Table button.*

1 × 3 Table

Ⓑ *Position the mouse pointer in the top left corner of the grid, then slide the mouse to the right until a 1 × 3 block is selected. There is no need to press the mouse button.*

Ⓒ *Click the last highlighted cell to insert a 1 × 3, table as shown here.*

*Notice that all columns are of equal width. The **Insert Table** button always inserts tables with equal column widths.*

3. Save the document as **Hands-On Lesson 10.**
   You will continue to develop the resume throughout this lesson.

Entering Text

You can type text and numbers and insert graphics in table cells. When typing text, Word will wrap the text when it reaches the right edge of a cell. The cell height will also expand to accommodate the wrapped text. You can also use (ENTER) to insert blank lines in a cell and expand the cell height.

Navigating in Tables

You can position the insertion point in a cell by clicking in the desired cell. However, it is often more efficient to use the keyboard to move between cells. You use the (TAB) key to move forward one cell and (SHIFT)+(TAB) to move back one cell. If the insertion point is in the last cell of the table, then the (TAB) key adds a new row to the bottom of the table.

Aligning Entries

You can use the Align Left 🔲, Center 🔲, and Align Right 🔲 buttons to align entries horizontally within table cells. In addition, you can use nearly all paragraph formatting commands within table cells, including line spacing, spacing before and after, and indents.

1. Make sure the insertion point is positioned in the first table cell. If necessary, click in the first cell to position the insertion point there.

2. Type the name **Gladys Kline**, and tap (ENTER) once.
   Notice that the row height increases for all three cells.

3. Type **845 Maple Street** on the second line of the first cell.

4. Tap the (TAB) key to move the insertion point to the second cell.

5. Click the Center  button, and type **El Cerrito, CA 94803**.

6. Tap the (TAB) key to move the insertion point to the third cell.

7. Click the Align Right  button, and type **(510) 215-6902**.
   As you can see, tables are useful for mixing alignments on a single line.

8. Tap the (TAB) key again; Word will add a new row to the table.
   A new row is always added when the insertion point is in the last table cell and (TAB) is tapped.

9. Click Undo to remove the new row.

10. Save the changes, and continue with the next topic.

Table Selection Techniques

There are several methods you can use to select table text and table elements such as cells, rows, and columns. The following Quick Reference table defines the various table selection techniques.

TABLE SELECTION TECHNIQUES	
Item to Select	**Technique**
Text within a cell	Drag over the desired text. You can select a single word by double-clicking the word.
All text within a cell	Click in the left cell margin. The left cell margin is the area between the text and left cell edge. You can also choose Table→Select→Cell from the menu bar.
A row	Click in the left margin next to the row. You can also choose Table→Select→Row from the menu bar. You can select multiple rows by dragging down in the left margin.
A column	Click the top of the column. You can also choose Table→Select→Column from the menu bar. You can select multiple columns by dragging across the tops of the desired columns.
A group of cells	Drag the mouse over the desired cells.
An entire table	Choose Table→Select→Table from the menu bar.

1. Make sure the insertion point is in the table, and choose **Table→Select→Table** from the menu bar.
   The insertion point must be positioned within a table cell before you can use this command to select a table.

2. Set the font to Arial 10.

3. Click anywhere below the table to deselect it.

4. Drag the mouse over the name Gladys Kline to select only the name.

5. Increase the size to 16, and apply bold formatting to the text.

6. Click anywhere below the table to deselect the table.

The Tables and Borders Toolbar

The Tables and Borders  button on the Standard toolbar displays the Tables and Borders toolbar. The Tables and Borders toolbar lets you apply borders and shading to table cells. You can also use the Tables and Borders toolbar to adjust the alignment of text within table cells and to set other options.

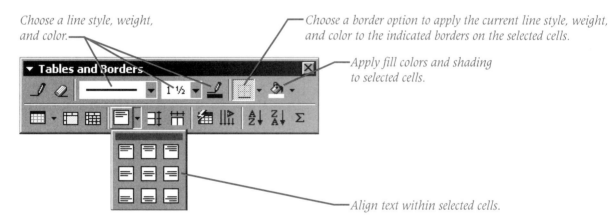

Choose a line style, weight, and color.

Choose a border option to apply the current line style, weight, and color to the indicated borders on the selected cells.

Apply fill colors and shading to selected cells.

Align text within selected cells.

TIP!   *You can also use the Tables and Borders toolbar to apply borders and shading to paragraphs within a document.*

Gridlines

When you insert a new table, Word formats the table by applying borders to all edges of all cells. If you remove the borders, then it is difficult to see the cell boundaries. For this reason, Word provides the gridline option. Gridlines are dotted lines that surround each cell. Gridlines are not printed, and you can display or hide them at your convenience. You use the **Table→Show Gridlines** and **Table→Hide Gridlines** commands to display and hide gridlines.

 Hands-On 10.4 Change the Vertical Alignment, and Remove Borders

Use Print Preview

1. Click the Print Preview ![] button on the Standard toolbar.

2. Zoom in by clicking the mouse pointer anywhere on the document.
   Notice that the table borders are visible in Print Preview. Later in this exercise, you will remove the borders and turn on gridlines. Gridlines look like borders; however, they are not printed and will not be visible in Print Preview.

3. Zoom out by clicking on the document.

4. Click the **Close** button on the Print Preview toolbar to exit from Print Preview.

Remove All Borders, and Apply a Thick Bottom Border

5. Locate the Tables and Borders ![] button on the Standard toolbar.

6. If necessary, click the Tables and Borders button ![] until it is recessed.
   This will display the Tables and Borders toolbar. If you just displayed the Tables and Borders toolbar, then your mouse pointer may take on the shape of a pencil. The pencil tool is used to draw new cells. You will use the pencil tool in the next exercise.

7. If the Pencil ![] icon is displayed, then click the Draw Table ![] button to turn it off.

8. Click in the table and use the **Table→Select→Table** command to select the table.

9. Follow these steps to remove all borders.

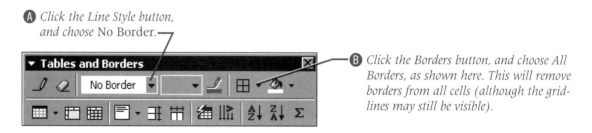

Ⓐ *Click the Line Style button, and choose* No Border.

Ⓑ *Click the Borders button, and choose All Borders, as shown here. This will remove borders from all cells (although the gridlines may still be visible).*

10. Follow these steps to apply a 1 1/2-point border to the bottom edge of each cell.

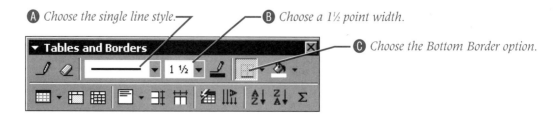

Ⓐ *Choose the single line style.*

Ⓑ *Choose a 1½ point width.*

Ⓒ *Choose the Bottom Border option.*

11. Follow these steps to set the vertical alignment of the text within the cells.

A *Click the Alignment drop-down button on the Tables and Borders toolbar.*

B *Take a few moments to examine the alignment options. Notice that the options set both the vertical and horizontal alignment.*

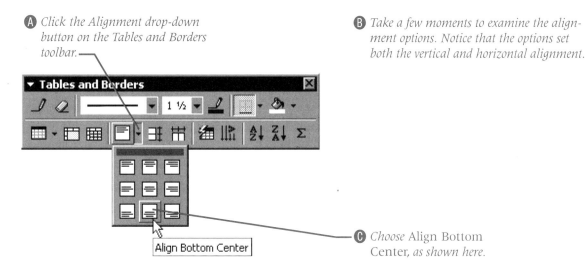

C *Choose* Align Bottom Center, *as shown here.*

The cell entries should now be aligned with the bottom edge of each cell and centered horizontally. Unfortunately, this is not the proper horizontal alignment for the first and last cells.

12. Click in the first cell, and click the **Alignment** drop-down button.

13. Choose Align Bottom Left ⊞ from the alignment list.

14. Apply the Align Bottom Right setting to the third table cell.

15. Click below the table, and a border should be visible at the bottom of each cell.

16. If necessary, choose **Table→Show Gridlines** to turn on table gridlines. The **Table→Show Gridlines** command will not be available if gridlines are already displayed. *Gridlines are light lines that appear on the cell borders.*

17. Click Print Preview ⊡.
    Notice that the gridlines are not displayed, but that the bottom border is displayed. Gridlines are not printed when the document is printed. They are only visible in the document window to assist you in seeing the cell borders.

18. Close the Print Preview window.

19. Choose **Table→Hide Gridlines** to hide the gridlines.

20. Choose **Table→Show Gridlines** to redisplay the gridlines.

21. Save the changes to your document, and continue with the next topic.

Drawing Tables

The Draw Table button displays a Pencil ✐ pointer that you can use to draw tables. This can be convenient if you want to create a table with a precise size and location within the document. To use the Draw Table tool, simply click the **Draw Table** button, and draw the outside border of the desired table in the document. After drawing the outside border, you can draw the desired rows and columns.

The Eraser Tool

The Eraser ✐ tool can be used to erase borders from tables. You can erase borders from tables created with the Draw Table tool and from tables inserted with the Insert Table button. If you erase an outside border, then you are simply removing the border style. If you erase an interior border, then you are erasing an actual row or column gridline. This will cause cells within the table to merge together to form larger cells.

Hands-On 10.5 Draw a Table, and Erase a Line

In this exercise, you will draw a table that will be used for the body of the resume.

1. Click below the existing table, and tap (ENTER) four times to insert blank lines.

2. Use the Line Weight ▭ ½ ▼ button on the Tables and Borders toolbar to set the line weight to ½.
   This will cause all lines to appear with a weight of ½ as you draw the table.

3. Click the Draw Table ▭ button to display the Pencil ✐ pointer.

4. Follow these steps to draw the outside border.

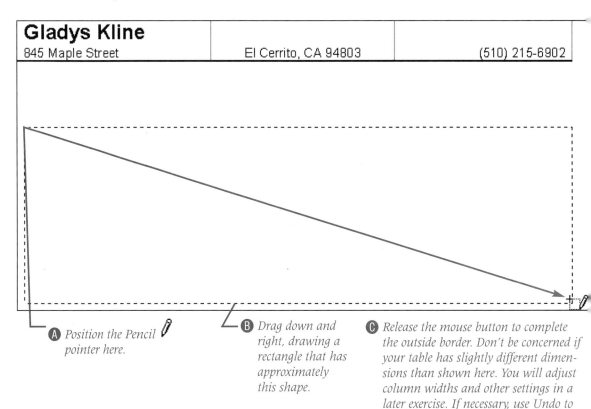

Ⓐ *Position the Pencil ✐ pointer here.*

Ⓑ *Drag down and right, drawing a rectangle that has approximately this shape.*

Ⓒ *Release the mouse button to complete the outside border. Don't be concerned if your table has slightly different dimensions than shown here. You will adjust column widths and other settings in a later exercise. If necessary, use Undo to remove the table and start over.*

5. Follow these steps to draw horizontal gridlines and vertical column gridlines.

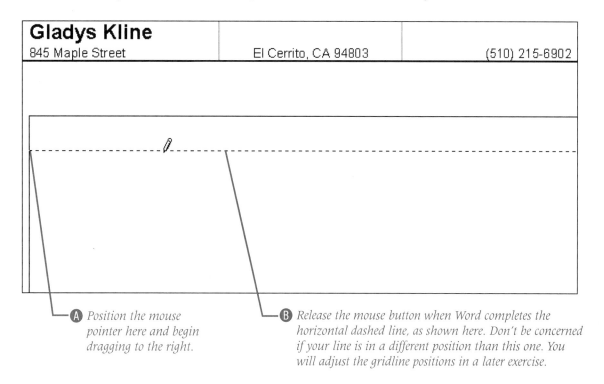

Gladys Kline
845 Maple Street   El Cerrito, CA 94803   (510) 215-6902

Ⓐ *Position the mouse pointer here and begin dragging to the right.*

Ⓑ *Release the mouse button when Word completes the horizontal dashed line, as shown here. Don't be concerned if your line is in a different position than this one. You will adjust the gridline positions in a later exercise.*

6. Draw three more horizontal gridlines and two vertical gridlines to complete a five-row by three-column table, as shown below. Once again, don't be concerned if your gridlines are in different positions than shown here.

Gladys Kline
845 Maple Street   El Cerrito, CA 94803   (510) 215-6902

(Continued on the next page)

7. Click the Eraser 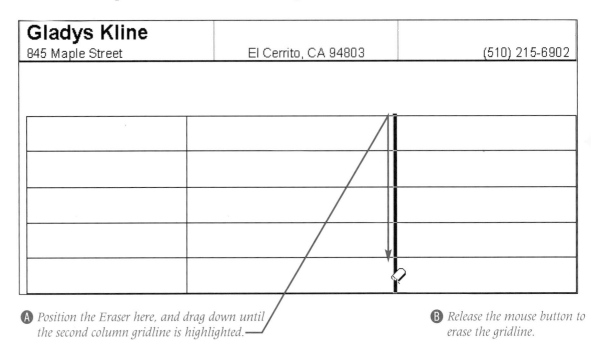 tool on the Tables and Borders toolbar.

8. Follow these steps to erase the second vertical gridline.

| Gladys Kline | | |
| 845 Maple Street | El Cerrito, CA 94803 | (510) 215-6902 |

Ⓐ *Position the Eraser here, and drag down until the second column gridline is highlighted.*

Ⓑ *Release the mouse button to erase the gridline.*

You should now have a five-row by two-column table. At this point, the row heights may be inconsistent, and the column widths will be unequal.

Sizing Rows and Columns

Word 2000 provides a variety of techniques for sizing rows and columns. Many of these techniques are new in Word 2000; others were available in previous versions of Word. Overall, Word 2000 gives you much greater control over the sizing of tables than previous versions of Word.

Distributing Rows and Columns

The Distribute Rows Evenly 🔠 and Distribute Columns Evenly 🔠 buttons on the Tables and Borders toolbar let you allocate the space in a table equally among the rows and columns. For example, if a table is six inches wide and has three columns, then the Distribute Columns Evenly command would adjust the width of each column to two inches. You can also issue these commands by choosing **Table→AutoFit** from the menu bar and choosing the desired command.

Hands-On 10.6 Distribute the Space Evenly

1. Make sure the insertion point is somewhere within the large table.

2. Click the Distribute Columns Evenly ⊞ button on the Tables and Borders toolbar. *Both columns should now be the same width.*

3. Click the Distribute Rows Evenly ⊟ button to make all rows the same height.

4. Click in the first cell, and type **OBJECTIVE:**.

5. Tap the (TAB) key, and type the text shown below in the second table cell.

OBJECTIVE:	To obtain an Administrative Assistant position where I can apply my computer skills and extensive work experience.

Adjusting Row Heights and Column Widths by Dragging

The adjust ⁺‖⁺ pointer appears whenever you position the mouse pointer on a row or column gridline. You can adjust column widths and row heights by dragging the gridline when the pointer appears. When you drag a column gridline, the width of the column to the left of the gridline is adjusted. When you drag a row gridline, the height of the row above the gridline is adjusted.

The width of the first column can be adjusted by dragging this gridline.

You can also adjust column widths and row heights by dragging column and row markers on the rulers

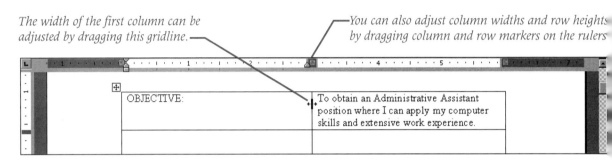

Hands-On 10.7 Adjust Column Widths

1. Position the mouse pointer on the column gridline as shown in the preceding illustration, and drag to the left and right.
   Both column widths will change as you drag. When you adjust the width of a column, the width of the column or columns to the right also changes.

2. Follow these steps to adjust the column widths by using the column marker on the ruler.

Ⓐ *Position the mouse pointer on the column marker on the ruler. The* Move Table Column *screen tip will appear as shown here.*

Ⓑ *Drag the marker to the left or right to adjust the column width.*

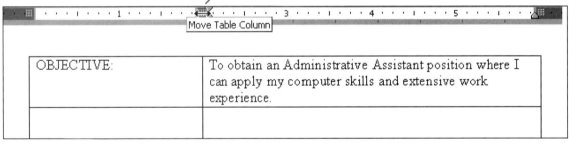

3. Adjust the column widths using either technique until the paragraph in the second cell occupies just two lines.

4. Save the changes to your resume, and continue with the next topic.

AutoFit Options

You can easily AutoFit a column to fit the widest entry in the column by double-clicking a column gridline. For example, the widest entry (and only entry) in the first column of your table is the word OBJECTIVE:. If you double-click the gridline between the columns, then the column width will be reduced to fit the OBJECTIVE: heading. You can also use this technique to AutoFit row heights. However, AutoFit has limitations, especially when table cells have paragraphs that wrap or when there are a large number of columns. AutoFit works best for adjusting column widths when cells have single-line entries.

AutoFit Options on the Table Menu

Word 2000 introduced three new AutoFit options available on the **Table→AutoFit** menu. You can use these options to AutoFit entire tables. The following table describes these options.

AutoFit Option	Description
AutoFit to Contents	AutoFits the widths of all table columns.
AutoFit to Window	Automatically resizes a table to fit within the text area (area between the margins). This feature is useful when tables are used on Web pages. The table size will automatically adjust to fit within the Web browser window.
Fixed Column Width	Sets each column to a fixed width using the current column widths.

 ## Hands-On 10.8 AutoFit Columns and Add Data

AutoFit Columns

1. Follow these steps to AutoFit the first column.

   A Position the mouse pointer on this gridline, and double-click when the adjust pointer appears. The column width will narrow, as shown here.

   B Notice that the overall table width has been reduced. The table no longer fills the space between the margins.

OBJECTIVE:	To obtain an Administrative Assistant position where I can apply my computer skills and extensive work experience.

2. Choose **Table→AutoFit→AutoFit To Contents** from the menu bar.
   Word will AutoFit the first column and expand the second column to the right margin. This command always expands or contracts the table to occupy the space between the margins.

(Continued on the next page)

3. Click in the cell below the heading OBJECTIVE:, and type **EXPERIENCE:**. Make sure you type in all caps, and include the colon after the word.
The column will automatically widen to accommodate the heading. Columns widen automatically when a single word is entered that is wider than the column.

4. Click in the cell below the heading EXPERIENCE:, and type **March 1995-Present**.
The text will wrap within the narrow column because it is composed of several words.

5. Now follow these guidelines to enter the data shown below into the table.

- Type the text using all caps and bullets where necessary.

- Tap (ENTER) after the last bulleted paragraph in each list, and turn off bullets. This will insert blank lines between the table rows. Also, use (ENTER) to insert a hard return after the large paragraph in the first row. This will create a blank line between the first and second table rows.

- Let word automatically wrap any lines that appear wrapped in the example below. The first column will automatically widen as you type text in certain cells.

OBJECTIVE:	To obtain an Administrative Assistant position where I can apply my computer skills and extensive work experience.
EXPERIENCE:	
March 1995—Present	ADMINISTRATIVE ASSISTANT FOR DIRECTOR OF MARKETING, Renquist Communications, Fulton, CA • Compose letters, memorandums, and other business correspondence. • Maintain the Director of Marketing's schedule. • Manage multiple projects assigned by the Director of Marketing.
January 1992—February 1995	WORD PROCESSING SPECIALIST, Smart Paging Systems, Berkeley, CA • Composed documents as required by supervisor, using Microsoft Word for Windows. • Used Microsoft Excel to create worksheets.
COMPUTER SKILLS:	Word 2000, Excel 2000, PowerPoint 2000, Outlook 2000, Windows 98, and Adobe Acrobat.

Table Properties

The **Table→Table Properties** command displays the Table Properties dialog box. The Table Properties dialog box lets you set various properties for tables, columns, rows, and cells. For example, you can adjust the position of an entire table horizontally on the page. You can also use table properties to specify precise settings for column widths and row heights.

Column Properties

The Column tab of the Table Properties dialog box lets you specify preferred column widths. For example, you can set the width of a column to a specific number of inches or a specified percentage of the total table width.

*When this box is checked, the column width(s) are set to the measurements specified in the **Preferred width** box.*

*The **Preferred width** is measured in inches or percent, depending upon the **Measure in** setting. The **Measure in** setting lets you specify the column width(s) in inches, as shown here, or as a percentage of the total table width.*

You can use these buttons to select columns while the dialog box is displayed. This lets you adjust the widths of more than one column without having to repeatedly open and close the dialog box.

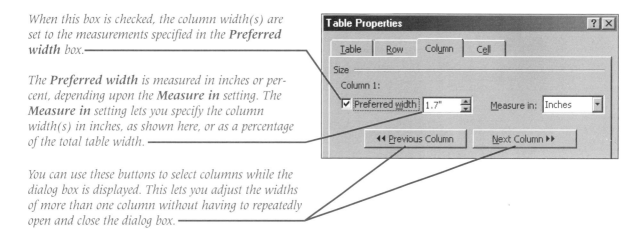

Row Properties

The Row tab of the Table Properties dialog box lets you specify row heights and other row options.

*When this box is checked, the row height(s) are set to the measurements specified in the **Specify height** and **Row height is** boxes.*

This option allows the text in a row to split across a page break. This is useful if rows have large paragraphs of text that fall at the bottom of a page.

You use this option to specify one or more rows as header rows. The header rows will print at the top of each page in a multi-page printout.

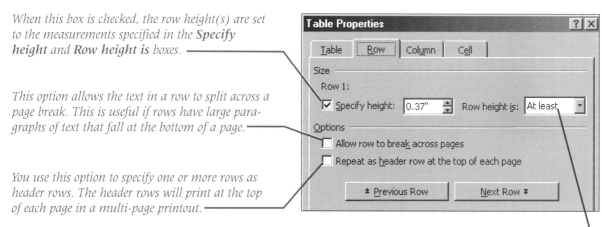

*The **Row height is** setting can be set to At least or Exactly. The At least setting makes the cell height at least the minimum specified in the **Specify height** box. If the text requires more space, the row height expands. The Exactly setting fixes the row height at the **Specify height** setting regardless of how much text is entered in the row.*

Set the Column Width

1. Click in the cell with the EXPERIENCE heading.

2. Choose **Table→Table Properties** from the menu bar.

3. Click the Column tab.

4. Click the Preferred width check box, make sure the Measure in setting is set to inches.

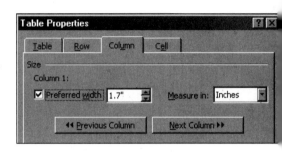

5. Set the Preferred width to **1.7″** as shown to the right, and click **OK**.
   You probably won't see much of a change in the column width. However, this setting will ensure that the column is just wide enough to display the March 1995–Present heading without it wrapping.

Adjust the Height of One Row

6. Make sure the insertion point is in the EXPERIENCE cell, and choose **Table→Table Properties.**

7. Click the Row tab.
   *Notice that the row height box is checked and the height is set to an **At least** measurement in inches. When you first create a table, the row height check box is unchecked for all rows in the table. This allows the row height to expand and contract depending upon the amount of text entered in the rows. The row heights in your table were changed to the **At least** setting when you used the **Distribute Rows Evenly** command in Hands-On Exercise 10.6.*

8. Uncheck the box, and click **OK**.
   *The row should now be just high enough to display the **EXPERIENCE** heading.*

Adjust the Heights of All Rows

9. Choose **Table→Select Table** to select the entire table.

10. Choose **Table→Table Properties,** and click the Row tab.

11. Click the Specify height check box once or twice until it is unchecked, and click **OK**.
    The heights of all rows will now automatically adjust to fit the text within the rows. However, some of your rows will have a blank line at the bottom of the rows because you inserted hard carriage returns in an earlier exercise. You can always adjust all row heights and column widths in a table by first selecting the entire table.

12. Save the changes to your resume, and continue with the next topic.

Inserting and Deleting Rows and Columns

You can insert new rows and columns after a table has been created. Word 2000's Table menu contains commands that let you insert rows above or below existing rows, and new columns to the right or left of existing columns. If you wish to insert more than one row or column, then you must first select the same number of rows or columns that you wish to insert. The following Quick Reference table describes techniques for inserting rows and columns.

INSERTING AND DELETING ROWS AND COLUMNS	
Task	**Procedure**
Insert rows.	■ Click in the desired row, or select the same number of rows that you wish to insert. ■ Choose Table→Insert→Rows Above or Table→Insert→Rows Below.
Insert columns.	■ Click in the desired column, or select the same number of columns that you wish to insert. ■ Choose Table→Insert→Columns to the Left or Table→Insert→Columns to the Right.
Delete rows or columns.	■ Select the desired rows or columns. ■ Choose Table→Delete→Rows or Table→Delete→Columns.

Hands-On 10.10 Insert and Delete Rows, and Add Text

1. Click anywhere in the last table row.

2. Choose **Table→Insert→Rows Above** to insert a row above the row with the insertion point.

3. Select the new row and the last row by dragging the mouse pointer in the left margin.
   The last two rows should be selected.

4. Choose **Table→Insert→Rows Below** to add two new rows to the end of the table.

(Continued on the next page)

5. Enter the text shown below into the new table rows. Notice that you are entering text in the row above the row with the COMPUTER SKILLS heading and in the two new rows below that row. Also, make sure you use (ENTER) to add hard returns and a blank line to the end of each bulleted list. The top portion of the table is not shown in this illustration.

January 1991—December 1992	STUDENT ASSISTANT, Contra Costa College, Pinole, CA • Assisted students with questions regarding financial aid. • Answered incoming telephone calls, filled out forms, and mailed literature.
COMPUTER SKILLS:	Word 2000, Excel 2000, PowerPoint 2000, Outlook 2000, Windows 98, and Adobe Acrobat.
EDUCATION:	Certificate of Completion, 1994, Bay Area R.O.P., Hayward, CA • Received extensive training in Microsoft Office applications, office procedures, and keyboarding.
	A. S. Business Administration, Contra Costa College, 1992, Pinole, CA • Worked as a student intern for the Vice President of Sales at Chevron Corporation. • Extra-curricular activities included participation in student body government, athletics, and tutoring of disadvantaged youths.

6. Save the changes to your resume, and continue with the next topic.

Moving and Copying Text, Rows, and Columns

You can move or copy text from a source cell to a destination cell with the Cut, Copy, and Paste buttons, or with drag and drop. If you move or copy a block of cells, then the cells are pasted as a block when the move or copy is completed. The moved or copied block will overwrite any text or graphics in the destination cells.

IMPORTANT!

The contents of destination cells are erased when you move or copy to those cells.

You can also move and copy entire rows and columns. To do this, simply select the rows or columns, and then use Cut, Copy, and Paste, or drag and drop. Word will restructure the table to accommodate the moved or copied rows or columns.

Hands-On 10.11 **Move Text and a Row**

In this exercise, you will use drag and drop to move text and a row. Use Undo if you make a mistake at any point in this exercise.

1. Follow these steps to move the text from the last cell to the cell above.

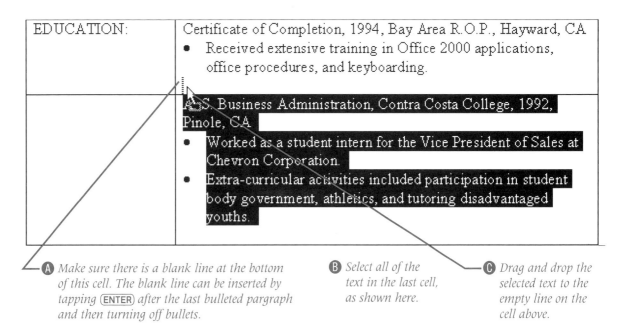

EDUCATION:	Certificate of Completion, 1994, Bay Area R.O.P., Hayward, CA • Received extensive training in Office 2000 applications, office procedures, and keyboarding.
	A.S. Business Administration, Contra Costa College, 1992, Pinole, CA • Worked as a student intern for the Vice President of Sales at Chevron Corporation. • Extra-curricular activities included participation in student body government, athletics, and tutoring disadvantaged youths.

Ⓐ *Make sure there is a blank line at the bottom of this cell. The blank line can be inserted by tapping* (ENTER) *after the last bulleted pargraph and then turning off bullets.*

Ⓑ *Select all of the text in the last cell, as shown here.*

Ⓒ *Drag and drop the selected text to the empty line on the cell above.*

You should now have an empty row at the bottom of the table.

2. Click anywhere in the empty row, and choose **Table→Delete→Rows** to remove the row.
   In a properly structured chronological resume, the education section should be above the skills section. In the next step, you will restructure the resume with drag and drop.

(Continued on the next page)

3. Follow these steps to move the education section above the computer skills section.

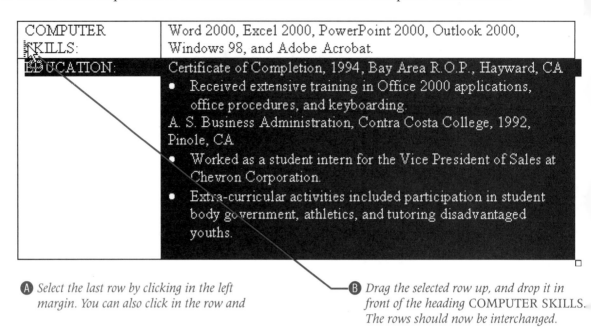

COMPUTER SKILLS:	Word 2000, Excel 2000, PowerPoint 2000, Outlook 2000, Windows 98, and Adobe Acrobat.
EDUCATION:	Certificate of Completion, 1994, Bay Area R.O.P., Hayward, CA • Received extensive training in Office 2000 applications, office procedures, and keyboarding. A. S. Business Administration, Contra Costa College, 1992, Pinole, CA • Worked as a student intern for the Vice President of Sales at Chevron Corporation. • Extra-curricular activities included participation in student body government, athletics, and tutoring disadvantaged youths.

A *Select the last row by clicking in the left margin. You can also click in the row and*

B *Drag the selected row up, and drop it in front of the heading* COMPUTER SKILLS. *The rows should now be interchanged.*

4. Now select the entire table, and remove all borders. Do not remove the border from the single row table at the top of the page.
At this point, your resume should match the one shown in the case study at the start of the lesson.

Vertical Alignment

You can set the vertical alignment of pages using the Vertical alignment option on the Layout tab of the Page Setup dialog box. The Page Setup dialog box is displayed with the **File→Page Setup** command. The vertical alignment can be set to top, center, bottom, or justified. The Top and Bottom options shift the enter page up or down to align with the top or bottom margins. The Center option centers the page between the top and bottom margins. The Justified option inserts space between all paragraphs so that the paragraphs are spread out evenly between the top and bottom margins.

1. Click the Print Preview button.

   The whole page should be visible in Print Preview. Notice that the top of the page is aligned with the top margin. The bottom of the table should be approximately 2" from the bottom of the page.

2. Click the **Close** button to close Print Preview.

3. Choose **File→Page Setup,** and click the Layout tab.

4. Set the Vertical alignment to Center, and click **OK.**

5. Click Print Preview , and the page should now be centered between the top and bottom margins.

   Many business documents look better when centered vertically on the page.

6. Click the **Close** button to exit from Print Preview.

7. Save the resume, and then close the document.

8. Continue with the questions and exercises on the following pages.

Concepts Review

True/False Questions

1. A chronological resume emphasizes skills and education.   TRUE   FALSE

2. The Insert Tables button inserts tables with unequal column widths.   TRUE   FALSE

3. Table gridlines are printed when the document is printed.   TRUE   FALSE

4. Table row heights are fixed to an exact height when a table is first inserted.   TRUE   FALSE

5. A new row is added to the bottom of a table whenever the (TAB) key is tapped.   TRUE   FALSE

6. Tables can be drawn using the Draw button on the Tables and Borders toolbar.   TRUE   FALSE

7. When you double-click a column gridline, the column to the right of the gridline is AutoFit.   TRUE   FALSE

8. Rows can be inserted above or below the row with the insertion point.   TRUE   FALSE

Multiple-Choice Questions

1. Which statement most accurately describes the way the row height functions in a new table?
   a. The row height automatically increases as text is typed.
   b. The row height is fixed at 12 point.
   c. The row height depends upon the number of columns in the table.
   d. None of the above

2. Where does the insertion point move to when it is in a table and (SHIFT)+(TAB) is used?
   a. Back one cell
   b. Forward one cell
   c. Above the table
   d. Below the table

3. Which keystroke adds a row to a table when the insertion point is in the last table cell?
   a. (TAB)
   b. (SHIFT)+(TAB)
   c. (ENTER)
   d. (CTRL)+(ENTER)

4. Which command is used to set the vertical alignment of pages?
   a. Format→Vertical Alignment
   b. Format→Paragraph
   c. Table→Vertical Alignment
   d. File→Page Setup

Skill Builders

Skill Builder 10.1 Create and Format a Table

In this exercise, you will create the table shown below. The amount of space allocated to the last column will be maximized. The space allocated to the first three columns will be minimized.

1. Start a new document, and use the Insert Table ⊞ button to insert a table with seven rows and four columns.

2. Enter the data shown in the table below.
   At this point, don't be concerned with the alignment, text wrapping, or formats.

3. Select the entire table, and choose **Format→Paragraph** from the menu bar.

4. Set the Spacing before to **6**, and click **OK.**
   This will create extra white space above each paragraph.

5. Select the first row, and set the Font to Arial 11 Bold.

6. Select the second column by clicking just above the top border, and center-align ▦ the text.

7. Select the third column and right-align ▦ the text.

8. Use the **Table→AutoFit→AutoFit to Contents** command to AutoFit the table.
   *Examine the first column; the phrase **Oil Pump** may be wrapping within the cell.*

9. Double-click the border between the first and second columns to AutoFit the first column.
   All text entries should now occupy just one line within the column.

10. If necessary, use the Tables and Borders ▦ button to display the Tables and Borders toolbar.

11. Select the first row, and use the Shading Color ▦ button on the Tables and Borders toolbar to apply a gray shade or color of your choice to the row.

12. Save the document as **Skill Builder 10.1,** and then close the document.

Item	Quantity	Cost	Description
Oil Pump	20	$78.20	Lubricates the engine by pumping motor oil.
Oil Filter	20	4.95	Cleans the oil as it circulates through the engine.
Battery	10	45.00	Provides electric current to start the engine.
Starter	10	150.00	Receives energy from the battery, and turns the crankshaft to start the engine.
Muffler	30	79.00	Muffles the sound produced by the engine.
Radiator	5	230.00	Holds and cools the antifreeze.

Skill Builder 10.2 **Restructure a Table**

In this exercise, you will open a document on your exercise diskette that contains a table. You will format the table, and you will use drag and drop to arrange the rows in alphabetical order.

1. Open the document named Skill Builder 10.2.

2. If necessary, use the **Table→Show Gridlines** command to turn on gridlines.

3. Select the fourth row (the row that begins with Allan).
   The Allan row should be the first row in alphabetical order.

4. Drag the row up and drop it in front of/above the Weinstein row.

5. Continue arranging the rows until they are in alphabetical order, as shown in the table on the following page.
   In the next few steps, you will reorder the columns.

6. Select the third column (the column labeled Q1) by clicking the top of the column.
   This column should be the second column.

7. Drag the column to the left, and drop it in front of the Q4 column.

8. Continue arranging the columns until they are in the order Q1, Q2, Q3, and Q4.

9. Select Columns 2–5, and right-align the text.

10. Select the entire table, and set the paragraph spacing before to **6**.

11. Use the Tables and Borders toolbar to choose a single-line style with a 1.5-point weight.

12. Apply the 1.5-point weight single line to the Outside Border .

13. Select only the first row, and use the Bottom Border button to apply the 1.5-point single line to the bottom border of the row.

14. Apply a 10% gray shade to the first row.

15. Format the text in the first row as Arial 12 Bold.

16. Hide the table gridlines, and the table should match the example below.

17. Save the changes to the document, and then close the document.

Sales Rep	Q1	Q2	Q3	Q4
Allan	3,000	5,000	6,000	9,000
Bolson	7,000	1,000	6,000	2,000
Colden	4,000	4,000	8,000	2,000
Davis	6,000	2,000	4,000	7,000
Johnson	5,000	3,000	2,000	5,000
Oliver	1,000	7,000	2,000	3,000
Smith	2,000	6,000	4,000	6,000
Weinstein	1,000	8,000	2,220	2,200
Ziegfried	2,000	5,000	1,000	9,000

Skill Builder 10.3 Use a Table in a Flyer

1. Follow these guidelines to create the document shown below.

   - ■ Use a drop cap in the first main paragraph.

   - ■ Place the bulleted lists in a one-row by two-column table. Remove all borders from the table.

   - ■ Use Times New Roman and Arial fonts. Use your best judgment when determining font sizes, alignment, and other settings.

2. Save the completed document as **Skill Builder 10.3,** and then close the document.

ARGS

Anne's Reliable Gift Service

My goal is to provide a wide variety of quality giftware, jewelry, home décor, and electronic items at reasonable prices.

We Have

Gifts From

Around The World

- Shop at home catalog
- Fund raising program available for churches, schools, and groups
- The latest products

- Income opportunities
- Gift, premium, and incentive program for businesses and offices
- Volume discounts

For more information or to place an order call…

(510) 236-1864

Satisfaction Guaranteed!

50% deposit required on all orders

Skill Builder 10.4 Create a Sign-In Sheet

In this Skill Builder, you will use a table to create a sign-in sheet.

1. Start a new document, and set the top, bottom, left, and right margins to .75".

2. Center align the title **Sign-in Sheet** at the top of the document, and tap (ENTER) twice to create two blank lines below the title.

3. Format the Sign-in Sheet title with an Arial 20 Bold font.

4. Position the insertion point on the second blank line below the title, and set the alignment to left.

5. Insert a table with 17 rows and 4 columns.

6. Use the Table Properties box to specify precise column widths as follows:

    Column 1—1.45"

    Column 2—2.25"

    Column 3—1.3"

    Column 4—2.15"

7. Use the Table Properties box to set the height of Row 1 to exactly 0.3".

8. Enter the headings **Name**, **Address**, **Phone**, and **Comments** in the cells in Row 1, and format the headings as Arial 12 Bold.

9. Use the Align Bottom Left 🔲 option on the Tables and Borders toolbar to align the headings in Row 1 with the bottom left edges of the cells.

10. Set the height of all other rows to exactly 0.5".

11. Apply a 2¼-point border to the outside of the table and to the bottom of Row 1. Leave all other borders as they are.

12. Apply a 10% gray shade to the cells in Row 1.

13. Center the page vertically.

14. Save the document as **Skill Builder 10.4,** and then close the document.

Skill Builder 10.5 Create Your Own Scannable Functional Resume

In this exercise, you will create a functional resume for yourself. Functional resumes emphasize skills, accomplishments, and achievements. You will format the resume so that it can easily be scanned into an electronic database. You may want to review the sample resumes at the start of this lesson before continuing.

1. Start a new document, and insert a table with one row and two columns.

2. Click in the right cell and use the Align Bottom Right ⊟ option on the Tables and Borders toolbar to set the alignment to bottom right.

3. Use the Tables and Borders toolbar to remove all borders.

4. Apply a single. ¾-point line to the bottom edge of both cells.

5. Enter your name, address, email address, and telephone number as shown below.

Your Name	
Your Street Address	Your Email Address
Your City, State Zip	Your Telephone Number

6. Position the insertion point below the table, and tap (ENTER) four times.

7. Insert a table with five rows and two columns.

8. Remove all lines from the table. Make sure table gridlines are turned on.

9. Use the Table Properties dialog box to set the width of the first column to 1.5″ and the width of the second column to 4.6″.

10. Enter your own personal information using the resume on the following page as an example. As you can see, this functional resume emphasizes skills and education. You should place your work experience before education if you have extensive work experience. Also notice that the resume lacks any type of character formatting. This is because it is designed for scanning into an electronic database. You should use keywords in the Office Skills section that are relevant to your skills and that will give your resume a high probability of being chosen by a potential employer's OCR software.

11. When you have finished, save your resume using a descriptive name such as Functional - Scannable Resume, and then close the document. You may want to use a separate Job Search diskette for all of your resumes, cover letters, and job search correspondence. Make sure you have a backup copy of your resume on another diskette, or in some other safe location.

Your Name
Your Street Address
Your City, State Zip

Your Email Address
Your Telephone Number

OBJECTIVE:	State your objective here

SKILLS:	Computer Skills
	    Windows 95, Word, Excel, Access, PowerPoint
	
	Office Skills
	    Bookkeeping, telephone reception, filing
	
	Personal Qualities
	    Flexible, team player, creative, excellent communication
	    skills

EDUCATION:	Degree, graduation date, school, location List any honors, accomplishments, or extra curricular activities that are relevant.
EXPERIENCE:	List job responsibilities, skills acquired, company, and date of employment.
OTHER:	You may include a community service section or some other section that details information relevant to the job for which you are applying.

Skill Builder 10.6 Enhance Your Functional Resume

In this exercise, you will enhance the appearance of the resume that you created in the previous exercise. The enhanced resume will be used as a functional resume but will not be designed specifically for scanning. However, you do not want to "go overboard" on formatting in case a potential employer unexpectedly scans the resume.

1. Open the resume that you created in the previous exercise.

2. Use **File→Save As** to save the resume with a new name, such as Functional Resume.

3. Enhance the appearance of the resume by formatting your name, the headings, and any other elements that you feel are necessary. You can use larger point sizes, bold, and other typefaces.

4. Save the changes to the resume, and then close it.

Skills Builder 10.7 Create Your Own Chronological Resume

In this exercise, you will open the resume that you developed in the Hands-On exercises. You will personalize the resume for your own use. This resume uses a chronological style that emphasizes paid work experience.

1. Open the Hands-On Lesson 10 document.

2. Change all information in the resume to your own personal information. Try to maintain the formatting by selecting a phrase or word, and typing a new phrase or word in its place.

3. Use the **File→Save As** command to save the completed resume to your job search diskette with a descriptive name, such as Chronological Resume.

4. Leave the resume open; you will continue to use it.

Skill Builder 10.8 Create Your Own Scannable Chronological Resume

In this exercise, you will convert the chronological resume into a scannable chronological resume.

1. Use the **File→Save As** command to save the resume to your job search diskette with a descriptive name, such as Chronological - Scannable Resume.

2. Select the entire document, and remove all text formats by setting the font to Times New Roman 12. You will need to turn off bold and any other text formats that may be present. The paragraphs should remain properly aligned because you used tables, indenting, bullets, and other alignment features.

3. Browse through the resume and try to insert key words in any locations where they may be important. For example, use words such as Word and Excel in a job description if you used those software applications as part of your job.

4. Save the changes, and then close the document.

Assessments

Assessment 10.1 Create and Format a Table

1. Start a new document, and follow these guidelines to create the table shown below.

   ■ Insert a table with six rows and five columns.

   ■ Set the width of the first four columns to one inch and set the width of the last column to two inches.

   ■ Use the paragraph Spacing Before option to add six points of spacing before each paragraph.

   ■ Center align the text in the second and third columns and right align the text in the fourth column.

   ■ Remove all borders from the table, and then apply a 1½-point border to the outside of the table and to the bottom border of Row 1.

   ■ Apply a 10% gray shade to Row 1, and format the text in Row 1 with bold.

2. Save the document as **Assessment 10.1,** and then close it.

Item	Status	Quantity	Value	Customer Name
A423	S	9	$100.90	Harold Johnson
A321	S	23	$45.87	Alexander Robertson
S345	I	7	$43.23	Bruce Pique
E567	H	6	$78.90	Al Chess
S230	I	5	$23.45	Roberta Brown

Assessment 10.2 **Use a Table in a Business Letter**

1. Follow these guidelines to create the document shown on the following page.

   ■ Start a new document, and type today's date on the first line of the document.

   ■ Create the block style letter shown on the following page.

   ■ Place the company, Word version, and contact person information in a six-row by three-column table. Leave the column widths set to the default widths that are used when the table is first inserted.

   ■ Remove all borders from the table.

   ■ Center-align the text in the middle column, and right-align the text in the third column.

   ■ Apply bold formatting as shown.

   ■ Center the completed letter vertically using the Vertical alignment option on the Page Setup dialog box.

2. Save the document as **Assessment 10.2,** and then close it.

Today's Date

Ms. Wanda Sample
HiTech Temps
1744 Lexington Avenue, Suite B
El Cerrito, CA 94530

Dear Ms. Sample:

Thank you for taking the time to speak with me yesterday. Per your request, I am providing you with the Word version and contact at each company where I have used Word.

Company	Word Version	Contact
BPI	6.0 for DOS	Dan Johnson
Exxon	6.0 for DOS	Maria Velasquez
City of Oakland	2.0 for Windows	Mary Smith
Centron	Word 97	Ralph Watson
Constructo	Word 2000	Ben Johnson

Ms. Sample, please contact me as soon as you have had the opportunity to review my application and check my references. I am eager to begin working with HiTech Temps and applying my excellent computer skills.

Sincerely yours,

Donna Benson

Critical Thinking

Critical Thinking 10.1 On Your Own

Christy Chan is the Human Resources Manager for Vectron, Inc. Christy requires all managers at Vectron to give new employees 30-, 60-, and 90-day reviews. In order to achieve consistency and help eliminate discrimination in the review process, Christy has asked you to set up a standardized form for evaluating employees. Christy has given you the following evaluation criteria and rating system.

Evaluation Criteria—Tardiness, job knowledge, communication skills, problem solving ability, team-oriented

Rating system—Poor, fair, good, excellent

Set up a Word document that can be used as an evaluation form. Include a table with the evaluation criteria and rating system. The user of the form should be able to check the appropriate box in the table to specify the evaluation criteria and rating. Use paragraph spacing before to increase the height of the table rows. Apply borders and shading as you deem appropriate. Also, include a title at the top of the form and a place where the employee's name, the date, and the type of review (30-, 60-, or 90-day) can be entered. Save your completed document as **Critical Thinking 10.1.** Close the document when you have finished.

Critical Thinking 10.2 On Your Own

After using the employee evaluation form for some time, Christy Chan has decided to make several changes to it. Open the Critical Thinking 10.1 document, and save it as **Critical Thinking 10.2.** Add the following two new evaluation criteria to the table: "Self-starter" and "Computer skills." Add a rating of "Very good" to the table. You may need to insert a column or row to accomplish this. Adjust all column widths as necessary to allow the table to fit within the margins. Rearrange the rows until they are in alphabetical order. Save the completed document, and then close it.

Critical Thinking 10.3 Web Research

Alexia Williams is the Information Systems Manager of Bellmont Health Care. Bellmont is a rapidly growing health care concern with over one billion dollars in FY 2000 revenues. Alexia has mandated that beginning in FY 2001 at least 50% of Bellmont's technology purchases will be made using online purchasing systems. Alexia believes this strategy will reduce costs and increase the efficiency of the procurement process. As a student intern working under the direction of Alexia, you have been assigned the task of locating five vendors that allow personal computers and accessories to be purchased online. Alexia has asked you to construct a Word document with a table that includes the vendor's name, Web site URL, and their customer service telephone number. Use Internet Explorer and a search engine of your choice to conduct your research. Record your results in a Word table, and save the document as **Critical Thinking 10.3.**

Critical Thinking 10.4 With a Group

You and your classmate have decided to prepare a customer survey form to be distributed by Health-e-Meals.com's drivers. Normally, you encourage customers to fill out survey forms online, but thus far the response has been small. For this reason, you want the drivers to hand out the forms when they deliver meals. Work with your classmate to determine the eight most important survey questions you can ask of your customers. The questions should be oriented towards helping you improve your product and service.

Prepare a Word document that includes a table with the customer survey questions and Yes and No columns so that customers can simply check yes or no to each question. The survey form should also include a location for the customer's name, mailing address, and telephone number. Incorporate the name, address, and telephone information into a table. Use the right column of the table to create lines where the customers can write their name, address, and telephone number. You can accomplish this by removing all lines from the table except for the horizontal lines where the name, address, and telephone number are to be placed. Save the completed document as **Critical Thinking 10.4.**

LESSON 11

Web Integration—Posting an Online Resume

Like all of the Office 2000 applications, Word 2000 makes it easy to interact with the Internet. You have already seen how Word helps you send documents by email. Now you will use Word to post a page on the Web. Word can convert any document into a Web page with a single command. The Web Page Preview command lets you see how the document will appear as a Web page before you convert it. Web Folders make it easy to save your Web pages to a Web server so that they can be accessed over the Internet. Word's Resume Wizard can help you create a professional-looking resume to post online. In this lesson, you will experience how Word's Web capabilities can help you communicate effectively over the World Wide Web.

In This Lesson

Case Study

Erin is about to graduate with an AA degree in Office Technology. She's going to transfer to a four-year college in the fall in a city 50 miles away. Erin is eager to get herself settled before the next semester and find a job that will let her study during the day and work in the evenings. She starts searching the want ads for work. But Erin also wants to advertise herself. So she decides to create an online version of her resume that she can post on the Web. There are many programs available for designing Web pages, but Word has all of the tools Erin needs to create and post a professional-looking resume on the Web.

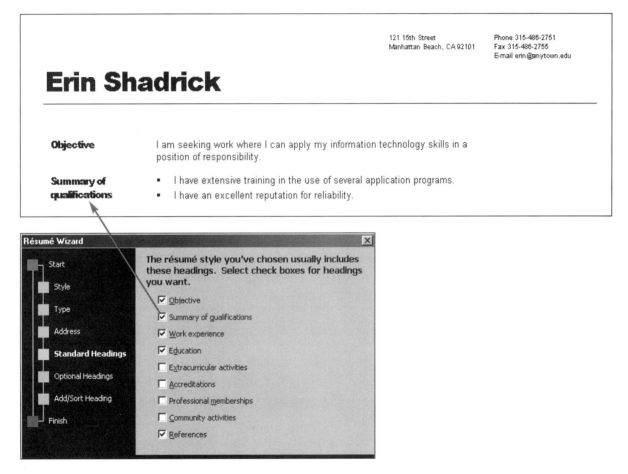

Word's Resume Wizard walks Erin through the steps of creating a resume. The Wizard recommends various headings for which Erin will later fill-in her personal information.

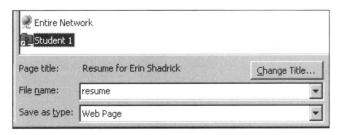

With a Web folder, Erin can save her resume as a Web page directly to the Web server at her Internet Service Provider (ISP).

Document Wizards

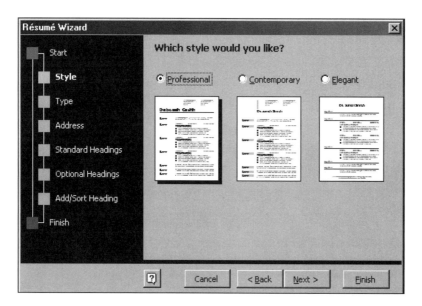

A Wizard is a small program that asks you questions about a task you wish to undertake. Word 2000 comes with Wizards to help you create meeting agendas, calendars, memos, resumes, and many other types of documents. In this lesson, you will use the Resume Wizard. Based upon the answers you give to several questions, a document Wizard can automatically format a document with the necessary sections and basic information. Then you edit the document to add details. Document Wizards make it easy to quickly create complex, well-formatted documents.

The Resume Wizard

The Resume Wizard is a good example of how Word can help you create a specialized document. This Wizard offers you choices of various resume styles and types. For example, you can tell the Resume Wizard to compose a chronological- or functional-type resume. Although the Resume Wizard will recommend several standard sections for your resume, it also lets you specify custom sections and the order of the various sections.

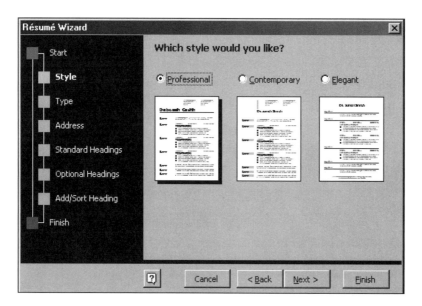

The Resume Wizard asks a series of questions to custom-design your resume.

USING A WIZARD

Task	Procedure
Find a Wizard to help create a specific type of document.	■ Choose *File→New* from the menu bar. ■ Click the tab for the type of document you wish to create, or click the *Other Documents* tab. ■ Double-click the icon of the Wizard for the type of document you wish to create. ■ You may be asked to insert the Office 2000 installation disc if the Wizard you need has not yet been installed on your computer.

In this exercise, you will use the Resume Wizard to create your own resume.

Start the Resume Wizard

1. Start Word; then choose **File→Close** from the menu bar. Choose **File→New** from the menu bar; then click the **Other Documents** tab.
   This tab contains wizards and templates for specific types of documents, such as a meeting agenda.

2. Double-click the *Resume Wizard* icon.
   The Wizard will open in a new dialog box. Along the left side you can see the various options that the wizard will ask you about.

3. Click the Help 🔳 button on the lower-left side of the dialog box; then click the *Help with this feature* option.
   An Office Assistant speech balloon will appear. This will display useful tips as you work your way through the Wizard's questions. It may be worthwhile to display the Office Assistant the first time you use a Wizard.

Specify the Resume Settings

4. Click **Next** to begin creating the resume. Read the text in the Office Assistant speech balloon.
   The Wizard displays the three style options available for your resume. You can change the style later on if you wish, and you will do so later in this exercise.

5. Click the *Contemporary* option; then click **Next.** Read over the description of your resume-type options in the Office Assistant speech balloon.

6. Choose the *Chronological resume* option, and click **Next.**
   If another student has used this wizard previously, you will see what they filled in. However, you can simply type over the old information with your own. Notice that the text in the Name box is already selected. When you start to type, your new data will replace the selection.

7. Fill in your first and last names; then tap the (TAB) key to jump to the next box.

8. Enter your street address; then tap (ENTER) and type your city, state, and zip code.

9. Using the (TAB) key to jump from one box to the next, fill in the rest of the information boxes. When you are done, click **Next.**

10. Click the Address ⬛ **Address** box on the left side of the Wizard window.
    You can navigate back through the previous steps of the Resume Wizard. This lets you change any of the settings before you finish.

11. Click the **Standard Headings** box.

12. If necessary, check the *Summary of qualifications* and *References* boxes to add them to your resume; then click **Next.**
    Here are additional headings you could choose. None of these are probably appropriate for this resume, but you will add one heading and remove it later.

13. Check the *Interests and activities* heading. Make sure that all of the other headings are unchecked; then click **Next.**

(Continued on the next page)

You are not limited to the Wizard's preset resume headings. You can also create your own and add them to the design.

14. Scroll down the headings list; then click the *Interests and activities* heading, and click **Remove.**
The heading is removed. You can add any number of headings or remove unwanted headings in this step of the Wizard.

15. Scroll through the list to see if *Software skills* is listed. If it is, select the *Software skills* heading; then click **Remove.**
This heading may have been added by a previous student. The Wizard always displays the most recently used settings each time you create a new resume.

16. Enter **Software skills** as a new heading; then click **Add.**
The new heading is added to the bottom of the resume headings list.

17. Scroll to the bottom of the headings list; then choose the *Software skills* heading. Click the **Move Up** button to change its position in the list; it should appear immediately beneath the *Work Experience* heading.
Now this heading should be listed fourth in the list. As you can see, the Wizard is very flexible. If you don't care for a heading or its position in the list, you can change it.

18. Click **Next.**
At this point, you could click on any step in the Wizard window and change your answers. Since what you have now should be satisfactory, you will finish.

19. Click **Finish.**
The Resume Wizard creates the new resume with your information. Notice that the speech balloon offers help on additional tasks such as creating a cover letter.

Fill Out the Resume

20. Click *Change the visual style of the resume* in the Office Assistant speech balloon.
Word jumps you to the appropriate step in the Resume Wizard.

21. Choose the *Professional style;* then click **OK.**
The resume is re-formatted to the newly chosen style.

22. Click the bracketed area where you can type your objective; then type a one- or two-line objective statement. For example: **I am seeking work where I can apply my information technology skills in a position of responsibility.**

    `[ Type Objective Here ]`

Notice how the bracketed text is replaced with your new statement. The wizard marks all of the areas where you must type with a description of the required information.

23. Click the Show/Hide ¶ button on the toolbar if the formatting marks are not displayed.
Notice that this resume is actually laid out on the page in a table. You can see the row markers along the right margin of the page.

24. Click the Show/Hide ¶ button to hide the formatting marks.
The preset information for the Summary of qualifications *heading is not really appropriate, so you will replace it with a bulleted list*

25. Follow this step to select the *Summary of qualifications* body text.
Now that the table cell is selected, you can start typing to replace the current content of the cell with your new information.

Ⓐ *Point near the 19xx until you see the right-pointing arrow here; then click to select the table cell.*

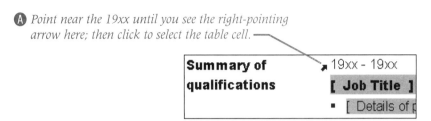

26. Type the two bulleted items shown below.

- I have extensive training in several application programs.
- I have an excellent reputation for reliability.

Notice that in the Work Experience *section there is room for just one job listing. Let's assume that you need to list your three most recent jobs. In the next steps you will add some new lines to list the additional jobs.*

27. Follow these steps to add two new job sections.

Ⓐ *Point here until you see the* I-beam *(not the small arrow); then start to drag down and to the right.*

Ⓑ *Release the mouse button immediately after the close-bracket character.*

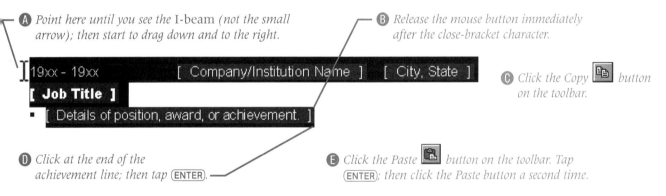

Ⓒ *Click the Copy button on the toolbar.*

Ⓓ *Click at the end of the achievement line; then tap* ⒺNTER.

Ⓔ *Click the Paste button on the toolbar. Tap* ⒺNTER; *then click the Paste button a second time.*

Now you should have two additional copies of the job description section in the resume.

28. Change the *19xx – 19xx* on the first job section to dates appropriate to the first job you will list.
As you fill in this section, you can either enter real jobs, or make up jobs as you prefer.

29. Click the *Company/Institution Name* item on the first job section. Type the name of the company or institution for this first job.

30. Continue clicking the other bracketed areas of the first job section and enter the appropriate information.

31. Fill in information for the other two jobs.

32. Click the bracketed area on the *Software skills* section. List the names of software application programs in which you are proficient or expect to become proficient. For example, Microsoft Word 2000; Windows 98; etc.

33. In the *Education* section, fill-in any diplomas, degrees, or other educational accomplishments.

34. In the *References* section, enter **Available upon request**.

35. Save 🖫 the document to your exercise diskette with the name **Resume**.

Delete Your Information from the Resume Wizard

The Resume Wizard always displays the most recently entered information. If you were the only user of this computer, that would be convenient. However, since other students will use this Wizard, you should delete your personal information now.

36. Choose **File→New** from the menu bar; then double-click the *Resume Wizard* icon.

37. Click the Address button on the left side of the Wizard window.

38. Select your personal information in each box; then tap (DELETE) to delete it. All of the boxes should be empty.

39. Click the Add/Sort Heading button on the Wizard window.

40. **Remove** the *Software skills* and *Summary of qualifications* headings from the headings list.

41. Click **Finish** to save the new Wizard settings.
    Now the items you deleted will not be displayed when the next student runs this Wizard.

42. Close 🗙 the Word window. Click **No** when you are asked if you wish to save the new document.
    Your original resume should now be in the open Word window.

The Save As Command

The **Save As** command lets you save additional copies of your documents with different names. There are several useful tasks you can accomplish with this command.

- You can save a copy of the document with a new name.

- You can save a copy of the document to a different folder or disk drive.

- You can create new folders for your documents.

- You can save a document in a new file format (export).

- You can delete and rename files from within the Save As dialog box.

Creating a Folder from Within Word

The Create New Folder 📁 button lets you create new folders from within Word's Save As and Open dialog boxes. The button is on the dialog box toolbar. This button lets you create new folders when you need them, without leaving Word.

In this exercise, you will save a copy of your resume with a new name. Then you will create a new folder and save a copy of the resume document there. You will also delete a document from within the Save As *dialog box.*

Save a Copy of a Document

1. Choose **File→Save As** from the menu bar.
   The current file name is selected in the Name box, ready for you to enter a new name.

2. Tap the (END) key on the keyboard; then tap the (SPACE BAR) and type **(original)** at the end of the filename. Tap the (ENTER) key to finish the **Save As** command.
   Now there are two versions of the document on your exercise diskette: Resume *and* Resume (original).

Create a New Folder, and Save the Document

3. Choose **File→Save As** from the menu bar.

4. Click the New Folder button on the Save As dialog box toolbar.

5. Enter **My Resume** as the new folder name; then tap (ENTER).
   Word automatically opens the new folder for you.

6. Delete **(original)** from the end of the document name; then click **Save** to save the document to the new folder.
   Now you have saved the resume to a new location. Notice that the name of the document is once again Resume. *At the moment, there are three copies of the document on your exercise diskette. You have a copy of the Resume document in the new folder and the other two copies in the base (root) level of the exercise diskette.*

Delete a File

7. Choose **File→Save As** from the menu bar; then click the Up button to navigate back to the base (root) level of your exercise diskette.

8. Scroll through the file list until the *Resume* document is visible; then *right-click* on the document, and choose **Delete** from the pop-up menu. Click **Yes** if you are asked to confirm the deletion.
   The document is deleted. If this document had been on the hard drive, you could still retrieve it from the Recycle Bin. Since it was deleted from the floppy disk, the document is permanently deleted.

9. Click **Cancel** to close the dialog box.
   This command cancels the **Save As** *command, not the delete command you just executed. This lets you manage files even when you don't actually need to save another copy of your document.*

Exporting Documents to Other File Formats

The *native* file format is how an application normally saves files. For example, Word has its own native *document* format. But what if you want to save a file in a different (non-native) file format? This is called **exporting.** The **Save As** command lets you export Word documents to any of the available file formats.

Example

You have a co-worker who still uses an older version of WordPerfect as her word processing program. You want to send her information from a Word document. You open the document normally in Word and use the **Save As** command to choose a different file format (export) and save it. Then you send the exported file to your co-worker. You end up with two different copies of the document, each in a different format.

Some Popular File Formats

There are many file formats for storing text documents. Three of the most useful are described in the table below.

File Format	Description
Text only	This file format saves only the alphabetic characters, tabs, and hard returns (where you tap the (ENTER) key). All other formatting information is lost. Text files have a filename extension of .txt at the end of the filename.
Rich Text Format (RTF)	This file format can store most of the formatting information for text. For example, it can store Font, Paragraph, and Tab settings. This is a good file format for exchanging Word documents with users who run other word processing programs. Rich Text Format files have a filename extension of .rtf at the end of the filename.
Web Page (HTML)	Word can save documents in the HTML language used for Web pages. This can be useful when you need to send content that will be transferred to a Web page. This format also lets you create your own Web pages within Word, as you will do later in this lesson.

TIP!

To visit the Microsoft Office Update Web site, choose Help→ Office on the Web *from Word's menu bar.*

Format Converters

In order to export your work to a different file format, Word must use a *converter* to convert the document file into the new format. Converters for several popular file formats are installed with Word. Other converters are ready for installation from the Office 2000 installation CDs. New converters are released as new file formats are introduced. New converters are often available from the Microsoft Office Update Web site and on the Web sites of other software vendors.

Limitations of File Formats

Some file formats will not be able to save all of the information in the document file. For example, a *text only* file won't be able to save any text formatting. Other types of special formatting, such as tables and comments, may be altered. Word will warn you about any features, formatting or data you might lose in the new file format. If you save to a non-Word file format, your original document file is always kept intact. The converted document is saved to different file. If however, you save the document in an older Word format (such as Word 6.0/95), your original file is overwritten with the new file format.

HOW TO EXPORT A DOCUMENT

Task	Procedure
Export a document to a different file format.	■ Open the document in Word; then choose *File→Save As* from the menu bar. ■ Click on the *Save As Type* box; then choose the desired file format; then click *Save*. ■ Read any warnings Word displays about the potential for lost formatting and/or other information in the new file; then click *OK*.

Hands-On 11.3 Export the Word Document

In this exercise, you will save the document in two different file formats.

1. Choose **File→Save As** from the menu bar.

2. Follow these steps to save the file with a different file format.

Ⓐ *Click at the end of the File name box; then add* **(text only)** *to the end of the filename, as shown here.*

Ⓑ *Click the* Save as type *drop-down list button. Scroll up and down the list to review the available file formats. Every format type in this list has a corresponding converter that was installed along with Word. It is possible to install additional converters later if they are needed.*

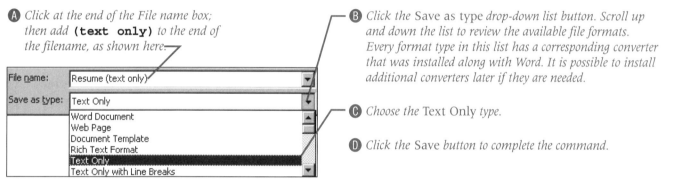

Ⓒ *Choose the* Text Only *type.*

Ⓓ *Click the* Save *button to complete the command.*

Word will warn you that that some features could be lost when you save to this file format.

3. Click **Yes** to approve saving the file in the new file format and accepting the loss of features such as formatting.
   The file is saved. Notice that the loss of formatting is not yet apparent. You will not see the text only version of this file until you open it.

4. Choose **File→Close** from the menu bar.

(Continued on the next page)

5. Click the Open button on the toolbar.
   Notice that the Resume (text only) file is not visible. This is because Word is presently set to display only Word documents. You must tell Word to display Text files (or all files) in order to see the file you just saved.

6. Scroll down the *Files of type* list at the bottom of the dialog box; then choose **Text files.**

   Files of type: Text Files

   Now only the Resume (text only) *file is displayed. This is because it is the only file of this file type in the* My Resume *folder.*

7. Double-click the **Resume (text only)** file.
   Notice that all text formatting has been stripped out of the file. All that remains are your words and line breaks. Text only *is an extreme example of how you can lose formatting when you change file formats. However, there are other file formats that preserve much of your formatting.*

8. Choose **File→Close** from the menu bar. Click **No** if you are asked to save any changes to the document.

Save the Document in Rich Text Format

Now you will export your resume to another file format. The Rich Text Format (RTF) can preserve most or all of the features of your document.

9. Click the Open button on the toolbar.
   Notice that the Resume (text only) file is visible. This is because Word is presently set to display only Text files. So you will reset the dialog box to display Word documents again.

10. Choose **Word Documents** from the *Files of type* list at the bottom of the dialog box; then double-click to open the **Resume** document.

11. Choose **File→Save As** from the menu bar; then choose **Rich Text Format** from the *Save as type* box. Add **(RTF)** to the end of the document name; then tap (ENTER) to save the document in the new file format.

12. Choose **File→Close** from the menu bar.
    Now let's see how well Rich Text Format preserved the look of your resume.

13. Click the Open button on the toolbar; then choose **Rich Text Format** from the *Files of type* list and double-click to open the *Resume (RTF)* document.
    There's really no visible difference at all between the Word document version and this RTF version of the resume. Since many other word processing programs can open (convert) RTF files, this format is an excellent choice to send formatted documents to non-Word users.

14. Choose **File→Close** from the menu bar. Click **No** if you are asked to save any changes to the document.

15. Click the Open button on the toolbar; then choose **All Word Documents** from the *Files of type* list at the bottom of the dialog box.
    Notice that the Resume (RTF) *document is also displayed now. This is because RTF is a file format that is also used to exchange documents with older versions of Microsoft Word.*

16. Double-click to open the **Resume** document.
    You are nearly ready to post your resume on the Internet. Before you do, take a moment to learn about some basic design considerations that can make your Web pages more effective.

Design Considerations for Web Pages

When you create Web pages, you should take several design considerations into account.

- Fonts
- Screen resolution
- Backgrounds
- Download speed

Fonts

You can use any fonts available on your computer when you design a Web page. However, if the person browsing your page does not have those fonts, the page will not appear as you designed it. A Web browser program will substitute other fonts that are as close a match as it can determine. If a match is not easy to determine, the Web browser program will substitute the **Courier** font. Thus, you might think your page is very attractive with several unusual fonts, but others won't see it that way. Below is an example of what can happen if someone browsing your Web page does not have those fonts on their computer.

Wow! Look at all of the cool fonts I am using.	W ow! Look at all of the cool fonts I am using.
I've got Comic Sans. In **Bold** too.	I've got Comic Sans. I n **Bold** t oo.
I've got Haettenschweiler.	I've got Haettenschweiler .
Then there's Corsiva; a script font.	Then there's Corsiva; a script font.

How the page would look on your computer. *How the page might look on a computer that does not have the same fonts installed.*

Screen Resolution

When you design a Web page, it is important that most people browsing your page can view it easily. This can place some limitations on the page design. For example, many users still have their video resolution set at 640 × 480 pixels. The video resolution sets how many pixels the computer uses to create the screen display.

640 pixels

480 pixels

The resolution of the computer display is measured in pixels horizontally and vertically.

This means if you design a page to fit an 800 × 600 screen, users set for 640 × 480 will have to scroll up and down, and from side to side, to view the contents of your page. For this reason, you may want to view your Web pages with the computer display set at 640 × 480 resolution to determine that they will still display well at that resolution.

TIP! *It is estimated that about 85% of computer users view Web pages at a screen resolution of 800 × 600 or higher.*

In this exercise, you will check the Display Properties window to view the resolution setting of the computer display.

NOTE!

Some computer labs lock the Display Properties window so you cannot enter or adjust it.

1. Minimize ▬ the Word window.

2. **Right-click** on a clear area of the Windows Desktop; then choose **Properties** from the pop-up menu.

3. Follow these steps to check the resolution of your monitor.

Ⓐ *Click the Settings tab.*

Ⓑ *Take note of the current resolution setting. It is probably set for 800 × 600 or 640 × 480 pixels. Now drag the Screen area slider control one increment to the right.*

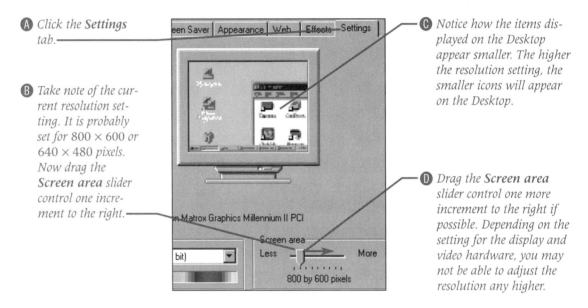

Ⓒ *Notice how the items displayed on the Desktop appear smaller. The higher the resolution setting, the smaller icons will appear on the Desktop.*

Ⓓ *Drag the Screen area slider control one more increment to the right if possible. Depending on the setting for the display and video hardware, you may not be able to adjust the resolution any higher.*

4. Click **Cancel** (not **OK**) to close the *Display Properties* window.

Backgrounds

If you set a color or an image as the background of a Web page, you should make your selection carefully. Many background colors can dazzle the browser's eyes so that it is almost painful to look at the page for any length of time. If you use dark text against a dark background color, the text may be almost impossible to read. Consider the comfort of your audience when you use colors for the background and text.

Download Speed

A Web page with lots of images may be quite attractive. However, a page with many images will load more slowly into Web browsers. In general, you should try make your Web pages download as quickly as possible. If you make people browsing your site wait very long, the result had better be worth it, or your audience will decide to browse elsewhere.

Saving Documents as Web Pages

Microsoft Word 2000 was designed to let you save documents as Web pages. This may save you the need to learn a more specialized Web page design program, such as Microsoft FrontPage or Adobe PageMill. Word includes commands to preview your Web pages and save any document as a Web page. When you save a document as a Web page, Word converts the document to HTML, the programming language for Web pages. When you convert a document, some formatting features may be lost. However, most of your documents should translate cleanly into attractive Web pages.

Web Page Preview

In previous lessons, you used the *Print Preview* command to see how a Word document workbook will appear in print. Word lets you preview your document as a Web page so you can see the results before you make the conversion. The *File→Web Page Preview* command launches your Web browser and displays the document exactly as it will appear on the Web.

HOW TO SAVE A DOCUMENT AS A WEB PAGE

Task	Procedure
Save a document so that it may be viewed on the Web.	■ Open the document in Word.
	■ Choose *File→Save As Web Page* from the menu bar.
	■ If desired, click the *Change Title* button to type the title that will appear in the Web browser when the document is displayed on the Web.
	■ Choose a destination for the Web page. This can be a folder on a disk drive or a Web folder (see page 349).
	■ Click *Save* to save the document in Web page format.
Preview a document in your Web browser.	■ Choose *File→Web Page Preview* from the menu bar.

Hands-On 11.5 Save a Document as a Web Page

In this exercise, you will use Web Page Preview and then save the resume document as a Web page.

Preview the Document as a Web Page

1. Click its button on the Windows Taskbar to restore the Word window to the Desktop.

2. Choose **View→Web Layout** from the menu bar.
This view lets you work with your document as it would appear in a Web browser, such as Internet Explorer. In this case, the page should appear similar to the Print Layout view you were using previously.

3. Choose **View→Print Layout** from the menu bar.

4. Choose **File→Web Page Preview** from the menu bar.
Word will start Internet Explorer *or your default Web browser program. The page is displayed just as it would appear if it were viewed over the Web. There's really not much difference between viewing the document in a Web browser and viewing it in* Web Layout *view. Most of the formatting should appear similar in both views.*

5. Close ☒ the Internet Explorer (or Netscape) window.
You are back to viewing the Word window.

Save the Document as a Web Page

Now you will save the document as a Web page on your floppy disk. Later, you will learn how to save the document as a Web page on the World Wide Web.

6. Choose **File→Save As Web Page** from the menu bar.

7. Click the **Change Title** button near the lower-right corner of the dialog box; then type the title: **Resume of [Your Name]**, and click **OK.**

8. Click the **Save** button.
There will be a pause as the document is converted to Web page (HTML) format; then Word will display your new Web page with the Web Layout *view.*

Open the Web Page

9. Minimize ▬ the Word window.

10. Double-click the *My Computer* icon on the Desktop; then double-click to open the *3½ Floppy (A:)* drive and double-click again to open the *My Resume* folder.
Notice that there is now a new folder in the My Resume folder. This folder holds any graphic images and other special information that controls the display of your Web page. In order to display your Web page properly, this folder must always be in the same folder as your Resume Web page.

11. Choose **View→Large Icons** from the menu bar.
    Notice that there are now two files named Resume; *one for each version of the document that you have saved as shown below.*

The Web page (HTML) version of the document.

The native Word format version of the document.

Resume   Resume

12. Double-click the **Resume** icon for the **Web page** version of your document.
    Internet Explorer (or another browser program) will start to display the document.

13. Scroll up and down in the Internet Explorer to view your new Web page.
    The resume should appear as it did in the Web Page Preview *view earlier in this exercise and as it appeared in the Word window immediately after the* **Save as Web Page** *command.*

14. Close ☒ the Internet Explorer window; then close the My Computer window.

Publishing with Web Folders

In order for others to view your Web pages over the Internet or an intranet, the pages must be **hosted** on a Web server. The act of placing your Web pages into a folder on a Web server is called **publishing** the pages. Most *Internet service providers* (ISPs) provide their subscribers with at least a megabyte or more of free Web space. Many ISPs have a variety of hosting plans and services to meet the needs of individuals, small businesses and large corporations.

Publishing Methods

You can choose from several methods to publish your Web pages to a Web server. The method you choose depends on the capabilities of the ISP or corporate network system that hosts the Web site. Some of the easiest methods are listed in the following table.

Method	When to Use It
Web folders	Use this method if your operating system supports Web folders. Windows 95, 98, NT 4.0 and Windows 2000 all support the use of Web folders to publish Web pages.
Via FTP	Use this method when there is no automated method to publish the pages. An FTP utility allows you to manually send your pages to the folder/directory in the hosting service system that will serve your pages.
ISP-provided utilities	Use this method when the ISP that hosts the Web site provides a special utility for publishing your Web pages.

Naming Web Pages

When you create your own Web pages, you should pay careful attention to their names. Many Web servers run on an operating system called UNIX that has rules for naming files that differ from Windows. The following points will help you name the workbook files that you publish to the Web so that they are compatible with most Web server systems:

- **Never use spaces in the filenames of Web pages and graphics**—UNIX systems do not allow spaces in filenames.

- **Give the primary page on your Web site the name *index.htm*—**If someone browses to your folder with the URL, but does not type a filename, most Web servers will display the index.htm page automatically. If you do not have an index.htm page on your Web site, someone browsing your site may get an error message.

- **Try not to use uppercase letters in filenames**—Web page filenames are case-sensitive. On UNIX servers for example, *MyHomePage.htm* and *myhomepage.htm* represent different filenames. If you consistently use lower-case letters in the filenames for Web pages and graphics on your Web site, it is less likely that those browsing your site will receive an error message.

Using Web Folders

Web Folders

Web folders allow you to publish Web pages and graphics with drag-and-drop ease. A Web folder is a folder on the computer that is directly associated with a folder on a Web server system. When you move or copy files to a Web folder, the files are automatically copied to the associated folder on the Web server system. If you delete files from a Web folder, they are also deleted from its associated Web server folder.

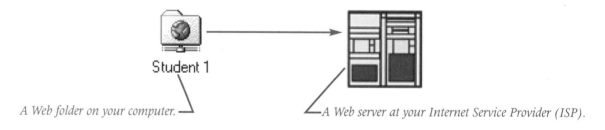
Student 1

A Web folder on your computer. ⌐   ⌐*A Web server at your Internet Service Provider (ISP).*

Quick Reference

HOW TO SAVE A DOCUMENT TO A WEB FOLDER	
Task	**Procedure**
Publish to a Web site with a Web folder.	■ Choose *File→Save as Web Page* from the menu bar.
	■ Click the *Web Folders* button on the left side of the dialog box, or click the *My Network Places* button if you are running Windows 2000.
	■ Double-click to open the desired Web folder.
	■ Complete the Save command normally.
Delete files from a Web site with a Web folder.	■ Open a *My Computer* or *Exploring* window; then open the *Web folders* folder; then open the Web folder from which you wish to delete files.
	■ Select any files you wish to delete; then click the *Delete* button on the toolbar.

In this Hands-On exercise, you will save your resume in Web page format to a Web folder. You will open the page in the Web folder to view your resume over the Internet or your school's intranet.

NOTE! *If your computer does not have a Web folder installed, you should skip this exercise and go on to the next topic.*

Before you Begin: *Ask your instructor for the Web folder name and, if necessary, the user name and password required to access your Web folder.*

Web Folder Name: _____

User Name: _____ *(optional)*

Password: _____ *(optional)*

Publish to a Web Folder

1. Click its button on the Windows Taskbar to restore the Word window to the Desktop.

2. Choose **File→Save as Web Page** from the menu bar.
   Now you will navigate to your Web folder.

3. Click the **Web Folders** button, or click **My Network Places** if you are running *Windows 2000.* The dialog box will display all of the available Web folders. This may be just one folder, or several.

4. Follow these steps to save the workbook to a Web folder.

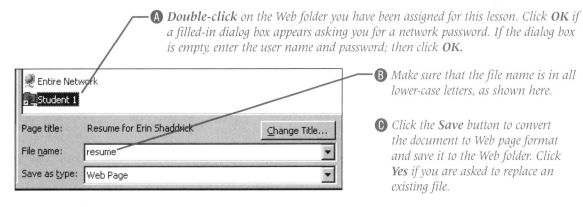

Ⓐ *Double-click on the Web folder you have been assigned for this lesson. Click **OK** if a filled-in dialog box appears asking you for a network password. If the dialog box is empty, enter the user name and password; then click **OK.***

Ⓑ *Make sure that the file name is in all lower-case letters, as shown here.*

Ⓒ *Click the **Save** button to convert the document to Web page format and save it to the Web folder. Click **Yes** if you are asked to replace an existing file.*

A Transferring File *dialog box will appear to show the progress of the transfer as the document is transmitted to the associated Web server folder. Your resume is now available over the Internet!*

(Continued on the next page)

5. Choose **File→Close** from the menu bar; then minimize ▬ the Word window.

6. Open a My Computer window; then follow the instructions for your version of Windows as listed below:

   ▪ **Windows 95, 98, NT 4.0**—If necessary, scroll down the My Computer window until the **Web Folders** icon is visible; then *double-click* to open Web Folders. If you do not see a Web Folders icon like the one at right toward the bottom of the My Computer window, then the Web folders feature is not installed on your computer. See your instructor for assistance.

   Web Folders

   ▪ **Windows 2000**—Click the Up one Level [⬆] button; then double-click on the *My Network Places* icon. You may see one or more Web folders along with other network resources.
   This window will display all of the available Web folders to which you may publish. Depending on how your system is configured, there may be just one folder, or several.

   My Network Places

7. Double-click to open your assigned Web folder. Click **OK** if you are prompted to enter a user name and password, and the password is already filled in. Otherwise, fill in the user name and password, and click **OK.**
   After a pause, the contents of the folder will be displayed. There may be some files displayed in this folder published by previous students.

8. After the contents of the Web folder are displayed, double-click the **resume** file in the Web folder window.
   The Internet Explorer Web browser will start and display your workbook Web page over the Internet. Notice the URL (Universal Resource Locator) *in the* Address bar *near the top of the Internet Explorer window. It should start with* http://www *and end with* resume.htm. *The URL serves as the address of your Web page.*

   After you have completed this exercise, feel free to tell others the URL of your Web workbook. Your resume will be displayed until another student uses this computer to perform a Hands-On exercise that uses this Web folder to post a resume.

   Write down the URL here:
   http://www. _____

9. Scroll down the page to confirm that the resume appears as it did in the Web Page Preview view.
   Leave the Internet Explorer window open.

■

Converting Documents from HTML

When you save a document as a Web page, some features of the document may change or become unavailable. Several types of format settings are not supported in the HTML format. For example, if your text is arranged in columns, those columns will disappear when the document is saved as a Web page. However, all of the data in your document (including any comments, columns, and page layout settings) are still stored in the Web page version. If you load the Web page version of the document back into Word, you can restore the file to the native Word document format. Once this has been done, all of the formatting features of the document will become active again.

Round Trips from HTML to Document Format

The process of taking a Word document from document (native) format to Web page (HTML) format and back again to document format is called a **round trip.** This process is shown in the diagram below.

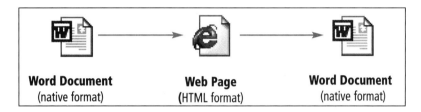

Word Document (native format)   **Web Page** (HTML format)   **Word Document** (native format)

An example of the round-trip concept. A Word document can be transformed to Web page format then back to Word format without any loss of data or special formatting.

CONVERT A WEB FORMAT DOCUMENT BACK TO NATIVE FORMAT	
Task	**Procedure**
Save a Word document that is posted on the Web.	■ Open the document in Internet Explorer.
	■ Click the *Edit* button on the Internet Explorer toolbar; then choose *Microsoft Word* from the drop-down list.
	■ Click *OK* if you are asked for a network password.
	■ After the file has loaded in Word, choose *File→Save As* from the menu bar.
	■ Change the *Save as type* to *Word Document* format, and click *OK*.

Hands-On 11.7 Perform a Round Trip with a Word Document

In this exercise, you will load the Web page version of your document into Word and then save it as a normal Word document.

 This exercise will not work if Netscape Navigator is set as your default Web browser. You must open the Web page in Internet Explorer to perform a round trip. You may need to start Internet Explorer; then choose File→Open from the menu bar. Click the Browse button and navigate to open your resume on the floppy disk. After your resume is displayed in Internet Explorer, you may proceed with Step 2 of this exercise.

1. Make sure that the Web page version of your resume is still displayed in the Internet Explorer window. If you were unable to perform Hands-On Exercise 11.6, follow the steps below to display your resume Web page.

   ■ Choose **File→Close** from the Word menu bar.

   ■ Minimize 🔲 the Word window.

   ■ Double-click to open a *My Computer* window; then double-click to open the *3½ Floppy (A:)* drive and the *My Resume* folder.

   ■ Double-click the *Resume* Web page. Your resume should now appear in an Internet Explorer window.

2. Follow these steps to load the Web page version workbook into Word.

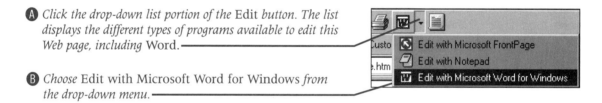

Ⓐ *Click the drop-down list portion of the* Edit *button. The list displays the different types of programs available to edit this Web page, including* Word.

Ⓑ *Choose* Edit with Microsoft Word for Windows *from the drop-down menu.*

You may receive a prompt that some files for this Web page are not in the expected location. This is a security feature to help you avoid files that might contain a computer virus. Since you created this file yourself, there is no need to worry.

3. Click **Yes** if you receive a notification that some files on this Web page are not in the expected location.

4. Click **OK** if you receive a prompt to enter a Web folder password.

5. Click its button on the Windows Taskbar to restore the Word window.

6. Examine the document for a moment to confirm that the Web page was loaded successfully from the Web site.

7. Choose **File→Save As** from the menu bar.

8. Follow these steps to finish saving the document in Word format to complete the round trip.

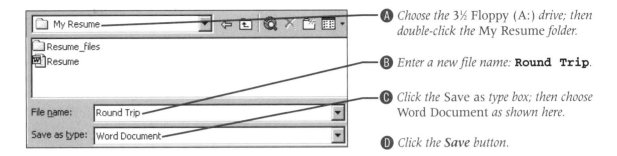

A. *Choose the* 3½ Floppy (A:) *drive; then double-click the* My Resume *folder.*

B. *Enter a new file name:* **Round Trip**.

C. *Click the* Save as *type box; then choose* Word Document *as shown here.*

D. *Click the* **Save** *button.*

9. Choose **File→Save As** from the menu bar.
   Notice that the Save as type *box now reads* Word Document. *This indicates that you have successfully converted the document from the Web page format to the native Word format (a* round trip*).*

10. Click **Cancel;** then choose **File→Close** from the menu bar.

11. Right-click on the Web Folder button on the Windows taskbar; then choose **Close** from the pop-up menu.
    This is a handy shortcut for closing unneeded windows.

Adding Bitmap Images to Documents

Images can add a great deal of visual interest and variety to documents. You learned how to place images on document pages in Lesson 8. There are several sources of graphics for your documents. For example, there are many free clip art sites on the Web that offer free graphics for noncommercial use. You can also use images from a digital camera, or scan a photograph. Many photo developing services can give you a disk with your photos in digital format.

There are two major categories of images you can place into your documents:

- **Bitmap Images**—these images are called **bitmaps** because they are composed of thousands (sometimes millions) of tiny dots called *pixels.* Each pixel is set to a specific color. Bitmap images are excellent for displaying photographs on Web pages. However, if you change the size of a bitmap image very much, you also reduce the image quality. *GIF* and *JPEG* files (see the following page) are examples of bitmap images.

- **Vector Images**—these images are composed of lines, curves, and fill patterns. Most of the clip art that comes with Microsoft office is in a vector image format. One advantage of vector images is that you can make them larger and smaller without reducing the quality of the image. *Windows Metafile* is an example of a vector image.

Types of Images for the Web

If you plan to publish a Word document as a Web page, and there are images on the document, you need to consider how this will affect the display of your Web page. Computer image files can be very large. For example, a three-inch square image suitable for printing in a book can be up to three megabytes in size. Fortunately, there are ways to compress image files so that they are not so large. This is important because most people access Web pages over a modem line, and modems are relatively slow when downloading large image files. For example, a three-megabyte file would take about 14 minutes to download over a 28.8K modem connection. If the same file were compressed, it might take just a few seconds to download. The two most popular file formats for images on the Web are described below.

- **GIF (Graphic Interchange Format)**—The GIF format compresses a file by examining the image for consistent patterns and then rewriting the digital image in a form of short-hand based on those repeated patterns, reducing the number of colors used to display the picture. The GIF format can compress images by about 4:1. Most of the buttons and small pieces of art you see on Web pages were saved as GIF images.

- **JPEG (Joint Photographic Experts Group)**—JPEG format compresses a file by tossing out subtle color differences in the image that human eyes are less likely to recognize. Depending on the level of image quality you require, JPEG can accomplish compression ratios between 10:1 and 100:1. Most of the photos you see on Web pages are saved as JPEG images.

TIP!

Try not to place too many images on a Web page or it will appear very slowly when others try to browse it.

INSERTING IMAGES	
Task	**Procedure**
Insert an image onto a document.	■ Click where you wish to insert the image.
	■ Choose *Insert→Picture→From File* from the menu bar; then click *Browse*.
	■ Navigate to the disk drive and folder where the image is stored, and double-click to insert the image.

Scaling Images

You can make an image larger or smaller after you have placed it in a document. You do this by dragging on the *handles* of the image. Every image on a page has handles at the corners and on each side. The handles appear as small white squares around the image when you click on it.

TIP!

When you scale an image larger than actual size, it will lose resolution and become fuzzier on the screen and on the printed page.

Each small square around the edge of this image is a handle.

In this exercise, you will use two methods to place bitmap images on a Word document.

Insert an Image with the Insert Command

1. Click the New Document 🔲 button on the Word toolbar.

2. Choose the **Heading 1** style; then type **We had a harrowing hike back to our camp.**

3. Tap the (ENTER) key to start a new line.

4. Choose **Insert→Picture→From File** from the menu bar.
   The Insert dialog box will appear.

5. Follow these steps to insert an image file.

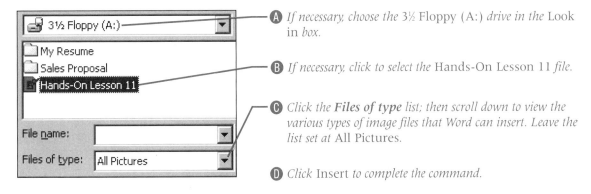

Ⓐ *If necessary, choose the 3½ Floppy (A:) drive in the Look in box.*

Ⓑ *If necessary, click to select the Hands-On Lesson 11 file.*

Ⓒ *Click the Files of type list; then scroll down to view the various types of image files that Word can insert. Leave the list set at All Pictures.*

Ⓓ *Click Insert to complete the command.*

Scale the Image

Now you will practice changing the size of the image by dragging on its handles.

6. Click anywhere on the image.
   Notice the small black squares around the edge of the image. These are its handles.

7. Follow these steps to scale the image to a smaller size.

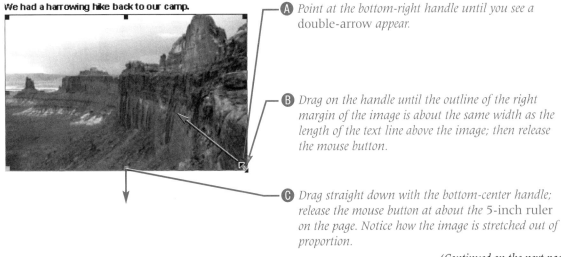

Ⓐ *Point at the bottom-right handle until you see a double-arrow appear.*

Ⓑ *Drag on the handle until the outline of the right margin of the image is about the same width as the length of the text line above the image; then release the mouse button.*

Ⓒ *Drag straight down with the bottom-center handle; release the mouse button at about the 5-inch ruler on the page. Notice how the image is stretched out of proportion.*

(Continued on the next page)

8. Click the Undo  button to undo the last scaling command.
   Now the image should be back in proportion.

9. Drag down and to the right on the bottom-right handle to scale the image larger; then drag back up and to the left to make the image about as wide as the text line above it.
   Regardless of its initial size, you can scale an image to just the size you need.

10. Tap the (END) key to jump to the end of the document; then tap (ENTER) twice to add two new lines.

11. Choose the **Heading 1** style; then type the following text:

    But we also had a magnificent view from our camp.

12. Tap (ENTER) to start a new line.

Insert an Image with Drag and Drop

Now you will navigate to a Web page and use the drag-and-drop technique to place an image onto your document directly from a Web page.

13. Click its button on the Taskbar to make the *Internet Explorer* window active.

14. Click in the Internet Explorer **Address bar,** and type the following URL:

    Address 🔲 http://www.offtowork.com/word/lesson11

    www.offtowork.com/word/lesson11

15. Click the **Web Image** hyperlink at the bottom of the page.
    A Web page with an image will appear.

16. Follow these steps to arrange the Word and Internet Explorer windows side by side.

🅐 Right-click *on a clear area near the right side of the Windows taskbar (near the system time).*

🅑 *Choose* Tile Windows Vertically *from the pop-up menu.*

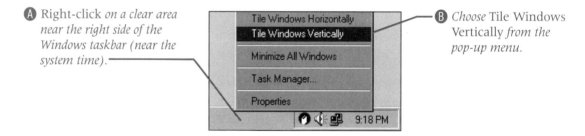

17. Follow these steps to drag and drop the image onto your document page.

Ⓐ *Point on the image in the Internet Explorer window; then start to drag the image to the bottom of the Word document.*

Ⓑ *Release the mouse button when you see the this pointer arrow on the document, immediately beneath the second caption in the document.*

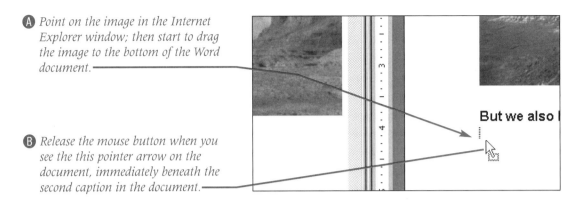

After a brief pause, the Web image will appear on the page.

18. Close ☒ the Internet Explorer window; then maximize ☐ the Word window.

The Office Clipboard

Normally, the Windows clipboard can only hold the most recently cut or copied item for pasting. With Office 2000, Microsoft introduced an enhanced Office Clipboard that can hold up to 12 recently cut or copied items at one time. You can choose which of these items to paste, and even preview text items on the Office Clipboard toolbar. The Clipboard toolbar displays the icon of each Office application program from which you have cut or copied items.

Paste Special and the Office Clipboard

You learned about Word's **Paste Special** command in Lesson 6. This command lets you paste clipboard data in various formats, such as text-only, rich text, and HTML. You can also use the **Paste Special** command in conjunction with the Office Clipboard. The **Paste Special** command lets you paste the most recently pasted item from the Office Clipboard.

A ScreenTip displays the first 50 characters of text items copied to the clipboard.

Non-text items, such as pictures, are identified only by an item number of the order in which they were copied.

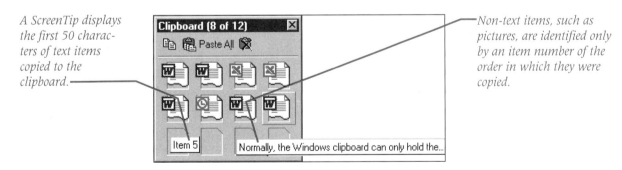

In this example, the Office Clipboard displays items copied from Word, Excel, and Outlook.

USING THE OFFICE CLIPBOARD

Task	Procedure
Display the Office Clipboard toolbar.	■ *Right-click* anywhere on a Word toolbar; then choose Clipboard from the pop-up menu.
Preview the contents of an Office Clipboard item.	■ Display the Office Clipboard toolbar. ■ Point over the desired clipboard icon for about two seconds. *The first 50 characters of any text item will display, or you will see a number for any copied images.*
Paste a specific Office Clipboard item.	■ Display the Office Clipboard toolbar. ■ Click on the icon for the desired item to be pasted.
Clear all items from the Office Clipboard.	■ Click the *Clear Clipboard* button on the clipboard toolbar.
Use Paste Special with the Office Clipboard	■ Paste the desired item from the Office Clipboard; then click the *Undo* button on the Word toolbar. ■ Choose *Edit→Paste Special* from the menu bar; then choose the desired paste format and click *OK*.

Hands-On 11.8 Use the Office Clipboard

In this exercise, you will copy several items to the Office clipboard and then selectively paste items from the clipboard onto the document.

1. Right-click on the Word toolbar; then choose **Clipboard** from the pop-up menu.
   The Clipboard toolbar will float over the Word window. Depending on what you have copied to the clipboard previously, there may be one or more items on the clipboard. You can move the Clipboard toolbar by dragging on its title bar if the toolbar ends up in an inconvenient location.

2. Click the *Clear Clipboard* button on the Clipboard toolbar.
   All clipboard items are cleared. Now you will begin copying items from your document onto the clipboard.

Copy Items to the Clipboard

3. Select the first line of text at the top of the document; then click the **Copy** button on the Clipboard toolbar.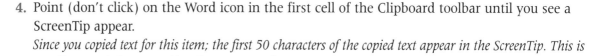
   A Word icon will appear on the Clipboard toolbar. This indicates that you copied something from a Word document.

4. Point (don't click) on the Word icon in the first cell of the Clipboard toolbar until you see a ScreenTip appear.
   Since you copied text for this item; the first 50 characters of the copied text appear in the ScreenTip. This is usually enough for you to identify any particular text item that you have copied.

5. Click to select the first image at the top of the document.
   The appearance of handles around the image will confirm that it is selected.

6. Click the Copy  button on the Word toolbar.
   *The standard toolbar **Copy** button and the **Copy** button on the Clipboard toolbar both function identically.*

7. Point at the new Word icon in the second cell of the Clipboard toolbar until you see a ScreenTip.
   This time the ScreenTip just shows Item 2. *When you copy an image without any text, each image you copy to the clipboard receives an item number.*

8. Drag to select the second line of text *and* the second image on the page.

9. Click the Copy  button to copy the entire selection. Point at the third icon on the Clipboard toolbar until the ScreenTip appears.
   Since the selection included both text and a graphic, the first 50 letters of the text are displayed.

Paste Items from the Office Clipboard

10. Use (CTRL)+(END) to jump to the bottom of the document; then tap (ENTER) twice.

11. Hold down the (CTRL) key; then tap (ENTER) to create a page break.
    You should now be viewing a blank page.

12. Click on the third (last) icon on the Clipboard toolbar.
    The text and image should be pasted at the top of the new page.

13. Click the second (middle) icon on the Clipboard toolbar.

14. Tap the (ENTER) key to start a new line; then click the first Clipboard item icon.
    The Office Clipboard lets you mix the order of any items you have copied.

15. Use (CTRL)+(ENTER) to create a page break.

16. Click the **Paste All** button on the Clipboard toolbar.
    All clipboard items are pasted on the new page in the same order they were originally copied. The Office Clipboard lets you gather multiple items in whichever order you need; then lets you paste them with a single command. Notice that the second line of text appears immediately after the first image. This is because you copied only the image, without the hard return that appeared after the image on your first page.

Use Paste Special with the Clipboard

17. Use (CTRL)+(ENTER) to create a page break.

18. Click the first Clipboard item icon to paste the caption of the top image.
    Notice that the caption is still formatted in the Heading 1 style.

19. Click Undo  on the Word toolbar; then choose **Edit→Paste Special** from the menu bar.
    Word displays a list of the various formats in which you can paste the most previously pasted selection. The format selection list depends on the type of item most recently pasted from the Office Clipboard.

20. Choose the *Unformatted Text* format; then click **OK.**
    The text no longer has the Heading 1 format. It was pasted as plain text characters.

21. Click the **Clear Clipboard** button on the Clipboard toolbar.
    All clipboard items are cleared once again.

22. Close  the Clipboard toolbar.

Working with Themes

Word has a slick feature that can instantly add color and visual variety to your Web pages. Themes are a combination of text formatting, bullets, and background colors that you can apply to any document. You can change a document from one theme to another. It is also easy to remove a theme from a document.

USE THEMES WITH DOCUMENTS	
Task	**Procedure**
Apply a theme to a document.	■ Display the document in Word; then choose *Format→Theme* from the menu bar.
	■ Select the theme you wish to apply. Many of the available themes may not be installed.
	■ Click *OK* to apply the theme to the entire document.
Remove a theme from a document.	■ Display the document in Word; then choose *Format→Theme* from the menu bar.
	■ Choose (No Theme) at the top of the theme list; then click *OK*.

Hands-On 11.9 Apply a Theme

In this exercise, you will apply a theme to your document. After you view a few themes, you will remove the theme from the document.

1. Use CTRL+HOME to jump to the first page of your document.

2. Choose **Format→Theme** from the menu bar.
   A list of available themes will appear. The right side of the dialog box displays a preview of the theme's visual elements.

3. Click the **Artsy** theme in the list on the left side of the dialog box.
   The preview shows that this theme is very dark. Let's try another one.

4. Tap the E key on the keyboard until the **Expedition** theme is selected.
   This theme seems better suited to the topic.

5. Click **OK** to apply the theme to your document.
   Notice that the text color and font has changed. Each theme has special text formatting designed for it.

6. Choose **Format→Theme** from the menu bar; then uncheck the *Background Image* box at the bottom-left corner of the dialog box.
   You can selectively add and remove some features from the theme.

7. Check the *Background Image* box to restore the background image to the theme.

8. Try previewing a few of the other installed themes, such as *Blends, Citrus Punch, Rice Paper,* and *Sumi Painting.*
   Most of the themes are not available from the standard installation of Office 2000. To view the uninstalled themes, you would need the Office 2000 installation CD.

9. When you are done sampling the themes, choose **(No Theme)** from the top of the list; and then click **OK.**

10. Close ☒ the Word window. Click **No** when you are asked if you wish to save the document. Close the Internet Explorer and My Computer windows.

Concepts Review

True/False Questions

1. A Wizard can help you create complex documents more easily.   TRUE   FALSE

2. Once you enter a setting into the Resume Wizard, you cannot change it.   TRUE   FALSE

3. In order to create a new folder when you save a Word document, you must first create the folder in a My Computer window.   TRUE   FALSE

4. The **Save As** command lets you change the file format of a Word document.   TRUE   FALSE

5. When you display a Web page over the Internet, the fonts on the page will always appear exactly the way the author designed them.   TRUE   FALSE

6. A Web folder lets you save pages directly to a Web server connected to the Internet.   TRUE   FALSE

7. A round trip consists of saving a Word document as a Web page, then saving the Web page back into Word format.   TRUE   FALSE

8. You can change the size of a bitmap image in any direction without distorting it.   TRUE   FALSE

9. The Office Clipboard requires you to paste items in the same order they were cut or copied.   TRUE   FALSE

10. The **Paste Special** command does not work with the Office Clipboard.   TRUE   FALSE

Multiple-Choice Questions

1. Which filename is most appropriate for a document saved as a Web page?

   a. My Resume

   b. MyResume

   c. myresume

   d. None of the above

2. What happens when you save document as a Web page to a Web folder?

   a. The Web page is transferred to a Web server folder.

   b. The document is converted to HTML format.

   c. The Web page is available for viewing over the Internet.

   d. All of the above

3. How do you start a Word Document Wizard?

   a. Click the New [ ] button on the Word toolbar.

   b. Choose **Tools→Templates and Add-Ins→Wizard** from the menu bar; then select a Wizard for the type of document you wish to create.

   c. Choose **File→New** from the menu bar; then select a Wizard for the type of document you wish to create.

   d. None of the above

4. Which statement best describes a *native* file format for Word?

   a. A file format for which Word has a converter.

   b. A file format that stores a Word document as a Web page.

   c. A file format which Word does not need a converter to open.

   d. A file format for a similar program, such as WordPerfect.

Advanced Table Techniques

Tables are a powerful tool for organizing and laying out documents. In Word 2000, tables are flexible and easy to modify and format. For example, you can merge or split table cells, sort rows, center tables between the margins, and perform calculations in tables. For situations requiring complex calculations and number formatting, you can embed Excel worksheets within Word documents. This way, you can take advantage of the power of Excel while still working within a Word document. Finally, Word's powerful **Table AutoFormat** command lets you create impressive, professionally formatted tables with a few mouse clicks.

In This Lesson

Case Study

Al Adams is an Administrative Assistant for Diamond Financial Services. Ted Johnson, a Diamond customer, has asked Al to prepare an account statement for his accounts. Normally, Al would prepare a standard statement using Diamond's financial software. However, Ted has requested a customized format for this particular statement. Al uses Word 2000's powerful tables feature to prepare the custom report requested by Ted.

Account Information
Ted Johnson (1/15/2000)

Account Summary (1999 vs. 2000)		
	1999	**2000**
Stocks	$125,000	$160,000
Bonds	$ 20,000	$ 18,000

Account TJ 1053

Stock Holdings

Company	Symbol	Purchase Price	Current Price	Gain/Loss
Apple	APPL	$4,000	$5,000	$1,000.00
BioSys	BIS	$21,000	$30,000	$9,000.00
CalGen	CLG	$19,000	$20,500	$1,500.00
Galileo	GLC	$10,000	$4,500	($5,500.00)
GemCo	GEC	$8,000	$35,000	$27,000.00
IBM	IBM	$37,000	$30,000	($7,000.00)
SysTech	SYT	$12,500	$10,000	($2,500.00)
Vectron	VCT	$20,000	$25,000	$5,000.00
Totals		$131,500.00	$160,000.00	$28,500.00

Merging and Splitting Cells

The Merge Cells 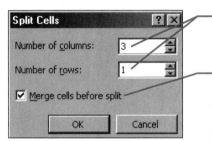 button on the Tables and Borders toolbar lets you merge any rectangular block of table cells. Merged cells behave as one large cell. This option is often used to center a heading across the top of a table. You merge cells by selecting the desired cells and then clicking the **Merge Cells** button. Once cells have been merged, you can change the alignment of text within the merged cell, and format the merged cell as you would format any other cell.

Account Summary (1999 vs. 2000)		

Cells in the heading row are merged, and the text is then centered within the merged cell.

The Split Cells button lets you split a cell into multiple cells. You can split a merged cell or a cell that has never been merged. A dialog box appears when you click the **Split Cells** button. The dialog box lets you specify the number of columns and rows to create from the split cell.

You can specify the number of columns and rows to create from the Split Cells menu.

This option is available if multiple cells are selected before the Split Cells button is clicked. If this box is checked, Word will first merge the selected cells, and then split the merged cell into the number of columns and rows specified.

Hands-On 12.1 Merge and Split Cells

In this exercise, you will set up the first table in the account statement.

Merge Cells

1. Start Word, and use the (ENTER) key to space down to approximately the 2" position.

2. Click the Center Align button, and type the heading **Account Information**.

3. Tap (ENTER), and type **Ted Johnson (1/15/2000)**.

4. Tap (ENTER) four more times, and insert a table with two columns and two rows.

5. If necessary, click the Tables and Borders button on the Standard toolbar to display the Tables and Borders toolbar.

6. If the mouse pointer takes on a pencil shape, then click the Draw Table button on the Tables and Borders toolbar to dismiss the icon.

7. Select the cells in the first row, and click the Merge Cells button on the Tables and Borders toolbar.

8. Click anywhere outside the table, and the cells should be merged.

9. Click in the merged cell, and type **Account Summary (1999 vs. 2000)**.
Notice that the entry is centered within the merged cell. The alignment is set to center in all of the table cells because the alignment was set to center when the table was created.

10. Click the Left Align button to change the alignment to left.

11. Click the Center Align button to recenter the entry.

12. Make sure that the insertion point is within the merged cell, and click the Split Cells ▦ button on the Tables and Borders toolbar.

    Notice that the Merge cells before split *option is not available. This option is only available if cells are selected prior to clicking the button.*

13. Click **OK** to split the cell into the original configuration of two columns and one row.

14. Click outside the table, and notice that the table is in the original configuration.

15. Click Undo ↻ to restore the merged cell.

16. Save the document as **Hands-On Lesson 12,** and continue with the next topic.

Changing the Text Direction

The Change Text Direction ▥ button on the Tables and Borders toolbar lets you rotate text in table cells. Text is rotated in 90-degree increments each time the button is clicked.

Hands-On 12.2 Rotate Text

Rotate the Text

1. Position the insertion point in the first cell of the second row.

2. Type **Account**, and tap (ENTER).

3. Type **TJ 1053** on the second line.

4. Click the Change Text Direction ▥ button on the Tables and Borders toolbar.

    The text will rotate 90 degrees in a downward configuration.

5. Click the Change Text Direction ▥ button again.

    The text will rotate into an upward position and move to the left edge of the cell.

AutoFit the Column Width, and Explore the Toolbar

6. Position the mouse pointer on the border between the columns, and double-click to AutoFit the first column.

    The first column should be just wide enough to hold the rotated text.

7. Click in the cell with the rotated text.

    Notice that the insertion point has a horizontal configuration. Also, notice that the buttons on the Formatting toolbar have a rotated appearance, as shown above.

8. Save the changes to the document, and continue with the next topic.

Embedding Excel Worksheets in Word Documents

The Insert Microsoft Excel Worksheet button on the Standard toolbar lets you embed Excel worksheets in Word documents. You can embed worksheets in the body of a document and within tables. When an embedded worksheet is activated, Excel's toolbars and menus replace Word's toolbars and menus. This allows you to use Excel's commands and tools within a Word document. You can use Excel to develop a polished worksheet that is placed within a Word document.

Editing Embedded Worksheets

You can edit an embedded worksheet by first double-clicking the worksheet. Once the worksheet becomes active, you can use Excel to edit,

Embedding a three-column by three-row worksheet

format, and modify the worksheet. When you have finished editing the worksheet, you can click outside the worksheet, and Word's toolbars and menus will reappear. Excel's toolbars and menus appear only after an embedded worksheet has been activated with a double-click.

Hands-On 12.3 Embed a Worksheet in a Table

Embed the Worksheet

1. Click in the large empty cell at the bottom right corner of the table.

2. Click the Insert Microsoft Excel Worksheet ⊞ button on the Standard toolbar.

3. Draw the mouse over a 3 × 3 block in the grid that appears, and release the mouse button.
   A worksheet will be inserted in the table, and Excel's menus and toolbars will replace Word's menus and toolbars.

4. Take a few moments to examine the toolbars.
   If you have worked with Excel 2000, you will recognize these as Excel's toolbars. All Excel tools and commands are available to you because you have embedded a worksheet.

5. Follow these steps to enter data in the Excel worksheet.

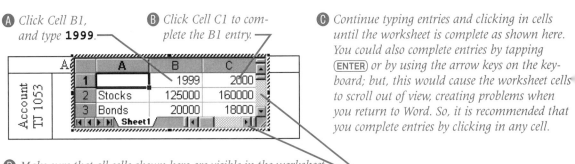

Ⓐ *Click Cell B1, and type* **1999**.

Ⓑ *Click Cell C1 to complete the B1 entry.*

Ⓒ *Continue typing entries and clicking in cells until the worksheet is complete as shown here. You could also complete entries by tapping* (ENTER) *or by using the arrow keys on the keyboard; but, this would cause the worksheet cells to scroll out of view, creating problems when you return to Word. So, it is recommended that you complete entries by clicking in any cell.*

Ⓓ *Make sure that all cells shown here are visible in the worksheet. If necessary, use the scroll bars until all cells shown here are visible.*

6. Click anywhere outside the worksheet to insert the worksheet in the table.
Notice that Word's menus and toolbars have reappeared. It is possible that you may not be able to see the entire worksheet in the table or

Account Summary (1999 vs. 2000)		
	1999	2000
Stocks	125000	160000
Bonds	20000	18000

Account TJ 1053

that extra worksheet cells may be visible. You will be able to correct these and other problems when you edit the worksheet in the following steps. At this point, your worksheet should match the worksheet shown above.

Edit the Worksheet

7. Click the embedded worksheet, and notice that it becomes selected.
If desired, you could delete the selected object by tapping the (DELETE) *key, or you could drag it to a different location (but not now).*

8. Double-click the embedded worksheet.
Excel's toolbars and menus will reappear, and the worksheet will once again be displayed in the Excel worksheet window.

9. Select the four cells shown to the right by dragging the mouse over them. The first cell in the block will not appear to be selected, as shown here. However, it will be part of the selection.

	A	B	C
1		1999	2000
2	Stocks	125000	160000
3	Bonds	20000	18000

Sheet1

10. Click the Currency Style [$] button on Excel's Formatting toolbar to apply a Currency format to the selected numbers.
The Currency Style displays a dollar sign, a comma between every third digit, and two decimal places.

11. Click the Decrease Decimals [.00 / +.0] button twice on Excel's Formatting toolbar.
This will remove the zeros to the right of the decimal points.

12. Click in the Word document below the table.
This will complete the changes and position the insertion point below the table.

Prepare to Create Another Table

13. Tap (ENTER) four times, and type **Stock Holdings**.
The Stock Holdings heading should be centered on the line. Later in this lesson, you will format the document and the table you just created. In addition, you will center the table horizontally on the page.

14. Tap (ENTER) twice, and continue with the next topic.

Sorting Tables, Lists, and Paragraphs

Word lets you sort tables, lists, and paragraphs. The most common type of sort is when table rows are sorted based upon the entries in one or more of the table's columns.

Sort Keys

When sorting table rows, Word must know which rows you want to sort and which column to use as the sort key. Word uses the sort key to decide how to arrange the rows. For example, imagine a table has a list of company names in the first column (Column A). If you wanted to sort the rows according to the names, then you would specify Column A as the sort key. You specify a column as a sort key by clicking in the desired column prior to sorting.

The Sort Buttons

The Sort Ascending and Sort Descending buttons on the Tables and Borders toolbar let you rapidly sort lists. A list is a group of table rows that are isolated from other rows in the table. Being isolated means there is at least one empty row above and below the list. Because a list is isolated from other rows, Word can easily determine which rows to sort when you click the Sort Ascending or Sort Descending button. Word sorts all rows in the list unless it determines that the list has a header row. A header row is the row at the top of a list containing column headings. To sort a list, you first click within the list in the column that you want to use as the sort key. Then, you click either the **Sort Ascending** or **Sort Descending** button.

Sorting Paragraphs

You can sort paragraphs that are not part of a table. To sort paragraphs, select the desired paragraphs and click the **Sort Ascending** or **Sort Descending** button. Word sorts the paragraphs based upon the first word or number in each paragraph.

Multilevel Sorts

The **Table→Sort** command displays the Sort dialog box. The Sort dialog box lets you specify more than one sort key for multilevel sorts. For example, imagine you had a table with last names in Column A and first names in Column B. Using the Sort dialog box, you could instruct Word to first sort the rows by last name and then by first name. This way, all rows with the same last name would be grouped together. Then, the rows would be sorted by first name within each group.

In this exercise, you will insert a stock holdings table and sort the table rows.

Set Up the Table

1. Make sure the insertion point is positioned on the second blank row below the Stock Holdings heading.

2. Click the Align Left ▤ button.

3. Insert a table with 9 rows and 5 columns (a 9 × 5 table).

4. Enter the data shown below into the table. Notice that there are no entries in the last column.

Company	Symbol	Purchase Price	Current Price	Gain/Loss
Vectron	VCT	$20,000	$25,000	
SysTech	SYT	$12,500	$10,000	
BioSys	BIS	$21,000	$30,000	
GemCo	GEC	$8,000	$35,000	
IBM	IBM	$37,000	$30,000	
Apple	APPL	$4,000	$5,000	
Galileo	GLC	$10,000	$4,500	
CalGen	CLG	$19,000	$20,500	

Sort the Table

5. Click in the cell with the company name Vectron.
   When you sort the table in the following steps, Word will sort entire rows. The rows will be sorted according to the text entries in Column A.

6. Click the Sort Ascending ▤ button on the Tables and Borders toolbar.
   Notice that the header row remained at the top of the table. Word was able to determine that the table included a header row. The Apple row now should be the first row below the header row followed by BioSys, etc.

7. Make sure that the insertion point is in Column A, and click the Sort Descending ▤ button to reverse the sort order.

8. Click anywhere in Column B, and sort the rows in Ascending order based upon the stock symbols.

9. Click anywhere in Column D, and sort the rows in Descending order.

10. Finally, sort the rows in Ascending order based upon the company names in Column A.

Performing Calculations in Tables

Word's **Table→Formula** command lets you insert simple formulas into table cells. You can use formulas to perform calculations on numbers. Word's table formulas aren't nearly as sophisticated as Excel's; however, they are adequate for simple calculations.

The Formula Dialog Box

In Word, all formulas are inserted using the Formula box. To insert a formula, you click in the desired cell, choose **Table→Formula,** and construct the desired formula.

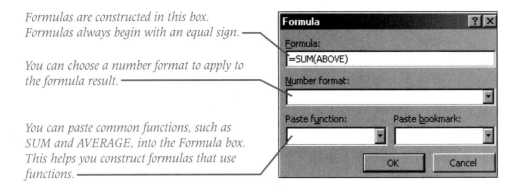

Formulas are constructed in this box. Formulas always begin with an equal sign.

You can choose a number format to apply to the formula result.

You can paste common functions, such as SUM and AVERAGE, into the Formula box. This helps you construct formulas that use functions.

Constructing Formulas

You construct formulas by typing directly into the Formula box. In Word, formulas can contain a combination of the following elements:

- **Arithmetic operators**—The most common arithmetic operators are + (addition), – (subtraction), / (division), and * (multiplication).

- **Functions**—Functions are predefined formulas that perform calculations on cells. The most common functions are SUM, AVERAGE, MIN, and MAX. These functions perform calculations on ranges (rectangular blocks) of cells.

- **Cell references**—In Word tables, the columns are labeled A, B, C, etc., and the rows are numbered 1, 2, 3, etc. Each cell has a reference formed by the column letter and row number. For example, Cell A1 refers to the cell formed by the intersection of Column A and Row 1. You can use cell references in formulas. For example, the formula =D2–C2 subtracts the number in Cell C2 from the number in Cell D2.

- **Direction references**—In Word, functions can use direction references to reference cell ranges. The direction references are ABOVE, BELOW, LEFT, and RIGHT. For example, the formula =SUM(ABOVE) would sum all numbers above the cell containing the formula.

AutoSum

The AutoSum Σ button on the Tables and Borders toolbar automatically sums columns of numbers. You can sum a column by clicking in the cell directly below the column of numbers and then clicking AutoSum.

Formula Limitations

In Word, you cannot copy formulas from one cell to another. Also, you must construct formulas one cell at a time. For these and other reasons, you should embed an Excel worksheet in your document if you need more sophisticated formulas and formula-management techniques.

In this exercise, you will use formulas to calculate the Gain/Loss column. You will also add a Totals row to the table, and you will use the SUM function to calculate the column totals.

Calculate the Gain/Loss

1. Make sure the table rows are sorted in ascending order on Column A. The Apple row should be the first row below the header row.

2. Click in the Gain/Loss cell for the Apple row, and choose **Table→Formula.**
   Word will propose the formula =SUM(LEFT) in the formula box.

3. Use the (BACKSPACE) key to remove the proposed formula, and type **=D2-C2**.
   This formula will subtract the purchase price in Column C (the third column) from the current price in Column D (the fourth column).

4. Click **OK** to complete the formula; the result should equal $1,000.00.
   Notice that Word applied a number format to the result. The number format inserts a dollar sign in front of the number, a comma between every third digit, and two decimal points.

5. Click in the next cell down, and choose **Table→Formula.**

6. Use (BACKSPACE) to remove the current formula, and type the new formula **=D3-C3**.

7. Click the **Number format** drop down-button, and notice the various number format codes.
   The third number format begins with a dollar sign $. Word automatically applied this Currency format to the previous formula. Word applied the Currency format because you used dollar signs when entering the data in Columns C and D. Another limitation of formulas in Word is that the number formats are not very flexible. For example, the Currency format displays a decimal point and two decimal digits. In your table, the decimals aren't necessary because the numbers in Columns C and D don't have decimals. Unfortunately, removing the decimal display is quite cumbersome in Word. If you had embedded an Excel worksheet, it would have been easy to remove the decimal display.

8. Tap the (ESC) key to dismiss the Number format drop-down list, and click **OK** to insert the formula.
   The result should equal $9,000.00.

9. Calculate the remaining Gain/Loss numbers in Column E. All of the formulas will continue to reference Columns D and C, but the row numbers will increase. For example, the next formula will be =D4–C4, followed by =D5–C5, etc. Also, some of the results will be surrounded by parentheses. Parentheses indicate that the result is negative.

Add a Totals Row

10. Click in the last table cell, and tap the (TAB) key to add a new row to the table.

11. Type the word **Totals** in the first cell of the new row.

12. Click in the third cell of the new row, and choose **Table→Formula.**
    Word will propose the formula =SUM(ABOVE).

13. Click **OK** to accept the proposed formula.
    The result should equal $131,500.00.

(Continued on the next page)

14. Click in the next cell, and then click the AutoSum Σ button on the Tables and Borders toolbar.

   The result should equal $160,000.00. The AutoSum button provides a convenient method of summing columns.

Use a Range Reference in a Formula

15. Click in the last table cell, and click the AutoSum Σ button.

   Word will insert the incorrect result $2,500.00. The correct summation for the column should be $28,500.00. Word calculated the total incorrectly because it stopped summing when it reached the first negative number ($2,500.00). It summed this negative number with the number $5,000.00 below it to achieve the incorrect result. You will overcome Word's limitation by using a range reference in the formula. Range references let you specify a range of cells by separating the first and last cell in the range with a colon.

16. Click Undo ↺, and then choose **Table→Formula.**

17. Use the (BACKSPACE) key to delete the closing parenthesis and the word ABOVE from the current formula. The formula should read =SUM(when you have finished using Backspace.

18. Type **E2:E9)** to complete the formula as =SUM(E2:E9). Make sure you type a colon (not a semicolon) between the references E2 and E9, and make sure beginning and ending parenthesis surround the range reference.

   You can use range references with functions such as SUM, AVERAGE, MIN, and MAX.

19. Click **OK.** The result should equal $28,500.00.

20. Save the changes to your document, and continue with the next topic.

Table AutoFormat

The **Table→Table AutoFormat** command lets you choose from a variety of predefined table formats. The predefined formats automatically apply borders, shading, font colors, font sizes, and other formats to tables. You may be pleasantly surprised when you see the professional formatting that AutoFormat can apply. To apply an AutoFormat, click anywhere in the table, choose **Table→Table AutoFormat,** choose an AutoFormat style, and click **OK.**

The Table AutoFormat box displays a preview of the currently selected AutoFormat. You can scroll through the list to view additional AutoFormats. The first format on the list is the (none) format, which removes all formats from a table.

If desired, you can specify particular Formats to apply.

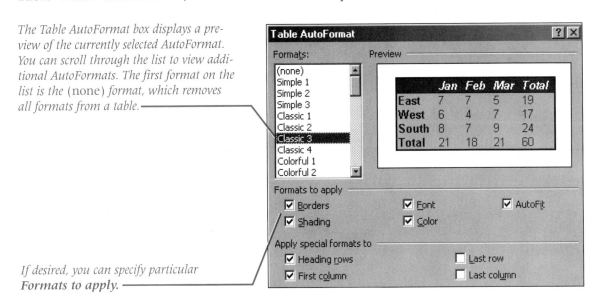

In this exercise, you will apply table AutoFormats to the stock holdings table, and to the embedded work-sheet in the account summary table.

Apply an AutoFormat to the Stock Holdings Table

1. Make sure the insertion point is somewhere within the stock holdings table, and choose **Table→Table AutoFormat.**

2. Choose the Classic 3 style, and click **OK.**
   Your table should now have impressive formatting!

3. Choose **Table→Table AutoFormat,** choose the **(none)** option from the top of the list, and click **OK.**
   Notice that the (none) *option removes all formatting from the table. You can use this option to remove all formats from a table even if an AutoFormat was never applied to the table.*

4. Choose **Table→Table AutoFormat** again.

5. Scroll through the list of formats until you locate the List 3 format.

6. Choose List 3, and click **OK.**

Apply an AutoFormat to the Embedded Excel Worksheet

In the next few steps, you will apply an AutoFormat to the embedded Excel worksheet in the account summary table. To accomplish this, you will activate the embedded worksheet by double-clicking it. Then, you will use Excel's AutoFormat command to apply the List 3 format. Excel's AutoFormat tool is quite similar to Word's AutoFormat tool.

7. Scroll to the top of the document, and double-click the embedded Excel worksheet located within the account summary table.

8. Position the mouse pointer over the first cell (the empty cell).

9. Drag two cells to the right, and then down two rows to select the cells with the data.
   In Excel, you must select the desired cells before applying an AutoFormat.

10. Choose **Format→AutoFormat** from the menu bar.

11. Scroll through the list of formats, choose List 3, and click **OK.**

12. Click outside the worksheet to complete the editing change to the embedded worksheet.
    Notice that the List 3 formats are consistent between Word and Excel.

13. Save the changes to the document, and continue with the next topic.

Additional Table Properties

In Lesson 10, you were introduced to column and row table properties. In this lesson, you will work with cell properties and properties affecting the entire table. The Table Properties dialog box is displayed with the **Table→Table Properties** command.

Cell Properties

The Cell tab of the Table Properties dialog box lets you specify precise sizes for cells. In addition, the Cell tab lets you specify the vertical alignment of text and objects within cells. You can specify cell properties for a single cell or you can select multiple cells and apply the desired properties to the selection.

Table Properties

The Table tab of the Table Properties dialog box lets you specify the overall table size, the horizontal alignment of the table on the page, and the wrapping options. You can use the horizontal alignment options to left-, center-, or right-align a table. You can also specify a measurement that will indent the table a precise distance from the left margin. The wrapping options can be used to position tables within paragraphs, allowing the text to wrap around the table.

 Hands-On 12.7 Use Table Properties

Set Vertical Cell Alignment

1. Position the insertion point in the first row of the account summary table, and choose **Table→Select→Table.**

2. Choose **Table→Table Properties,** and click the Cell tab in the Table Properties dialog box.

3. Choose the Center vertical alignment option, and click **OK.**
   Notice that the embedded worksheet becomes centered vertically within the cell. The alignment options affect text and objects within cells.

Center-Align the Tables

4. Choose **Table→Table Properties,** and make sure the Table tab is active.

5. Choose the Center alignment option, and click **OK.**
   The entire table should now be center-aligned on the page.

6. Scroll down, and click anywhere in the stock holdings table.

7. Use the **Table→Table Properties** command to center align the table.

8. Select Columns C, D, and E in the stock holdings table, and right-align the entries.

Format the Worksheet

9. Select the Stock Holdings heading located just above the stock holdings table.

10. Format the selection with a 14pt, bold, blue font.

11. Scroll to the top of the worksheet, and select the Account Information heading.

12. Format the selection with an 18pt, bold, blue font.

13. Format the Ted Johnson subheading with a 14pt, bold, blue font.

14. Save the changes to the document, and then close the document.

15. Continue with the end-of-lesson questions and exercises.

Concepts Review

True/False Questions

1. Cells can be merged horizontally, but not vertically.   TRUE   FALSE

2. The split command is used to split merged cells only.   TRUE   FALSE

3. Text is rotated in 45-degree increments each time the **Change Text Direction** button is clicked.   TRUE   FALSE

4. An embedded worksheet can be edited by double-clicking the worksheet.   TRUE   FALSE

5. Table rows can be sorted in both Ascending and Descending order.   TRUE   FALSE

6. The Sort Ascending button can be used to perform multilevel sorts.   TRUE   FALSE

7. The **Insert→Formula** command is used to insert formulas into table cells.   TRUE   FALSE

8. Table AutoFormats can apply borders, shading, and font colors to tables.   TRUE   FALSE

Multiple-Choice Questions

1. Which of the following can be set with the Table tab of the Table Properties dialog box?
   a. Horizontal alignment of the table
   b. Overall table size
   c. Wrapping options
   d. All of these

2. Which command is used to apply AutoFormats to tables?
   a. Table→Table AutoFormat
   b. Format→AutoFormat
   c. Insert→AutoFormat
   d. None of these

3. Which of the following is a valid element in formulas within Word tables?
   a. +
   b. SUM
   c. LEFT
   d. All of these

4. How are multilevel sorts conducted?
   a. Click the **Sort Ascending** button.
   b. Click the **Sort Descending** button.
   c. Choose **Table→Sort.**
   d. Both a and b

Skill Builders

Skill Builder 12.1 Set Up an Order Tracking Table

Set Up a Table, and Sort the Table

1. Start a new document, and insert a six-row by five-column (6 × 5) table.

2. Enter the data shown below into the table.

Customer ID	Order Status	Item #	In Stock?	Order Total
341	S	A423	Y	$100.91
234	S	A321	Y	$45.87
567	I	S345	N	$43.23
879	H	D567	N	$78.92
233	I	S230	Y	$23.45

3. Click anywhere in Column C (the Item column).

4. Click the Sort Ascending 🔼 button on the Tables and Borders toolbar.
   The rows should now be sorted based upon the item numbers.

5. Now sort the table based upon the Customer IDs in Column A.

Add a Title Row and a Total Row

6. Select the first two rows of the table.

7. Choose **Table→Insert→Rows Above** from the menu bar.

8. Click anywhere in the table, and two empty rows should be visible at the top of the table.

9. Select the empty rows, and click the Merge Table Cells 🔲 button on the Tables and Borders toolbar.

10. Type the title **Order Tracking Sheet** in the large merged cell.

11. Click the Center Align 📑 button on the Formatting toolbar to center the entry horizontally in the merged cell.

12. Now add a row to the bottom of the table, and type the phrase **Total Orders** in the first cell.

Use AutoSum, and Align the Entries

13. Click in the last table cell, and click the AutoSum Σ button on the Tables and Borders toolbar.
    The total should equal $292.38.

14. Select the entries in Columns B, C, and D, and Center Align 📑 them.

15. Right-align the entries in the Column E (the last column).

(Continued on the next page)

Format the Table

16. Choose **Table→Table AutoFormat,** and apply the Classic 2 AutoFormat.

17. Select the entire table, and use the **Table→AutoFit→Fit to Contents** command to AutoFit all columns.

18. Choose **Table→Table Properties,** and apply the Center alignment option on the Table tab to center the table on the page.

Insert Blank Lines Above the Table

The following steps will show you how to use (ENTER) *to push the table down and insert blank rows above the table.*

19. Press (CTRL)+(HOME) to position the insertion point at the top of the document.
    Notice that the insertion point is inside the table. You could also have clicked in front of the word Order *in the title row. However, the* (CTRL)+(HOME) *keystroke is a convenient way to position the insertion point at the top of any document.*

20. Tap (ENTER) once.
    The table will move down, and the insertion point will be positioned on the blank row above the table.

21. Tap (ENTER) four more times to push the table down to approximately the 2″ position.
    If desired, you could now type text and insert objects on the blank lines above the table.

22. Save the completed table as **Skill Builder 12.1,** and then close the document.

Skill Builder 12.2 Embed an Excel Worksheet

Set Up the Worksheet

1. Start a new document, and click the Center Align ![icon] button.

2. Type **2000 Home Budget**, and tap (ENTER) three times.

3. Select the 2000 Home Budget title, and format it with the font, size, and color of your choice.

4. Position the insertion point on the last blank line below the title.

5. Click the Insert Microsoft Excel Worksheet ![icon] button, and insert a seven-row by four-column worksheet.

6. Enter the data shown to the right into the worksheet. Keep in mind that the worksheet on the right shows Column A widened slightly. In your worksheet, the entries in Column A will not be completely visible after you enter the entries in Column B. The column widths will be adjusted later in this exercise.

	A	B	C	D
1	Item	January	February	March
2	Car Insurance	180	0	0
3	Car Payment	325	325	325
4	Mortgage	1325	1325	1325
5	Food	285	285	285
6	Utilities	125	125	125
7	Totals			

Calculate the Totals and Format the Worksheet

7. Follow these steps to calculate the totals and to apply the Currency number format.

Ⓐ *Select the January, February, and March cells, and right align the entries.*

Ⓑ *Select the Totals cells by dragging the mouse over them.*

Ⓒ *Click the AutoSum* Σ *button on Excel's Standard toolbar.*

Ⓓ *Click the Currency Style* $ *button on Excel's Formatting toolbar.*

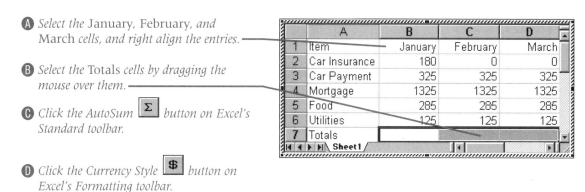

	A	B	C	D
1	Item	January	February	March
2	Car Insurance	180	0	0
3	Car Payment	325	325	325
4	Mortgage	1325	1325	1325
5	Food	285	285	285
6	Utilities	125	125	125
7	Totals			

Notice how easy it was to use AutoSum on multiple cells. It was also quite easy to apply the Currency Style. Once again, it is usually better to insert an Excel worksheet if the table requires calculations, number formats, and other modifications that are handled more efficiently in Excel.

8. Now select all of the cells and use Excel's **Format→AutoFormat** command to apply the AutoFormat of your choice. The completed document shown below uses the Classic 3 AutoFormat.

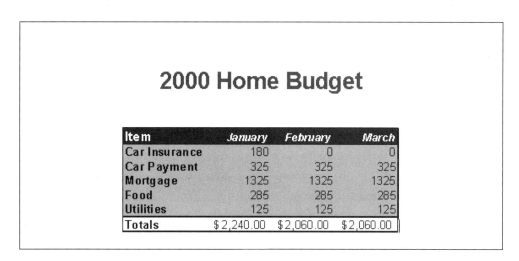

2000 Home Budget

Item	January	February	March
Car Insurance	180	0	0
Car Payment	325	325	325
Mortgage	1325	1325	1325
Food	285	285	285
Utilities	125	125	125
Totals	$2,240.00	$2,060.00	$2,060.00

9. Save the document as **Skill Builder 12.2,** and then close the document.

Skill Builder 12.3 Insert Pictures in Tables

Besides being useful for organizing text and numbers, tables can be used to organize pictures and other objects. In this exercise, you will use a table to set up the flyer shown on the following page.

Set up the Table

1. Start a new document, and click the Center Align 📑 button.

2. Type **Third Annual**, and tap (ENTER).

3. Type **County Fair**, and tap (ENTER) five more times.

4. Insert a three-row by three-column table.

5. Select the entire table, and choose **Table→Table Properties** from the menu bar.

6. Click the Row tab, and specify the row height as exactly 1.5″.

Insert and Size a Picture

7. Type **Horse Rides** in the first cell, and tap (ENTER) twice.

8. Choose **Insert→Picture→Clip Art** from the menu bar.

9. Choose the Animals category, and insert the horse head clip as shown to the right.

10. Close the clip gallery; a very large horse head will appear in the table cell.

11. Click the horse head to select it, and then choose **Format→Picture** from the menu bar.

12. Click the Size tab in the Format Picture box, set the height to 1″, and click **OK.**

13. Select the Horse Rides heading, and set the font to Arial Bold 14.

Complete the Table

14. Insert the remaining pictures and picture headings in the table as shown on the following page. The pictures and headings are only inserted in the corner cells and center cell of the table. The completed table will have four blank cells. All of the pictures are located in the Animals category except for the car, which is located in the Transportation category. Set the height of all pictures to 1″, and use the Format Painter to copy the Arial Bold 14 format from the Horse Rides headings to the other headings.

15. Remove all borders from the table.

16. Position the insertion point below the table, and tap (ENTER) three times.

17. Complete the document as shown on the following page. You will need to type and format the text. Use whichever text formats you desire.

18. When you have finished formatting the document, choose **File→Page Setup,** click the Layout tab, and set the vertical alignment to center.
    This will center the entire page vertically.

19. Save the completed document as **Skill Builder 12.3,** and then close the document.

Third Annual
County Fair

Horse Rides

Exotic Animals

Classic Cars

Frog Jumping

Magic Shows

July 15 through August 30

County Fairgrounds

Skill Builder 12.4 Tables, Pictures, and Custom Tabs

1. Follow these guidelines to create the document shown on the following page.

   - Use whichever fonts and fonts sizes you desire.

   - Use centered custom tab stops and right-aligned custom tab stops with leaders to set up the staff list.

   - Format the table as shown. Use thick borders, thin borders, and shading as shown.

   - The pictures are located in the Sports & Leisure and Special Occasions categories. Set the height of all pictures to 1".

   - Apply 3 points of paragraph spacing before and 2 points of paragraph spacing after each paragraph in the table. You can apply the spacing with a single command by first selecting the entire table. The paragraph spacing settings will create a small amount of space between the cell edges and the text and pictures.

   - Center align Columns B and C in the table.

   - Set the vertical alignment of the page to center.

2. Save the completed document as **Skill Builder 12.4,** and then close the document.

1999 Outstanding Players

Alameda Sports and Recreation Staff

Coordinator .... Roland Hindsman 411-3176
Coach .... Robert Rubio 432-9098
Coach .... Bill Chamblee 345-6789
Secretary .... Lucy Chamblee 426-7689

Player	Age	Sport Played
Gregory Ashford	12	
Roger Chamblee	12	
Frank Pelland	10	
Brandon Williams	11	

Assessments

Assessment 12.1 Use Table AutoFormat and Merge Cells

1. Follow these guidelines to create the memorandum shown below.

   ■ Use proper spacing and formatting for a business memorandum.

   ■ Set up the table as shown, merging the cells in the first row.

   ■ Apply the Colorful 2 AutoFormat to the completed table.

   ■ Center-align the entries in the merged cell and in Columns B, C, and D.

   ■ Apply three points of paragraphs spacing before to each paragraph in the table.

2. Save the completed document as **Assessment 12.1,** and then close the document.

Memo To: Linda Lewis

From: Bernie Willis

Date: Today's Date

Subject: FastTrack Contractors

Per your request, I am providing you with a list of independent contractors who are qualified to work on the FastTrack project. I have included their names, hourly rates, availability, and telephone numbers.

Independent Contractors for FastTrack			
Name	Rate	Availability	Phone
Barbara Denny	$35/hour	April 15	223-4565
Jason Simms	$40/hour	Immediate	234-8980
Ted Brown	$30/hour	April 21	450-9090
Isaac Stone	$55/hour	Immediate	235-9988
Pat Thomas	$40/hour	May 1	236-0090

Assessment 12.2 Embed an Excel Worksheet

1. Follow these guidelines to create the memorandum with embedded Excel worksheet shown below.

   - Use proper spacing and formatting for a business memorandum.

   - Set up the worksheet as an embedded Excel worksheet.

   - Use Excel's AutoSum Σ button to calculate the totals.

   - Use Excel's **Format→AutoFormat** command to apply the Classic 3 AutoFormat to the worksheet. You must select the cells before applying the AutoFormat.

2. Save the completed document as **Assessment 12.2,** and then close the document.

Memo To: Barry Livingston

From: Vivian Chu

Date: Today's Date

Subject: Employee Time Log

Per your request, I am providing you with an employee time log for the past five days. As you can see, the number of employee hours is decreasing due to the automation technology we recently installed. On an annualized basis, I expect the total employee hours to decrease by at least 20%.

Computer Depot Employee Time Log

Employee	Wednesday	Thursday	Friday	Saturday	Sunday
Mary Johnson	6.5	0.0	5.0	6.5	4.0
Cliff Packard	4.0	6.0	6.5	6.5	4.0
Helen Martinez	4.0	6.0	6.5	6.5	0.0
Sarah Stonestown	0.0	4.0	4.0	4.0	0.0
Totals	14.5	16.0	22.0	23.5	8.0

Critical Thinking

Critical Thinking 12.1 On Your Own

Fred Watson is the owner of Fred's Quality Lawn Care service. Fred has provided high-quality lawn care and landscaping services for over 25 years. Recently, Fred purchased a personal computer with Office 2000 preinstalled. He intends to use his new computer and Office 2000 to improve his customer service, conduct mailings, computerize his billing processes, and increase his profits. He recently took a Word class at a local community college. Fred wants to use Word tables to track his activities and help maximize his profits.

You have been assigned the task of setting up a job log for Fred. The job log should be set up in a table. If necessary, reduce the left and right margins to allow the table to fit on the page. Use an Arial 10 font for all table text. Include the title "Fred's Quality Lawn Care" in the first row of the table. Merge the cells in the first row, and center the title in the merged cell.

The table should include a column to allow Fred to assign a job number to each job. In addition, it should include the customer name, day of the week, type of work performed, the number of hours required to complete the activity, and the total dollar amount billed for the job. Use a formula in another column to calculate the effective hourly rate for each job. This calculation will allow Fred to determine the types of work that yield the highest hourly rates. Apply a currency to the cells that contain the formulas. Include enough jobs to account for an entire week of activity with perhaps one or two jobs per day. Use the following categories of work performed:

- Mowing
- Irrigation system installation
- Tree trimming
- General maintenance

Save your completed document as **Critical Thinking 12.1**.

Critical Thinking 12.2 On Your Own

Cathy Adams works for George Miller at Speedy Package Delivery Service. Cathy has assigned you the task of setting up a Word document to record mileage, gasoline usage, and other expenses for Speedy drivers. Cathy provides you with the following information for the month of March.

Driver	Miles Driven	Gasoline Used (gallons)	Gasoline Expense	Tolls
Harold Robinson	4,850	202	$267	$152
Jane Allen	5,232	194	$256	$165
Bill Peterson	4,100	158	$208	$90
Janine Rockwell	5,050	240	$317	$158

Set up the information in a Word table. If necessary, reduce the left and right margins to allow the table to fit on the page. Use an Arial 10 font for all table text. Include the title Fred's Quality Lawn Care in the first row of the table. Use formulas to calculate the miles/gallon for each driver. Also, use formulas to calculate the total expenses for each driver as the gasoline expense plus tolls. You can include dollar signs and commas in the numbers when you enter them in the table as shown on the previous page. Apply the Currency format when calculating the total expenses. Merge the cells in the first table row and center a descriptive title in the row. Save your workbook as **Critical Thinking 12.2.**

Critical Thinking 12.3 **Web Research with a Group**

You and your classmate have been so successful with Health-e-Meals.com that it is time to invest some of your profits. Use Internet Explorer and a search engine of your choice to locate a Web site that offers free stock quotes. Get quotes on the symbols shown in the table below. Set up an Excel worksheet that includes all of the information shown below plus the company name associated with each stock symbol. Include the current price of each stock and a formula that calculates the current value of each stock holding. Include a total row, and use Excel's AutoSum button to calculate the total portfolio value.

Symbol	Current Price	Shares Purchased
CORL	_____	500
ORCL	_____	100
LU	_____	200
MSFT	_____	300
GLC	_____	60
HAL	_____	250

Format the worksheet using Excel's **Format→Autoformat** command. Choose any AutoFormat, and make sure you select all of the data before issuing the command. Save the completed worksheet as **Critical Thinking 12.3—Excel Worksheet.**

Write a personal business letter to Gerald Livingston of Livingston Capital Management. Let Gerald know that you are interested in investing with his firm. You decide upon an address for Gerald's firm. Embed the Excel worksheet that you just created into your word document. Explain to Gerald that this worksheet represents your current investment portfolio. Save the completed Word document as **Critical Thinking 12.3—Word Document.**

Newpaper Style Columns and Excel Integration

Many organizations publish internal newsletters for their employees and members. Word's Columns tool makes it easy to set up multi-column layouts for use in newsletters and other documents. The Columns tool also lets you easily modify the layout of columns after they have been set up. Word also lets you embed charts in documents. Charts are useful for graphically depicting trends, comparisons, and other relationships for numerical data.

In This Lesson

Case Study

Maria Gonzalez is an Administrative Assistant for the Farber Investment Group. The Farber Investment Group provides comprehensive financial management for a select group of clients. Maria has been assigned the task of setting up a newsletter that will be distributed to clients enrolled in the Farber Group's Balanced Portfolio program. The Balanced Portfolio provides complete financial management of all assets contributed to the portfolio. Maria use Word's Columns tool to effortlessly lay out the newsletter. In addition, she inserts charts to graphically depict the portfolio's performance. Maria also links an Excel workbook into her newsletter. Linking to an Excel workbook allows Maria to use the power of Excel to develop and maintain her worksheets, while reflecting the resulting worksheet(s) in a Word document.

The Farber Investment Group
Balanced Portfolio Report
Today's Date

The Economic Outlook

The U.S. economy continues to charge forward, growing at an annual rate of 4.3 percent. We anticipate this growth to continue throughout this year, although the rate may slow slightly depending upon the Federal Reserve's position on interest rates. In a recent speech before the Economic Council of New York, the Fed Chairman noted that inflation was once again their primary concern. The Chairman noted that the Fed will preempt any inflationary pressure with interest rate hikes. The Fed has had an interest rate increase bias for the past three quarters.

As a rule of thumb, stock prices tend to fluctuate with interest rates. Investors are generally willing to pay higher multiples for stocks when interest rates are low. Thus, an increase in interest rates will tend to have a dampening effect on the stock market. It is our opinion that an interest rate increase of 50 basis points in the first six months of this year will cause an overall decrease in stock prices of around 10 percent. Even with rising interest rates, our Balanced Portfolio has recorded an impressive gain.

Stock Holdings

It is our opinion that technology will continue to be the driving force in the U.S. economy. Even though technology stocks tend to reactive negatively to interest rate increases, we believe that any negative effects that interest rates may have will be more than offset by the steep growth curves of many technology companies. We particularly like companies that are building the new Internet infrastructure and semiconductor companies. Our top stock holdings appear in the following table. As you can see, technology companies dominate the list.

Company	Shares	Value
IBM	840,000	$98,280,000
Oracle	900,000	$58,500,000
Etek Dynamics	450,000	$44,100,000
Cisco Systems	350,000	$39,900,000
Citigroup	450,000	$27,000,000
Corel	800,000	$23,200,000
Amazon.com	200,000	$17,000,000
Boeing	350,000	$16,800,000

Balanced Portfolio Breakdown

Our Balanced Portfolio experienced a large influx of capital this year as more and more investors opted for the professional management and diversification this product offers. When compared to last year, the Balanced

Section Breaks

In Word, many page-formatting commands affect every page of the document unless the document is organized in **sections.** Section breaks let you divide a document into different sections. You can then apply formatting options to individual sections. You may need to insert a section break when changing the vertical alignment, margins, page size, orientation, page numbering, headers, footers, and columns. These formatting options are applied to every page in a section, or to every page in the document if the document has just one section.

Inserting Section Breaks

You use the **Insert→Break** command to insert section breaks. The Break dialog box lets you choose from four types of section breaks. The only difference between the four break types is where the break begins. The following table discusses the various sections breaks.

Section Break Type	Description
Next Page	The new section begins on the next page.
Continuous	The section break is inserted at the insertion point, and the new section begins immediately.
Odd Page	The new section begins on the next odd numbered page. This option is used for documents with multiple chapters where each chapter begins on an odd page.
Even Page	The new section begins on the next even-numbered page.

Removing Section Breaks

You can remove a section break by first clicking the Show/Hide ¶ button on the Standard toolbar to display the nonprinting characters. Then you can click on the break and use the (DELETE) key to remove the break. When you delete a section break, the formats from the section below the break are applied to all pages in the combined section.

In this exercise, you will begin developing a newsletter by inserting three title lines, a picture, and a section break.

Set Up the Title Lines and Insert a Section Break

1. Start Word, and click the Center Align  button.

2. Follow these guidelines to insert the text and picture shown below.

   - Type the text, tapping (ENTER) twice after the last line.

   - Format the text using the formats of your choice.

   - The picture can be found in the Business category of the Office 2000 Clip Gallery.

   - Adjust the height of the picture to 1″.

   - Add a ½ pt border to the picture. You can add a border by right-clicking the picture, choosing Borders and Shading, and then using the Box option on the Borders and Shading dialog box.

The Farber Investment Group
Balanced Portfolio Report
Today's Date

3. Tap (ENTER) three times after the picture, and switch to left alignment.

4. Choose **Insert→Break** from the menu bar.
   Notice that this is the same dialog box that can be used to insert page breaks. You will also use the column break option later in this lesson.

5. Choose the Continuous section break option, and click **OK.**
   The status bar at the bottom of the Word window will indicate that the insertion point is on Page 1, Sec 2. The status bar always indicates the page, section, and line position of the insertion point.

   (Continued on the next page)

Delete and Reinsert the Section Break

6. Click the Show/Hide button on the Standard toolbar to display the nonprinting characters. *Notice the Section Break line.*

7. Click on the Section Break line, and the insertion point will be positioned near the beginning of the line.

8. Tap the (DELETE) key to remove the section break.
    If the second section had different formats (such as different left and right margins) then the combined section would have those margins. However, in your document, both sections had the same formatting, so the formatting of the first section has not changed.

9. Click Undo 🔙 to restore the section break.

10. Position the insertion point in front of the last paragraph mark in the document.

11. Save the document as **Hands-On Lesson 13.**

Inserting Files

You can use the **Insert→File** command to insert a file into the current document. Files are inserted at the insertion point location. For this reason, you should always position the insertion point at the desired location before inserting a file.

Hands-On 13.2 Insert a File

In this exercise, you will insert a file with a large amount of text. The text will be used throughout the Hands-On exercises in this lesson, so you will not have to type large amounts of text.

1. Make sure the insertion point is positioned in front of the last paragraph mark.

2. Choose **Insert→File** from the menu bar.

3. Navigate to your exercise diskette, and insert the file name **Hands-On Lesson 13—Text.**
    Take a moment to browse through the document, and you will notice there are approximately 1½ pages of text.

4. Save the changes to your document, and continue with the next topic.

Newspaper Style Columns

You can use newspaper style columns to lay out text in multiple columns. In a multicolumn layout, text flows down the first column and then continues at the top of the second column and so forth. Word automatically reformats the column layout as you insert or delete text.

Setting Up Columns

The Columns  button on the Standard toolbar lets you easily create a multicolumn layout where each column is of equal width. You can also use the **Format→Columns** command to display the Columns dialog box. The Columns dialog box can be used to set up and format more sophisticated columns. For example, you can set up columns of unequal width, insert lines between columns, and end a multicolumn layout.

*Inserting columns with the **Columns** button*

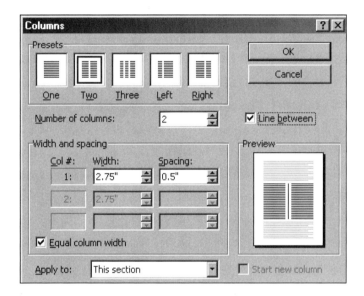

The Columns dialog box

Revising Column Structure

You can revise the column structure after columns have been set up. For example, you can change the number of columns, specify precise widths for columns, or insert a line between columns. Word will automatically reformat the columns and adjust the text flow to accommodate the new column layout. The modifications affect only the column layout in the current section (or the entire document if there is only one section).

Adjusting Column Widths with the Ruler

You can adjust the widths of columns by dragging margin boundaries on the horizontal ruler. The horizontal ruler displays margin boundaries for the left and right edges of each column in a multicolumn layout. Dragging the margin boundaries changes the widths of the associated columns. You can also adjust indents for selected text in multicolumn layouts by dragging indent markers on the ruler.

Hands-On 13.3 Set Up and Revise Columns

Set Up a Three-Column Format

1. Scroll up, and position the insertion point on the *The Economic Outlook* heading.
   The column formatting you apply will affect all text in the current section.

2. Click the Columns ▥ button on the Standard toolbar.

3. Drag the mouse over the first three columns on the drop-down menu as shown to the right, and release the mouse button.
   Word will lay out all text in the second section in a three-column format. Notice that all columns are of equal width. Also, notice that the text and picture in the first section are unaffected by the column format in the second section.

Revise the Column Layout

4. Look at the horizontal ruler, and notice that it is divided into sections.
   You can adjust column widths by dragging the margin boundaries on the edges of each section (but don't do it now).

5. Choose **Format→Column** from the menu bar.

6. Follow these steps to revise the column layout.

   Ⓐ *Choose a two-column format.*

   Ⓑ *Check the **Line between** box to insert a line between the columns.*

   Ⓒ *Notice the **Width** and **Spacing** options. You can create columns of unequal width by specifying the width of each column and the spacing between columns.*

   Ⓓ *Click **OK** to apply the new layout.*

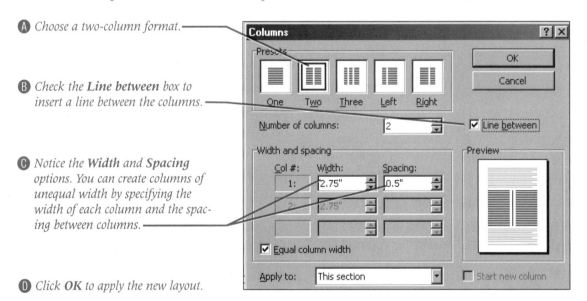

   Scroll through the document to view your work thus far. As you can see from this exercise, working with columns is quite straightforward. The key to working with columns is to insert section breaks before and after the section(s) with columns so that the column layouts only affect the desired sections.

7. Save the changes to your document, and continue with the next topic.

Linking Excel Worksheets

In the previous lesson, you learned how to embed an Excel worksheet into a Word document. You can also insert an Excel worksheet into a Word document with object linking. When you insert a worksheet using object linking, the worksheet in the Word document is linked to the original Excel worksheet. If the worksheet is opened in Excel and modified, the modifications are immediately reflected in the linked worksheet in the Word document. This powerful capability ensures that the worksheet in your Word document always reflects the revisions made in the original Excel worksheet.

LINKING AN EXCEL WORKSHEET

To Link an Excel Worksheet to a Word Document

- ■ Open the worksheet in Excel, and select the desired data.
- ■ Click the Copy 📋 button in Excel.
- ■ Switch to Word, and position the insertion point at the location where the linked worksheet is to be placed.
- ■ Choose Edit→Paste Special from the menu bar.
- ■ Choose Microsoft Excel Worksheet Object, choose the Paste Link option, and click OK.

Editing Linked Worksheets

You can edit a linked worksheet by first double-clicking it in Word or opening the source worksheet in Excel. If you double-click the linked worksheet in Word, Excel will start, and the worksheet will be displayed. Once the worksheet is displayed, you can make any editing changes, and they will be reflected in the Word document.

Hands-On 13.4 Link a Worksheet

*In this exercise, you will open an Excel worksheet on your exercise diskette. You will paste the worksheet into Word using the **Paste Special** command, thus establishing a link.*

Link the Worksheet

1. Start the Excel program, and open the workbook on your exercise diskette named **Hands-On Lesson 13—Stock Data.**

2. Select all cells containing data (the range A1:C9) by dragging the mouse over the cells.

3. Click the Copy 📋 button on Excel's Standard toolbar.

4. Switch to Word by clicking the **Hands-On Lesson 13** button on the Windows Taskbar.

5. Position the insertion point on the second blank line above the *Balanced Portfolio Breakdown* heading in the right column of the newsletter.

6. Choose **Edit→Paste Special** from the menu bar.

7. Choose Microsoft Excel Worksheet Object from the top of the object list.

8. Choose the Paste Link option, and click **OK.**
   The linked worksheet should be pasted into the document.

(Continued on the next page)

9. Notice that the linked worksheet currently shows 840,000 IBM shares.

   In the next few steps, you will change this number in the source Excel worksheet. The change will be reflected in the linked worksheet in the Word document.

10. Switch to Excel by clicking the **Hands-On Lesson 13—Stock Data** button on the Windows Taskbar.

11. Click in Cell B2 (the cell with the 840,000 entry).

12. Type **800,000**, and tap (ENTER) to complete the entry.

    The formula in Cell C2 will recalculate the investment value.

13. Switch to Word by clicking the Word button on the Windows Taskbar, and the changes should be reflected in the linked worksheet.

14. Click below the worksheet, and tap (DELETE) to remove one of the blank lines.

15. Feel free to modify the source Excel worksheet in any way you desire.

    All changes will be reflected in the linked worksheet in Word.

16. Save the changes to the Word document when you have finished.

17. Save the changes to the Excel worksheet, close the worksheet, but leave the Excel program open.

Linking Excel Charts

Excel has powerful charting capabilities that allow you to create a variety of charts. You can use Excel's charting tool to create charts and then link them to your Word documents. Any changes made to the original Excel worksheet data are reflected in the Excel chart in the Word document. You use the same technique to link an Excel chart that you used to link an Excel worksheet.

LINKING AN EXCEL CHART

To Link an Excel Chart to a Word Document

- Set up an Excel worksheet and chart, and select the chart.
- Click the Copy button in Excel.
- Switch to Word, and position the insertion point at the location where the linked chart is to be placed.
- Choose Edit→Paste Special from the menu bar.
- Choose Microsoft Excel Chart Object, choose the Paste Link option, and click OK.

Set Up the Worksheet and Chart

1. Switch to Excel, and click the New ⬜ button to start a new worksheet.

2. Enter the following data into the new worksheet.

	A	B	C	D
1	Balanced Portfolio Stock Value			
2				
3		1997	1998	1999
4	Value	200	245	365

3. Select the cells in the range A3:D4 by dragging the mouse over them. This range includes all cells with data in Rows 3 and 4.
   In the next few steps, you will use Excel's Chart Wizard to set up the chart.

4. Click the Chart Wizard 📊 button on Excel's Standard toolbar.
   The Chart Wizard will prompt you to choose a chart type.

5. Click the **Next** button to accept the column chart.
   Excel will display a sample of the chart with three vertical columns.

6. Click **Next** to accept the proposed data range and three-column layout.
   The Step 3 of 4 dialog box will let you choose various chart options.

7. Enter the title **Balanced Portfolio Stocks (millions)** in the Chart Title box.

8. Click the Legend tab on the Step 3 of 4 dialog box.

9. Uncheck the Show Legend box, and the legend will be removed from the chart in the preview window.

10. Click the **Finish** button to complete the chart.
    Excel will embed a simple column chart in your worksheet. The chart should also be selected with sizing handles visible on the edges of the chart.

11. Save the worksheet as **Hands-On Lesson 13—Excel Chart.**

Link the Chart

12. Click the Copy 📋 button on Excel's Standard toolbar.

13. Switch to Word by clicking the **Hands-On Lesson 13** button on the Windows Taskbar.

14. Position the insertion point on the second blank line above the *Management Team and Strategy* heading on the second page.

15. Choose **Edit→Paste Special** from the menu bar.

16. Choose Microsoft Excel Chart Object from the top of the object list.

17. Choose the Paste Link option, and click **OK.**
    The linked chart should be pasted into the document.

(Continued on the next page)

Size the Chart

18. Right-click on the chart, and choose **Format→Object** from the pop-up menu.

19. Click the Size tab in the Format Object dialog box.

20. Set the height to **1.5″**, and click **OK.**
    The chart should now fit within the column.

Modify the Excel Worksheet Data

21. Switch to Excel by clicking the **Hands-On Lesson 13—Excel Chart** button on the Windows Taskbar.

22. Click in Cell B4.

23. Type **300**, and tap (ENTER) to complete the entry.

24. Switch to Word by clicking the **Word** button on the Windows Taskbar.
    The first chart column should reflect the new value of 300.

25. Save the changes, and continue with the next topic.

Column Breaks

From the Keyboard

(CTRL)+(SHIFT)+(ENTER)
to insert column break

You can force a column to end prematurely, thus moving text to the top of the next column, by inserting a column break. This technique is often used to begin headings at the tops of columns and to balance columns on the last page of a multicolumn layout. You insert column breaks by choosing **Insert→Break** from the menu bar and choosing the Column break option. You can remove column breaks by displaying the nonprinting characters and deleting the column break.

 ## Hands-On 13.6 Insert and Remove Column Breaks

1. Scroll to the bottom of the first page, and the Stock Holdings heading should be visible near the bottom of the first column.

2. Position the insertion point just in front of the Stock Holdings heading.

3. Choose **Insert→Break** from the menu bar, choose the Column break option, and click **OK.**
   The Stock Holdings heading should move to the top of the second column.

4. If necessary, use the Show/Hide ¶ button to display the nonprinting characters.

5. Position the insertion point on the Column break at the bottom of the first column, and tap (DELETE) to remove the break.

6. Click Undo ↶ to restore the break.

7. Scroll to the second page and position the insertion point in front of the Management Team and Strategy heading near the middle of the first column.

8. Insert a column break to move the heading and text to the top of the second column.

Ending Column Sections

You must end column sections if you want to return to a single-column layout following a multicolumn section. You can accomplish this by inserting a continuous section break and setting the column layout to single for the new section. However, Word provides a command on the Columns dialog box that takes care of both the section break and the single-column layout with a single command. To accomplish this, choose **Format→Columns** to display the Columns dialog box. Choose the *One column* format at the top of the dialog box, and then choose *This point forward* from the *Apply to* list at the bottom of the dialog box. Word inserts a continuous section break, and formats the new section with the column layout you chose. This technique can actually be used to begin any column layout in a new section.

Hands-On 13.7 End the Column Layout

1. Press (CTRL)+(END) to position the insertion point at the end of the document.

2. Choose **Format→Columns** from the menu bar.

3. Choose the *One column* layout at the top of the dialog box.

4. Choose *This point forward* from the *Apply to* list at the bottom of the dialog box, and click **OK.**
    The new section has a single-column layout. You can see this by noticing that the horizontal ruler no longer displays markers for multiple columns.

5. Position the insertion point on the section break line at the bottom of the second column, and tap (DELETE) to remove the line.
    Notice that the entire section is now in a single-column layout. This is because a new section formed from deleting a break between two sections takes on the formatting of the second section. In this example, the second section had a single-column layout, so the new combined section has that format as well.

6. Click Undo to restore the break.
    Keep in mind that there wasn't really any reason to end the column layout and begin a new section in this document. This technique is only necessary if you want to return to a single-column format and continue entering text into the document.

7. Feel free to experiment with any of the techniques you have learned in this lesson.

8. Save the changes to your document when you have finished, and close the document.

Concepts Review

True/False Questions

1. Vertical alignment, page size, and column formats can be applied to individual sections.   TRUE   FALSE

2. The Odd Page section break type applies formats only to the odd pages in a document.   TRUE   FALSE

3. Section breaks are removed with the **Edit→Delete Section Break** command.   TRUE   FALSE

4. Files are always inserted at the top of documents.   TRUE   FALSE

5. Text flows from one column to the next in newspaper style columns.   TRUE   FALSE

6. The **Columns** button on the Standard toolbar can be used to insert lines between between columns.   TRUE   FALSE

7. Linked worksheets are updated in the Word document when the source worksheet is modified in Excel.   TRUE   FALSE

8. Page breaks are used to force text to the top of the next column.   TRUE   FALSE

Multiple-Choice Questions

1. Which command is used to insert section breaks?
   a. Insert→Break
   b. Edit→Break
   c. Format→Break
   d. None of these

2. Which command is used to set up newspaper style columns?
   a. Format→Columns
   b. Insert→Columns
   c. Insert→Table→Columns
   d. None of these

3. Which of the following techniques can be used to adjust column widths?
   a. Drag margin boundaries on the horizontal ruler.
   b. Specify the desired widths in the Columns dialog box.
   c. Column widths cannot be adjusted.
   d. Both a and b

4. Which command is used to set up linked worksheets?
   a. Insert→Link
   b. Edit→Paste Special
   c. Format→Excel Link
   d. Edit→Past Link

Skill Builders

Skill Builder 13.1 Set Up a Newsletter

In this exercise, you will set up a newsletter. The newsletter will use a text box to display a block of text in the columns and will contain a picture that floats over several columns.

Set Up Columns

1. Start a new document, type **The Hope Report**, and tap (ENTER).

2. Type **January 2000**, and tap (ENTER) three times.

3. Insert a continuous section break.

4. Choose **Insert →File**, and insert the document on your exercise diskette named **Skill Builder 13.1—Text.**

5. Click the Columns ▦ button, and choose a three-column format.
   The inserted text should be laid out in three columns.

6. Increase the size of the title and subtitle at the top of the newsletter, and apply the font color of your choice to the text.

7. Apply the font color of your choice to the headings within the newsletter.

Insert a Text Box

Text boxes were introduced in the Desktop Publishing lessson. Text boxes are useful in newsletters because they let you place formatted blocks of text that stand out from the rest of the newsletter text. You can set the wrapping options for text boxes so that the text flows around the text boxes within a column, or you can straddle a text box across multiple columns.

8. Scroll to the bottom of the newsletter.
   You will insert a text box at the bottom of the first column.

9. Click the Text Box ▣ button the Drawing toolbar.

10. Follow these steps to place the text box at the bottom of the first column.

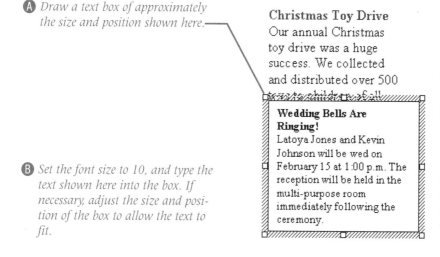

A *Draw a text box of approximately the size and position shown here.*

B *Set the font size to 10, and type the text shown here into the box. If necessary, adjust the size and position of the box to allow the text to fit.*

Christmas Toy Drive
Our annual Christmas toy drive was a huge success. We collected and distributed over 500

Wedding Bells Are Ringing!
Latoya Jones and Kevin Johnson will be wed on February 15 at 1:00 p.m. The reception will be held in the multi-purpose room immediately following the ceremony.

commitment of all who participated. We would like to extend a special thank you to Winnie Wilson for organizing and planning the event. Donna Thomas also deserves a commendation for orchestrating the successful toy gathering campaign. Donna was able to secure large toy donations from several

(Continued on the next page)

Format the Text Box

11. Right-click any edge of the text box, and choose Format Text Box from the pop-up menu.

12. Click the **Fill Color** drop-down button on the Colors and Lines tab, and choose a gray shade or a dark fill color.

13. Click the **Line Color** drop-down button, and choose No Line.
    This will remove the border from the box.

14. Click the Layout tab, choose the Square wrapping style, and click **OK.**
    The Square wrapping style will force the text to flow around the text box. Initially, the text box floated over the text.

15. Select all of the text in the text box, and use the Font Color button to choose a white font color.
    Placing white text on a dark background is known as "reversing out" the text.

16. Select the heading line Wedding Bells are Ringing! and apply bold formatting.

17. Click anywhere outside of the text box to view the completed box.

18. If necessary, adjust the text size and the size and position of the text box.

Insert a Picture that Straddles Columns

19. Scroll up to the middle of the newsletter, and click anywhere on the *What a Magic Show* heading.

20. Insert the picture shown to the right, which is located in the Entertainment category of the Clip Gallery.
    Pictures are initially inserted inline with the text. The picture behaves like a text character positioned within a line of text. In the next few steps, you will change the wrapping style, which will allow you to position the picture anywhere on the page.

21. Right-click the picture, and choose Format Picture from the pop-up menu.

22. Click the Size tab, and set the height to **2″**.

23. Click the Layout tab, choose the Tight wrapping style, and click **OK.**

24. Scroll down until the picture is visible.

25. Drag the picture to the right until it is centered between the second and third columns. Also, drag the picture up about an inch or two to help balance the page.
    The Tight wrapping style should force the text to wrap around the contours of the picture.

26. Click outside of the picture to deselect it.

27. Choose **Format→Borders and Shading** from the menu bar.

28. Click the Page Border tab.

29. Choose a border color and set the width to 2¼ pt.

30. Choose the Box style, and click **OK** to apply an attractive border to the page.
If your newsletter had more than one page, then the page border would appear on every page. You would need to insert one or more section breaks and apply page borders to specific sections to prevent them from printing on every page of a document.

31. Scroll to the bottom of the newsletter.

32. If necessary, adjust the position of the text box so that the bottom edge is aligned with the bottom of the second column.
The text box may have moved down when you inserted the picture. Your completed newsletter should fit on one page.

33. Feel free to enhance the newsletter in any way you desire.

34. Save the completed newsletter as **Skill Builder 13.1,** and close the document.

Skill Builder 13.2 Link an Excel Worksheet

1. Start a new document, and set up the memorandum shown below. Use proper spacing and formatting for a business memorandum. Also, double-space after the last line of the memorandum.

Memo To: Ralph Richardson

From: Carl Wilson

Date: Today's Date

Subject: Sales Volume Comparisons

Per your request, I am providing you with 98 vs. 99 sales volume comparisons for the months of April, May, and June. Notice that Store 3 had strong percentage increases in both April and June. I attribute this to the leadership of the new store manager, Nate Williams.

2. Save the memorandum as **Skill Builder 13.2.**
Leave the memorandum open, as you will insert a linked worksheet.

(Continued on the next page)

3. Start Excel, and open the workbook on your exercise diskette named **Skill Builder 13.2—Worksheet Data.**

4. Select all cells that have data and formatting (the range A1:E16).

5. Click the Copy 🔳 button on Excel's toolbar.

6. Switch to Word by clicking the Skill Builder 13.2 button on the Windows Taskbar.

7. Position the insertion point on the second blank line below the memorandum text.

8. Choose **Edit→Paste Special** from the menu bar.

9. Choose Microsoft Excel Worksheet Object, choose the Past link option, and click **OK.**
   The worksheet should be inserted. This worksheet is linked to the source worksheet in Excel.

10. Switch to Excel, and change the number in Cell B4 to **10,000,000**.

11. Switch back to Word, and the change should be reflected in the Word document.

12. Feel free to make additional changes to the Excel worksheet.

13. Save the changes to your memorandum, and then close it.

14. Save the changes to the Excel workbook, and close it.

Skill Builder 13.3 Insert a Next Page Section Break

In this exercise, you will open the document you created in Skill Builder 13.1. You will modify the document by positioning the title text on a separate page using a next page section break. You will apply different page formats to the title page and the page with the newsletter. Normally, newsletters do not have separate title pages. However, a title page will be added to this newsletter for the purposes of demonstrating section formatting.

Insert a Section Break

1. Switch to Word, and open the document named **Skill Builder 13.1.**
   You will need to complete Skill Builder 13.1 if you skipped over that exercise earlier in the lesson.

2. Use the **File→Save As** command to save the document as **Skill Builder 13.3.**

3. If necessary, click the Show/Hide ¶ button to display the nonprinting characters.

4. Position the insertion point on the Section Break line, and choose **Insert→Break** from the menu bar.

5. Choose Next page from the Section breaks section, and click **OK.**
   Word will push the newsletter to a new page creating a separate title page.

Format Text and Insert a Picture

6. Scroll up to the title page and select the heading The Hope Report.

7. Change the font to Arial Bold 26pt, and apply the font color of your choice.

8. Select the date, format the text with an Arial 20 Bold Italic font, and apply the font color of your choice.

9. Click on the second line below the date.

10. Insert the picture shown to the right. The picture can be found in the House and Family category.

11. Adjust the height of the picture to 2″.

12. Select the title lines, the picture, and the blank lines between the picture and title lines.

13. Click the Center Align [icon] button to center the title, date, and picture.

Format the Title Page

14. Choose **Format→Borders and Shading** from the menu bar.

15. Click the Page Border tab.

16. Choose the *None* option at the top-left corner of the dialog box (but don't click OK).

17. Choose *This Section* from the *Apply to* list at the bottom right corner of the dialog box, and click **OK.**
    This option will remove the border from the title page, leaving it only on the newsletter page.

18. Click on the title line to deselect the text.

19. Choose **File→Page Setup** from the menu bar.

20. Choose the Layout tab, and set the Vertical alignment to center (but don't click OK yet).

21. Choose This Section from the *Apply to* list, and click **OK.**
    Commands that affect entire pages will always give you the option of applying the command to the entire document or to the current section only.

22. Click the Print Preview [icon] button on Word's standard toolbar to view the document.
    The title page should be centered vertically.

23. Scroll down to the newsletter page, and the page border and original vertical alignment should still be in effect.
    The page formatting options you set on the title page did not affect the newsletter page because a section break separates the pages. The page formatting commands were applied to the current section only (the title page section).

24. Exit from Print Preview.

25. Save the changes, and close the document.

Assessments

Assessment 13.1 **Format a Newsletter**

1. Open the document on your exercise diskette named **Assessment 13.1.**
   Normally, newsletters do not have separate title pages. However, a title page will be added to this newsletter for the purposes of demonstrating section formatting.

2. Position the insertion point on the first blank line below the three title lines, and insert a section break that begins on the next page.

3. Follow these guidelines to format the title page.

   ■ Center the three title lines horizontally on the page, and format them with the font, color, and size of your choice.

   ■ Insert the picture shown to the right three lines below the last title line. The picture can be found in the Animals category of the clip gallery.

   ■ Set the height of the inserted picture to 2″.

   ■ Set the vertical alignment of the title page only to centered.

4. Follow these guidelines to format the second page.

   ■ Apply a three-column layout to the page.

   ■ Format the bolded headings with the font color of your choice.

   ■ Apply the page border of your choice only to the section with the three-column layout.

5. Follow these guidelines to insert a picture in the newsletter.

   ■ Insert the picture shown to the right. The picture can be found in the Animals category of the clip gallery.

   ■ Set the height of the picture to 2.5″, and change the wrapping style to Tight.

   ■ Position the picture in the center of the page, allowing the text in the middle column to wrap around the picture as necessary.

6. Save the changes to the document, and close it.

Assessment 13.2 Link an Excel Workbook

1. Setup the memorandum and linked Excel worksheet shown below. The source Excel worksheet can be found on your exercise diskette with the name **Assessment 13.2—Worksheet Data.** The worksheet must be linked so that any changes made in the original Excel worksheet are reflected in the Word document.

2. Save the changes to the document, and close it.

Memo To: Tony Ramos

From: Denise Lapine

Date: Today's Date

Subject: Customer Complaint Survey Results

Per your request, I have organized the customer complaint survey results and placed them in an Excel workbook. I have linked the Excel workbook to this Word document. As you can see, we did significantly better in 1998. I suggest we conduct a meeting next week to determine the cause of the increase.

Quality Greeting Cards - 1999 Customer Complaints			
	Christmas	*Easter*	*Valentines*	*Thanksgiving*
Boston	27	43	14	34
Los Angeles	31	47	19	39
New York	35	51	24	44
St. Louis	39	55	29	49
Total	132	196	86	166
Average	33	49	21.5	41.5

Quality Greeting Cards - 1998 Customer Complaints			
	Christmas	Easter	Valentines	Thanksgiving
Boston	19	31	16	24
Los Angeles	22	34	18	26
New York	25	37	20	28
St. Louis	28	40	22	30
Total	94	142	76	108
Average	23.5	35.5	19	27

Differences Between 1999 and 1998			
Totals	38	54	10	58
Averages	9.5	13.5	2.5	14.5

Critical Thinking

Critical Thinking 13.1 On Your Own

Cathy Richardson is the Director of Marketing for the Chewy Chocolate Company. The Chewy Chocolate Company makes a variety of gourmet chocolate treats to satisfy the palettes of chocolate connoisseurs. Recently, they decided to create a new line of high-quality confections. Cathy has decided to create a marketing and sales strategy document to be distributed to the sales force. The strategy document will include the following mandatory topics.

Availability date of confections
Sales strategies for selling confections
Competitors
Discount policy
Sampling policy

Create a cover page for the document that includes the title, date, and a "Prepared by Cathy Richardson" line. Include a picture/logo on the cover page that relates to chocolate. You can download a picture from Microsoft's Clip Online Web site. Use a section break to separate the cover page from the body of the document. Set the vertical alignment of the title page to center.

Use your creativity when writing the marketing and sales strategy document. Make sure you include all of the mandatory topics listed above and any optional topics that you think are appropriate. Save the completed document as **Critical Thinking 13.1.**

Critical Thinking 13.2 On Your Own

Beth Jones is the Sales Manager for Creative Clothing Stores. On a weekly basis, Beth sends a price change memo with a linked worksheet to the store managers at each of her three store locations. Beth links the worksheet so that she can change it on a weekly basis and have the results reflected in the Word memo.

Set up an Excel worksheet with the data shown below. Calculate the discounted prices as the original prices multiplied by 80%. This will effectively create a 20% discount. Save the completed worksheet as **Critical Thinking 13.2—Excel Worksheet.**

Item	Original Price	Discounted Price
Track and Walk Footwear	$34.50	_____
Action Aerobics Clothing	$19.00	_____
Jay's Designer Jeans	$50.00	_____
Sherman Cowboy Boots	$67.95	_____
Jensen Back Packs	$34.55	_____

Set up a memo from Beth to the store managers. Inform them that the weekly price changes are effective immediately. Link the Excel worksheet to the memorandum. Save the completed memorandum as **Critical Thinking 13.2—Word Document.**

Critical Thinking 13.3 Web Research with a Group

As you and your classmate have grown the Health-e-Meals.com business, you realize that communicating regularly with your employees is important. You decide to set up a quarterly newsletter to be distributed to all employees.

Set up a newsletter for Health-e-Meals.com. Include the same logo that you used in the Health-e-Meals letterhead template in Critical Thinking exercise 8.4. The logo should appear somewhere in the title area of the newsletter. Set up your newsletter with two columns. Include the following topics in the newsletter. You will need to write the text to accompany these topics.

Another Big Quarter	401K Plan
Employee Discount Program	Annual Company Picnic

Include a linked Excel worksheet depicting the tax advantages of investing in the 401K plan. Include the sample data shown below in the worksheet. Format the worksheet with an attractive Excel AutoFormat. This worksheet should be linked somewhere in the 401K Plan topic. Save the worksheet as **Critical Thinking 13.3—Excel Worksheet.**

Contribution	Marginal Bracket	Tax Savings
$1,000	20%	$200
$5,000	25%	$1,250
$10,000	32%	$3,200

Apply a border to the page and format the newsletter with whatever font formats you think are appropriate. Save the completed newsletter as **Critical Thinking 13.3—Newsletter.**

LESSON 14

Creating a Research Paper

Research papers are a requirement for nearly every undergraduate and graduate student and many professionally employed individuals. In this lesson, you will use Word to develop a research paper using widely accepted style conventions. Your research paper will include footnotes, endnotes, and a header and footer.

In This Lesson

Case Study

Sam Perkins is an undergraduate student majoring in marketing at a small private college. Sam has been assigned the task of writing a research paper on Internet commerce. This project is of particular interest to Sam since he intends to specialize one day in ecommerce marketing. Sam uses Word 2000 to set up the research paper. He uses headers and footers that print at the top and bottom of every page. In addition, he uses footnotes and endnotes to comment on passages and cite his sources.

Richardson 1

George Richardson

Professor Wilkins

Office Technology 122

May 22, 2000

Internet Commerce

The Internet had its origins in the 1960s when the Department of Defense developed a communications network to connect the computers of various military installations. The Department of Defense removed its computers from this network in the 1980s and turned over the control to the National Science Foundation (NSF). In 1992, the U.S. government withdrew funding from the NSF and encouraged private companies to administer and control the "Internet." It was at this point that Internet commerce was born. Companies both large and small suddenly realized the enormous marketing potential of this global computer network. In fact, the Internet could become the largest global marketplace by 2005.[1]

The commercial potential of the Internet stems from the fact that it is a global network with inexpensive access.[2] The Internet is also available 24 hours a day – seven days a week. The World Wide Web has added multimedia capabilities to the Internet, which is useful for marketing and advertising. Quick product delivery, automated order-taking and low overhead are several more factors that are driving Internet commerce.[3]

The Internet accounted for over $10 billion in retail sales in 1999.[1] This number could reach $50 billion by the year 2002. However, the largest portion of the Internet commerce pie

---

[1] This is the opinion of many business leaders and economists.
[2] This is true in the United States, but many foreign nations still have high rates due to limited competition among Internet service providers.
[3] These factors depend upon the capabilities of individual companies.

Research Paper Styles

The Modern Language Association publishes the *Modern Language Association Handbook for Writers of Research Papers*. This publication is the definitive style guide for research papers. The MLA style guidelines have been the standard used in academia for many years. You can visit the MLA Web site at www.mla.org. The following illustration provides an overview of the MLA style guidelines.

The MLA style requires a header with the student name followed by the page number. The header should be right-aligned ½" from the top of every page.

The student name, professor, course, and date are positioned at the top of the title page and double-spaced.

Double-space between all lines in the paper, and indent the first line of each paragraph ½".

The MLA handbook also provides detailed specifications for citing works, references, and other documentation.

Richardson 1

George Richardson

Professor Wilkins

Office Technology 122

May 22, 2000

Internet Commerce

The Internet had its origins in the 1960s when the Department of Defense developed a communications network to connect the computers of various military installations. The Department of Defense removed its computers from this network in the 1980s and turned over the control to the National Science Foundation (NSF). In 1992, the U.S. government withdrew funding from the NSF and encouraged private companies to administer and control the "Internet." It was at this point that Internet commerce was born. Companies both large and small suddenly realized the enormous marketing potential of this global computer network. In fact, the Internet could become the largest global marketplace by 2005.[1]

The commercial potential of the Internet stems from the fact that it is a global network with inexpensive access.[2] The Internet is also available 24 hours a day – seven days a week. The World Wide Web has added multimedia capabilities to the Internet, which is useful for marketing and advertising. Quick product delivery, automated order-taking and low overhead are several more factors that are driving Internet commerce.[3]

The Internet accounted for over $10 billion in retail sales in 1999.[1] This number could reach $50 billion by the year 2002. However, the largest portion of the Internet commerce pie

---

[1] This is the opinion of many business leaders and economists.
[2] This is true in the United States, but many foreign nations still have high rates due to limited competition among Internet service providers.
[3] These factors depend upon the capabilities of individual companies.

Footnotes and Endnotes

Footnotes and endnotes are an important part of most research papers. Footnotes are usually used to provide comments and additional details on topics. Footnotes appear at the bottom of each page. Endnotes are used to cite works, references, and information sources. Endnotes appear at the end of a document on a "Works Cited" page. Footnotes and endnotes are inserted using the Footnote and Endnote dialog box. You display the Footnote and Endnote dialog box with the **Insert→Footnotes** command.

From the Keyboard

(ALT)+(CTRL)+F to insert footnote

(ALT)+(CTRL)+D to insert endnote

You can choose to insert a footnote or endnote.

Word automatically numbers footnotes and endnotes when the AutoNumber option is chosen. Footnotes are numbered with Arabic numerals. Endnotes are numbered with roman numerals.

*The **Options** button lets you change the numbering style for both footnotes and endnotes. You can also specify a starting number. Changing the starting number can be useful if you have a large research project that is organized into multiple documents. In this situation, you could specify a starting number for the footnotes and endnotes in each document.*

Footnote and Endnote	? X
Insert	
⊙ Footnote	Bottom of page
○ Endnote	End of document
Numbering	
⊙ AutoNumber	1, 2, 3, ...
○ Custom mark:	
	Symbol...
OK	Cancel	Options...

Footnote and Endnote Links

When you insert a footnote or endnote, Word inserts a footnote or endnote marker in the document. The marker is displayed in a superscript font. The marker is linked to a corresponding footnote or endnote. Word automatically renumbers footnotes and endnotes as you add or remove them from a document. The following illustration shows a footnote marker and the corresponding footnote at the bottom of the page.

suddenly realized the enormous marketing potential of this global computer network.

Internet could become the largest global marketplace by 2005.[1]

---

[1] This is the opinion of many business leaders and economists.

The footnote text is typed at the bottom of the page. Word adds a separator line above the footnote and inserts the appropriate number.

This is the footnote marker. Footnote markers identify the location at which the footnote was inserted.

Set Up the Paper

1. Start Word, and set the left and right margins to 1".
   These are the recommended margin settings for an MLA-style research paper.

2. Set the line spacing to double.

3. Type the text shown below. You will need to tap (ENTER) just once after each paragraph except after the date, where you should tap (ENTER) twice.

George Richardson

Professor Wilkins

Office Technology 122

May 22, 2000

Internet Commerce

　　The Internet had its origins in the 1960s when the Department of Defense developed a communications network to connect the computers of various military installations. The Department of Defense removed its computers from this network in the 1980s and turned over the control to the National Science Foundation (NSF). In 1992, the U.S. government withdrew funding from the NSF and encouraged private companies to administer and control the Internet. It was at this point that Internet commerce was born. Companies both large and small suddenly realized the enormous marketing potential of this global computer network. In fact, the Internet could become the largest global marketplace by 2005.

---

4. Position the insertion point to the right of the period at the end of the last paragraph.

5. Choose **Insert→Footnote** from the menu bar.

6. Make sure the Footnote and AutoNumber options are chosen, and click **OK.**
   The Footnote area will appear at the bottom of the page. Word automatically inserted a separator line and the correct number.

7. Type the following text directly into the footnote area.

---

   [1] This is the opinion of many business leaders and economists.

8. Click to the right of the footnote marker, which is located at the end of the large paragraph in the body of the document.

9. Tap (ENTER) to begin a new paragraph, and then tap (TAB) to indent the first line of the new paragraph.

10. Type the following paragraph using the **Insert→Footnote** command to insert footnotes at the footnote marker locations 2 and 3. Use the footnote text shown in the footnote area below.

> The commercial potential of the Internet stems from the fact that it is a global network with inexpensive access.[2] The Internet is also available 24 hours a day – seven days a week. The World Wide Web has added multimedia capabilities to the Internet, which is useful for marketing and advertising. Quick product delivery, automated order-taking, and low overhead are several more factors that are driving Internet commerce.[3]
>
> ---
>
> [1] This is the opinion of many business leaders and economists.
> [2] This is true in the United States, but many foreign nations still have high rates due to limited competition among Internet service providers.
> [3] These factors depend upon the capabilities of individual companies.

Display the Footnote Pane

11. Use the **View→Normal** command to switch to Normal view.
    Notice that the footnote area is not visible at the bottom of the page. The footnote area is only visible in Print Layout view. In Normal, Outline, or Web Layout views, the footnotes appear in a separate window pane whenever you double-click one of the footnote markers.

12. Scroll up and double-click any of the footnote markers in the body paragraphs.
    The Footnote pane will appear at the bottom of the window.

13. Use the **View→Print Layout** command to switch back to Print Layout view.

(Continued on the next page)

Insert Endnotes

14. Click to the right of the footnote marker located at the end of the last paragraph.

15. Tap (ENTER) to begin a new paragraph, and then (TAB) tab to indent the first line of the new paragraph.

16. Follow these guidelines to type the text shown below and to insert endnotes.

   ■ Type the body paragraphs using the **Insert→Footnote** command to insert endnotes at the locations where the roman numerals i, ii, and iii appear. You will need to choose the Endnote option in the Footnote and Endnote dialog box. The first paragraph you type will be split by a page break.

   ■ Use the text shown in the endnote area below. You will need to turn italics on and off when typing the endnotes as shown.

   ■ Your endnotes will most likely be positioned above the footnotes when you first begin typing them. However, they will move to the end of the document as it increases in length.

The Internet accounted for over $10 billion in retail sales in 1999.[i] This number could reach $50 billion by the year 2002. However, the largest portion of the Internet commerce pie went to commerce between businesses. Business to business Internet commerce could be as large as $2.7 trillion by 2004.[ii] No matter how you slice the pie, the Internet will provide huge dividends for retailers, brokerages, banks, and other types of businesses.

Perhaps the biggest obstacle to online commerce has been the potential lack of security. Many consumers are hesitant to enter credit card numbers in an electronic form on some computer system in cyberspace. Even though recent studies have shown that electronic commerce is more secure than offline commerce; consumers are still cautious.[iii] Privacy is also a concern for many consumers. Most consumers are already overwhelmed with junk mail, illicit telephone calls, and deceptive advertising.

---

[i] Richard J. Smith, *Internet Commerce,* New York Technology Press, New York, NY, 1999, p. 235
[ii] Steven Crosby, *Investing in the New Millennium,* Silicon Valley Press, San Jose, CA 1999, p. 180
[iii] Steven Crosby, *Investing in the New Millennium,* Silicon Valley Press, San Jose, CA 1999, p. 221

---

17. Save the document as **Hands-On Lesson 14,** and continue with the next topic.

Editing Footnotes and Endnotes

In Print Layout view, you can edit footnote or endnote text in the footnote or endnote area at the bottom of the page or document. If you are working in Normal, Web Layout, or Outline views, you must double-click a footnote or endnote marker to display the Footnote or Endnote panes. You can then edit the footnotes and endnotes in those panes. Also, the position of a footnote or endnote marker can be changed by dragging it to another location.

Deleting Footnotes

You can delete a footnote or endnote by selecting the desired footnote or endnote marker and tapping the (DELETE) key. The footnote or endnote text associated with the marker will be deleted from the footnote or endnote areas. It is important that you delete footnotes and endnotes in this manner. You should never attempt to delete footnotes or endnotes by deleting the text from the footnote or endnote area. The markers will remain in the document if you try to delete in this manner. However, you can delete some of the text in the footnote or endnote areas for the purpose of editing the text.

Hands-On 14.2 Delete an Endnote, Edit a Footnote, and Add Text

1. Follow these steps to delete an endnote.

    A *If necessary, scroll up or down until this endnote marker is visible in the last paragraph.*

    B *Select the marker by dragging the mouse over it.*

    consumers are still cautious.ⁱⁱⁱ Privacy is also a

    C *Tap (DELETE) to remove the marker. Notice that the endnote has been removed from the endnote area located below the paragraph.*

2. Scroll up to the bottom of page 1 to view the footnotes.

3. Select the words *and economists* at the end of the first footnote, and tap (DELETE) to remove the words.

4. Now add the following text to the end of the document.

    In order to alleviate the concerns of consumers, many large companies are now guaranteeing credit cards against theft during Internet commerce. These companies include AB & B International, which has promised to pay the $50 liability deductible that most credit card issuers require. AB & B will pay this fee if a consumer's credit card number is stolen during online commerce with AB & B.

    In summary, Internet commerce will be a driving force in the global economy of the twenty-first century. There are still obstacles to overcome, but technology and market forces will propel this new commercial medium forward at a rapid pace.

5. Save the changes, and continue with the next topic.

Text Flow Options

The Line and Page Breaks tab of the Paragraph dialog box has several check boxes that let you control the text flow of paragraphs. The table below describes the various text flow options. You can apply the options by selecting the desired paragraphs, choosing **Format→Paragraph,** and checking the desired check boxes on the Line and Page Breaks tab of the Paragraph dialog box.

Option	Description
Widow/Orphan control	A widow line occurs when the last line of a paragraph appears at the top of a new page by itself. An orphan line occurs when the first line of a paragraph appears at the bottom of a page by itself. The Widow/Orphan control check box prevents widow and orphan lines from occurring.
Keep lines together	Prevents pages breaks from occurring within paragraphs. If a paragraph falls on a page break, then the entire paragraph moves to the new page.
Keep with next	Keeps the following paragraph together with the selected paragraph. The two paragraphs will always appear on the same page.
Page break before	Inserts a manual page break before the selected paragraph.

 ## Hands-On 14.3 Use Text Flow Options

1. Scroll through the document until the page break is visible.
   The page break will most likely split a paragraph. In the following steps, you will prevent the paragraph from splitting by setting the Keep lines together *option.*

2. Press (CTRL)+A to select the entire document.
   This shortcut keystroke is a convenient way to select an entire document.

3. Choose **Format→Paragraph,** and click the Line and Page Breaks tab in the Paragraph dialog box.

4. Check the *Keep lines together* box (ignore the other options), and click **OK.**
   The Keep lines together *setting is applied to all selected paragraphs.*

5. Now scroll through the document, and notice that the paragraph that was initially split by the page break has moved to the second page.

6. Feel free to experiment with the text flow options, and then continue with the next topic.

Headers and Footers

There are times that you will want text to appear on every page of a document. For example, the MLA style guidelines for research papers require the author's name followed by the current page number to appear at the top right corner of every page. This is easily accomplished by placing the name and a page number code in the header. Headers appear at the top of every page while footers appear at the bottom of every page.

Creating Headers and Footers

The **View→Header and Footer** command is used to set up headers and footers. This command displays the header area at the top of the document and the footer area at the bottom of the document. You can type text in the header and footer areas and insert date, time, and page number codes using buttons on the Header and Footer toolbar. You can also format text, insert graphics, apply borders and shading, and use virtually any other formats within the header and footer areas. Word also includes two preset custom tab stops in the header and footer areas that make it easy to center-align and right-align text within headers and footers. The following illustration describes the buttons on the Header and Footer toolbar.

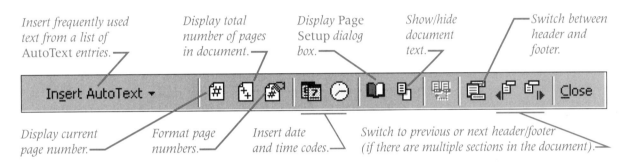

Insert frequently used text from a list of AutoText entries.

Display total number of pages in document.

Display Page Setup dialog box.

Show/hide document text.

Switch between header and footer.

Display current page number.

Format page numbers.

Insert date and time codes.

Switch to previous or next header/footer (if there are multiple sections in the document).

Hands-On 14.4 Set Up a Header

1. Press (CTRL)+(HOME) to move the insertion point to the top of the document.

2. Choose **View→Header and Footer** from the menu bar.

3. Follow these steps to explore the header area and set up the header.

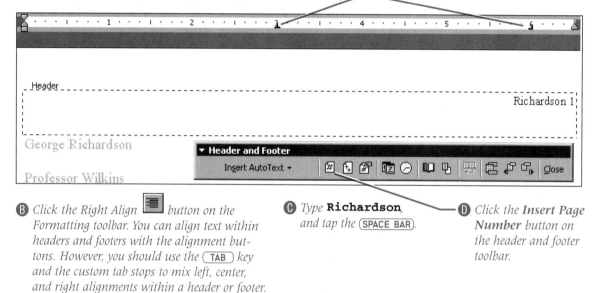

Ⓐ *Notice the center and right tab stops on the ruler. They can be used to center-align or right-align text in a header or footer. But, notice that the right tab is about ½" from the right margin. This is because you reduced the left and right margins to 1" at the start of this lesson. The custom tab stop positions in the header and footer do not move when the margins are adjusted. Fortunately, you can drag the custom tab stops on the ruler if you need to adjust their positions (but don't do it now).*

Ⓑ *Click the Right Align* ▤ *button on the Formatting toolbar. You can align text within headers and footers with the alignment buttons. However, you should use the* (TAB) *key and the custom tab stops to mix left, center, and right alignments within a header or footer.*

Ⓒ *Type* **Richardson**, *and tap the* (SPACE BAR).

Ⓓ *Click the* **Insert Page Number** *button on the header and footer toolbar.*

4. Click the **Close** button on the header and footer toolbar.

5. Scroll down and notice that the header is visible at the top of the second page.
   Headers and footers appear on every page unless you set options that restrict where they appear.

6. Now double-click the header area (on either the first or second page) to activate it.
   If desired, you could edit the header at this point.

7. Click the **Close** button on the header and footer toolbar, and continue with the next topic.

Header and Footer Options on the Page Setup Dialog Box

The **File→Page Setup** command displays the Page Setup dialog box. The Layout tab of the Page Setup dialog box contains a Header and Footer section with two check boxes you can use with headers and footers.

Different Odd and Even Option

When the *Different odd and even* box is checked, you can set up different headers and footers on odd and even pages. This is often used with bound documents where even pages are on the left and odd pages are on the right.

Different First Page Option

When the *Different first page* box is checked, Word initially removes the header and footer from the first page of the document or section. This is often used with documents that have title pages where the header or footer is not to appear on the title page. If desired, you can also check the *Different first page* box and then set up a different header and footer on the first page.

Navigation Buttons on the Header and Footer Toolbar

The Switch Between ⊞, Show Previous ⊞, and Show Next ⊞ buttons on the Header and Footer toolbar let you navigate among the headers and footers in a document. The **Switch Between** button simply toggles you between the header and footer. The **Show Previous** and **Show Next** buttons let you move between the headers and footers in documents with more than one header and footer. You may have more than one header or footer if you use the *Different first page* option, *Different odd and even* headers/footers option, or if your document has multiple sections. You can have different headers and footers in each section.

Hands-On 14.5 Use Header/Footer Options and Navigate

Experiment With Navigation Buttons

1. Double-click the header, and the Header and Footer toolbar will appear.

2. Click the Switch Between Header and Footer ⊞ button to display the footer.
   The footer should be blank.

3. Click the Switch Between Header and Footer ⊞ button again to display the header.

4. Try clicking the Show Previous ⊞ and Show Next ⊞ buttons.
   There is only one header and footer, so nothing will happen.

5. Click the **Close** button on the Header and Footer toolbar.

(Continued on the next page)

Remove the Header from the First Page

6. Choose **File→Page Setup,** and click the Layout tab.

7. Check the *Different first page* box, and click **OK.**
    The header should be removed from the first page.

8. Scroll to the second page, and double-click the header.

9. Click the Show Previous button on the Header and Footer toolbar.
    The blank first page header will appear. The first page header is now a separate header from the second page header. You could type text and insert codes in this header without affecting the second header (but don't do it now).

Restore the First Page Header

10. Click the Page Setup button on the Header and Footer toolbar.
    This button is located on the toolbar to allow you to easily access the Page Setup dialog box.

11. Uncheck the *Different first page* box, and click **OK.**
    Notice that the header has been restored.

12. Try clicking the Show Previous and Show Next buttons.
    Once again, the buttons will be inactive because the document has just one header and footer.

13. Close the Header and Footer toolbar, and continue with the next topic.

Browsing Objects

From the Keyboard

ALT + CTRL + HOME
to display Browse
Object menu

You can rapidly browse through various document objects, including pages, footnotes, endnotes, and tables. You browse objects by first choosing the desired object type from the Browse Object menu at the bottom of the vertical scroll bar. Then, you use the **Previous Object** and **Next Object** buttons on the vertical scroll bar to browse through the objects.

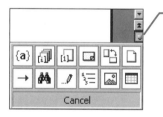

The Browse Object *menu is displayed when you click the* Browse Object *button at the bottom of the vertical scroll bar.*

Hands-On 14.6 **Browse Objects**

Browse By Page

1. Press (CTRL)+(HOME) to position the insertion point at the top of the document.

2. Position the mouse pointer on the Next Object  button at the bottom of the vertical scroll bar.
   A Next Page *screen tip should pop up. The object type is set to page by default.*

3. Click the Next Object button to display the second page.

4. Click the Previous Object button to redisplay the first page.

Browse By Footnote

5. Click the Select Browse Object button on the vertical scroll bar.

6. Choose Browse by Footnote from the object list.
   The insertion point will move to the first footnote marker.

7. Click the Next Object button to move to the second footnote marker.

8. Click the Next Object button again.

9. Use the Select Browse Object button and the Next Object button to browse for endnotes.

10. Feel free to experiment with the object browsing buttons.

11. When you have finished, save the changes to the document, and then close it.

Concepts Review

True/False Questions

1. Footnotes are positioned at the bottom of the page on which they are inserted.   TRUE   FALSE

2. Endnotes are positioned at the end of the page on which they are inserted.   TRUE   FALSE

3. Footnotes are typically used to cite references.   TRUE   FALSE

4. Endnotes are typically used for explanatory text or to provide additional details on a topic.   TRUE   FALSE

5. The header and footer area can be accessed by choosing **Edit→Header and Footer.**   TRUE   FALSE

6. The header and footer area can be accessed by single-clicking on a header.   TRUE   FALSE

7. Page numbers can be inserted in a header or footer.   TRUE   FALSE

8. The Select Browse Object [icon] button is used to move the insertion point to the next occurrence of a selected object.   TRUE   FALSE

Multiple-Choice Questions

1. Which of the following objects can you browse through?
   a. Pages
   b. Footnotes
   c. Endnotes
   d. None of these

2. Which command is used to insert an endnote?
   a. Insert→Footnote
   b. Insert→Endnote
   c. Edit→Endnote
   d. Format→Endnote

3. Which command is used to insert a footnote?
   a. Insert→Footnote
   b. Insert→Footnote
   c. Edit→Footnote
   d. Format→Footnote

4. Which command is used to insert a header in a new document?
   a. Edit→Header and Footer
   b. View→Header and Footer
   c. Insert→Header and Footer
   d. None of these

Skill Builders

Skill Builder 14.1 Set Up Headers, Footers, and Endnotes

In this exercise, you will open a document on your exercise diskette. You will set up a header and footer using left-, center-, and right-aligned text. You will also insert a footnote.

Examine the Document

1. Open the document named **Skill Builder 14.1.**

2. Click the Select Browse Object ⬚ button on the vertical scroll bar, and choose the *Browse by Page* option.

3. Use the Next Page ⬚ button to browse through the document page-by-page.
   How many pages are in the document? This question is easily answered by examining the Status bar at the bottom of the window.

4. Press (CTRL)+(HOME) to move to the top of the document.

5. Click the Next Page ⬚ button again to move to the top of the second page.

Insert a Footnote

6. Scroll down several lines until the bottom of the first paragraph is visible.

7. Click just to the right of the period at the end of the paragraph.

8. Choose **Insert→Footnote** from the menu bar.

9. Make sure the Footnote option is chosen, and click **OK.**

10. Type the following footnote text in the footnote area at the bottom of the page.

   ---

   [1] There are actually five main characters in this novel.

Set Up the Header

11. Choose **View→Header and Footer** to display the header area.

12. Type the word **Heart** on the left end of the header.

13. Tap the (TAB) key to position the insertion point below the center-aligned tab stop.

14. Type **Oriental Languages 133B**, and the text will be centered below the tab stop.

15. Tap the (TAB) key again to position the insertion point at the right margin.

16. Type **Gerry Jefferson**, and the text will move to the left as you type.
   This is because a right-aligned tab stop is positioned at the right margin. The preset custom tab stops let you easily create a combination of left-, center-, and right-aligned text within headers and footers. Your completed header should match the following example.

Header		
Heart	Oriental Languages 133B	Gerry Jefferson

(Continued on the next page)

Set Up the Footer

17. Click the Switch Between Header and Footer [icon] button to display the footer area.

18. Click the Insert Date [icon] button on the Header and Footer toolbar.
    The current date is inserted as a field. The date will be updated to reflect the current date whenever the document is opened.

19. Tap the (TAB) key twice to position the insertion point at the right margin.

20. Click the Insert Page Number [icon] button to insert the current page number.

21. Tap the (SPACE BAR) once, type the word **of**, and tap (SPACE BAR) again.

22. Click the Insert Number of Pages [icon] button (not the **Insert Page Number** button).
    This button inserts the total number of pages in the document. Your completed footer should match the following example (although the date will be different).

```
  Footer
  1/27/00                                                                                  1 of 9
```

23. Click the **Close** button on the Header and Footer toolbar.

24. Click the Print Preview [icon] button on the Standard toolbar.

25. Use the (PGUP) and (PGDN) keys to browse through the document.
    If necessary, click the document to zoom in and out as necessary. Notice the way the page numbering occurs throughout the document. You will remove the header from the title page in the next few steps.

Use a Different First Page Header and Footer

26. Close the Print Preview window, and then double-click the header.

27. Click the Page Setup [icon] button on the Header and Footer toolbar.

28. Click the Layout tab in the Page Setup dialog box.

29. Check the *Different first page* box, and click **OK.**

30. Scroll to the top of the document, and the header and footer will no longer be visible on the title page.

31. Feel free to experiment with the headers and footers in this document.

32. Close the Header and Footer toolbar, save the changes to the document, and then close the document.

Skill Builder 14.2 Set Up Headers and Footers on Even and Odd Pages

Set Up Headers

1. Open the document named **Skill Builder 14.2.**

2. Choose **File→Page Setup,** and click the Layout tab in the Page Setup dialog box.

3. Check both the *Different odd and even* and *Different first page* boxes, and click **OK.**

4. Choose **View→Header and Footer** to display the header area.
   Notice that the header area is labeled First Page Header. If you were to create a header at this point, it would only display on the first page. You do not want a header on the title page, so you will move to the even page header in the next step.

5. Click the Show Next ⬚ button on the Header and Footer toolbar.
   You currently have three headers in your document: a first page header; an even page header; and an odd page header. The even page header should now be displayed.

6. Type the name **Gerry Jefferson**.
   This header will appear on the left side of even pages.

7. Click the Show Next ⬚ button to display the odd page header.

8. Click the Align Right ⬚ button, and type the phrase **Anthropology 151**.
   This text will only appear on the right side of odd numbered pages.

Set Up Footers

9. Click the Switch Between Header and Footer ⬚ button.

10. Click the Show Previous ⬚ button to display the even page footer.

11. Use the Header and Footer toolbar to insert the current date.

12. Click the Show Next ⬚ button to display the odd page footer.

13. Click the Align Right ⬚ button and use the Header and Footer toolbar to insert the current page number.

14. Close the Header and Footer toolbar.

15. Scroll through the document and examine the various headers and footers.

16. Save the changes to the document, and then close it.

Skill Builder 14.3 Use Text Flow Options

1. Open the **Skill Builder 14.1** document.

2. Scroll through the document and notice the way the paragraphs break at the bottom and top of each page.
   There shouldn't be any pages where a single line from a paragraph appears at the bottom or top of a page by itself. This is because Widow/Orphan control is turned on.

3. Press (CTRL)+A to select the entire document.

4. Choose **Format→Paragraph,** and click the Line and Page Breaks tab.

5. Remove the check from the Widow/Orphan control box, and click **OK.**

6. Scroll through the document, and you will most likely see at least one widow or orphan line.
   It is impossible to ensure that you will see a widow or orphan because the locations at which paragraphs wrap depends on the printer driver used on your system.

7. Save the changes to the document, and close the document.

Assessments

Assessment 14.1 Footnotes, Headers, and Footers

1. Open the document named **Assessment 14.1** on your exercise diskette.

2. Create the following header to print on every page of the report except the cover page.

   Header
   The Salem Witchcraft Trials   Donna Adams

3. Create the following footer to print on every page of the report except the cover page. Insert the time and date using buttons on the Header and Footer toolbar. Your date will reflect the current date.

   Footer
   1/27/00   Page 2

4. Insert the following footnote immediately to the right of the period at the end of the first paragraph.

   _____

   [1] There were 23 other people arrested, but they were released soon after their arrests.

5. Insert the following footnote to the right of the period at the end of the second paragraph.

   _____

   [2] Most of the arrests involved lower-class and socially disadvantaged people.

6. Save the changes to the document, and close it.

Critical Thinking

Critical Thinking 14.1 On Your Own

Open the newsletter you created in Critical Thinking 13.3. Add a footer to the newsletter that prints the page number and date at the bottom of every page. Save the changes to the newsletter, and then close it.

Critical Thinking 14.2 Web Research

Samantha Jackson is majoring in business at Mid State University. Samantha's interest is in ecommerce marketing. Professor Davidson's Marketing 101 course gives the students the option of writing a research paper on the marketing topic of their choice. Samantha chooses to write a paper on the growth of ecommerce.

Set up a research paper on the growth of ecommerce using the MLA style guidelines for research papers. Make sure you include the appropriate header and cover page text required in the MLA guidelines.

Use Internet Explorer and a search engine of your choice to locate an article on the Web that discusses the growth of ecommerce. Select the article text, and copy and paste it into your Word document. If necessary, copy text from several articles until you have 1½–2 pages of text. It is OK to copy selected text in this manner as long as you do not intend to distribute it commercially or claim ownership of it. You are copying the text in this exercise simply to fill a document with text. Select all of the copied text and format it with a Times New Roman 12 font. You may want to bold headings and format the text in other ways.

Work through the document and insert at least three footnotes that expand upon topics you feel are inadequately covered in the text. Make up humorous footnotes if you are unsure what to write in a footnote. Save your completed paper as **Critical Thinking 14.2.**

Critical Thinking 14.3 As a Group

You and your classmate have grown Health-e-Meals.com to the point where you are considering taking the company public. This is a bold move that may require investment from venture capital firms. In addition, you will need to recruit experienced executives to run the company. You have decided to write an executive-level paper describing the success of your company and the marketing opportunities available to you. This paper will be presented to potential investors and managers to acquaint them with the company and the growth opportunities awaiting them.

Work with your classmate to write a paper as discussed above. You work on the part of the paper that describes Health-e-Meals successes thus far, and have your classmate work on the growth opportunities portion of the paper. Once your classmate has completed his/her portion of the paper, insert the text into your paper to create one large paper. If necessary, search the Web for articles on growth opportunities in the online food service industry. Copy and paste the text into your paper.

Include a cover page on your paper with the Health-e-Meals.com logo. Include a header or footer with the page number and date. Save your completed document as **Critical Thinking 14.3.**

Creating an Employee Policy Manual

Word provides a variety of tools that are useful with large multipage and multichapter documents. Styles are a powerful formatting tool that help ensure formatting consistency throughout large documents. Word's outlining view can be quite useful for organizing and rearranging large documents. Word even provides sophisticated table of contents and indexing tools to help you add a table of contents and an index to your documents.

In This Lesson

Case Study

Lisa Barons is the Administrative Assistant for TrainRight, Inc.—a successful computer training company. Lisa has been asked to produce an employee policy manual to be distributed to all TrainRight employees. In her present and past occupations, Lisa has learned to take advantage of the variety of tools available to her in Word. Lisa uses Word's built-in styles to format the headings in the employee policy manual, thus ensuring consistent formatting throughout the document. She uses the outline feature to organize her work and headers, footers, and page numbering to provide structure. In addition, Lisa effortlessly generates a table of contents and index to help TrainRight's employees easily locate the information they need.

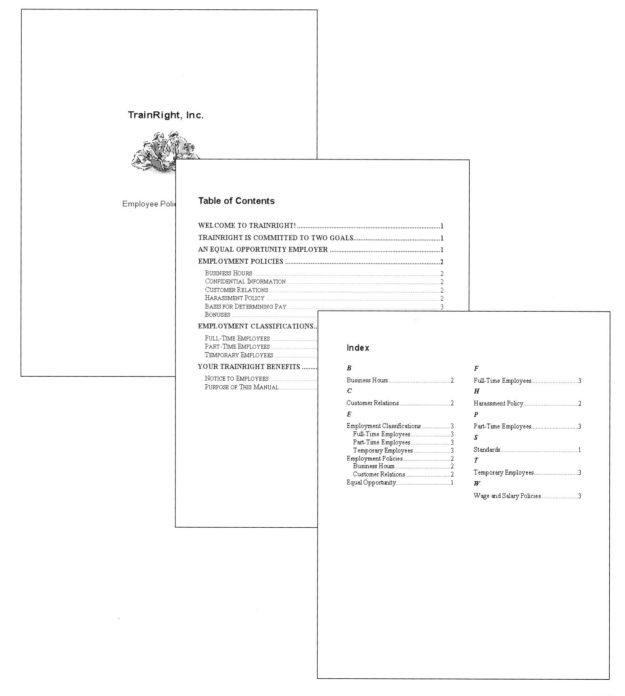

TrainRight, Inc.

Employee Poli

Styles

Styles are perhaps the most powerful formatting tool in Word. A style is a group of formats identified by a unique style name. You can rapidly format text and paragraphs by applying styles to them. Styles create consistent formatting throughout a document. In addition, styles allow you to make global formatting changes by changing style definitions. When a style definition is changed, the changes are applied to all text or paragraphs formatted with the style.

Types of Styles

Word supports both character and paragraph styles as discussed below:

- **Paragraph styles**—Paragraph styles are applied to all text in selected paragraphs. You can use any text or paragraph formats in paragraph styles. Paragraphs styles are often used to format headings. For example, you may want to format a heading with a large bold font and apply paragraph spacing before and after the heading.

- **Character styles**—Character styles are applied to selected text only. Character styles can only contain text formats. You can apply character styles to text within a paragraph that is formatted with a paragraph style. The character style overrides the text formats applied by the paragraph style.

Applying Styles

Word provides built-in styles that are available in all documents. You can redefine the built-in styles or create your own custom styles to suit your particular needs. All styles are accessed through the Style box on the left end of the Formatting toolbar. You apply styles to paragraphs by selecting the paragraph(s) and choosing the desired style from the Style list. The following illustration shows the styles that appear on the style list in new documents.

This button displays the style list. Both built-in and custom styles are displayed on the list.

This paragraph is formatted with the Heading 1 style. The Heading 1 style applies both text and paragraph formats.

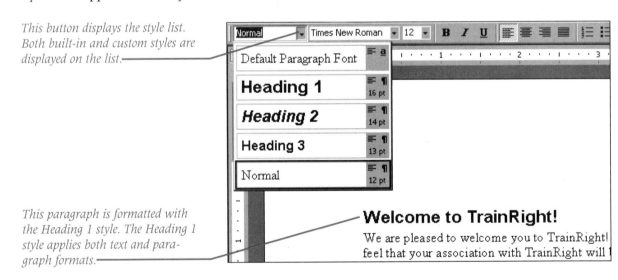

Heading Styles

Word provides a series of built-in styles named Heading 1, Heading 2 . . . Heading 9. These heading styles have special significance in Word. For example, they are used with Word's Outline and Table of Contents features. You will use these styles with the Outline and Table of Contents features later in this lesson.

Type Text, and Insert a Picture

1. Start Word, or start a new document.

2. Click the Center ▦ button, type the phrase **TrainRight, Inc.**, and tap ⟨ENTER⟩ twice.

3. Insert the picture shown to the right. The picture can be found in the Business category of the Office 2000 Clip Gallery.

4. Adjust the size of the picture until it is approximately 1″ high.

5. Click to the right of the picture, tap ⟨ENTER⟩ four times, and type **Employee Policy Manual**.

6. Set the vertical alignment of the page to center. You will need to use the Page Setup dialog box to accomplish this.

7. Set the zoom control to Whole Page to view the entire page.
   You will format the title and subtitle with styles in a later exercise.

Insert a New Section, and Change the Vertical Alignment

8. Set the zoom control to Page Width.

9. Tap ⟨ENTER⟩ after the subtitle, and set the alignment to left ▦.

10. Insert a section break that begins on the next page.

11. Use the Page Setup dialog box to set the vertical alignment to top for the new section.
    The vertical alignment should still be set to center for the first section.

Apply Styles

12. Look at the Style box │Normal ▾│ on the left end of the Formatting toolbar, and notice that a style named Normal is in effect.
    The Normal style is active when you create new documents. The Normal style formats text with a Times New Roman 12 pt font. All text in the current document is formatted with the Normal style.

13. Click the Style list │Normal ▾│ button.
    There should be five styles on the list. These styles are a small subset of the built-in styles. There are many more built-in styles that are not on this list. You will learn how to access the remaining built-in styles in the next topic. Notice that the phrases Heading 1, Heading 2, etc., are formatted on the list. The formatting you see is the same formatting that will be applied when you use the indicated style in your document.

14. Choose Heading 1 from the list, and type the phrase **Welcome to TrainRight!**
    Notice that the text is formatted with an Arial 16 bold font. This font is part of the Heading 1 style definition.

15. Tap ⟨ENTER⟩ once, and notice that the Normal style is once again in effect.
    Every built-in paragraph style (such as Heading 1) sets the style for the following paragraph when ⟨ENTER⟩ is tapped. The Heading 1 style sets the style of the following paragraph to Normal.

(Continued on the next page)

16. Now type the following paragraph.

> We are pleased to welcome you to TrainRight. Congratulations on joining our company. We want your employment to be rewarding and mutually beneficial. You have joined an organization with a reputation for quality computer training and outstanding customer service. We understand that our success depends on our employees. For this reason, we believe in nurturing our employees through proper training, above average compensation, and challenging job responsibilities. It is our sincere hope that you will enjoy your employment and thrive in this dynamic company.

17. Tap (ENTER) once, and type the phrase **You're Part of Our Team.**

18. Tap (ENTER) again, and then click anywhere on the phrase "You're Part of Our Team."

19. Click the **Style list** button, and choose Heading 2.
    The entire phrase will be formatted with an Arial 14 Bold Italic font. Heading 2 is also a paragraph style and paragraph styles impact all text in the paragraph. Therefore, you only need to position the insertion point within a paragraph when applying paragraph styles; there is no need to select the entire paragraph. Also notice that the paragraph has been pushed down about one line. This is because the Heading 1 and Heading 2 styles apply 12 points of paragraph spacing before the paragraph. Paragraph styles can include any paragraph formats in their style definitions.

20. Choose **Format→Paragraph** from the menu bar.
    Notice that the Spacing Before is 12 pt and the Spacing After is 3 pt.

21. Click the **Cancel** button to close the dialog box.

22. Now click below the heading "You're Part of Our Team," and type the following text.

> As a member of the TrainRight team, you will have the opportunity to grow with our company. You will be given responsibility and challenging job assignments. It is up to you to take advantage of this opportunity by contributing your time, creativity, and skills. The success of our company depends on each member of our team. Together, we can achieve our goals and have fun in the process.

23. Save the document as **Hands-On Lesson 15,** and continue with the next topic.

Displaying All Built-in Styles

Only five of Word's built-in styles appear on the Style list when you click the **Style list** button. This short list displays the five most commonly used styles. There are many other built-in styles, but most of them are not used often. These additional styles would clutter the Style list; therefore, they do not appear on the short list. You can display the complete style list by pressing (SHIFT) while clicking the **Style list** button.

In this exercise, you will use built-in styles that are not displayed on the short list.

Use a Number Style

1. Tap (ENTER) after the second large paragraph.

2. Type **TrainRight Is Committed to Two Goals**, and tap (ENTER) again.
   You will format the heading later in this exercise.

3. Press the (SHIFT) key while you click the **Style list** button.

4. Scroll up and down through the list, and notice the various styles.

5. Locate the *1. List Number* style, and choose it.
   Notice that this style numbers the paragraph just as if you had used the Numbering button on the Formatting toolbar. Styles such as this one are also advantageous if you want paragraph spacing, indentations, or other paragraph formats to be applied along with the numbering.

6. Type the following text, tapping (ENTER) after both paragraphs.

---

1. To provide our customers with the best quality products and services at the most competitive prices.
2. To provide our employees with above average compensation and a working environment that allows them to grow professionally.
3.

---

7. Make sure the insertion point is on the paragraph with the number 3.
   You will remove the numbering by applying the Normal style to the paragraph.

8. Click the **Style list** button.
   Notice that the 1. List Number *style is now on the short list. Styles are added to the short list once they have been used in a document. However, they only appear on the short list in the current document.*

9. Choose Normal to remove all formatting from the paragraph.
   Applying the Normal style effectively removes all formatting from paragraphs.

10. Type the following two paragraphs. You will format the heading paragraph in a moment.

An Equal Opportunity Employer
TrainRight is an equal opportunity/affirmative action employer. We welcome and encourage diversity in the workplace. At TrainRight, we recognize that people have different needs and different lifestyles. That's why we work hard to accommodate the individual needs of our employees.

(Continued on the next page)

Use Styles on the Title Page

11. Scroll up to the title page and click anywhere on the "TrainRight, Inc." title.

12. Press the (SHIFT) key while you click the **Style list** button.

13. Tap the letter **T** on the keyboard to display style names beginning with the letter *t*.
You can use this technique to scroll most drop-down lists, including the style and font lists.

14. Choose the Title style.
The Title style applies an Arial 16 Bold font and center-aligns the title.

15. Click on the "Employee Policy Manual" subtitle.

16. Press the (SHIFT) key while you click the **Style list** button.

17. Tap the letter **S** on the keyboard to display style names beginning with the letter *s*.

18. Choose the Subtitle style.

Apply Styles with the Format Painter

You can use the Format Painter to apply styles by copying them from one paragraph to another.

19. Scroll down, and click anywhere on the heading "You're Part of Our Team."
The insertion point can be anywhere within a paragraph when copying paragraph formats with the Format Painter.

20. Double-click the Format Painter ⬙ .

21. Click the mouse pointer 📝 in the left margin just in front of the "TrainRight Is Committed to Two Goals" heading. This heading is currently formatted with the Normal style, and it is located just below the "You're Part of Our Team" body paragraph.
This will copy the Heading 2 style to the paragraph. Clicking in the margin ensures that the style is applied to all text in the paragraph. If desired, you can also drag the mouse over the paragraph.

22. Click in front of the "An Equal Opportunity Employer" paragraph to apply the Heading 2 style to that paragraph as well.

23. Click the Format Painter ⬙ to turn it off.

Insert a File

In the next few steps, you will insert a file containing four pages of text.

24. Position the insertion point at the end of the last paragraph, and insert a manual page break.

25. Choose **Insert→File** from the menu bar.

26. Navigate to your exercise diskette, and insert the file named **Hands-On Lesson 15—Text.**

27. Scroll up through the text you just inserted.
Notice that some paragraphs are formatted with a blue color, and some are formatted with a red color.

28. Apply the Heading 1 style to all paragraphs that have a blue color, and apply the Heading 2 style to all paragraphs with a red color. You can accomplish this by clicking on the various paragraphs and choosing the desired style from the Style box. However, you may be able to save time by copying the Heading 1 and Heading 2 styles from paragraphs you have already formatted to the new paragraphs using the Format Painter.

29. Save the changes and continue with the next topic.

The Style Dialog Box

The **Format→Style** command displays the Style dialog box. The Style dialog box lets you modify styles, create new styles, and delete styles.

*You can modify or delete a style by choosing it from this list and clicking the **Modify** or **Delete** buttons. However, you cannot delete the built-in styles. Only custom styles can be deleted.*

Determines which styles are displayed in the Styles dialog box.

Create a new style or modify or delete the style chosen on the list.

Apply changes made to a style throughout the document.

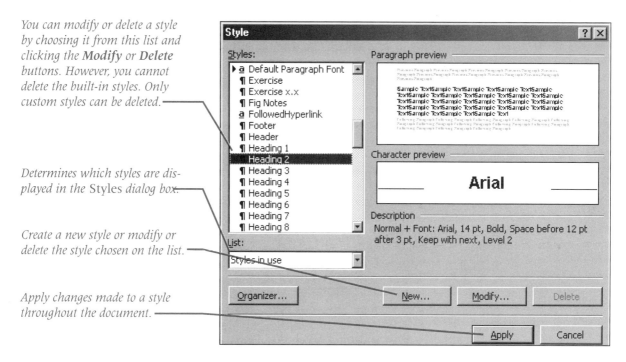

Modifying Styles

The **Modify** button on the Styles dialog box displays the Modify Style dialog box. You use the Modify Style dialog box to modify style definitions. When you modify a style and apply the changes, the changes affect all text formatted with the style throughout the document. This is perhaps the most powerful capability of styles.

When you format a paragraph with a style and tap (ENTER), the style specified here is used to format the next paragraph.

All styles are based on other styles. Most of the built-in styles are based on the Normal style.

Style modifications are applied only in the current document unless this box is checked. Checking this box updates the style in the template that the document is based on. For the built-in styles, this will change the Normal template thus affecting the style definition for all new documents.

Modify the text, paragraph, and other style formats.

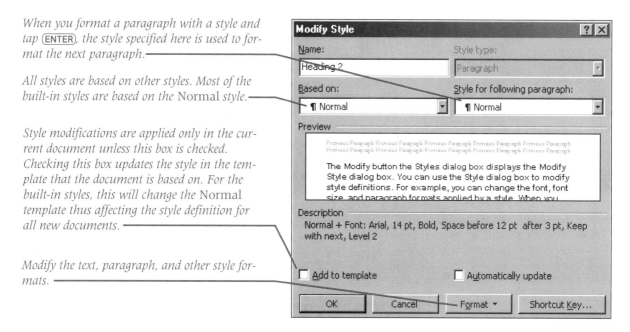

Hands-On 15.3 Modify a Style

In this exercise, you will add additional paragraph spacing to the Heading 2 style, and you will remove italics from the style.

1. Scroll to Page 2, and notice the three headings that are formatted with the Heading 2 style.
    The Heading 2 style applies 12 points of spacing before the paragraphs. In the next few steps, you will change the spacing to 18 points in the Heading 2 style definition. You will also remove italics from the style. These changes will affect all paragraphs that are formatted with the Heading 2 style.

2. Click on any heading that is formatted with the Heading 2 style.
    The Style box should indicate that the paragraph has been formatted with the Heading 2 style.

3. Choose **Format→Style** from the menu bar.
    The Heading 2 style should be chosen in the Styles list. Notice that the Description area lists all formats for the style.

4. Click the **Modify** button.

5. Click the **Format** button at the bottom of the dialog box, and choose Font.
    The Font dialog box will appear.

6. Change the Font style setting from Bold Italic to Bold, and click **OK.**

7. Click the **Format** button, and choose Paragraph.

8. Set the Spacing before to **18**, and click **OK.**

9. Click **OK** on the Modify Style box, and then click the **Apply** button on the Style box.
    Scroll through the document, and notice that italics have been removed from every paragraph with the Heading 2 style. The paragraphs will also have additional spacing above them.

10. Save the changes to your document, and continue with the next topic.

Defining New Styles

You can define your own custom styles if the built-in styles don't satisfy your needs. You can define styles by example, or you can define them using the Styles dialog box. Both paragraph and character styles can be defined; however, the style by example technique can only be used to define paragraph styles. Paragraph styles affect all text within a paragraph, whereas character styles can be applied to selected text within a paragraph.

DEFINING STYLES

Define Styles by Example

- Format a paragraph with the text and paragraph formats you would like included in the style definition.

- Select the paragraph, and click in the Style box on the Formatting toolbar.

- Type the name you would like to assign to the style, and tap (ENTER).

Define Styles Using the Style Dialog Box

- Choose Format→Style to display the Style dialog box.

- Click the New button.

- Type a style name, choose Paragraph or Character from the Style type list, choose a based-on style, and a style for the following paragraph.

- Use the Format button to apply the desired text and paragraph formats to the style.

- Click OK on the New Style box and on the Style box.

Hands-On 15.4 Define a Style by Example

Define the Style

1. Scroll to the third page, and position the insertion point on the "Annual Party or Outing" paragraph. This paragraph is located just below the large text paragraph at the top of the page.

2. Click the Bullets button on the Formatting toolbar.

3. Choose **Format→Paragraph** from the menu bar.

4. Set the Spacing Before to **3**, and click **OK.**

5. Click in the Style box on the left end of the Formatting toolbar.

6. Type **My Bullets**, and tap (ENTER).
   You have just defined a style named My Bullets that applies bullets and three points of spacing before.

Apply the Style

7. Click on the "Credit Union Membership" paragraph (the next paragraph).

8. Click the **Style list** button, and choose the My Bullets style.

9. Now select the next eight paragraphs, and apply the My Bullets style to all eight paragraphs with a single command.

10. Feel free to experiment with creating new styles.
    Any styles you create will be available in the current document only.

11. Save the changes, and continue with the next topic.

Outlines

Word has a powerful Outline view that can help you organize documents. Outline view works with the heading styles, Heading 1 through Heading 9. In Outline view, you can easily show or hide heading levels. For example, imagine that you are working on a large document with several chapters. You may have several levels of headings in your document. Using Outline view, you can easily see the "big picture" by showing only the Heading 1 paragraphs. Just as easily, you can view both the Heading 1 and Heading 2 paragraphs and all body text for a particular chapter. Outline view gives you great flexibility in the way you view and organize documents. You switch to Outline view by choosing **View→Outline** or by clicking the Outline view button on the left end of the Scroll bar. Take a moment to study the following illustration, which discusses the Outlining toolbar.

Promote, Demote, and Demote to Body Text let you increase or decrease heading levels. For example, you could convert Heading 1 to Heading 2 and vice-versa.

Move Up and Move Down let you rearrange headings, subordinate headings and body text.

Expand and collapse heading levels. Expanding displays additional levels, and contracting displays fewer levels.

The Show Levels buttons let you show or hide the indicated number of heading levels.

The Plus icon indicates that a heading has subheadings and/or body text.

The Minus icon indicates that a heading has no subheadings or body text.

This icon appears in front of body text.

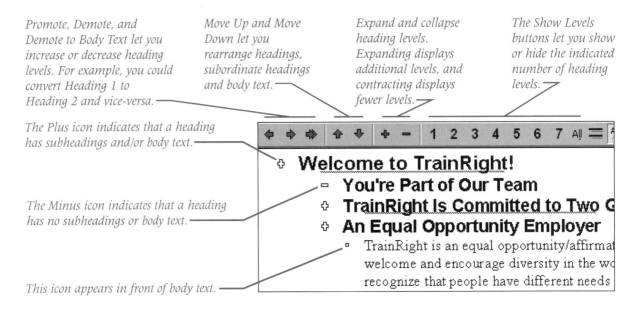

Hands-On 15.5 Work with Heading Levels

1. Choose **View→Outline,** or click the Outline view [image] button on the left end of the horizontal scroll bar.
   Notice that the Outlining toolbar appears. Also, notice that the document contains various heading levels.

2. Click the Show Heading 1 **1** button on the Outlining toolbar.
   Only the headings and paragraphs with the Heading 1 style will be displayed. Notice that viewing just the Heading 1 level gives you the "big picture" of your document.

3. Click the Show Heading 2 **2** button.
   The Heading 2 headings will appear below the Heading 1 headings. The Show Heading 3 through Show Heading 7 buttons will have no effect in this document because you only used two heading levels (Heading 1 and Heading 2).

4. Scroll up, and click anywhere on the "Welcome to TrainRight!" heading.

5. Click the Collapse **–** button.
   The Heading 2 headings under TrainRight will be hidden.

6. Now click the Expand ⊞ button, and the Heading 2 headings will reappear.

7. Click Expand ⊞ again, and the body text will be visible under the "Welcome to TrainRight!" heading and all of its subheadings.

8. Experiment with the Show Levels buttons (buttons 1 through 7) and the **Expand** and **Collapse** buttons.
   Keep in mind that these buttons give you various views of the document. At this point, you have not edited or modified the document in any way.

Promoting and Demoting Headings

The Promote ◄ and Demote ► buttons let you increase or decrease heading levels. For example, you can convert Heading 1 to Heading 2 and vice versa.

Hands-On 15.6 Promote Headings

1. Follow these steps to promote a heading.

Ⓐ *Click on the* Welcome to TrainRight! *heading.*

Ⓑ *Use the Collapse ▭ button to collapse the headings as shown here.*

⇩ **Welcome to TrainRight!**
   ⇩ **You're Part of Our Team**
   ⇩ **TrainRight Is Committed to Two Goals**
   ⇩ **An Equal Opportunity Employer**

Ⓒ *Click on the* TrainRight Is Committed to Two Goals *heading.*

Ⓓ *Click the Promote ◄ button to promote the heading to Heading 1.*

⇩ **Welcome to TrainRight!**
   ⇩ **You're Part of Our Team**
⇩ **TrainRight Is Committed to Two Goals**
   ⇩ **An Equal Opportunity Employer**

2. Promote ◄ the "An Equal Opportunity Employer" heading to Heading 1.

3. Demote ► the "Notice" heading to Heading 2.

Reorganizing Documents in Outline View

The Move Up ⬆ and Move Down ⬇ buttons let you move headings and all subordinate subheadings and body text. This lets you easily reorganize a document while still viewing the "big picture."

 Hands-On 15.7 Reorganize the Document

Move a Subheading and Body Text

1. Click anywhere on the "Notice" subheading.
   This is the subheading you demoted in the previous exercise.

2. Click the Expand ➕ button.
   Notice the text that is below this subheading. In a moment, you will move the subheading above the "Purpose of This Manual" subheading. The body text will be moved along with the subheading.

3. Click the Collapse ➖ button to hide the body text.

4. Click Move Up ⬆ to move the subheading above the "Purpose of This Manual" subheading.

5. Click the Expand ➕ button, and notice that the body text has been moved as well.

6. Click the Collapse ➖ button to hide the body text.

Move an Entire Page

In the next few steps, you will move the "Employment Policies" heading and all of its subheadings and body text.

7. Notice the heading named "Employment Classifications" and the three subheadings below it.
   The "Employment Policies" headings will be moved above the "Employment Classifications" headings.

8. Follow these steps to select a heading and all subheadings.

   Ⓐ *Position the mouse pointer on the plus sign in front of the* Employment Policies *heading and a four-headed arrow will appear.*

   Ⓑ *Click the plus sign to select the heading and subheadings as shown here.*

   Employment Policies
   ⇧ **Business Hours**
   ⇧ **Confidential Information**
   ⇧ **Customer Relations**
   ⇧ **Harassment Policy**

9. Click the Move Up ⬆ button.
   The selected headings will move up slightly, and the "Temporary Employees" subheading will move below the headings. The "Temporary Employees" subheading was the last subheading under "Employment Classifications" prior to the move.

10. Click Move Up ⬆ three more times, and the headings will be positioned on the page above the "Employment Classifications" headings.

11. Click the Print Layout ▤ view button on the horizontal scroll bar.

12. Browse through the document, and notice the structural changes that have been made.

13. Save the changes, and continue with the next topic.

Inserting a Table of Contents

Word's table of contents feature automatically builds a table of contents by gathering up the headings that are formatted with heading styles. Word sorts the headings in the order in which they appear in the document. In addition, the table of contents feature applies styles to the headings depending upon the heading level. The styles format the table entries and indent them based upon the heading level. For example, Heading 2 entries are subordinate to Heading 1 entries, so they are indented slightly. You display the table of contents dialog box with the **Insert→Index and Tables** command.

A preview of the styles that will be applied to the table entries is displayed here.

You can choose an overall table style from this list. The table style determines the styles applied to the table entries.

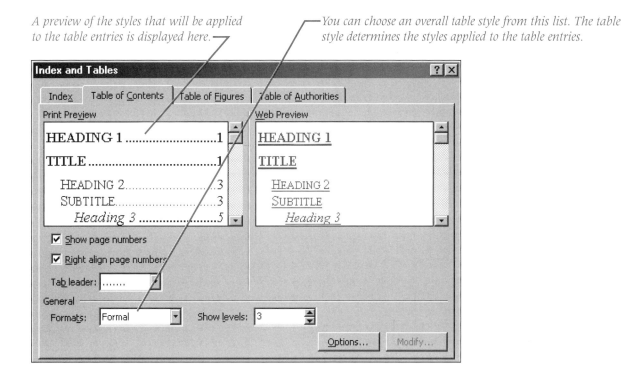

Table of Contents Structure

A table of contents is inserted as a large field composed of the various table entries. Each entry within a table of contents is formatted as a hyperlink. You can navigate to a page within the document by clicking a hyperlinked entry in the table of contents. In addition, you can edit and delete table of contents entries after the table of contents has been inserted.

Table of contents entries are formatted with styles that show the hierarchical structure of the document. Notice that this Heading 2 entry is subordinate to the Heading 1 entry.

Table of Contents

You can navigate to a page by clicking anywhere on a table of contents entry.

Hands-On 15.8 Insert a Table of Contents

Create a New Page for the Table

1. Make sure you are in Print Layout view, and set the zoom control to Page Width.

2. Scroll to page 2, and position the insertion point in front of the "Welcome to TrainRight!" heading.
   In the next step, you will insert a section break. This will create a blank page between the cover page and page 2. You will insert the table of contents on the blank page.

3. Insert a section break that begins on the next page.

4. If necessary, use the Show/Hide ¶ button to display the nonprinting characters.

5. Scroll up, and position the insertion point at the top of page 2 (the blank page) just in front of the section break.
   Look at the Style box, and notice that the style of the current paragraph is set to Heading 1. This is because the style of the "Welcome to TrainRight!" heading on the next page is Heading 1. The insertion point was on that paragraph when you inserted the section break. Therefore, the new paragraph on the empty page has the same style.

6. Type the title **Table of Contents**, and tap (ENTER) three times.

7. Choose **Insert→Index and Tables,** and click the Table of Contents tab.
   Notice that the Formats *box at the bottom left corner of the dialog box is currently set to* From Template. *The **Modify** button on the right side of the dialog box is available when the* From Template *option is chosen. You can use the **Modify** button to customize the table of contents styles thus creating your own table format.*

8. Choose Formal from the Formats list, and click **OK.**
   Word will gather up the headings in your document and insert the table of contents.

Navigate Using Hyperlinks

9. Click the Show/Hide ¶ button to hide the nonprinting characters.

10. Slide the mouse pointer anywhere over the table of contents, and the hyperlink pointer (pointing finger) will be visible.

11. Click the "Employment Policies" heading near the middle of the table to navigate to that heading.
    Word will scroll the document and position the insertion point in front of the "Employment Policies" heading.

12. Scroll up to the table of contents, and continue with the next topic.

Editing Table of Contents Entries

NOTE!

Changes made to a table of contents are overwritten if the table is updated.

You can edit and delete entries and even add new entries to a table of contents. The easiest way to delete an entry is to select the entry by clicking in the left margin and then tapping the (DELETE) key. Editing entries can be tricky since the mouse pointer becomes a hyperlink pointer whenever it is positioned over a table of contents. The easiest way to select part of a table entry is to use the arrow keys to navigate to the desired location and then press the (SHIFT) key while moving the cursor with the arrow keys. Once the desired text is selected, you can edit or delete it as desired.

Updating a Table of Contents

From the Keyboard

Position insertion point in table, and press (F9) to update TOC.

A table of contents is usually inserted after the document is complete. However, if the pagination changes or if you need to insert or delete headings, then you will need to update the table of contents. You can update a table of contents by right-clicking the table and choosing Update Field from the pop-up menu. The Update Table of Contents box lets you update just the page numbers or the entire table.

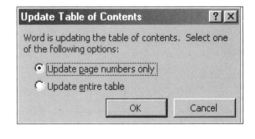

Hands-On 15.9 Delete and Edit Entries

Delete Entries

1. Follow these steps to select the first three entries.

Ⓐ *Position the mouse pointer ⬚ in the left margin in front of the first entry, and click when the pointer is a right-pointing-arrow shape. The entire table will become selected. You can select most table entries using this technique; however, selecting the first entry can be tricky.*

Table of Contents

TRAINRIGHT, INC. 1

EMPLOYEE POLICY MANUAL 1

TABLE OF CONTENTS...2

WELCOME TO TRAINRIGHT!...3

YOU'RE PART OF OUR TEAM... 3

Ⓑ *Click to the right of the table in the right margin to deselect.*

Ⓒ *Position the mouse pointer I to the right of the third heading, and drag up and left until just the first three headings are selected, as shown here. If the entire table becomes selected, then click in the right margin and try again.*

2. Tap the (DELETE) key to remove the entries.

3. Select the *"You're Part of Our Team"* subheading by clicking in front of it in the left margin.

4. Tap (DELETE) to remove the entry.

Edit an Entry

5. Tap the ↓ key until the insertion point is on the "Notice" heading in the table of contents.
   The arrow keys allow you to position the insertion point within a table of contents.

6. Tap → until the insertion point is just to the right of the word "Notice."

7. Tap the (SPACE BAR), and type **to Employees**.
   The table of contents Heading 2 style will automatically format the text with a small caps format.

8. Save the changes, and continue with the next topic.

Page Numbers

The **Insert→Page Numbers** command displays the Page Numbers dialog box. The Page Numbers dialog box lets you insert page numbers by specifying the position and alignment of the page numbers within a header or footer. This has the same effect as inserting page numbers in a header or footer with the Header and Footer toolbar.

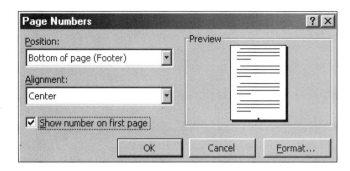

Formatting Page Numbers

The **Format** button on the Page Numbers dialog box displays the Page Number Format dialog box. You can use this dialog box to choose a number format for page numbers and to specify a starting page number for a section. The available number formats include Arabic (1, 2, 3), lowercase Roman numerals (i, ii, iii), uppercase Roman numerals (I, II, III), lowercase letters (a, b, c), and uppercase letters. The Page Number Format dialog box can also be used to specify chapter numbers. Chapter numbers are printed in front of page numbers. For example, the page number for the third page in Chapter 2 of a multiple chapter book could be displayed as II-3.

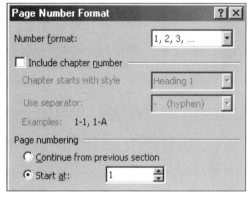

 Hands-On 15.10 Insert and Format Page Numbers

In this exercise, you will insert page numbers. You will also change the starting page number of the page following the table of contents.

Format and Insert Page Numbers

1. Look at the table of contents, and notice that the "Welcome to TrainRight!" heading is on page 3.
   Page 3 is the first main page of the policy manual. For this reason, you will change the starting page number to 1. Keep in mind that you are able to do this because you inserted a section break between the table of contents and the next page of the manual. You will be changing the starting page number for the first page of Section 3. This change will have no impact on the preceding sections.

2. Scroll down, and click anywhere on page 3.
   Look at the Status bar; it should indicate that you are on Page 3 Section 3.

3. Choose **Insert→Page Numbers** from the menu bar.
   The Page Numbers *dialog box lets you choose the position and alignment of the page numbers. You will do this in a moment.*

(Continued on the next page)

4. Click the **Format** button, and follow these steps to explore the dialog box and specify a starting page number.

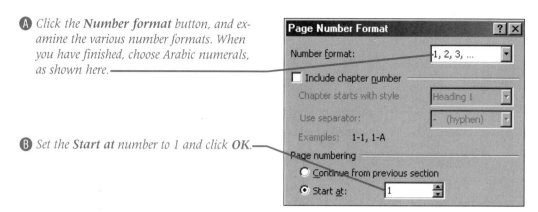

Ⓐ *Click the **Number format** button, and examine the various number formats. When you have finished, choose Arabic numerals, as shown here.*

Ⓑ *Set the **Start at** number to 1 and click **OK**.*

The Page Number Format *box will close, and the* Page Numbers *box will still be displayed.*

5. Set the position to Bottom of page (Footer), the Alignment to Center, and click **OK.**

Examine the Page Numbers and Update the Table of Contents

6. Scroll up to the cover page, and then scroll down through the document.
   Notice that the page numbering appears at the bottom of every page. Also notice that the page numbering starts over at 1 on the third page. The reason the page numbers appear on every page is because Word created a footer in all three sections of the document. The footers in all three sections are connected, so the page numbering appears in all three footers. You will learn how to disconnect the footers in the next exercise.

7. Scroll to the second page and notice that the table of contents incorrectly indicates that the "Welcome to TrainRight!" heading begins on page 3.
   The table of contents must be updated to reflect the page numbering changes you just made.

8. Right-click (click the right mouse button) anywhere on the table of contents, and choose Update Field from the pop-up menu.

9. Choose *Update page numbers only,* and click **OK.**
   If you had chosen the Update entire table *option, then the headings from the title page and table of contents page would have once again appeared in the table of contents. You deleted these entries from the table of contents in an earlier exercise.*

10. Save the changes, and continue with the next topic.

Working with Multiple Headers and Footers

Initially, Word uses the same header and footer in each section of a multiple section document. If you want different headers and footers in different sections, then you must "break the connections" between the sections. Breaking a connection effectively isolates a header and footer from those in the previous section.

The Same As Previous ⊞ button on the Header and Footer toolbar lets you break the connections between headers and footers. Once the connections are broken, you can edit the header or footer in the current section without affecting the headers and footers in other sections. Likewise, you can connect a header or footer in the current section to the previous section by activating the **Same As Previous** button.

Deleting Headers and Footers

You can delete a header or footer by selecting all of the text in it and tapping the (DELETE) key. However, if the document has multiple sections and you want to delete a header or footer from just one section, then you should "break the connections" before deleting the header or footer text.

 ## Hands-On 15.11 Work with Multiple Footers

Delete Footers

1. Scroll to the bottom of any page, and double-click the page number in the footer.
   The Header and Footer toolbar will appear.

2. If necessary, click the Show Next ⊡ or Show Previous ⊡ buttons on the Header and Footer toolbar until Footer-Section 3 is visible.
   At this point, the footers in all three sections are identical. Your objective is to break the connection between the footers in Sections 2 and 3 and then delete the footers from Sections 1 and 2.

3. Notice the Same as Previous ⊞ button on the Header and Footer toolbar.
   This button should be recessed (pushed in). This means that the footers in Sections 2 and 3 are identical. Any changes made to the footer in Section 2 would also be applied to the footer in Section 3. Likewise, if you were to delete the footer in Section 2, then you would also delete the footer from Section 3.

4. Click the Same as Previous ⊞ button to break the connection with Section 2.

5. Click the Show Previous ⊡ button to move to the footer in Section 2.
   Notice that the Same as Previous button is recessed. This means that the footers in Sections 1 and 2 are the same. Any changes you make to the footer in Section 1 will also be applied to the footer in Section 2. In a moment, you will delete the footer in Section 1. This will also delete the footer in Section 2 since the two are connected. However, the footer in Section 3 will remain unchanged because you already broke the connection between it and the footer in Section 2.

6. Click the Show Previous ⊡ button again to move to the Section 1 footer.

7. Select the page number by first clicking it and then clicking on an edge of the box that surrounds the number.

8. Tap the (DELETE) key to remove the page number.

9. Click the Show Next ⊡ button to move to the Section 2 footer.
   Notice that the page number has been removed.

(Continued on the next page)

10. Click the Show Next ⬚ button again to move to the Section 3 footer.
    Notice that the page number is still intact.

Format Page Numbers

In the next few steps, you will format the page number in Section 3. You can format text and fields (such as page numbers) in headers and footers just as you would in any other part of a document.

11. Select the page number by first clicking it and then clicking on an edge of the box that surrounds the number.

12. Format the page number with an Arial 12 Bold font.

13. Click the **Close** button on the Header and Footer toolbar.

14. Scroll through the document. The first and second pages should no longer have page numbers. The page numbers in Section 3 should have an Arial 12 Bold font.

15. Save the changes, and continue with the next topic.

Creating an Index

Word's index feature automatically generates an index using marked words and phrases. The marked words and phrases are inserted in the index, sorted alphabetically, and grouped according to the first letter of the entry. Like the table of contents feature, the index feature lets you choose a style. The index style formats the main entries and subentries and applies other formats to the index. You display the Index and Tables dialog box with the **Insert→Index and Tables** command.

Index

B

Business Hours 2

C

Customer Relations 2

This is a main entry. ── *E*

Employment Classifications 3
  Full-Time Employees 3
These are subentries. ── Part-Time Employees 3
  Temporary Employees 3
Employment Policies 2
  Business Hours 2
  Customer Relations 2

F

Full-Time Employees 3

H

Harassment Policy 2

P

Part-Time Employees 3

S

Standards 1

T

Temporary Employees 3

Marking Index Entries

The first step in creating an index is to mark the main index entries and subentries. Main entries and subentries are the words and phrases to be inserted in the index. A main entry can have one or more subentries. Entries are marked using the Mark Index Entry dialog box. The dialog box can be displayed by clicking the **Mark** button on the Index and Tables dialog box.

From the Keyboard

 ALT + SHIFT +X to open Mark Index Entry dialog box

Mark Index Entry ? X

Index
Main entry: Employment Po
Subentry: Business Hours

Options
○ Cross-reference: See
◉ Current page
○ Page range
Bookmark:

Page number format
☐ Bold
☐ Italic

This dialog box stays open so that you can mark multiple index entries.

[Mark] [Mark All] [Cancel]

MARKING INDEX ENTRIES

To Mark a Main Entry

■ Select the desired word or phrase in the document.

■ Display the Mark Index Entry dialog box. The easiest way is with the ALT + SHIFT +X shortcut keystroke. The selected text will appear in the Main entry box.

■ Click the Mark button. You can also modify the text in the Main entry box before clicking the Mark button. The modified text will appear in the index.

■ The Mark Index Entry dialog box remains open, allowing you to select and mark additional entries.

To Mark a Subentry

■ Click on the desired word or phrase in the document.

■ Display the Mark Index Entry dialog box if it is not currently displayed.

■ Type the main entry in the Main entry box that the subentry should appear under.

■ Type the desired subentry text in the Subentry box.

■ Click the Mark button.

■ The Mark Index Entry dialog box remains open, allowing you to mark additional main entries and subentries.

Mark Main Entries

1. Scroll to the page immediately following the table of contents.

2. Use the Show/Hide ¶ button to display the nonprinting characters.

3. Select the heading "TrainRight Is Committed to Two Goals."

4. Choose **Insert→Index and Tables,** and, if necessary, click the Index tab.
   Notice that the options are similar to those for the table of contents.

5. Click the **Mark** button at the bottom of the dialog box.

6. Type **Goals** in the Main entry box, and it will replace the text currently in the box.
   The text that was in the box was taken from your selection in the document. You can always replace or edit the suggested entry text in this manner.

7. Click the **Mark** button at the bottom of the dialog box.
   The Mark Entry box remains open, allowing you to scroll through the document and mark additional entries and subentries.

8. If necessary, drag the dialog box to the side, and notice that Word inserted an {XE "Goals"} code in the document.
   This code identifies "Goals" as a main index entry.

9. Click in the document anywhere on the heading "An Equal Opportunity Employer."

10. Click in the Main entry box, and type the phrase **Equal Opportunity**.

11. Click the **Mark** button.

Mark Subentries

12. Scroll down to the page with the "Employment Policies" heading.

13. Select the "Employment Policies" heading.

14. Click in the Main entry box, and then click the **Mark** button to use the proposed text as the main entry.
    In the next few steps, you will mark main entries and subentries. For example, you will mark a main entry named "Business Hours." You will also mark "Business Hours" as a subentry of "Employment Policies." Thus, the phrase "Business Hours" will appear twice in the index; once as a main entry and once as a subentry of "Employment Policies."

15. Select the "Business Hours" heading in the document.

16. Click in the Main entry box, and click the **Mark** button.

17. Select the phrase "Business Hours" in the Main entry box.

18. Type the replacement phrase **Employment Policies** (being careful to spell it correctly).

19. Click in the Subentry box, and type the phrase **Business Hours**.

20. Click the **Mark** button to complete the entry.
    Notice that Word inserts an {XE Employment Policies:Business Hours} code. Also, notice that a colon separates the phrases. The colon indicates that "Business Hours" is a subentry of "Employment Policies."

21. Scroll down, and select the "Customer Relations" heading.

22. Click in the Main entry box, and mark the entry.

23. Select the "Customer Relations" main entry in the Main entry box, and type the replacement phrase **Employment Policies**.

24. Click in the Subentry box, type **Customer Relations**, and click the **Mark** button.
    You just created another subentry of "Employment Policies," which now has two subentries. Both subentries will appear below "Employment Policies" when the index is inserted.

25. Select the "Harassment Policy" heading, and mark it as a main entry.

26. Scroll through the next two pages and mark the entries shown in the following table.

Heading	What to Mark
Employment Classifications	Mark a main entry named "Employment Classifications."
Full-Time Employees	Mark a main entry named "Full-Time Employees" and a subentry of "Employment Classifications" named "Full-Time Employees."
Part-Time Employees	Mark a main entry named "Part-Time Employees" and a subentry of "Employment Classifications" named "Part-Time Employees."
Temporary Employees	Mark a main entry named "Temporary Employees" and a subentry of "Employment Classifications" named "Temporary Employees."
Wage and Salary Policies	Mark a main entry named "Wage and Salary Policies."

27. Click the **Close** button on the Mark Entry dialog box when you have finished.

28. Use the Show/Hide ¶ button to hide the nonprinting characters.

29. Save the changes, and continue with the next topic.

Inserting the Index

Once the entries have been marked, you can insert the index using the Index and Tables dialog box. The Index and Tables dialog box lets you choose the overall format for the index and several other options. An index is usually inserted at the end of a document on a new page or section. If the index is to be inserted in another part of the document, then you should insert section breaks before and after the index location. This way, the index formats will not affect other parts of the document.

Specify the indentation style for the page numbers and the number of columns.

A preview of the styles that will be applied to the index entries is displayed here.

*You can choose an overall index style from the **Formats** list. The index style determines the styles applied to the main entries and subentries.*

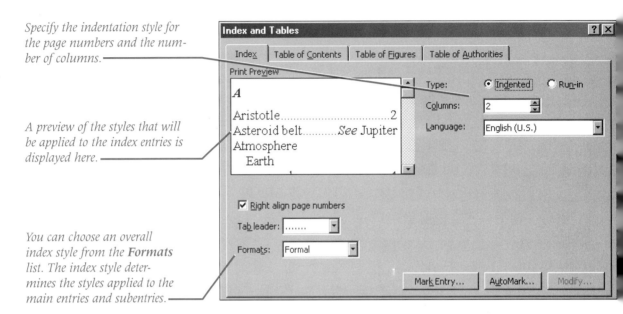

 Hands-On 15.13 **Insert and Modify the Index**

Set Up a New Page

1. Press (CTRL)+(END) to position the insertion point at the bottom of the document.

2. Insert a manual page break.

3. Type the heading **Index**, and tap (ENTER) twice.

4. Select the "Index" heading, and format the text as Arial 16 Bold.

5. Position the insertion point on the second blank line below the "Index" heading.

Insert the Index

6. Choose **Insert→Index and Tables** from the menu bar.

7. Choose the Formal style from the Formats list at the bottom left corner of the dialog box.

8. Click **OK,** and Word will insert the index.

9. Click anywhere in the index, and choose **Insert→Index and Tables** from the menu bar.

10. Choose the *Run in* option at the top right corner of the dialog box.
    Notice the effect that this option has on the page numbers in the preview area.

11. Click **OK,** and then click **OK** again when Word asks if you want to replace the current index.
    The new index will be inserted with the Run in *number style. Notice that the* Run in *style only affects the subentries.*

12. Click Undo [↺] to reverse the change.

13. Use Print Preview to examine your index and the rest of your document.

14. Feel free to enhance your document in any way you desire.

15. Save the changes when you have finished, and then close the document.

Master Documents and Subdocuments

In this lesson, you have worked with many features that are often used with large, multichapter documents. Word's master documents feature makes it easy to manage a number of subdocuments that comprise one large document. Using master documents and subdocuments, you can apply formatting, create a table of contents and index, insert continuous page numbers, and perform other document management tasks in a master document while maintaining the actual body of the subdocuments in separate files. The Outlining toolbar provides a number of buttons that are used with master documents and subdocuments. A complete discussion of master documents and subdocuments is beyond the scope of this course. For more information, see master documents and subdocuments in Word 2000's online Help.

Concepts Review

True/False Questions

1.	One of the benefits of styles is that they ensure consistent formatting between documents.	TRUE	FALSE
2.	A paragraph style affects all text in a paragraph.	TRUE	FALSE
3.	You must select the entire paragraph in order to apply a paragraph style.	TRUE	FALSE
4.	The **Same As Previous** button is used to "break the connections" between headers and footers in different sections.	TRUE	FALSE
5.	The (F9) key is used to update a table of contents.	TRUE	FALSE
6.	Each main entry in an index can have only one subentry.	TRUE	FALSE
7.	You can use Outline view to apply different heading styles to paragraphs.	TRUE	FALSE
8.	Each section of a document can have a different header and footer.	TRUE	FALSE

Multiple-Choice Questions

1. Which command displays the Style dialog box?
   a. Insert→Style
   b. Format→Style
   c. Insert→Paragraph style
   d. None of these

2. Which command displays the Page Numbers dialog box?
   a. Insert→Page Numbers
   b. Format→Page Numbers
   c. Tools→Page Numbers
   d. All of these

3. What function does the [←] button have in Outline view?
   a. Expands the current paragraph
   b. Promotes the current heading
   c. Demotes the current heading
   d. All of these

4. Which command is used to format the page numbers in a table of contents as hyperlinks?
   a. Format→Table of Contents→Hyperlinks
   b. Insert→Hyperlinks
   c. Click in the table, and tap the (F9) key.
   d. This is unnecessary. Table of contents entries are automatically formatted as hyperlinks when the table is inserted.

Skill Builders

Skill Builder 15.1 **Work with Styles**

Apply Built-in Styles to Headings

1. Open the document named **Skill Builder 15.1.**

2. Apply the built-in Title style to the "TrainRight Instructor Profiles" title. You will need to press the (SHIFT) key while you click the **Style box** button.

3. Apply the built-in Heading 2 style to the "Tanya Walton" heading.

Modify the Heading 2 style

4. Choose **Format→Style** from the menu bar.

5. Make sure that Heading 2 is selected on the list, and then click the **Modify** button.

6. Click the **Format** button.

7. Choose Font from the menu, set the font size to **16**, and click **OK.**

8. Click the **Format** button again, choose Paragraph, set the Spacing Before to **0**, and click **OK.**

9. Click **OK** on the Modify Style dialog box, and then close the Style dialog box.
   The "Tanya Walton" heading should have a 16 pt font size and less space above the heading.

10. Click the Show/Hide ¶ button to show the symbols in the document.

Copy Styles with the Format Painter

11. Click anywhere on the "Tanya Walton" heading.

12. Double-click the Format Painter ⌷.

13. Click in the margin to the left of the "Burt Jones" heading, and the Heading 2 style will be applied to that paragraph.

14. Scroll through the document, and click in the margin to the left of the next four names.

15. Click the Format Painter ⌷ when you have finished.

16. Save the changes to the document, and then close it.

Skill Builder 15.2 Create and Apply a Character Style

In this exercise, you will create and use a character style to help you format the paragraph below. Character styles can be applied to individual characters, words, or phrases within a paragraph.

Create the Style

1. Start a new document, and choose **Format→Style** from the menu bar.

2. Click the **New** button in the Style dialog box.

3. Change the name in the Name box to **flex**, and change the style type to character.

4. Click the **Format** button, and choose Font.

5. Set the font to Arial Bold Italic 12, and click **OK.**

6. Click **OK** on the New Style dialog box, and then close the Style dialog box.

Apply the Style

7. Choose the *flex* style from the Style Box.

8. Type **Flexico**, and tap the (SPACE BAR) once.
   In the next step, you will turn the character style off by choosing the Default Paragraph Font style.

9. Choose the Default Paragraph Font style from the Style Box.
   Notice that the font has been returned to the default setting (Times New Roman 12). The Default Paragraph Font style is used to restore the default font. The default font is the font that is used by the current paragraph style prior to any additional formatting.

10. Type the remainder of the paragraph shown below without applying the style.
    You will apply the style in the next few steps.

11. Select the word "Flexico" at the beginning of the second sentence in the first line.

12. Apply the flex style to the selected word.
    Notice that the character style affects only the selected word and not the entire paragraph.

13. Apply the *flex* style to the remainder of the document, as shown below.

14. Save the document as **Skill Builder 15.2,** and then close it.

> *Flexico* is proud of its newest product lines. *Flexico* constantly strives to improve its products. With the new *Tempest* line, *Flexico* has once again proven that it is the industry leader. *Flexico* has a tradition of affordable quality. This tradition and the *Tempest* products will help *Flexico* remain the industry leader.

Skill Builder 15.3 Apply Styles and Add a Title Page

In this exercise, you will open a six-page document on your exercise diskette. You will apply built-in heading styles throughout the document.

Apply Styles

1. Open the document named **Skill Builder 15.3.**

2. Apply the Title style (you will need to use the (SHIFT) key) to the heading "Proposed Courses."

3. Apply the Heading 1 style to the heading "Word 2000."

4. Apply the Heading 2 style to the "Overview," "Topics Included," and "Prerequisites" headings.

5. Apply the List Bullet style (you will need to use the (SHIFT) key) to the eight topics below the "Topics Included" heading.

6. Scroll through the next five pages, and perform the following steps.

   ▪ Apply the Heading 1 style to the course names, such as "Excel 2000."

   ▪ Apply the Heading 2 style to the "Overview," "Topics Included," and "Prerequisites" headings.

   ▪ Apply the List Bullet style to the topics under the "Topics Included" headings.

   Don't forget that you can use the Format Painter ![format painter icon] *to copy the styles from one paragraph to another. Every page should have the same formatting as the first page when you have finished.*

Modify a Style

7. Click on any paragraph formatted with the List Bullet style.

8. Choose **Format→Style,** and choose List Bullet style from the Styles list.

9. Click the **Modify** button, and the click the **Format** button.

10. Choose Font from the menu.

11. Set the font size to 12, and click **OK.**

12. Click **OK** on the Modify box, and then click the **Apply** button.
    The font size of all text formatted with the List Bullet style should now be 12 point.

(Continued on the next page)

13. Use the (CTRL)+(HOME) keystroke combination to position the insertion point at the top of the document.

14. Insert a section break that begins on the next page.

15. Position the insertion point on the title page, and follow these guidelines to set up the title page text and picture shown to the right.

TrainRight, Inc.

- Type the title and subtitle shown to the right, and insert the picture as shown.

- Apply the Title style and the Subtitle style to the title and subtitle.

- The picture can be found in the Business category of the clip gallery. Set the height of the picture to 1".

- Center-align the title, subtitle, and picture.

Proposed Courses

- Set the vertical alignment of the title page only to center.

16. Save the changes to the document, and then close it.

Skill Builder 15.4 Use Multiple Headers and Footers

In this exercise, you will create a document with several sections. You will create a different header and footer in each section. You will also restart the page numbering at the beginning of each section, and you will format title pages with built-in styles.

Build the Document

1. Start a new document, and follow these guidelines to set up a title page.

   - Type the text shown to the right, tapping (ENTER) four times after the title "TWO GREAT PAPERS" and after the name "Gerry Jefferson." Double-space between all other paragraphs.

   - Later in this exercise, you will format the text on the various title pages using the Title and Subtitle styles.

   ```
   TWO GREAT PAPERS
   Prepared by
   Gerry Jefferson
   Submitted to
   Hamilton Publishing Company
   Today's Date
   ```

2. Insert a section break that begins on the next page, and set up another title page using the text shown to the right. Tap (ENTER) four times after the title and after the name "Gerry Jefferson." Double-space between all other paragraphs.

   ```
   HEART
   Submitted by
   Gerry Jefferson
   Prepared for
   Professor Chin
   Oriental Languages 133B
   Today's Date
   ```

3. Insert a section break that begins on the next page.

4. Insert the file named **Skill Builder 15.4—Text 1** into the new section.
   This file contains six pages of text. The insertion point should be at the end of the document.

5. Insert a next-page section break, and set up another title page using the text shown to the right. Tap (ENTER) four times after the title and after the name "Gerry Jefferson." Double-space between all other paragraphs.

```
FOREST
Submitted by
Gerry Jefferson
Prepared for
Professor Donaldson
Anthropology 150
Today's Date
```

6. Insert a next-page section break.

7. Insert the file named **Skill Builder 15.4—Text 2.**
   This file contains four pages of text. You should now have a document with 13 pages of text.

Format the Cover Page and Title Pages

8. Press (CTRL)+(HOME) to position the insertion point at the top of the document.

9. Select all text on the title page, and center-align the text.

10. Set the font to 16, and apply bold formatting to all of the text.

11. Scroll down through the document, and format the two title pages (pages 2 and 9) in the same manner.

12. Set the vertical alignment of the cover page and two title pages to center. Make sure you apply the vertical alignment settings to those sections only (not to the body sections).

Set Up Headers and Footers

13. Position the insertion point on the third page of the document.
    This is the first body page of the Heart document and the first page in Section 3.

14. Choose **View→Header and Footer** from the menu bar.

15. Type the following header text using the (TAB) key to align the word "Heart" on the right side.

```
 Header
 Oriental Languages 133B                                                      Heart
```

16. Click the Switch Between Header And Footer ⊞ button.

17. Type the following footer text using the Insert Page Numbers # button to insert the page numbers.

```
 Footer
 Gerry Jefferson                                                             Page #
```

18. Click the Switch Between Header And Footer ⊞ button to view the header.

(Continued on the next page)

19. Look at the header area, and notice that you are viewing the header in Section 3.
    Your document has five sections. Earlier in this lesson, you learned that each section can have a different header and footer. However, the headers and footers are initially connected in all sections. In the next few steps, you will examine the headers and footers in the various sections.

20. Notice that the Same as Previous ⊞ button is recessed on the Header and Footer toolbar.
    This indicates that the header in Section 3 is connected to (is the "same as") the header in Section 2.

21. Click the Show Previous ⊞ button on the Header and Footer toolbar.

22. Look at the header area, and notice that you are viewing the header in Section 2.
    Your objective is to delete the header and footer from the cover page and title page. However, if you were to do this now, then you would also delete the header and footer from all sections of the document. This is because the headers and footers in all sections are connected. Any changes made in one section will affect the others. Before you can delete the header and footer from Sections 1 and 2, you must break the connections in Section 3.

23. Click the Show Next ⊞ button to move forward to the header in Section 3.

24. Click the Same as Previous ⊞ button to break the connection with Section 2.

25. Click the Switch Between Header And Footer ⊞ button to view the footer.

26. Click the Same as Previous ⊞ button to break the connection with Section 2.

Delete the Header and Footer

27. Click the Show Previous ⊞ button to move to the footer in Section 2.

28. Select all text in the footer, and tap (DELETE) to remove the footer.

29. Click the Switch Between Header And Footer ⊞ button to view the header.

30. Select the header text, and tap (DELETE) to remove the header.

31. Click the Show Next ⊞ button once to move to Section 3.
    Both the header and footer should still be intact in this section.

Delete the Header and Footer in Section 4

In the next few steps, you will delete the header and footer in Section 4. Before doing this, you will break the connections between the headers and footers in Sections 3 and 4 and between Sections 4 and 5.

32. Click the Show Next ⊞ button once to move to the header in Section 4.

33. Click the Same as Previous ⊞ button to break the connection with Section 3.

34. Select the header text, and tap (DELETE) to remove the header.

35. Click the Switch Between Header And Footer ⊞ button to view the footer.

36. Use the Same as Previous ⊞ button to break the connection, and then delete the footer text.

37. Move to the footer in Section 5, and break the connection between it and Section 4.

38. Enter the following footer text into the Section 5 footer.

```
Footer
Gerry Jefferson                                                    Page #
```

39. Switch 🔲 to the header, break the connection, and enter the following header text.

```
Header
Anthropology 150                                                   Forest
```

40. Scroll through the document, and examine the headers and footers.
Only the sections with the body text should have headers and footers.

Change Starting Page Numbers

41. Close the Header and Footer toolbar, and navigate to the second page of the document.
This page should be page 1 of the "Heart" document.

42. Choose **Insert→Page Numbers** from the menu bar.

43. Click the **Format** button.

44. Set the Start at option to **1**, and click **OK** on the Page Number Format dialog box.
*The Page Numbers dialog box will still be displayed. In the next step, you will click the **Close** button on the Page Numbers dialog box. It is important that you click the **Close** button on this dialog box and not the OK button. This is because page numbers are already appearing in the footer. If you were to click the **OK** button, then Word would insert another page number in the header or footer using the parameters in the Page Numbers dialog box. By clicking the **Close** button, you will prevent this from occurring, and you will preserve the current page numbering format and position in the footer. However, the Start at option will still be set to 1, so the page numbering will begin at 1.*

45. Click the **Close** button.

46. Scroll down through the document.
The page numbering should begin at 1 on the title page of the "Heart" document; however, the page numbering will only be displayed in the body pages of the document. This is because you removed the header and footer from the title page.

47. Scroll down to the title page of the fourth section, and click anywhere on the page.

48. Set the starting page number to 1.

49. Feel free to practice the techniques discussed in this Skill Builder.

50. Save the document as **Skill Builder 15.4,** and then close it.

Assessments

Assessment 15.1 Apply Styles and Modify Styles

1. Open the document named **Assessment 15.1.**

2. Apply the Title style to the title "Our Qualifications."

3. Apply the Heading 1 style to the following headings:

   Overview
   Our Training Philosophy
   Our Classrooms
   On-Site Training
   Client List
   Client Evaluations

4. Apply the 1. List Number style to the following paragraphs. These paragraphs are below the "Our Training Philosophy" heading.

   Each student has unique needs, which can only be met if class sizes are small.
   Students learn best in a comfortable environment.
   Training materials must be of superior quality.

5. Modify the 1. List Number style so that the font size is 12 instead of 10.

6. Apply the List Bullet style to the following company name paragraphs. These paragraphs are below the "Client List" heading.

   Frito Lay
   Meyers
   General Dynamics
   Freemont Forest Products

7. Modify the List Bullet style so that the font size is 12 instead of 10.

8. Apply the Heading 2 style to the following names. These names/paragraphs are below the "Client Evaluations" heading.

   Bobby Smith
   Jaunita Lopez
   Burt Jones

9. Save the changes to the completed document, and then close it.

Assessment 15.2 Multiple Headers and Footers

In this assessment, you will create a title page for a college-style research paper. You will insert a file containing the text of the research paper. Finally, you will create a "Works Cited" page in a different section at the end of the paper.

1. Start a new document and set the line spacing to double.

2. Type the following text, tapping (ENTER) once after each paragraph, and center-align the title as shown.

Cynthia Thomas

Professor Jackson

American History 120

Today's Date

The Salem Witchcraft Trials

3. Position the insertion point on the line below the centered title, and set the alignment to left.

4. Insert the file named **Assessment 15.2—Text.**

5. Create the following header, allowing it to print on all pages, including the title page. Insert page numbering where the # sign is shown.

Header

Thomas #

6. Position the insertion point at the bottom of the document, and insert a section break that begins on the next page.

7. Create the following "Works Cited" page. You will need to center-align the title and use hanging indents of ½" for the cited works. The line spacing should already be set to double, so you will only need to tap (ENTER) once after each paragraph.

Works Cited

Stuart, Richard W. *An Historical Perspective On the Salem Witchcraft Trials*, Chicago,

The Heartland Publishing Group, 1987.

Tillson, Ted B. *Early American Witchcraft*, New York, Purcy Publishing, 1992.

Alexander, William T. *Early American Folklore, Witchcraft, and Cults*, San Francisco,

Jones, Leahman, and Vaughn Publishing, 1990

8. Break the connection between the headers in Sections 1 and 2.

9. Delete the header from Section 2 but leave the header in Section 1 intact.
This will remove the header from the "Works Cited" page.

10. Save the document as **Assessment 15.2,** and then close it.

Critical Thinking

Critical Thinking 15.1 Web Research on Your Own

Joel Simmons is the Communications Director for the Chewy Chocolate Company. The Chewy Chocolate Company is a small company with just 85 employees. Each year, Joel prepares an annual report listing the accomplishments of the company and outlining the goals for the next year. The report is distributed to employees, investors, advisors, and other people affiliated with the company. Joel has asked you to help him prepare this year's report. He has given you the following outline of topics and subtopics.

Topic	Subtopic(s)
FY 1999 Revenue Results	Chocolate Sales Merchandise Sales
FY 2000 Revenue Forecast	
New Product Plans	Confections Ice Cream Line
Internet Strategy	
Employee Benefits	401K Plan Profit Sharing Plan

Prepare a document with the topics and subtopics listed above. Apply the Heading 1 style to topics and the Heading 2 style to subtopics. Begin each Heading 1 on a new page. Write a brief paragraph (as short as one sentence) for each topic and subtopic. Be creative and imagine that you are the CEO of a company trying to motivate your employees. If necessary, use Internet Explorer and a search engine of your choice to locate Web sites with information about 401K plans and other topics in your document. You can copy and paste text into your document or use the information to help you write more descriptive paragraphs. Use the spell checker to spell check the document and use the thesaurus to find replacement words for important words or phrases.

Open the document that you created in Critical Thinking exercise 13.1. Copy the entire title page, and paste it into a new section at the top of the document. Modify the report title and the author's name. Make sure the vertical alignment of the page is centered.

Create a new section between the title page and first body page. Set the starting page number of the first body page to 1. Insert a table of contents in the new section between the title page and body page. Use whichever table style you desire, and include a descriptive title for the page. If necessary, delete entries from the title page that appear in the table of contents.

Navigate through the document, and mark at least five main index entries and at least five subentries. You determine which entries belong in the index. Insert a new section at the end of the document, and insert an index using the same style that was used for the table of contents. Save the completed document as **Critical Thinking 15.1.**

Critical Thinking 15.2 **With a Group**

You and your classmate have seen the annual report prepared by the Chewy Chocolate Company and would like to prepare a similar report for the employees of Health-e-Meals.com. Open the Critical Thinking 15.1 document and save it as **Critical Thinking 15.2.** Follow these guidelines to modify the document to serve the needs of Health-e-Meals.com.

- Edit the cover page text and replace the Chewy Chocolate logo with the Health-e-Meals.com logo.

- Replace the Chocolate Sales and Merchandise Sales subtopics with Online Sales and 800 Number Sales. Change the descriptive paragraphs for the heading and subheadings on this page as necessary.

- Replace the Confections and Icc Cream Line subtopics with Desert Items and Beverages. Change the descriptive paragraphs for the heading and subheadings on this page as necessary.

- Modify all other headings and text as necessary to accommodate the needs of Health-e-Meals.com.

Replace the table of contents so that it includes the new headings and subheadings. Use the **Show/Hide** button to display the nonprinting characters in the document. You will notice that index entries have been inserted with an {XE: Index Entry} format. Delete any unnecessary index entries by selecting the entries and tapping the (DELETE) key. Work through the document and mark new index entries as necessary. Replace the index at the end of the document. Save the changes to the document when you have finished.

Macros and Forms

Most organizations have tasks that are unique to the organization and that are repeated frequently. Word allows you to create macros to automate such tasks. Macros can set up formatting, enter text, and perform nearly all Word commands. In addition, Word lets you assign macros to shortcut keys and custom toolbar buttons to make it easy to run them. Word and other Office 2000 applications also let you use the Visual Basic for Applications (VBA) programming language to edit recorded macros and customize Word. Word also lets you set up sophisticated forms to facilitate the collection of data. Forms can be distributed to users and filled out in printed form, electronically in Word, or via the Web.

In This Lesson

Case Study

Carol Parkins works in the Human Resources department of Geneva Health Care Services. Geneva is a rapidly growing health care company that takes great care of its employees. Recently, the company has considered offering additional benefits to its 76 employees. Carol has been assigned the task of setting up a form to be distributed to the employees. The purpose of the form is to gather updated employee information and to determine which benefits are of most interest to the employees. Carol decides to set up the form in Word and email it to all employees. This way, the employees can fill out the form electronically and email it back to her. Word lets Carol include text boxes, check boxes, and drop-down lists on her form to enable the employees to easily enter the data.

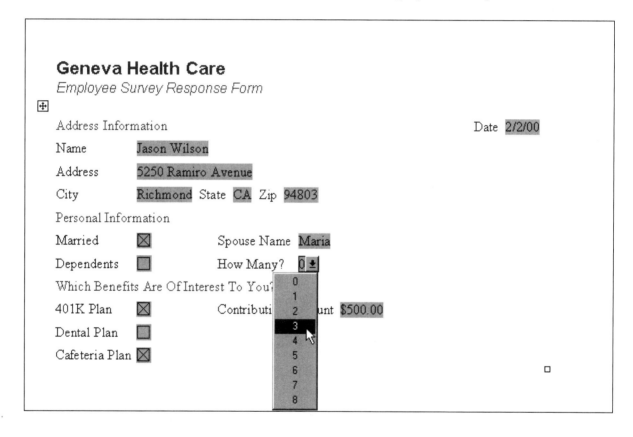

Page Orientation and Paper Size

The Paper Size tab on the Page Setup dialog box lets you set the size and orientation of the page. You can choose to print in portrait (vertical) orientation or landscape (horizontal) orientation. The Paper Size tab lets you choose from several predefined paper sizes, or you can specify a custom size by entering measurements in the Width and Height boxes.

 Hands-On 16.1 Set Page Orientation and Paper Size

1. Start Word to display a new document.

2. Choose **File→Page Setup,** and click the Paper Size tab.

3. Choose Landscape orientation.

4. Set the width to **7″**, the height to **5″**, and click **OK.**

5. If necessary, adjust the zoom control until you can see the entire page.
   Notice that the horizontal and vertical rulers display the page measurements. To print this page, you would need 5″ by 7″ paper.

6. Click the Undo button once, and both the orientation and paper size will return to the default settings.
   All settings you make in the Page Setup dialog box are applied as a single command. This is why you were able to undo both the orientation setting and page size with a single click of the Undo button. In the next exercise, you will use a macro to adjust the orientation and paper size.

Macros

A macro is a set of instructions that can be played back at a later time. Macros are useful for automating routine tasks, especially if those tasks are lengthy.

Recording Macros

Word's macro recording feature can record your keystrokes and the commands you issue. You can then play back a recorded macro at a later time. This is similar to the automatic redial feature on telephones. The redial feature allows you to record frequently used phone numbers and subsequently redial them by pressing one or two keys. Similarly, macros can easily play back recorded keystrokes and commands.

Assigning Macros

Macros should be designed to save time and help you become more productive. In order for this to occur, macros must be easy to run, especially if you use the same macro repeatedly. Word lets you assign macros to shortcut keystrokes and to various objects, including toolbar buttons, menus, and form controls. You can run a macro by issuing a shortcut keystroke or clicking the object to which the macro is assigned.

Macro Storage Locations

Macros can be stored in documents, templates, or in the Normal template. The default storage location for macros is the Normal template. Macros stored in the Normal template are available to all documents on the system. It is usually best to store macros in the Normal template unless you are distributing a document or template to associates and you want your macros to be available in the distributed document or template. In such a situation, it is best to store the macros in the distributed document or template. You choose the storage location of macros when setting up macros in the Record Macro dialog box as shown to the right.

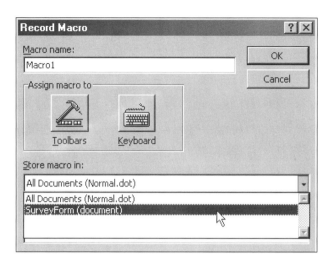

Usefulness Of Macros

Word 2000 has numerous features and tools that automate routine tasks and assist you with a variety of formatting tasks. These tools include AutoCorrect, templates, the Format Painter, AutoFormat, and styles. Prior to such tools, macros were used to automate many formatting tasks. For this reason, you should decide whether a macro is the proper tool to use for a particular task or whether one of these formatting tools is more appropriate. You may find that macros have fewer practical applications than you had initially assumed.

Recording Limitations

Certain mouse motions such as scrolling, selecting, and resizing windows cannot be recorded by macros. You may also find that certain commands are not available while recording macros. However, you can often overcome these limitations with alternative techniques. For example, instead of scrolling with the mouse (which cannot be recorded) you can use the arrow keys on the keyboard. Macros can record the movement of the insertion point when issued from the keyboard. Likewise, instead of selecting text with the mouse you can press the (SHIFT) key and use the arrow keys to select.

RECORDING A MACRO

■ Develop the document to the point where you are prepared to record the macro.

■ Choose Tools→Macro→Record New Macro from the menu bar.

■ Type a descriptive name in the Macro Name box. Do not use spaces in the name, because spaces are not allowed in macro names.

■ Click OK to begin recording.

■ Execute the commands and procedures you want the macro to record.

■ Click the Stop ■ button on the Macro toolbar when you have finished recording.

Hands-On 16.2 Record a Macro

In this exercise, you will record a macro that sets up the orientation, margins, and page size of the survey form. In addition, the macro will insert and format text.

Set Up the Macro

1. Save the blank document to your exercise diskette with the name **SurveyForm**.

2. Choose **Tools→Macro→Record New Macro** from the menu bar.
   The Record Macro dialog box appears.

3. Follow these steps to name the macro and begin the recording process.

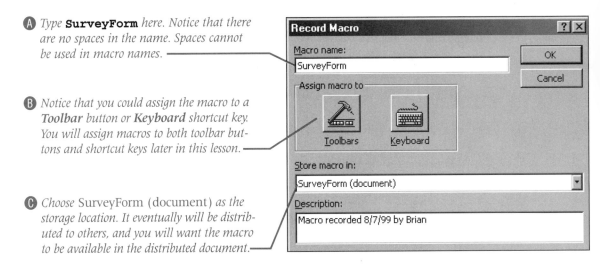

Ⓐ *Type* **SurveyForm** *here. Notice that there are no spaces in the name. Spaces cannot be used in macro names.*

Ⓑ *Notice that you could assign the macro to a* **Toolbar** *button or* **Keyboard** *shortcut key. You will assign macros to both toolbar buttons and shortcut keys later in this lesson.*

Ⓒ *Choose SurveyForm (document) as the storage location. It eventually will be distributed to others, and you will want the macro to be available in the distributed document.*

4. Click **OK** to begin the recording process.
   The macro is now recording your actions. The Stop Recording button and toolbar should be displayed somewhere in the document. If the toolbar isn't visible, then display it with the **View→Toolbars→Stop Recording** *command.*

Record the Macro

5. Set the font to Arial 14 Bold, and use the Font Color button to choose a color.
   The macro recorded each of these actions.

6. Type the title **Geneva Health Care Services**.

7. Choose **File→Page Setup,** and click the Paper Size tab.

8. Choose Landscape orientation.

9. Set the width to **7″** and the height to **5″**.

10. Click the Margins tab.

11. Set the top and bottom margins to **0.4″**, the left and right margins to **0.5″**, and click **OK**.

12. Click the Stop Recording button to stop the recording process.
    The macro is now ready to be played back.

Running Macros

Macros can be run in a variety of ways. The method used to run a macro depends upon how the macro was assigned during the recording process. In the previous exercise, you created a macro without assigning it to a toolbar button or shortcut key. For this reason, you must run the macro with the standard procedure shown in the following Quick Reference steps. This procedure can be used to run any macro.

RUNNING MACROS

- Choose Tools→Macro→Macros from the menu bar.
- Choose the desired macro from the Macro Name list.
- Click the Run button.

Hands-On 16.3 Run the Macro

1. Select the title "Geneva Health Care Services," and delete it.

2. Set the font to Times New Roman 12, and turn off bold.

3. Choose **File→Page Setup,** and click the Paper Size tab.

4. Choose Portrait orientation.

5. Set the width to **8.5″** and the height to **11″**.

6. Click the Margins tab.

7. Set all four margins to **1″**, and click **OK.**
   Restoring these settings will allow you to see the effects the macro has when it is run.

8. Choose **Tools→Macro→Macros** from the menu bar.

9. Follow these steps to run the SurveyForm macro.

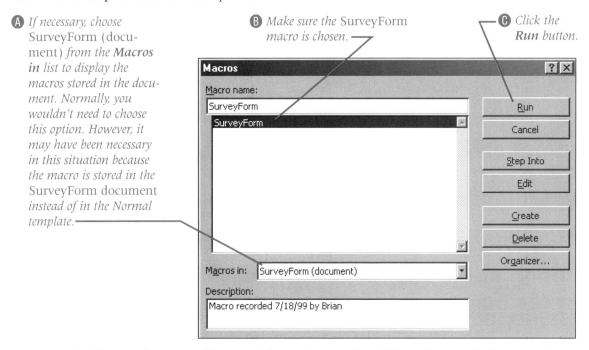

Ⓐ *If necessary, choose* SurveyForm (document) *from the Macros in list to display the macros stored in the document. Normally, you wouldn't need to choose this option. However, it may have been necessary in this situation because the macro is stored in the* SurveyForm document *instead of in the Normal template.*

Ⓑ *Make sure the* SurveyForm *macro is chosen.*

Ⓒ *Click the* **Run** *button.*

The macro should set up the page and insert and format the text. You will learn how to edit the macro in the next topic.

Visual Basic for Applications

Visual Basic for Applications (VBA) is a programming language that runs within Office 2000 applications. Visual Basic can be used to automate processes within applications and to customize applications. When you record a macro in Word, you are creating a Visual Basic module that contains programming instructions. Word's macro recorder constructs a sequence of Visual Basic statements that are executed when the macro is run. This topic will introduce you to Visual Basic. However, a complete discussion of Visual Basic is beyond the scope of this course.

Using the VBA Editor to Edit Macros

A module is a place where Visual Basic code is entered during the recording of a macro. Modules are normally hidden from view. You can edit a recorded macro by displaying the macro's Visual Basic module and deleting or modifying Visual Basic code. You can also add new code to a module. To display a module, you choose **Tools→Macro→Macros** from the menu bar, choose the desired macro, and click the **Edit** button. This command sequence starts the Visual Basic Editor, and the module appears in the Visual Basic Editor window. The Visual Basic Editor is a program independent of Word. The Visual Basic Editor has its own menus, toolbars, and commands that allow you to develop, edit, and test Visual Basic applications. The following illustration shows the Visual Basic Editor window. The programming code shown in the right side of the window is the code from the SurveyForm macro that you just recorded.

From the Keyboard

ALT + F11 to open VBA editor

The Visual Basic Editor menu bar and toolbar. —

*VBA applications are organized in projects. Projects contain modules and other elements. This window displays the **NewMacros module**. It contains the VBA code for the various macros associated with the current project. The code shown here was constructed during the recording of the* SurveyForm Macro. —

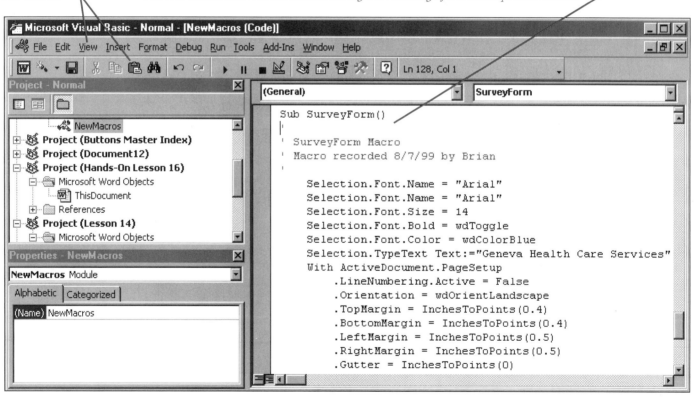

1. Choose **Tools→Macro→Macros** from the menu bar.

2. Make sure the SurveyForm macro is chosen on the Macro name list, and click the **Edit** button. *The Microsoft Visual Basic editor will open in a separate program window. The* SurveyForm *macro code will be displayed in the right pane of the window.*

3. Examine the macro statements, and notice that they correspond to the formatting settings you made while recording the macro.

4. Leave the window open, and continue with the next topic.

Objects, Methods, and Properties

Visual Basic recognizes all Word items as **objects.** Some examples of objects include an entire document, a picture, and selected text. Object names form an important part of the syntax of many Visual Basic statements. For example, the first significant statement in the macro you just recorded is:

Selection.Font.Name = "Arial"

This Visual Basic statement specifies an object (the selected text), a method (Font), a property (Name), and a property setting (Arial). This Visual Basic statement simply instructs Word to set the font name to Arial. This instruction was inserted in the module when you set the font name to Arial while recording the macro.

Modifying Code in Visual Basic Modules

Once the Visual Basic Editor window is open, you can modify the code within the module window. For example, in the SurveyForm macro you may want to change the font size property from 14 to 16, or perhaps you would like to change the text that is inserted by the Selection.TypeText statement. You can make these changes directly in the module window and then close the Visual Basic Editor when finished. The modified VBA code will play back the next time you run the macro.

Hands-On 16.5 Edit the Macro

The Visual Basic Editor window should be displayed from the previous exercise. The SurveyForm VBA code should be displayed on the right side of the window.

Edit the Macro

1. Follow these steps to modify the VBA code.

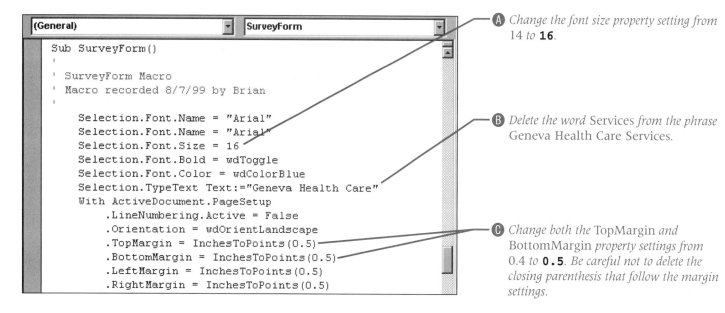

Ⓐ *Change the font size property setting from 14 to* **16**.

Ⓑ *Delete the word* Services *from the phrase* Geneva Health Care Services.

Ⓒ *Change both the* TopMargin *and* BottomMargin *property settings from 0.4 to* **0.5**. *Be careful not to delete the closing parenthesis that follow the margin settings.*

```
(General)                          SurveyForm

Sub SurveyForm()
'
' SurveyForm Macro
' Macro recorded 8/7/99 by Brian
'
    Selection.Font.Name = "Arial"
    Selection.Font.Name = "Arial"
    Selection.Font.Size = 16
    Selection.Font.Bold = wdToggle
    Selection.Font.Color = wdColorBlue
    Selection.TypeText Text:="Geneva Health Care"
    With ActiveDocument.PageSetup
        .LineNumbering.Active = False
        .Orientation = wdOrientLandscape
        .TopMargin = InchesToPoints(0.5)
        .BottomMargin = InchesToPoints(0.5)
        .LeftMargin = InchesToPoints(0.5)
        .RightMargin = InchesToPoints(0.5)
```

2. Take a few moments to review the code in the module window.
   Try to understand the objects, methods, and properties associated with the various statements.

3. When you have finished reviewing the code, click the Close ☒ button at the top right corner of the Visual Basic Editor window.
   The changes will automatically be saved.

Run the Edited Macro

4. Select the title "Geneva Health Care Services" and delete it.

5. Set the font to Times New Roman 12, and turn off bold.

6. Choose **Tools→Macro→Macros** from the menu bar.

7. Make sure the SurveyForm macro is chosen, and click the **Run** button.
   Notice that the word "Services" has been removed from the title, and the title size is now 16. If desired, you can use the **File→Page Setup** *command to verify that the top and bottom margins have been increased to 0.5.*

8. Save the changes to the document, and continue with the next topic.

Copying and Renaming Macros

The **Organizer** button on the Macros dialog box displays the Organizer. The Organizer lets you organize styles, macros, and other types of objects. You can use the organizer to rename and copy macros. Copying macros may be necessary if you want to make macros available in another document or template.

*The **Organizer** displays the macro projects for two different documents or templates.*
The NewMacros project contains all macros recorded in a document or template.

The projects can be copied, deleted, or renamed.

Organizer   ? ✕

| Styles | AutoText | Toolbars | Macro Project Items |

In SurveyForm: To Hands-On Lesson 16:
NewMacros   NewMacros

[Copy ▶▶]
[Delete]
[Rename...]

Macro Project Items available in: Macro Project Items available in:
SurveyForm (Document)   Hands-On Lesson 16 (Template)

[Close File]   [Close File]

Description

These buttons toggle between closing and opening,
allowing you to close or open the desired documents or templates.

Hands-On 16.6 Copy Macros

In this exercise, you will copy the macro project from the SurveyForm document to a new template. Later in this lesson, the template will be used as the basis for an electronic form. When the template is distributed to various users, the SurveyForm macro will be stored in the template.

Save a New Document as a Template

1. Click the New [ ] button to start a new document.

2. Click the Save [ ] button to display the Save As dialog box.

3. Choose Document Template from the Save as type list at the bottom of the dialog box.

4. Use the Save in list to navigate to your exercise diskette.

5. Save the blank template as **Hands-On Lesson 16—Template.**

(Continued on the next page)

6. Click the **SurveyForm** button on the Windows Taskbar to switch to the SurveyForm document.

7. Choose **Tools→Macro→Macros** from the menu bar.

8. Click the **Organizer** button at the bottom of the dialog box.
   Notice that the SurveyForm *document and its* NewMacros *project are displayed on the left side of the dialog box. Currently, the* Normal *template and its* NewMacros *project are displayed on the right side. In the next few steps, you will close the* Normal *template and open the* Hands-On Lesson 16—Template. *You will copy the* NewMacros *project from the* SurveyForm *document to the* Hands-On Lesson 16— Template *thus making the* SurveyForm *macro available to the* Hands-On Lesson 16—Template.

9. Follow these steps to copy the macro project.

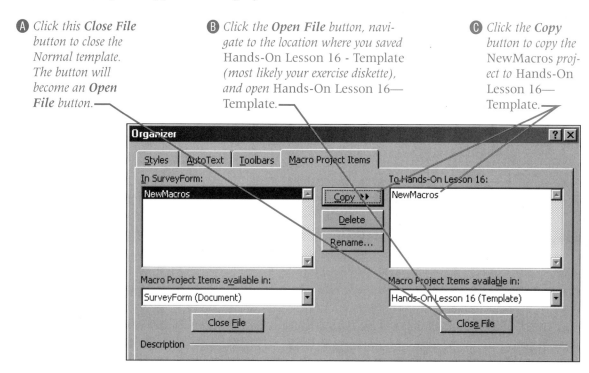

Ⓐ *Click this* **Close File** *button to close the* Normal *template. The button will become an* **Open File** *button.*

Ⓑ *Click the* **Open File** *button, navigate to the location where you saved* Hands-On Lesson 16 - Template *(most likely your exercise diskette), and open* Hands-On Lesson 16— Template.

Ⓒ *Click the* **Copy** *button to copy the* NewMacros *project to* Hands-On Lesson 16— Template.

10. Click the **Close** button at the bottom of the Organizer dialog box to return to the SurveyForm document.

Run the Macro

11. Save the changes to the SurveyForm document, and then switch to Hands-On Lesson 16— Template.

12. Choose **Tools→Macro→Macros** to display the Macros dialog box.
    Notice that the SurveyForm *macro is now available in the template.*

13. Click the **Run** button to run the macro.

Deleting Macros

You can delete macros by displaying the Macros dialog box with the **Tools→Macro→Macros** command, choosing the desired macro, and clicking the Delete button.

Hands-On 16.7 Delete the Macro from the SurveyForm Document

1. Switch to the SurveyForm document, and choose **Tools→Macro→Macros** from the menu bar.

2. Choose the SurveyForm macro, and click the **Delete** button in the dialog box.

3. Click **Yes** to confirm the deletion, and then close the dialog box.

4. Save the changes to the SurveyForm document, and then close it.

Customizing Toolbars

Word and other Office 2000 programs allow you to add custom buttons to toolbars. You can assign macros to custom toolbar buttons, thus providing a convenient method of running macros. You may want to do this if you have macros that are used frequently.

CUSTOMIZING TOOLBARS

To assign a macro to a toolbar button:

- Right-click any toolbar, and choose Customize from the pop-up menu.
- Click the Commands tab, and choose the Macros category.
- Drag the desired macro from the dialog box to any toolbar.
- Click the Modify Selection button, click in the Name box, and type the text that you would like to appear on the button.
- Close the Customize dialog box.

Forms

Many organizations use forms to collect data. Forms contain fields where information is entered and objects such as check boxes and drop-down lists to assist users with data entry. Word lets you easily set up forms to meet the needs or your organization. You can create forms that are distributed using any of the following methods:

- **Printed**—Printed forms are printed and then filled out on paper.

- **Electronic**—Electronic forms are distributed to Word users and filled out in Word. These forms use form-field objects such as check boxes and drop-down lists to facilitate data entry. These forms are often distributed via a network or email.

- **Web-Based**—Web-based forms are posted to the Web and filled out using a Web browser. The data is stored in an electronic database. Word 2000 lets you set up forms and save them as Web pages.

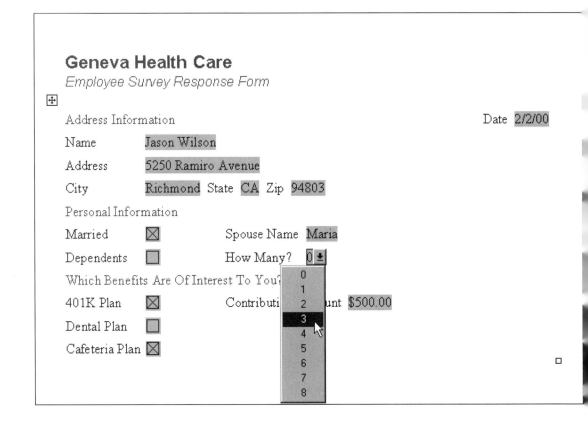

Setting Up Forms

You can set up forms using the same tools and techniques that are used to set up any other type of document. However, certain Word features are particularly useful with forms. For example, tables are frequently used to set up forms because they allow you to lay out forms with an orderly structure. Word also provides a Forms toolbar with buttons specifically designed for use with forms. The Forms toolbar is displayed with the **View→Toolbars→Forms** command.

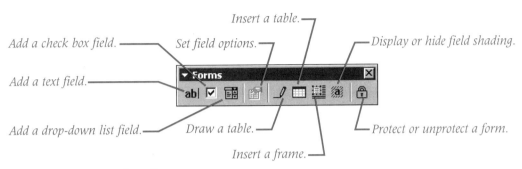

Add a check box field. — *Set field options.* — *Insert a table.* — *Display or hide field shading.*

Add a text field. —

Add a drop-down list field. — *Draw a table.* — *Protect or unprotect a form.*

Insert a frame. —

 ## Hands-On 16.8 Set Up the Form

In this exercise, you will begin setting up a form in Hands-On Lesson 16—Template. You will use a table and custom tab stops to align objects within the form.

Prepare for the Table

1. Tap (ENTER) after the title to position the insertion point on a new line.

2. Set the font size to 12, turn off bold, and turn on italics.

3. Type **Employee Survey Response Form** as the subtitle.

4. Tap (ENTER), set the font to Times New Roman, turn off italics, and set the font color to black.

5. Tap (ENTER) again to create a double space below the subtitle.

Set Up a Table

The form will be contained within a table to give it an orderly structure.

6. Insert a table with three rows and two columns.

7. Drag the vertical border that separates the columns to the right until the second column is approximately 1.5″ wide.
   This will create a wide first column.

8. Select the entire table and choose **Format→Paragraph.**

9. Set the spacing before to **6**, and click **OK.**
   This will create space above each paragraph in the table. You will appreciate this extra space as you develop the form.

(Continued on the next page)

10. Type **Address Information** in the first table cell, and tap (ENTER).

11. Type **Name** on the second line of the first cell, and follow this step to set a custom tab stop.

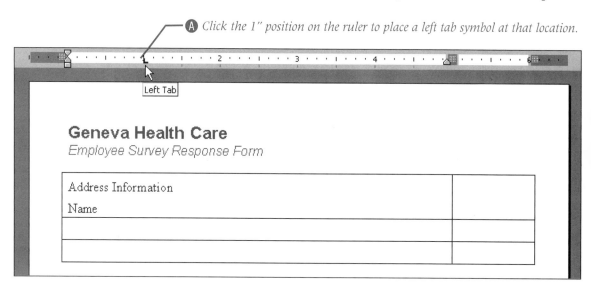

Ⓐ *Click the 1" position on the ruler to place a left tab symbol at that location.*

12. Press (CTRL)+(TAB) to move the insertion point to the tab stop at the 1" position.
    This keystroke combination allows you to move the insertion point to tab stops within table cells. If you had pressed just the (TAB) key, then the insertion point would have moved to the next table cell.

13. Save the changes to the template, and continue with the next topic.

Form Fields

The Forms toolbar lets you insert text, check box, and drop-down list fields in forms. Text box fields let users enter text in electronic forms. Check box fields let users check or uncheck boxes. Drop-down list fields let users choose options from drop-down lists. You insert fields by clicking at the desired location in the form and then clicking the desired field button on the Forms toolbar. You can delete a field by selecting it and tapping the (DELETE) key.

 Hands-On 16.9 Insert Fields

Insert and Delete a Text Form Field

1. Choose **View→Toolbars→Forms** to display the Forms toolbar.

2. Click the Text Form Field **abl** button on the Forms toolbar.
   Word will insert a shaded text field at the insertion point. You won't actually enter data in the fields until the form is complete and it has been protected. When you eventually enter data, the length of the text field will increase to accommodate the text you type unless you restrict the field length with property settings.

3. Select the field by dragging the mouse over it.
   The field will become black when it is selected.

4. Tap (DELETE) to remove the field.

5. Click Undo **↶** to restore the field.

Insert Additional Text Form Fields

6. Tap (ENTER) and type **Address**.
   Notice that a custom tab stop is set at the 1″ position on the ruler. Custom tab stops are paragraph formats, so they are carried to new paragraphs when you tap (ENTER).

7. Press (CTRL)+(TAB), and click the Text Form Field **abl** button to insert another text field.

8. Tap (ENTER), type **City**, press (CTRL)+(TAB), and insert a text field.

9. Tap the (SPACE BAR) twice, type **State**, tap the (SPACE BAR) twice, and insert a text field.

10. Tap the (SPACE BAR) twice, type **Zip**, tap the (SPACE BAR) twice, and insert a text field.

Insert a Text Field to Be Used for the Date

11. Tap the (TAB) key to move the insertion point to the next table cell to the right.

12. Click the Right Align **≣** button.

13. Type **Date**, tap the (SPACE BAR) twice, and insert a text field.
    In the next exercise, you will set the properties of this field to allow only dates to be entered in it.

14. If the date line wrapped within the table cell, then widen the right column slightly.

15. Tap the (TAB) key to move to the next table cell.

Insert Check Box Fields

16. Click at the 1″, 2″, and 3″ positions on the horizontal ruler to place custom tab stops at those locations.

17. Type **Personal Information**, and tap (ENTER).

18. Type **Married**, and press (CTRL)+(TAB).

19. Click the Check Box Form Field **☑** button on the Forms toolbar.
    You will use the check box field after the form has been protected.

20. Press (CTRL)+(TAB) to move to the next custom tab stop.

21. Type **Spouse Name**, press (CTRL)+(TAB), and click the Text Form Field **abl** button to insert a text box field.

22. Tap (ENTER), type **Dependents**, press (CTRL)+(TAB), and click the Check Box **☑** button to insert a check box field.

Insert a Drop-Down List Field and Complete the Form Design

23. Press (CTRL)+(TAB), and type **How Many?**

24. Press (CTRL)+(TAB), and click the drop-down list **▦** button to insert a drop-down list field.
    The drop-down list field will look like a text field until you enter data.

25. Tap the (TAB) key twice to move the cell in the bottom left corner of the table.

26. Set custom tab stops at the 1″ and 2″ positions on the ruler.

(Continued on the next page)

27. Follow these guidelines to complete the form design as shown below.

- ■ Type text and insert fields as shown. The "Contribution Amount" field is a text field.

- ■ Use the custom tab stop at the 1" position to align the check box fields.

- ■ Align the "Contribution Amount" text with the custom tab at the 2" position. Tap the (SPACE BAR) twice after the "Contribution Amount" text and insert the text field.

28. Save the changes and continue with the next topic.

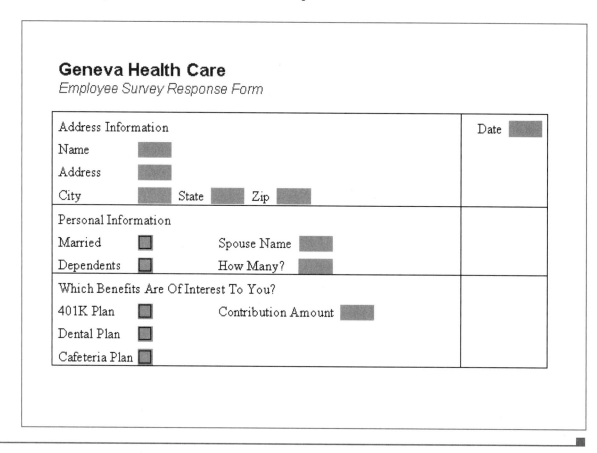

Field Properties

Each field type has various properties associated with it. For example, you can restrict the type and length of data entered in text fields, and you can have Word automatically format the data. You display the Properties box for a field by double-clicking the field on the form. Once the Properties box is displayed, you can specify one or more properties for the field.

Set Text Field Properties

1. Double-click the date text field at the top of the right column.
   The Text Form Field Options box will appear.

2. Follow these steps to specify a date format for the field.

Ⓐ *Choose* Date *from the* **Type** *list. Choosing this option will restrict data entry in the field to valid date formats.*

Ⓑ *Choose this* **Date format**. *Word will style, accordingly, any dates that you enter.*

Ⓒ *Take a moment to examine the other properties in the dialog box. You will use some of these properties in the following steps.*

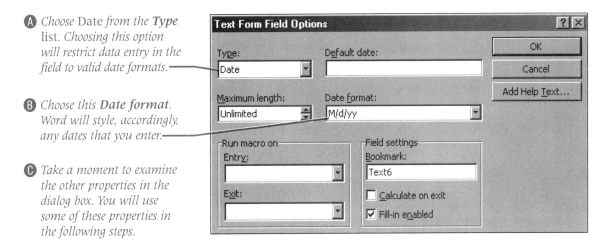

3. Click **OK** to complete the property settings.

4. Double-click the "State" field.

5. Set the Maximum length property to **2**, and click **OK.**
   This will force users to enter just the state abbreviations.

6. Double-click the "Zip" field, set the maximum length to **10**, and click **OK.**

7. Double-click the "Contribution Amount" field.

8. Set the Type to Number, the Number format to the Currency format ($#,##0.00 . . .), and click **OK.**
   Word will format any numbers entered with a dollar sign, commas between every third digit, a decimal point, and two decimals.

(Continued on the next page)

9. Double click the "How Many?" field.

10. Follow these steps to specify the list items.

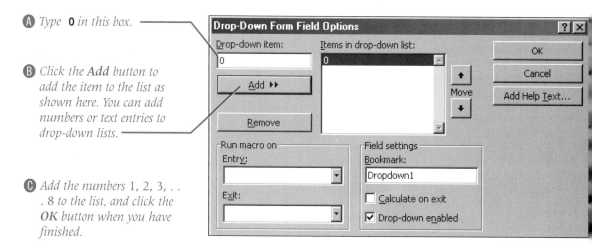

A *Type* **0** *in this box.*

B *Click the* **Add** *button to add the item to the list as shown here. You can add numbers or text entries to drop-down lists.*

C *Add the numbers 1, 2, 3, . . . 8 to the list, and click the* **OK** *button when you have finished.*

Complete the Form Design

11. Format the "Address Information," "Personal Information," and "Which Benefits Are of Interest to You?" headings by selecting the text and applying the font color of your choice.

12. Select the entire table, and remove all borders.

13. Use the **File→Page Setup** command to set the vertical alignment of the page to center.

14. Save the changes to your template, and continue with the next topic.

Saving and Protecting Forms

Forms that are designed to be printed and distributed on paper can be saved as regular Word documents. However, forms that are to be filled out electronically in Word or via a Web browser must be protected and saved using special techniques.

Saving Electronic and Web Forms

You should save electronic forms as templates. This way, a user can base a new document upon the template and fill out the form without changing the template. Forms designed to be accessed via a Web browser should be saved as Web pages. The original form will remain intact when a user enters data using a Web browser.

Protecting Forms

The Protect Form ⬚ button on the Forms toolbar protects electronic and Web-based forms and prepares them for use. Protecting a form prevents a user from modifying the form. Protecting a form also allows the form to behave like a form. For example, tapping the (TAB) key will move the insertion point to the next form field, and clicking a check box will insert or remove a check marker. When a form is unprotected, your actions have the same effect that they have in regular Word documents. You unprotect a form when designing or modifying the form, and you protect it when you are ready to use it.

Using Forms

Once the design of a form is complete you can protect the form to prepare it for use. A paper form can simply be printed and distributed to users. An electronic form should be protected, saved as a template, and distributed to users. Users can base a new document/form upon the template, fill out the form, save it as a document, and then return the completed document/form to the person responsible for collecting the data. Web-based forms should be protected, saved as Web pages, linked to a database, and then posted to the Web.

 ## Hands-On 16.11 **Protect and Use the Form**

Protect and Save the Form

1. Click the Protect Form 🔒 button on the Forms toolbar.

2. Try clicking on the title at the top of the form or on any of the text headings.
   When a form is protected, the insertion point can only be positioned within fields.

3. Tap the (TAB) key several times to move the insertion point from one field to another.

4. Tap (SHIFT)+(TAB) to move backwards through the fields.

5. Save the changes to the template, and then close it.

Use the Template to Open a New Form

In the next few steps, you will use Window's My Computer tool to display the contents of your exercise diskette. You will base a new form upon Hands-On Lesson 16—Template.

6. Click the Show Desktop 🖼 button on the Windows Taskbar to hide all program windows. If you don't have a **Show Desktop** button on your Taskbar, then right-click on an open part of the Taskbar and choose Minimize All Windows from the pop-up menu.

NOTE! *In Steps 7 through 9, you can click once instead of double-clicking if you point to the objects and they appear as underlined hyperlinks.*

7. Double-click the My Computer 🖥 icon on the Desktop.

8. Double-click the 3½ Floppy (A:) icon to display the contents of your exercise diskette.

9. Double-click **Hands-On Lesson 16—Template.**
   A new form will appear with the same text and fields as the template.

(Continued on the next page)

Fill Out the Form

The insertion point should be positioned in the first form field.

10. Type **Jason Wilson**, and tap the (TAB) key.
    Notice that the field width expanded to accommodate the text.

11. Type **5250 Ramiro Avenue**, and tap the (TAB) key.

12. Type **Richmond**, and tap the (TAB) key.

13. Try entering **California** in the "State" field, and notice that Word restricts the number of characters to two.
    This is because you set the maximum field length property of this field to two.

14. Type **CA** in the "State" field, tap (TAB), and type **94803** in the "Zip" field.

15. Tap (TAB), type **January 30, 2000** in the date field, and tap (TAB) again.
    Word will format the date as 1/30/00 because of the date format property you set for this field.

16. Click the "Married" check box, and type the name **Maria** in the "Spouse Name" field.

17. Click the "Dependents" check box, and then click the "How Many?" field.
    Word will display a drop-down list with the list entries you set up in the previous exercise.

18. Choose **3** from the drop-down list.

19. Click the "401K" check box, and type **500** in the "Contribution Amount" box.

20. Click the "Dental Plan" check box, and Word will format the contribution amount with a Currency format.
    You set a Currency format for this field in the previous exercise.

Save the Completed Form

21. Click the Save ![Save button] button, and save the completed form to your exercise diskette as **Hands-On Lesson 16—Completed Form.**

22. Use Print Preview ![Print Preview button] to preview the form, but don't try to print it unless you have a 5" by 7" sheet of paper.

23. Close Print Preview, and then close the form.

24. Close any open documents, and then close the My Computer window.

25. Continue with the end-of-lesson questions and exercises.

Concepts Review

True/False Questions

1. Macros can record keystrokes and commands.   TRUE   FALSE

2. Macro names can contain spaces.   TRUE   FALSE

3. Macros can be assigned to shortcut keys and toolbar buttons.   TRUE   FALSE

4. The **Format→Page Orientation** command is used to set landscape orientation.   TRUE   FALSE

5. The Customize dialog box is used to assign macros to toolbar buttons.   TRUE   FALSE

6. Visual Basic code can be edited in the Visual Basic Editor window.   TRUE   FALSE

7. Forms allow you to edit macros.   TRUE   FALSE

8. The Tables and Borders toolbar is used to insert fields in forms.   TRUE   FALSE

Multiple-Choice Questions

1. Which of these commands is used to record a new macro?
   a. Tools→Record New Macro
   b. Tools→Macro→Macros
   c. Tools→Macro→Record New Macro
   d. None of these

2. Which of the following techniques can be used to run macros?
   a. Click a toolbar button that has been assigned a macro.
   b. Use a shortcut key assigned to a macro.
   c. Use the **Tools→Macro→Macros** command.
   d. All of these

3. Where is the Visual Basic code for Word macros stored?
   a. Module
   b. Object
   c. Property
   d. Method

4. How can the property box for a field be displayed?
   a. Protect the form, and click the field.
   b. Unprotect the form, and click the field.
   c. Protect the form, and double-click the field.
   d. Unprotect the form, and double-click the field.

Skill Builders

Skill Builder 16.1 Record a Section Break Macro

In this Skill Builder, you will create a macro that inserts a section break and formats the title page with different page setup options than the remaining pages in the document.

Assign the Macro

1. Start a new document, and choose **Tools→Macro→Record New Macro.**

2. Type the name **TitlePage** in the Macro name box, and click the **Keyboard** button. Replace the macro if it already exists.
   You will assign this macro to a shortcut key.

3. Follow these steps to assign a shorcut key to the macro.

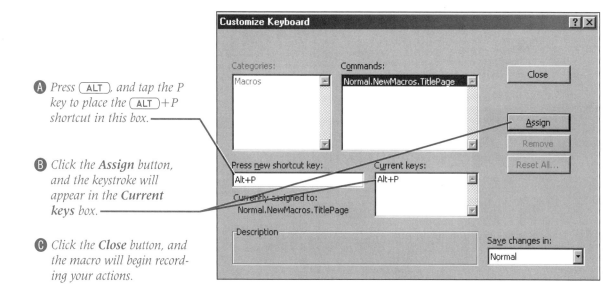

Ⓐ *Press* (ALT), *and tap the P key to place the* (ALT)+*P shortcut in this box.*

Ⓑ *Click the **Assign** button, and the keystroke will appear in the **Current keys** box.*

Ⓒ *Click the **Close** button, and the macro will begin recording your actions.*

Record the Macro

4. Insert a section break that begins on the next page.

5. Set the left and right margins to 1″ in the new section.

6. Press (CTRL)+(HOME) to position the insertion point on the title page.

7. Choose **File→Page Setup,** and make the following settings in the Page Setup dialog box.

   ▪ Set the left and right margins to 1″.

   ▪ Set the vertical alignment to center.

   ▪ Choose the *Different first page* option for the header and footer.

8. Click **OK** on the Page Setup dialog box to apply the Page Setup options.

9. Choose the Title style from the style list. You will need to press the (SHIFT) key while clicking the **Style list** button.

10. Click the Stop ▪ button to stop the macro recording.

11. Close the document without saving it, and then start a new document.

12. Press (ALT)+P to run the TitlePage macro.
    The macro was available in the new document because it was saved to the Normal template when you recorded it. Macros saved in the Normal template are available to all new documents on the system that are based upon the Normal template.

13. Type **This Is a Title Page** on the title page.
    The title should be formatted with the Title style.

14. Press (CTRL)+(END) to position the insertion point in the second section.

15. Choose **View→Header and Footer** to display the header area.

16. Type **This Is a Test Header**, and then close the Header and Footer toolbar.

17. Scroll to the title page, and the header should be suppressed on that page.
    This is because of the Different first page *option set by the macro. As you can see, this macro could be conveniently used to set up documents requiring a title page.*

18. Save the document as **Skill Builder 16.1,** and then close it.

Skill Builder 16.2 Record a Page Border Macro

In this exercise, you will record a macro that applies a page border.

1. Set up a macro named PageBorder, and assign the macro to the (ALT)+M shortcut key. Replace the macro if it already exists.
   The macro should now be recording your actions.

2. Use the **Format→Borders and Shading** command to apply a page border with a 2¼ pt line width and the Box style.
   The macro should have recorded these actions.

3. Stop the macro recording.

4. Close the document without saving, and start a new document.

5. Use the (ALT)+M shortcut keystroke to run the macro and apply the page border.

6. Save the document as **Skill Builder 16.2,** and then close it.

Skill Builder 16.3 **Create a Table Macro**

In this exercise, you will record a macro that inserts a table with three columns and four rows, merges the cells in the first row, and applies a table AutoFormat to the table.

1. Start a new document, and use the Tables and Borders ▦ button to display the Tables and Borders toolbar.

   Often, it is important to display toolbars, position the insertion point, and do other types of preparation prior to recording a macro. For example, in this exercise you will use the Tables and Borders toolbar to format a table while the macro records those actions. If you needed to display the Tables and Borders toolbar while the macro was recording, then that action would become part of the recorded macro steps.

2. Set up a macro named MyTable, and replace the macro if it already exists. There is no need to assign the macro to a shortcut key.

3. Choose **Table→Insert→Table** from the menu bar.

4. Set the number of columns to **3**, the number of rows to **4**, and click **OK.**

   You could have inserted the table using the Insert Table *button on the Standard toolbar; however, it is often better to use precise methods such as dialog box controls when a macro is recording.*

5. Choose **Table→Select→Row** to select the first table row.

6. Click the Merge Cells ▦ button on the Tables and Borders toolbar.

   The merged cell will be selected. In the next step, you will type a heading in the merged cell. The selection will vanish as you begin typing.

7. Type **My Table** in the merged cell, and click the Center ▤ button.

8. Choose **Table→Table AutoFormat** from the menu bar.

9. Choose the Colorful 2 AutoFormat, and click **OK.**

10. Click the Stop ▣ button to stop the macro recording.

11. Close the document without saving it, and then start a new document.

12. Choose **Tools→Macro→Macros** from the menu bar.

13. If necessary, choose Normal.dot from the Macros in list to display the macros in the Normal.dot template.

14. Choose the MyTable macro, and click the **Run** button.

   The table should automatically be inserted and set up. Keep in mind that this task could just as easily have been accomplished by creating an AutoCorrect entry for the completed table. AutoCorrect could have been used to insert the formatted table. In addition, the macros recorded in the previous two Skill Builder exercises could be replaced by setting up templates with the formats in place. Macros have fewer uses in Word 2000 than they did in earlier versions of Word due to AutoCorrect, templates, and other tools.

15. Save the document as **Skill Builder 16.3,** and then close it.

Skill Builder 16.4 **Record a Postcard Macro**

In this exercise, you will record a macro that formats a postcard-size page. In the next Skill Builder, you will use the macro to set up the page in preparation for the creation of a form.

1. Record a macro named PostCard, and replace PostCard if it already exists.

2. Use the **File→Page Setup** command to make the following settings.

   ▪ Set the page orientation to landscape.

   ▪ Set the page width to **5″** and the height to **3″**.

   ▪ Set all four margins to **0.5″**.

3. Stop the macro recording, and test the macro to ensure that it is functioning correctly. Close all open documents without saving them.

Skill Builder 16.5 **Create an Electronic Form**

In this exercise, you will use the macro created in Skill Builder 16.4 to set up a new document. You will place form fields in the document and save it as a template.

Set Up the Document

1. Start a new document, and run the PostCard macro recorded in Skill Builder 16.4.

2. Set the zoom control percentage to 150%.
   This will give you better visibility as you lay out the postcard.

3. Type **TrainRight Discount Voucher**, and tap (ENTER).

4. Insert a table with two columns and two rows.

5. Click below the table, and type **Return card by December 15 to receive discount credit!**

6. Click the Center 📄 button to center the line below the table.

7. Select the title on the first line, format the text as Times New Roman 14 Bold, and apply the color of your choice to the title.

8. Click the Center 📄 button to center the title above the table.

Insert Text and Fields

9. Select the first table row, and use the **Format→Paragraph** command to apply 3 points of spacing before.
   This will create a small amount of space between paragraphs as you enter text and fields in the table.

10. Select the second table row, and apply 6 points of spacing before.

11. Select the entire table, and set the font size to 10.

(Continued on the next page)

12. Use the **View→Toolbars→Forms** command to display the Forms toolbar.

13. Type text and insert fields in the table cells as shown below. The fields in the first table cell are check box fields. The "Credit card type" field is a drop-down list field. All fields in the right column of the table are text fields. Don't be concerned if the "Zip" field wraps to a second line.

```
┌─────────────────────────────────────────────────────────────┐
│              TrainRight Discount Voucher                      │
│ ┌─────────────────────────────┬─────────────────────────────┐│
│ │ Please check one:           │ Name  ▭                     ││
│ │ ☐ Three classes (10%)       │ Address ▭                   ││
│ │ ☐ Five classes (20%)        │ City ▭ State ▭ Zip ▭        ││
│ │ ☐ Ten classes (30%)         │ Email ▭                     ││
│ ├─────────────────────────────┼─────────────────────────────┤│
│ │ Credit card type ▭          │ Number ▭                    ││
│ └─────────────────────────────┴─────────────────────────────┘│
│    Return card by December 15 to receive discount credit!     │
└─────────────────────────────────────────────────────────────┘
```

Set Field Properties

14. Double-click the "Credit card type" field to display the Drop-Down Form Field Options box.

15. Add the credit card types **Visa, Mastercard, Discover,** and **American Express** to the drop-down item list, and click **OK.**

16. Double-click the "State" field, and set the maximum length to **2.**

17. Set the maximum length of the "Zip" field to **10.**

Format the Table and the Page

18. Select the entire table, and remove all borders.

19. Apply a ½ pt border to the right edge of the first cell.
    The only border in the table should be the vertical border between the first two cells.

20. Reduce the width of the first column by approximately ½" by dragging the border between the two columns.
    This will narrow the first column and widen the second column.

21. Apply a 1½ pt page border to the page. Choose the same color for the border that you chose for the title line.

22. Choose **File→Page Setup,** and click the Layout tab.

23. Set the vertical alignment to Justified, and click **OK.**
    The Justified setting will work particularly well in this document. The Justified setting spreads the paragraphs out evenly between the top and bottom margins.

24. Use Print Preview ![icon] to preview the form. At this point, your form should match the following example.

```
┌─────────────────────────────────────────────────────────┐
│                TrainRight Discount Voucher                │
│                                                           │
│   Please check one:      │  Name  ▓▓▓                     │
│   ☐ Three classes (10%)  │  Address ▓▓▓                   │
│   ☐ Five classes (20%)   │  City ▓▓▓  State ▓  Zip ▓▓▓    │
│   ☐ Ten classes (30%)    │  Email ▓▓▓                     │
│                                                           │
│                                                           │
│   Credit card type Visa      Number ▓▓▓                   │
│                                                           │
│      Return card by December 15 to receive discount credit!│
└─────────────────────────────────────────────────────────┘
```

Protect and Save the Form

25. Close Print Preview, and click the Protect Form ![icon] button on the Forms toolbar.

26. Click the Save ![icon] button, and choose Document Template from the Save as type list at the bottom of the dialog box.

27. Navigate to your exercise diskette, save the form as **Skill Builder 16.5—Template,** and then close the template.

Use the Form

28. Click the Show Desktop ![icon] button on the Windows Taskbar to hide all program windows. If you don't have a **Show Desktop** button on your Taskbar, then right-click on an open part of the Taskbar, and choose Minimize All Windows from the pop-up menu.

29. Double-click the My Computer ![icon] icon on the Desktop.

30. Double-click the 3½ Floppy (A:) icon to display the contents of your exercise diskette.

31. Double-click **Skill Builder 16.5—Template.**
    A new form will appear with the same text and fields as the template. The insertion point will be positioned in the first check box.

32. Click the first check box to place a check in it.

33. Click in the "Name" field, and type your name.

34. Tap the (TAB) key, and enter your address.

35. Fill out the remainder of the form using your own address information. Choose any credit card type from the card type drop-down list, and use a fictitious card number. If either of the columns is too narrow to hold the information, then you will need to close the document without saving, use Word's Open dialog box to open the original template, unprotect the form, modify the form, reprotect the form, save the template, and then base a new form upon the template.

36. Save your completed form as **Skill Builder 16.5—Form,** and then close it.

37. Close any open documents, and then close the My Computer window.

Assessments

Assessment 16.1 **Record and Play a Macro**

1. Record a macro named LegalPage that records the following options. Replace the macro if it already exists.

   ■ Set the paper size to Legal 8½ × 14, and set the left and right margins to 1″.

   ■ Use the **Format→Tabs** command to set a center-aligned custom tab stop at the 3.25″ position and a right-aligned custom tab stop at the 6.5″ position.

2. Stop the macro recording, and close the document.

3. Play back the macro to verify that it functions correctly.

Assessment 16.2 **Create and Fill Out an Electronic Form**

1. Start a new document.

2. Set the page orientation to landscape, the width to 7″, the height to 5″, and all four margins to 0.75″.

3. Insert an eight-row by two-column table.

4. Select the entire table, and set the paragraph spacing before to 4 points and the paragraph spacing below to 3 points.

5. Remove all borders from the table.

6. Follow these guidelines to set up the form shown on the following page.

   ■ Enter the data in the table rows as shown on the following page.

   ■ The "Account Holder Information" and "Financial Information" headings can be formatted by merging the cells in those rows, setting the fill color to a dark color, and setting the font color to white. The example on the following page uses an Arial 10 font for these rows.

   ■ Insert fields as shown. The "Investment Experience" and "Risk Tolerance" fields should use drop-down lists. All other fields are either text fields or check box fields. Use the list entries "Little," "Moderate," and "Extensive" for the "Investment Experience" list. Use the list entries "Conservative," "Moderate," and "Aggressive" for the "Risk Tolerance" list.

   ■ Set the maximum field length of the "State" field to 2, the "Zip" field to 10, the "Social Security Number" field to 11, and the "Driver's License Number" field to 8.

   ■ Format the "Annual Income" and "Net Worth" fields with a Number type and a currency number format.

   ■ Create the line above the signature row by applying a border to the row.

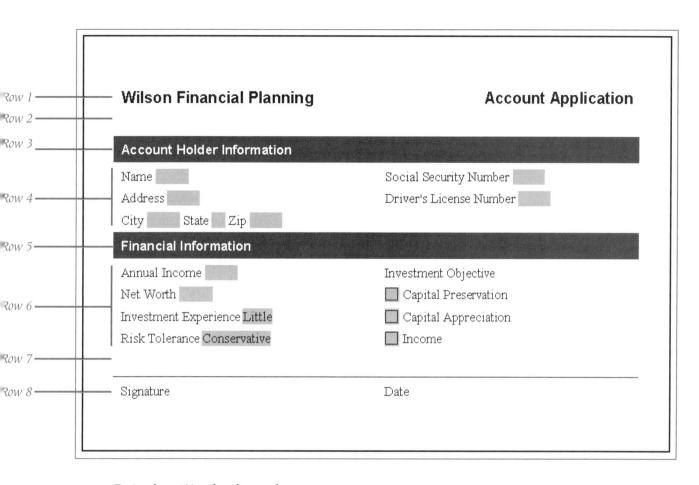

7. Apply a 1½ pt border to the page.

8. Set the vertical alignment of the page to center.

9. Protect the form, and save it to your exercise diskette as a template with the name **Assessment 16.2—Template.**

10. Base a new document upon the template, fill out the form using the data of your choice, and save the completed document as **Assessment 16.2—Completed Form.**

11. Close all open documents and windows.

Critical Thinking

Critical Thinking 16.1 On Your Own

Jack Dennings has set up his recipes in 8.5″ × 11″ Word documents. However, he decides to copy the recipes to Word documents sized to 5″ × 3″ so that he can print them on index cards. Start a new document and make the following page setup adjustments:

- Set the paper size to 5″ × 3″ with a landscape orientation
- Set all four margins to 0.3″

Open the document you created in Critical Thinking 5.2. Copy and paste all text into the new index card page you just set up. Reduce the font size of all text until it fits on the new page size. If you can't fit the text on the page using a point size of 8 or higher, then organize the bulleted ingredient list in a two-column table. This should allow the text to fit on a single 5″ x 3″ page. Save the completed document as **Critical Thinking 16.1.**

Critical Thinking 16.2 On Your Own

Marina Thomas is the owner of Marina's Persian Carpets. Many of Marina's customers are quite wealthy and return frequently to purchase additional carpets. Marina's customers often ask if she can invoice them with Net 30 terms. This will give her customers 30 days to pay the bill. Until recently, Marina granted the requests assuming she would be paid. However, after speaking with a friend who is also a business owner, she has decided to have her client's fill out a short credit application. Rather than have them fill out the application by hand, Marina sets up the form in a Word document so customers can fill it out online. Marina decides that she needs the following information on the credit application form.

Name, address, and telephone number	Social security number
Annual income range	Driver's license number
Two credit references with account numbers	

Set up a form on a 7″ × 5″ page in landscape orientation. Set all four margins to 0.75″. Follow these guidelines to include the information described above on the form.

- Use text boxes for the name, address, telephone number, social security number, and driver's license number.
- Use check boxes for the income range. The income ranges are Less than $50,000, $50,000–$100,000, and Above $100,000. The customers should be able to check the box that matches their income range.
- Use two fields for Credit Reference 1 and two fields for Credit Reference 2. Use a drop-down list as the first field for each credit reference. The drop-down list should include the entries Visa, MasterCard, American Express, and Bank Account. Use a text box as the second field for each credit reference. The customers will enter the account number in the text box.

Include a signature line and a date line on the form. Centralize the form both vertically and horizontally on the page. Apply a page border to the page. Protect the form and save it as a template named **Critical Thinking 16.2.** Test your form to verify that it functions properly.

Critical Thinking 16.3 **With a Group**

You and your classmate have decided to set up a work schedule for the Health-e-Meal office staff using a Word table. To maximize the width of the table, you have decided to lay out the page in landscape orientation. In addition, you have decided to reduce the left and right margins to 1″ to create uniform page margins. After meeting with your classmate, you have agreed that the table must contain the following information:

- The title Work Schedule should be centered across the first table row.

- The title Week of February 16 should be displayed vertically in the left column. The title should occupy the entire height of the column except for the first row.

- A header row should be used for the days of the week Sunday through Saturday.

- A header column should be used for the employee names Jason, Ted, Lisa, Pat, Barry, and Ned.

- Each cell formed by the intersection of a header cell and column cell will contain one of these entries: Shift 1, Shift 2, Shift 3, Vacation, Off, or Training. The entries should be centered both horizontally and vertically within the cells. These cells and the header row and column display the work schedule for the employees.

Set up the page and the table using the parameters described above. Apply shading or fill color to all cells in the title rows/columns and the header rows/columns. Format the text as you feel is appropriate. Set the height of all rows to exactly 0.75″ except for the title row and header row. Set the height of the title row to 0.5″ and the height of the header row to 0.35″. Center the entire table horizontally and vertically on the page. Make any other formatting enhancements to the table that you think are necessary. Save the completed document as **Critical Thinking 16.3.**

LESSON 17

Integration: Workgroup Collaboration

The Internet has made it much easier for project teams to collaborate in the drafting of a document. Now documents can be exchanged across the country as easily as they can across the hall. In Lesson 6, you learned how to place comments in a document. Word has several other features that can make group collaboration activities more efficient. For example, Word can track all of the changes made on a document by each group member and then let you merge all of the changes into a single document for review. Word can also automatically archive various versions of a document for you. Workgroup templates help standardize the page layout and styles of documents created by a workgroup. It is also possible to place a watermark that prints lightly in the background of a document.

In This Lesson

Case Study

Ariana is a grant administrator at Columbia State College. One of her responsibilities is to submit a quarterly report for the Connections grant. This grant supports the development of new courses and programs in Information Technology at the college. Although she is responsible for writing the report, Ariana needs the input and review of faculty and staff members who are working on the project. Ariana uses Word's collaboration features to make the process of input and review more efficient. For example, she taught everyone working with her on the project how to insert comments into documents.

Now Ariana is working on the end-of-year report for the Connections project. This is four pages long and requires the input of several people at the college. Ariana uses Word's *Track Changes* command to make it easier for her workgroup to collaborate in the drafting and editing of this document.

> **Approval of a new ~~Technical Support~~<u>Help Desk</u> degree program**
>
> The curriculum committee <u>has</u> approved the institutionalization of a new Technical Support degree/certificate program. This program is closely modeled upon the successful program at Bellevue Community College. The details of the program are adapted to local conditions. <u>Local business donated time and funds to help CSC to develop this new program.</u>

Word automatically applies change marks, such as strikethrough, underscores and a different font color on every change made to the document.

Some standard documents must be created or attached to submit various reports on grant activities, so Ariana creates a common folder to hold Word templates for these standard documents. Then she teaches the members of her workgroup how to set this as a workgroup template folder. These templates will display on all of the workgroup member's computers when they use **File→New** to create a new document.

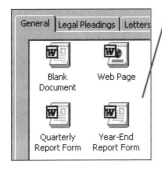

These document templates are stored in a folder on a network drive, yet display as if they were located on your computer.

Ariana also wants to maintain good documentation of each quarterly report. With Word's *Versions* feature, she is able to archive each significant version of her documents as they go through the process of drafting and review.

On some long documents, Ariana uses bookmarks to make it easy to navigate to specific pages quickly. *Bookmarks* can work in conjunction with hyperlinks and cross-references to jump readers to specific locations in a document.

Tracking Changes to Documents

When you need input on a document from several persons, it can be awkward to get this from printed documents. This is especially true if most of the workgroup members communicate by email. Word has tools to make collaborative review and editing of documents easier and more efficient. For example, in Lesson 6 you learned about the *comments* feature. The *Track Changes* feature is one of Word's most useful collaboration tools. With Track Changes switched on, Word records and marks each change to a document. Then Word helps you to review and approve or reject each change. It is also possible to make and distribute several copies of a document, then merge all of the changes back into a single document.

This change line indicates that these two lines were edited.

This strikethrough indicates that these words were deleted.

> **Approval of a new** ~~Technical Support~~ <u>Help Desk</u> **degree program**
>
> The curriculum committee <u>has</u> approved the institutionalization of a new Technical Support degree/certificate program. This program is closely modeled upon the successful program at Bellevue Community College. The details of the program are adapted to local conditions. <u>Local business donated time and funds to help CSC to develop this new program.</u>

This underscore indicates that this sentence was inserted.

Setting the User Name and Initials

Whenever you work on a document in conjunction with the track changes feature, you should make sure that your user name and initials are set correctly. You learned how to do this in Lesson 6. This is important because the Track Changes feature can use a different color to distinguish the edits of each author that works on the document. To set the user name, choose **Tools→Options,** from the menu bar; then click the *User Information* tab.

A Typical Editing and Review Process with Change Tracking

Below is a narrative of a typical document review process using the Track Changes feature.

1. You open the document in Word and activate the *Track Changes* command with **Tools→Track Changes→Highlight Changes.**

2. You send the document to the first author (reviewer).

3. The author makes sure that his or her user name and initials are properly entered in the **Tools→Options** dialog box, under the **User Information** tab.

4. As the author makes revisions, Word automatically marks each revision and notes the author name, type of revision, and date.

5. The first author passes the document along to the next author, who repeats steps 3 and 4. This process continues until all of the authors have edited the document. The last author returns the document to you.

6. You execute the *Accept or Reject Changes* command to review the revisions. As you review the document, Word displays the author name so you know who to ask a question about any particular revision.

7. You switch off the Track Changes feature and complete your work on the final draft of the document.

Example

Ariana works on a quarterly report for the grant she is directing. She decides to send the draft report to several other administrators for review. Ariana opens the draft report in Word; then switches on the *Track Changes* feature. She emails the document as an attachment to the first reviewer, with the request to add his changes and then pass the document along to the next reviewer. The last reviewer sends the document back to Ariana. She then uses the Accept or Reject Changes command to review each edit and decide which ones to incorporate in the final draft.

HOW TO SWITCH ON TRACK CHANGES FOR A DOCUMENT

Task	Procedure
Switch on the Track Changes feature for a document.	■ Choose *Tools→Track Changes→Highlight Changes* from the menu bar. ■ Check the *Track changes while editing* option. ■ Choose the options for the how changes will be highlighted on the screen or in print; then click *OK*.
Associate your initials with changes.	■ Choose *Tools→Options* from the menu bar. ■ Click the *User Information* tab. ■ Enter your name and initials; then click *OK*.

Hands-On 17.1 Switch on Track Changes

In this exercise, you will switch on Track Changes for the document. Then you will make several edits to the document.

Switch on Track Changes

1. Start Word; then open the *Hands-On Lesson 17* file on your exercise diskette.
   This eight-page document is an end-of-year report. Most of the paragraphs are composed of dummy text. However several paragraphs are normal text that you will edit.

2. Choose **Tools→Track Changes→Highlight Changes** from the menu bar.
   The Highlight Changes dialog box will appear.

3. Click the **Options** button.
   This dialog box lets you adjust the colors and other markings used to highlight changes to a document when the Track Changes feature is switched on. When the By Author *setting is used, Word will use a different color for each author. Normally, there should be no need to adjust these options.*

4. Make sure that the *Color* setting for the top three Options match the figure at right; then click **OK.**

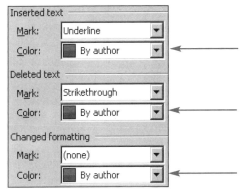

(Continued on the next page)

5. Check the *Track changes while editing* option. Make sure that the two options to highlight changes on the screen and when the document is printed are also checked; then click **OK**.
Most of the time, you will want changes to be highlighted on the screen and when the document is printed. Word is set to track and highlight every change to the document.

Set the User Name and Initials

Since Word can keep track of each author who makes revisions to a document, you should make sure that your name and initials are set properly.

6. Choose **Tools→Options** from the menu bar; then click the *User Information* tab.

7. Make sure that your user name and initials are entered; then click **OK**.

Edit the Document

Now you will make several edits to the document. Notice how Word highlight's each change as you work.

8. Use (CTRL)+G to display the *Go To* dialog box; then enter **4** as the page number and click **Go To**.
Page 4 should display the heading Best Practices *at the top of the page.*

9. Close ☒ the dialog box.

10. Follow these steps to insert a new bulleted item immediately beneath the introductory sentence of the *Payment for Services* section.

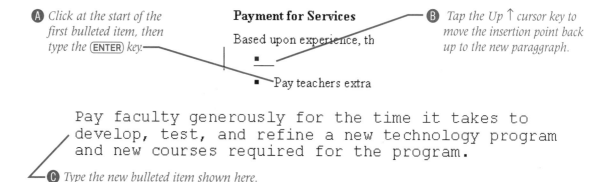

Ⓐ *Click at the start of the first bulleted item, then type the* (ENTER) *key.*

Payment for Services

Based upon experience, th

Ⓑ *Tap the Up ↑ cursor key to move the insertion point back up to the new paraggraph.*

■
■ Pay teachers extra

```
Pay faculty generously for the time it takes to
develop, test, and refine a new technology program
and new courses required for the program.
```

Ⓒ *Type the new bulleted item shown here.*

11. Scroll down the page; then make the following changes to bulleted items under the *Course Development Practices* heading as outlined in blue.

Course Development Practices
Several best practices have emerged in the area of developing new curriculum.

■ Review the skill standards survey often during the development process. It is easy to lose sight of the goal without frequent review.

■ Meet with faculty from various disciplines to get their input on general education courses. Non-technical courses are an important part of any information technology program.

■ Include general education requirements that can transfer easily to other four-year colleges. This makes it easier for students to transfer if they must relocate for a new job.

Ⓐ *Insert this new bulleted item.*

Ⓑ *Delete this bulleted item.*

12. Scroll to the bottom of page 4; then follow these steps to make three revisions of the last paragraph.

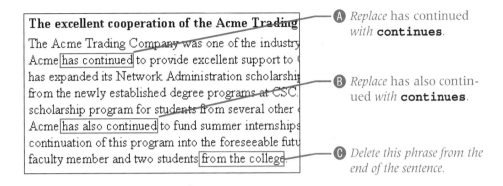

The excellent cooperation of the Acme Trading

The Acme Trading Company was one of the industry Acme has continued to provide excellent support to (has expanded its Network Administration scholarship from the newly established degree programs at CSC. scholarship program for students from several other (Acme has also continued to fund summer internships continuation of this program into the foreseeable futu faculty member and two students from the college

Ⓐ *Replace* has continued *with* **continues**.

Ⓑ *Replace* has also continued *with* **continues**.

Ⓒ *Delete this phrase from the end of the sentence.*

13. Save 🖫 the document.
Leave the document open, and go on to the next topic.

Reviewing Tracked Changes

You can review changes to a document that has the Track Changes feature switched on. When you review changes, Word can jump you from one change to the next and gives you the opportunity to accept or reject each change. After you have reviewed a change, Word will unmark the revision. The table below describes your review options.

Option	Result
Accept	An accepted change is kept in the document.
Reject	A rejected change is removed from document.
Accept All or Reject All	All of the changes that have not yet been reviewed can be rejected or accepted with a single command.

The dialog box shows the nature of the change (inserted, deleted, etc.) and who made it.

*The **Find** buttons help you navigate directly from one change to the next.*

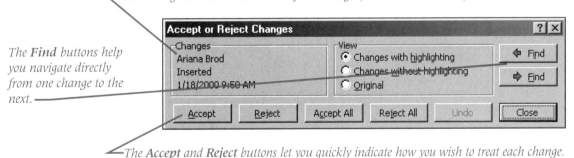

*The **Accept** and **Reject** buttons let you quickly indicate how you wish to treat each change.*

The Accept *or* Reject Changes *dialog box lets you review each change and decide whether it should be retained.*

Hands-On 17.2 Review Tracked Changes

In this exercise, you will review the changes to the document, accepting some changes and rejecting others.

1. Choose **Tools→Track Changes→Accept or Reject Changes** from the menu bar.
   The Accept or Reject Changes dialog box will appear.

2. Click anywhere in the body of the document, so that the dialog box is no longer the active window.
   You can freely navigate in the document while the dialog box is displayed. However, you cannot navigate while the dialog box is the active window.

3. Use (CTRL)+(HOME) to jump to the beginning of the document.
   Starting from page 1 lets you review the changes in their order in the document. Otherwise, the Find buttons will begin locating changes from the current location of the insertion point.

4. Follow these steps to begin reviewing the tracked changes.

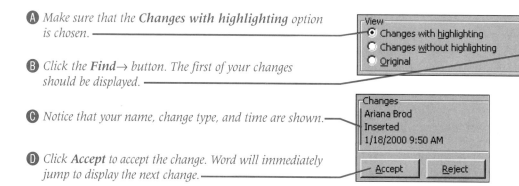

Ⓐ *Make sure that the **Changes with highlighting** option is chosen.*

Ⓑ *Click the **Find→** button. The first of your changes should be displayed.*

Ⓒ *Notice that your name, change type, and time are shown.*

Ⓓ *Click **Accept** to accept the change. Word will immediately jump to display the next change.*

5. Click anywhere on the document; then tap the (PGUP) key to display the top of the page. Examine the new bulleted item that you just approved.
   Notice that the change marks have been removed from the new bulleted item. After a change has been reviewed and accepted, it is no longer highlighted.

6. Click the [⇨ Find] button to return to the next change; then click **Reject.**
   The inserted bulleted item is removed from the document, since you rejected an insertion of new text. Notice that Word has jumped you to the next change item. There is no need to click Find after you accept or reject each change.

7. Click **Accept** on the currently displayed change.
   The deleted bulleted item is removed from the document since in this case you are accepting a deletion rather than an insertion.

   Notice that now the phrase has continued *is selected, but not the word* continues *that replaced it. Word treats the deleted text as a separate change from the replacement text.*

8. Click **Accept** on the deletion of *has continued* and the insertion of *continues.*

9. Click **Accept** on the deletion of *has also continued* and the insertion of *continues.*

10. Click **Reject** on the final change (deletion of the phrase *from the college*).
    Word will prompt you that it has reached the end of the document.

11. Click **OK** to confirm continuing the review from the beginning of the document.
    Word will continue the search until there are no more changes to review.

12. Click **OK** if Word displays a *no more changes* prompt.

13. Close the *Accept and Reject Changes* dialog box.

14. Save ![save icon] the document.

Switch Off Change Tracking

Now that you are done editing the document and reviewing the changes, you can switch change tracking off. You can always switch it on again later, and will do so shortly.

15. Choose **Tools→Track Changes→Highlight Changes** from the menu bar.
    The Highlight Changes dialog box will appear.

16. Uncheck the *Track changes while editing* option, and click **OK.**

17. Use (CTRL)+(HOME) to jump to the beginning of the document.
    Leave the document open.

Merging Tracked Changes

If you set up a document to track changes, you can also send out copies of that document for review by others. As these authors make revisions, Word tracks their changes in each individual copy of the document. When an author sends you his or her edited copy of the document, you can merge the tracked changes into a single document. Word can also mark each author's changes with a different color to make it easier to recognize input on the same text from different authors. After the changes have been merged, you can execute the Accept and Reject Changes command to review all of the authors' revisions in a single document.

A Typical Editing and Review Process with Merge Documents

A typical example of using the track changes feature with the merge documents command is described below:

1. You open the document in Word and activate the Track Changes command with **Tools→Track Changes→Highlight Changes.**

2. You use the **File→Save As** command to save a copy of the document for each author with a different name. For example *Draft (Grace reviews); Draft (Terry reviews);* etc.

3. Each author should make sure that his or her user name and initials are properly entered in the **Tools→Options** dialog box, under the *User Information* tab.

4. Each author reviews his or her copy of the document, making any desired revisions.

5. Each author returns his or her copy of the draft document to you.

6. You merge the various author copies of the draft document into a single document.

7. You execute the Accept or Reject Changes command to review and approve the revisions.

Example

Ariana works on a quarterly report for the grant she is directing. She decides to send the draft report to several other administrators for review. Ariana opens the draft report in Word and then switches on the *Track Changes* feature. She then saves one copy of the draft for each author and sends it to him or her by email. When the authors return their copies of the draft, Ariana merges the various review copies into her primary draft of the document. Then she uses the Accept or Reject Changes command to review the all of the changes in the primary draft and makes decisions on changes the document.

In this exercise, you will make changes to two documents and then merge the changes into one document. Finally, you will review the tracked changes from both documents.

Create a Copy of the Hands-On Lesson 17 Document

For this exercise, imagine that Ariana needs to create a copy of the report document for review by another workgroup member. Later, you will merge the revisions in this document with the original Hands-On Lesson 17 document. Since you want to merge the changes to these documents, you should switch on change tracking before you make a copy of the document for another reviewer.

1. Choose **Tools→Track Changes→Highlight Changes** from the menu bar. Then check the *Track changes while editing* option, and click **OK.**

2. Choose **File→Save As** from the menu bar. Save the document with the new name: **Merge**.
   Now you will reopen the Hands-On Lesson 17 document.

3. Use (ALT)+F to open the file menu; then tap the **2** key to open the *Hands-On Lesson 17* document.

Edit the Hands-On Lesson 17 Document

4. If necessary, scroll down until the two paragraphs beneath the *Approval of a new Technical Support degree/certificate program* heading are visible; then select and delete the second paragraph.
   As you would expect, change marks appear to highlight the deletion.

5. Save ⊟ the document.

Edit the Merge Document

6. Click the **Merge – Microsoft Word** button on the Windows taskbar to display the *Merge* copy of the document.
   Since another reviewer is supposed to be working with this document, let's change the User Name and Initials to simulate the situation.

7. Choose **Tools→Options** from the menu bar; then if necessary click the *User Information* tab.

8. Set the User Name to **Richard B.** and the initials to **RB**; then click **OK.**
   Now any changes to the document will be marked with this current user name.

   Richard doesn't like the use of an abbreviation for the college name. In the next steps you will perform a global replacement of the initials CSC *with* Columbia State College.

9. Use (CTRL)+H to display the *Find and Replace* dialog box.

(Continued on the next page)

10. Follow these steps to replace *CSC* with *Columbia State College*.

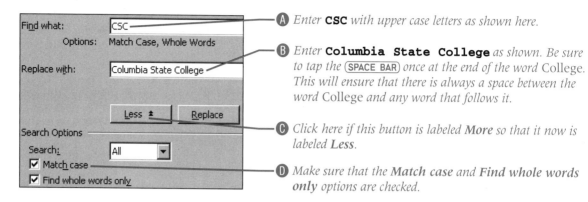

Ⓐ *Enter* **CSC** *with upper case letters as shown here.*

Ⓑ *Enter* **Columbia State College** *as shown. Be sure to tap the* (SPACE BAR) *once at the end of the word* College. *This will ensure that there is always a space between the word* College *and any word that follows it.*

Ⓒ *Click here if this button is labeled* **More** *so that it now is labeled* **Less**.

Ⓓ *Make sure that the* **Match case** *and* **Find whole words only** *options are checked.*

11. Click the **Find Next** button twice. Make sure that only the CSC item is selected each time.
Whenever you plan to give the Replace All *command, it is a good idea to use the* Find Next *button a couple of times to test that only the intended items will be replaced. This can help you avoid an unpleasant surprise. With the present settings, it is very unlikely that any incorrect replacements will take place—but it never hurts to check. If a* Replace All *command does give you an unexpected result, don't forget that you can click the* Undo *button to undo all of the replacements with a single command.*

12. Click the **Replace All** button.
Word should indicate that 12 replacements were made. Notice the change marks that are visible where replacements were made.

13. Click **OK** to dismiss the replacement information dialog box; then close ☒ the *Find and Replace* dialog box.

14. Save 🖫 the **Merge** document; then close ☒ it.
The Hands-On Lesson 17 *document should now be displayed.*

Perform the Merge

Now that you have edited the Merge *document, you will merge its changes to into the* Hands-On Lesson 17 *document.*

15. Choose **Tools→Merge Documents** from the menu bar.

16. Double-click to select the *Merge* document for this command.
The changes are immediately merged into your open document.

17. If necessary, scroll down the first page until the *Departure of the Information Technology Department Head* line is visible.
Notice that the change of CSC *to* Columbia State College *has been merged successfully into the* Hands-On Lesson 17 *document.*

18. Use (CTRL)+(HOME) to return to the top of the document.

19. Choose **Tools→Track Changes→Accept or Reject Changes** from the menu bar.

20. Click the ⟹ Find button.
Your first change to the Hands-On Lesson 17 *document will be highlighted. Notice your author name and time on the left side of the dialog box.*

21. Click the [⇒ Find] button again.

    Now the first change from the Merge *document is displayed and* Richard B. *is displayed as the author name. By the way, you can use the* Find *buttons to navigate through the changes without accepting or rejecting every change.*

22. Click the **Accept All** button.

    Word will ask you to confirm that you wish to accept all of the changes without reviewing them. Normally, it would be better to review each change. In this case, you will click OK so you can observe how the Accept All *option works.*

23. Click **Yes** to accept all changes without reviewing them; then **Close** the dialog box.

24. Choose **Tools→Track Changes→Highlight Changes** from the menu bar; then uncheck the *Track changes while editing* option, and click **OK.**

25. Save [💾] the document.

26. Use (CTRL)+F to display the *Find* dialog box.

    Notice that CSC is still listed in the dialog box. Word always remembers the most recently entered word in the Find and Replace commands for the current work session.

27. Click **Find Next** to search for CSC in the document.

    Word will indicate that the "word" was not found. This confirms that the changes you merged were implemented by the Accept All command.

28. Click **OK** to dismiss the search word not found dialog box; then click **Cancel** to close the **Find** dialog box.

Protecting Documents

Word's *Protect Document* command lets you protect a document from two specific types of alterations. In order to change either of these settings, a user may be required to enter a protect document password.

- You can protect a document from having the track changes command disabled. This means that every change to the document will be recorded and highlighted according to the options chosen in the *Track Changes* dialog box. In addition, no one can run the Accept or Reject Changes command while the document is protected.

- When you protect the document for *comments,* users can insert and edit comments in the document but cannot edit the document itself. Thus, although reviewers can comment on the text of the document, they will not be able to enter any changes to it.

TIP!

You can protect a document for track changes *or* comments, *but not both simultaneously.*

About Passwords

When you use a password with the document protection command, there are a few facts that you should keep in mind.

- **Passwords are case-sensitive**—Passwords are case-sensitive. This means that if you use capital letters in the password, these must be typed exactly when entering the password to open the workbook. For example, the passwords *OffToWork* and *offtowork* are not identical.

- **Don't forget the password**—If you set a password, then later forget it, you will be unable to remove the document protection setting. When you create a new password, it is a good idea to write it down and keep it in a secure, easy-to-find place.

- **Don't use obvious passwords**—the name of a spouse, a birthday, and other items that may be common knowledge are not good choices for passwords. The most effective passwords usually include one or more numbers as well as letters.

Some users rely on just one or two passwords for all of their documents. This reduces the number of passwords they need to memorize.

HOW TO PROTECT A DOCUMENT	
Task	**Procedure**
Turn on document Protection.	■ Choose *Tools→Protect Document* from the menu bar.
	■ Choose the desired protection option.
	■ If desired, enter a password for the protect document command.
	■ Click *OK*. Re-enter the password if you are prompted to do so. *Note: If you protected the document for Tracked changes, this feature is switched on automatically.*
Disable document protection.	■ Choose *Tools→Unprotect Document* from the menu bar.
	■ If prompted, enter the password, and click *OK*.

Hands-On 17.4 Protect a Document

In this exercise, you will switch on document protection for Tracked changes. You will use a password with this command so that unauthorized users will not be able to disable the Track changes feature.

1. Choose **Tools→Protect Document** from the menu bar.

2. Follow these steps to switch on document protection for Tracked changes.

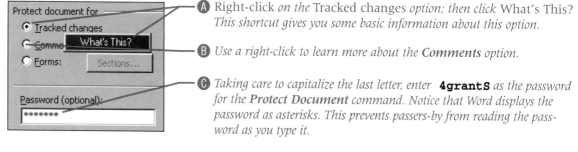

Ⓐ Right-click *on the* Tracked changes *option; then click* What's This? *This shortcut gives you some basic information about this option.*

Ⓑ *Use a right-click to learn more about the* **Comments** *option.*

Ⓒ *Taking care to capitalize the last letter, enter* **4grantS** *as the password for the* **Protect Document** *command. Notice that Word displays the password as asterisks. This prevents passers-by from reading the password as you type it.*

Ⓓ *Make sure that the* **Tracked changes** *option is chosen; then click* OK.

Word will prompt you to re-enter the password. This is a safeguard to ensure that you did not make a typo-graphic error the first time you entered the password.

3. Re-enter the password **4grantS**; then click **OK.** Re-enter the password, and click **OK** again if Word prompts you that the passwords did not match.

4. Choose **Tools→Track Changes→Highlight Changes** from the menu bar.
   Notice that this feature has been switched on again. (You had switched it off at the end of the previous exercise.) Notice also that the checkbox is grayed out. Now you cannot switch off change tracking from this dialog box.

5. Click **Cancel;** then use ⌨CTRL+⌨HOME to jump to the beginning of the document.

6. Tap the ⌨CAPS LOCK key; then insert the word **Project** immediately after the word *Recent* in the underscored heading near the middle of the page, so that it now reads *Recent Project Events.* Tap the ⌨CAPS LOCK key again.
   The change will be highlighted. No one can alter this document without a highlight marking each change.

7. Choose **Tools→Track Changes→Accept or Reject Changes** from the menu bar.
   Notice that the Accept, Reject, Accept All, *and* Reject All *buttons are grayed out. You cannot use these commands while the document is protected. However, the* Find *buttons are active, and you can still use them to jump from one change to the next.*

8. **Close** the dialog box.

Unprotect the Document

9. Choose **Tools→Unprotect Document** from the menu bar.

10. Taking care to capitalize the last letter, enter the password **4grantS**; then tap ⌨ENTER.

11. Choose **Tools→Track Changes→Highlight Changes** from the menu bar.
    Notice that the track changes *feature has been switched off again. However, your change in Step 6 is still highlighted. To remove the highlight, you will review the changes.*

12. Click **Cancel** to close the dialog box.

13. Choose **Tools→Track Changes→Accept or Reject Changes** from the menu bar; then click the **Accept All** button. Click **Yes** when you are asked if you wish to accept all changes without reviewing them.
    The highlight is removed, and the change remains inserted in the heading.

14. **Close** the dialog box; then save 💾 the document.

Creating Multiple Versions of a Document

A long, complex document may become difficult to manage. Sometimes information may be deleted that you later wish were still available. If you wish to save and archive previous versions of a Word document, you have two techniques to choose from.

- You can use **File→Save As** and change the name of the document each time you wish to save a new version. As you save various versions, the number of file names in the document folder will increase.

- Word's **Versions** command lets you save previous versions of a document within the document itself. This method lets you use a single document, with all version information archived within that document.

The Versions Command

The **File→Versions** command opens a dialog box from which you save different versions within the same document. You can save a version at any time. You can also set the Versions feature to create a new version of the document every time you close the document. When you save a version, Word makes a sort of "snapshot" of the document as it exists the moment you give the command. When you use the **Versions** command to open any previously saved version, Word displays the document exactly as it appeared when the version was created.

TIP! *Each version you save may increase the size of the file. The more revisions you make between versions, the greater the change in file size will be.*

Comments on Versions

When you save a new version of a document, Word gives you the option of entering a comment on the version. This information can help you keep track of major editing passes on the document, or significant additions of new content.

 ## Hands-On 17.5 Save a Version

In this exercise, you will save a new version of the document. You will add a comment to indicate the significance of the version.

1. Choose **File→Versions** from the menu bar.
   The Versions dialog box for the document will appear.

2. Click the **Save Now** button.
   A comments dialog box provides a space to type a comment about the version you are saving.

3. Type the text below in the comment box.

```
Second Draft: This version contains changes
recommended by Richard B. It does not contain
input from the other reviewers.
```

4. Click **OK.**

 There will be a pause as Word saves the version.

5. Choose **File→Versions** from the menu bar.

 Notice that only about the first 50 characters of the comment are displayed.

6. Click the **View Comments** button.

 Now you can read the entire comment. Notice that there is no way to revise the comment, however. The comment is a permanent part of the version.

7. **Close** the *View Comments* dialog box; then **Close** the *Versions* dialog box.

Auto-Saving Versions on Close

You can set an option in the Versions dialog box to save a new version every time you close a document. This automates the creation of new versions and relieves you of the need to open the dialog box and manually issue the **Save Now** command at the end of every editing session. Remember, however, that as you create more versions of a document, the file size may grow as well.

☑ Automatically save a version on close

This option tells Word to create a new version of the document every time you close it.

TIP!

This option must be set for each individual document. You cannot set Word to automatically save a new version on close for all new documents you create.

Opening Previous Versions

Word lets you open any previous version of a document whenever you need it. After you open a previous version, you can work with its contents as you would with any Word document. For example, you can copy portions of the previous version and paste them into other documents. However, in order to save the previous version as a document, you must save it with a new filename. Word does not allow you to directly replace a more recent version of a document with an older version. This is a safeguard to avoid inadvertently saving the older version of a document over a newer version.

Hands-On 17.6 Auto-Save, and Open a Version

In this exercise, you will set Word to automatically save a new version when you close the document.

1. Revise the first line of the report from *Year-End Narrative Report* to **Annual Report**. *This change will help you to identify the next version.*

2. Choose **File→Versions** from the menu bar.

3. Check the *Automatically save a version on close* box near the top-right corner of the dialog box; then **Close** the dialog box.

4. Save 🖫 the document; then choose **File→Close** from the menu bar.
   There will be a brief pause as a new version is saved automatically. This will not take as long as the first version you created, since now Word only needs to record the simple change you made in Step 1 *of this exercise.*

Open a Previous Version

5. Click the Open 📂 button on the toolbar; then open the *Hands-On Lesson 17* document.

6. Choose **File→Versions** from the menu bar.
   Notice that the first entry in the Versions *list has the comment* Automatic version. *The most recently created version is always at the top of the list. The* Automatic version *comment is given to every version created when you close the document. Remember that you can still save versions manually even while the* Automatically save a version on close *option is checked.*

7. Select the *Second Draft* version immediately below the *Automatic* version; then click the **Open** button.
   A new Word window will appear to display the version beneath the currently open document. This makes it convenient to compare the old version with the current version. Notice that the old heading for the report (Year-End Narrative Report) is retained in this version. You can also see the date and time of the version in the document window title bar.

> 📰 **Hands-On Lesson 17, 3-8-2000 version - Microsoft Word**

Save the Version as a Document

Imagine that you want to save this version as a stand-alone document. To do so, you must save it with another name, or to a different folder.

8. Click the Save 🖫 button on the toolbar of the *Second Draft* (lower) Word window.
   The Save As *dialog box opens. Notice that a name including the date and time of the version is proposed for this document. You can either accept the proposed name or revise the name as desired. But, Word will not let you simply save the older version with the same name as the most current version—unless you deliberately enter the same filename as the current version.*

9. Click **Save** to save the version as a stand-alone document with the proposed filename.

10. Close ❌ the *Second Draft* (lower) document window; then maximize ⬜ the *Hands-On Lesson 17* window.

Deleting Versions

You can delete unneeded versions of a document at any time. You may want to do this to reduce the file size. Or you may only want to keep significant revisions, and delete the incremental changes between significant revisions. You delete versions from the same dialog box you used to create them.

WARNING! *Once you delete a version it is impossible to undelete it. All version deletions are permanent.*

WORKING WITH VERSIONS

Task	Procedure
Manually create a new version of a document.	■ Choose *File→Versions* from the menu bar. ■ Click the *Save Now* button. ■ If desired, enter a comment on the new version.
Automatically create a new version every time a document is closed.	■ Choose *File→Versions* from the menu bar. ■ Check the *Automatically save a version on close* option.
Open a previous version of a document.	■ Choose *File→Versions* from the menu bar. ■ Select the desired version; then click the *Open* button.
Save a previous version of a document.	■ Choose *File→Versions* from the menu bar. ■ Select the desired version; then click the *Open* button. ■ Choose *File→Save As* from the menu bar. ■ Save the version with a different filename.
Delete a version.	■ Choose *File→Versions* from the menu bar. ■ Select the desired version; then click the *Delete* button.

Hands-On 17.7 Delete a Version

In this exercise, you will delete a version of the document.

1. Choose **File→Versions** from the menu bar.

2. Select the *Second Draft* version of the report; then click the **Delete** button.
   Word will warn you that you cannot undo this deletion. A version cannot be restored once it has been deleted.

3. Click **Yes** to confirm the deletion.
   The version disappears from the version list.

4. Close the dialog box.

Setting the Location of Workgroup Templates

When several people in a workgroup collaborate on a writing project, consistent use of templates is important. In addition to the standard *User Templates* folder, Word also lets you specify a *Workgroup Templates* folder. When a workgroup templates folder is specified, all template files located in that folder will also be displayed under the *General* tab in the New dialog box. Thus, a project administrator can create templates and place them in a single folder. Any project team member who creates a new document can access the templates from a central location (such as a network drive), rather than needing to copy the templates to their individual computers.

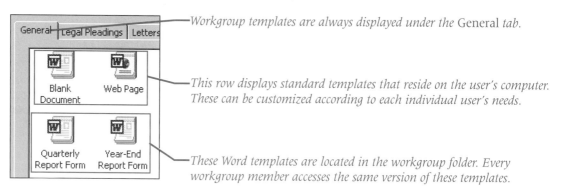

Workgroup templates are always displayed under the General *tab.*

This row displays standard templates that reside on the user's computer. These can be customized according to each individual user's needs.

These Word templates are located in the workgroup folder. Every workgroup member accesses the same version of these templates.

An example from the New dialog box of a workgroup member.

Why Have Workgroup Templates?

You learned how to create your own Word templates in Lesson 7. Templates offer several advantages for workgroups:

- Each template can contain a common set of styles. The use of styles can make the formatting in the documents much more consistent.

- Each template can contain common layout items, such as tables and images.

- Each template can contain common file properties, such as the project name, keywords, and custom properties.

Example

Ariana has a number of standard report forms and program description forms designed for the Connections grant workgroup. She places these forms in a folder on the network server. Ariana teaches each member of the workgroup how to set a default workgroup templates location in Word. Now whenever members of her workgroup choose the *File→New* command, all of the templates in their workgroup folders are displayed under the *General* tab. This helps everyone in the workgroup produce uniform documents with consistent features.

With a workgroup templates folder, Ariana can revise a template, and everyone in her workgroup has immediate access to the revised version. Without a workgroup templates folder, Ariana might have to distribute new or revised templates on floppy disks or as attachments to email.

HOW TO SET A DEFAULT LOCATION FOR TEMPLATES

Task	Procedure
Set a default location for Word workgroup templates.	■ Choose *Tools→Options* from the menu bar; then click the *File Locations* tab.
	■ Select the *Workgroup Templates* line in the dialog box; then click *Modify.*
	■ Navigate to the location on your hard drive or local area network (LAN) where the template folder is located; then click *OK.*
	■ Close the Options dialog box.
Create a new document based upon a workgroup template.	■ Choose *File→New* from the menu bar.
	■ Make sure that the *General* tab is selected.
	Any Word templates located in the Workgroup template folder will be displayed. However, you will not see any visual cues to distinguish your personal templates from the workgroup templates.
	■ Double-click the desired template to create a new document.

 ## Hands-On 17.8 Set the Folder for Workgroup Templates

In this exercise, you will use Word's Options dialog box to set a folder on your exercise diskette as the default location for templates.

Examine the Workgroup Folder and Templates

Before you designate the workgroup template folder, you will examine the workgroup templates in a folder on your exercise diskette. You will also examine the New dialog box to observe the existing templates available for use before you set the location of a workgroup templates folder.

1. Minimize ▬ the Word window.

2. Double-click the **My Computer** icon on the Desktop; then double-click to open the *3½ Floppy [A:]* drive.
   Notice the Grants Office *folder on your exercise diskette. This folder will simulate a folder that might be located on a network drive, which workgroup members can access over a local area network (LAN).*

3. Double-click to open the *Grants Office* folder.
   There are two Word template files in this folder. Each template contains the basic format of a report that the workgroup must submit periodically.

4. Close ✖ the My Computer window

5. Click the **Hands-On Lesson 17** button on the Windows Taskbar to restore the Word window.

6. Choose **File→New** from the menu bar; then make sure that the *General* tab is selected.
   Notice the standard templates listed in this dialog box.

7. Click **Cancel** to close the New dialog box.

(Continued on the next page)

Designate a Workgroup Templates Folder

8. Choose **Tools→Options** from the menu bar; then click the *File Locations* tab.

9. Click *Workgroup templates* in the File types list; then click the **Modify** button.
   A dialog box will appear, displaying the contents of your exercise diskette.

10. Navigate to your floppy disk in the dialog box; then double-click to open the **Grants Office** folder.
    Notice that the folder name and path (A:\) are displayed in the Folder name *box at the bottom of the dialog box.*

11. Click **OK** to set the workgroup template folder.
    The new location of the workgroup templates folder is now listed in the dialog box.

12. Click **Close** to close the Options dialog box.

Open a Workgroup Template

13. Choose **File→New** from the menu bar.
    Notice that both of the templates you observed in the Grants Office *folder are now displayed in the dialog box.*

14. Double-click to select the *quarterly report form* template.
    Word opens a new document based upon this template. If you needed to start a new quarterly report, all of the formatting and sections are already defined for you.

15. Close ☒ the Document window. Click **No** if you are asked if you wish to save the document.

Remove the Workgroup Template Designation

Now you will remove the workgroup template designation so that Word is properly set up for the next student to perform this exercise.

16. Choose **Tools→Options** from the menu bar.

17. Click *Workgroup templates* in the File types list; then click the **Modify** button.

18. Tap the (DELETE) key to erase the current workgroup template location; then tap (ENTER).
    Notice that the workgroup template folder location is now blank.

19. Click **Close** to close the Options dialog box.

Working with Bookmarks

A bookmark is a hidden code you can use to mark a specific location in a document, such as a piece of text or an image. Bookmarks are a useful way to mark a location and then jump to it quickly. Once you have inserted a bookmark, you can use the following methods to navigate to the bookmark location.

- **Hyperlink**—You can create a hyperlink that navigates the user to the bookmark location.

- **Go to Bookmark**—You can navigate to the bookmark with the **Go to** button in the Insert Bookmark dialog box.

- **Cross-reference**—You can create a cross-reference that refers to the bookmark name and can serve as a hyperlink to the bookmark location.

Example

Ariana is in the middle of editing a document at the end of the workday. She inserts a bookmark named "ContinueHere" where she stopped working for the day. The next morning, she opens the document; then chooses **Insert→Bookmark** from the menu bar. Ariana clicks to select the *ContinueHere* bookmark in the dialog box; then clicks the **Go to** button. Word jumps to the line where Ariana inserted the bookmark and she continues her work on the document. The bookmark lets Ariana mark her place in the document without inserting text or a highlight that she would need to remove later.

Inserting Bookmarks

TIP!

You cannot use spaces in a book-mark name.

You can create a new bookmark wherever you need it. Simply click in the text, select some text, or click on any image where you wish to set the bookmark location; then give the **Insert→Bookmark** command and add the bookmark name. You can insert any number of bookmarks into a document.

Task	Procedure
HOW TO CREATE AND NAVIGATE WITH BOOKMARKS	
Create a bookmark.	■ Click anywhere in the text, select some text, or click on an image where you wish to locate the bookmark.
	■ Choose *Insert→Bookmark* from the menu bar.
	■ Enter the bookmark name (you cannot use space characters in the name); then click the *Add* button.
	The bookmark is added, and the dialog box will close.
Jump to a bookmark location.	■ Choose *Insert→Bookmark* from the menu bar.
	■ Select the desired bookmark; then click the *Go to* button.
Create a hyperlink to a bookmark.	■ Select the text or image for the hyperlink.
	■ Choose *Insert→hyperlink* or click the *Insert Hyperlink* button on the toolbar.
	■ Click the *Bookmark* button in the dialog box.
	■ Select the desired bookmark; then click *OK*.
	■ Click *OK* again to complete the Insert Hyperlink command.
Create a cross-reference to a bookmark.	■ Click where you wish to locate the cross-reference; then choose *Insert→Cross-reference* from the menu bar.
	■ Choose *Bookmark* in the reference type list at the top-left corner of the dialog box.
	■ Choose the desired bookmark from the lower half of the dialog box.
	■ Choose the desired cross-reference type (text, page, etc.) from the list at the upper-right side of the dialog box.
	■ Click *OK* to complete the command.

In this exercise, you will insert a new bookmark. Then you will create a hyperlink that automatically jumps the reader to the bookmark.

Insert Bookmarks

1. Display page **2** of the document; then click on the *Progress Toward Objectives* heading line at the top of the page.

2. Choose **Insert→Bookmark** from the menu bar.

3. Type **progress** in the bookmark name box; then click the **Add** button.
    The bookmark name is added to the list.

4. Display page **4** of the document; then drag to select the *Best Practices* heading at the top of the page.

5. Choose **Insert→Bookmark** from the menu bar.

6. Type **Best Practices** in the bookmark name box.
    Notice that the Add button is grayed out. You cannot use spaces in a bookmark name.

7. Delete the space so that the bookmark name reads **BestPractices**; then click the **Add** button.

Navigate with the Bookmarks

8. Choose **Insert→Bookmark** from the menu bar.

9. Click to select the **progress** bookmark; then click the **Go To** button in the dialog box.
    Word displays the heading on page 2 where you placed the bookmark.

10. Double-click **BestPractices** in the bookmark list.
    This is a shortcut for the Go To command.

11. **Close** the *Bookmark* dialog box.

Create a Hyperlink to a Bookmark

You learned how to create a hyperlink to a Web page in Lesson 6. Now you will use a similar technique to create a hyperlink to a bookmark.

12. Use (CTRL)+(HOME) to jump to the beginning of the document.

13. Follow these steps to insert text for the hyperlink.

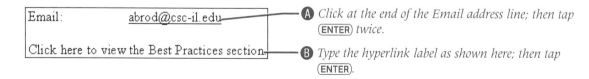

Ⓐ *Click at the end of the Email address line; then tap* (ENTER) *twice.*

Ⓑ *Type the hyperlink label as shown here; then tap* (ENTER).

14. Select the line you just typed; then click the Insert Hyperlink 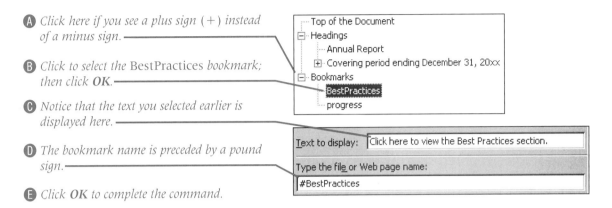 button on the toolbar.

15. Click the **Bookmark** button on the dialog box; then follow these steps to insert the hyperlink to a bookmark.

Ⓐ *Click here if you see a plus sign (+) instead of a minus sign.*

Ⓑ *Click to select the BestPractices bookmark; then click OK.*

Ⓒ *Notice that the text you selected earlier is displayed here.*

Ⓓ *The bookmark name is preceded by a pound sign.*

Ⓔ *Click OK to complete the command.*

Word adds color and an underscore to indicate visually that the text is now a hyperlink.

16. Point (don't click) anywhere on the hyperlink.
The pointer changes to a hand 🖑, again indicating that this text now functions as a hyperlink.

17. Click on the hyperlink.
Word jumps you to the page with the bookmark. Notice that the Web *toolbar has appeared as well. It will probably be immediately below the formatting toolbar.*

18. Click the Back ⬅ button on the Web toolbar to return to the hyperlink.

Editing Bookmarks

You can change the location of a bookmark or delete it entirely at any time. If you delete a bookmark to which a hyperlink has been created, the hyperlink will remain but will no longer function properly. Similarly, a cross-reference to a bookmark will remain in the document, but will display an error message the next time you update the cross-reference.

HOW TO EDIT BOOKMARKS

Task	Procedure
Delete a bookmark.	■ Choose *Insert→Bookmark* from the menu bar.
	■ Click to select the bookmark name; then click *Delete*.
Change the location of a bookmark.	■ Click anywhere in the text, select some text, or click on an image where you wish to relocate the bookmark.
	■ Choose *Insert→Bookmark* from the menu bar.
	■ Click to select the bookmark name; then click Add. *The bookmark location is changed, and the dialog box will close.*

Hands-On 17.10 Edit Bookmarks

In this exercise, you will change the location of a bookmark and then remove it.

Change the Location of a Bookmark

1. Display the top of page **4.** Scroll down the page until the *Course Development Practices* heading is visible; then click anywhere on the heading line.

2. Choose **Insert→Bookmark** from the menu bar.

3. Make sure that the *BestPractices* bookmark is selected; then click the **Add** button.
   Word immediately changes the location of the chosen bookmark to the current insertion point or selection. Now you will test the new location setting.

4. Use (CTRL)+(HOME) to jump to the top of the document.

5. Click on the *Best Practices* hyperlink you created on this page.
   Word should display the Course Development Practices *heading in middle of page 4 rather than the* Best Practices *heading at the top of the page. The bookmark location has been changed.*

6. Click the Back [⏎] button to return to page 1 of the document.

Delete a Bookmark

7. Choose **Insert→Bookmark** from the menu bar.

8. Make sure that the *BestPractices* bookmark is selected; then click the **Delete** button.
   The bookmark is deleted.

9. **Close** the dialog box.
   Notice that the hyperlink to the BestPractices *bookmark is still underlined as if it were still active.*

10. Click on the *Best Practices* hyperlink.
    The insertion point should now be blinking at the top of the page. The hyperlink exists but no longer functions properly.

11. *Right-click* on the hyperlink; then choose **Hyperlink→Remove Hyperlink** from the pop-up menu.
    The font color and underscore are removed along with the hyperlink.

12. *Right-click* anywhere on the Word toolbar; then click **Web** in the pop-up menu to dismiss the toolbar from the screen.

Working with Watermarks

A *Watermark* is an image that is only visible when a document is displayed in the Print Layout view and when it is printed out. Watermarks are not visible in the normal or outline views. Watermarks must always be placed in the header or footer of a document. However, you can place a watermark in such a way that it actually prints in the body area of each page. You can use any of the following types of graphic images as watermarks:

- Any AutoShape
- Any drawing object
- A WordArt object
- A text box with text
- Any picture or clipart image

TIP!

Although a watermark must be placed while you are in the Header/Footer *view, you are not limited to placing a watermark at the top or bottom of the page. You can place a watermark anywhere on the page, including the body area in the center of the page. However, to place clipart or a picture in the body area of the page, you must insert it within a text box.*

Example

When Ariana sends out a draft quarterly report document, she inserts a watermark in the header that reads "Draft." Since it only appears when the document is displayed with the *print layout* view or when it is printed out, the watermark does not clutter the view of the document on the screen. At the same time, the watermark helps ensure that the draft version will never be printed and sent out to the client by mistake.

HOW TO ADD A WATERMARK

Task	Procedure
Add a watermark to print on each page of a document.	■ Choose *View→Header and Footer* from the menu bar. ■ Click the *Show/Hide Document Text* 🔲 button on the Header and Footer toolbar. ■ Draw the desired AutoShape or text box. If you wish to place clipart or a picture outside the header/footer boundaries, draw a text box first; then use the *Insert→Picture* command to place the image inside of the text box. ■ Position the watermark anywhere on the page you desire, including anywhere in the body area of the page. You are not limited to the header/footer areas at the top and bottom of the page. ■ Click the *Close* button on the Header and Footer toolbar.
Preview a watermark.	■ Choose *View→Print Layout* from the menu bar, or click the *Print Preview* button on the Word toolbar.

In this exercise, you will use a picture as a watermark. You will add it to the header/footer area of the document so that it will print properly. Remember that you could also simply type text in a text box, use an AutoShape, or create a WordArt image rather than placing an image as you will do in this exercise.

1. Choose **View→Header and Footer** from the menu bar.

2. Click the Show/Hide Document Text 🔲 button on the Header and Footer toolbar.
   The body text of the document is no longer visible. This lets you focus on the placement of your watermark image.

3. Make sure that Word's Drawing toolbar is displayed. Click the Drawing 🔲 button on the toolbar, or *right-click* on a Word toolbar; then click the *Drawing* toolbar.

4. Follow these steps to draw a text box in the center of the page.

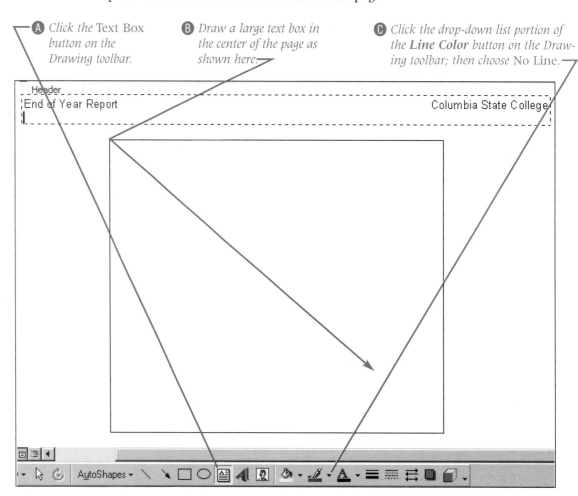

Ⓐ *Click the* Text Box *button on the Drawing toolbar.*

Ⓑ *Draw a large text box in the center of the page as shown here.*

Ⓒ *Click the drop-down list portion of the **Line Color** button on the Drawing toolbar; then choose No Line.*

Header
End of Year Report　　　　　　　　　　　　　　　　　　Columbia State College

5. Make sure that the insertion point is blinking inside the text box; then choose **Insert→Picture→From File** from the menu bar. Navigate to your exercise diskette in the Look in box; then double-click to insert the **Draft** picture on your exercise diskette.
   Notice that the picture is automatically scaled to fit within the text box you drew. You can also click on the picture and manually scale it (as you learned to do in Lesson 11). This picture was created with a graphics program. It is a light image so that text will still be visible over the picture. If necessary, you can adjust the brightness and contrast of the picture to ideally suit your needs and the characteristics of your printer.

6. Follow these steps to adjust the brightness of the watermark.

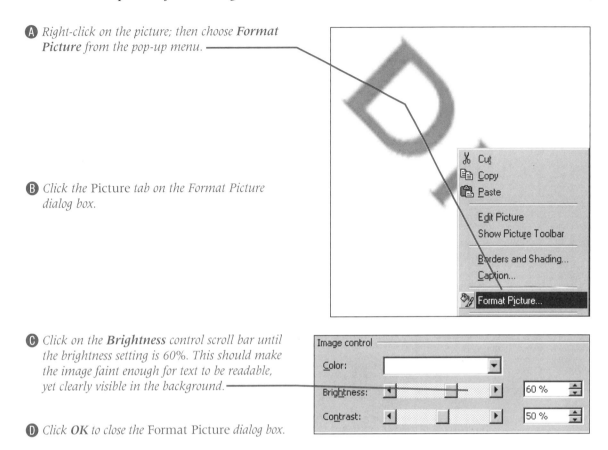

Ⓐ *Right-click on the picture; then choose* **Format Picture** *from the pop-up menu.*

Ⓑ *Click the* Picture *tab on the Format Picture dialog box.*

Ⓒ *Click on the* **Brightness** *control scroll bar until the brightness setting is 60%. This should make the image faint enough for text to be readable, yet clearly visible in the background.*

Ⓓ *Click* OK *to close the* Format Picture *dialog box.*

Your watermark image should lighten visibly on the screen. Depending on your monitor's settings, the image may be almost invisible. However, this does not mean that it will be invisible on the printed page.

7. Click the **Close** button on the Header/Footer toolbar to return to the normal page view.

8. Click the Print Preview ⬚ button to preview the printed pages.
   The watermark should be visible in the background of the document, with the body text printed over it.

9. Choose **File→Print** from the menu bar; then choose the **Current Page** option in the *Page Range* section of the dialog box and click **OK.** Retrieve the page from the printer.
   Printing of the watermark will vary depending on the type of printer you are using. If the watermark prints too dark or too light, you can always return to the Header/Footer view and adjust the brightness of the image. If you simply typed text in a text box, you can also vary the Font color of the text.

10. Choose **View→Print Layout** from the menu bar.
    The watermark should also be visible in the print layout view.

11. Choose **View→Normal** from the menu bar.
    The watermark disappears from view, along with the header and footer.

12. If you feel that the watermark prints too dark or too light, choose **View→Header and Footer** from the menu bar; then right-click on the image, and choose **Format Picture** from the pop-up menu. Try adjusting the *Brightness* and *Contrast* controls to adjust the lightness of the image. After you close the *Format Picture* dialog box, choose **File→Print** from the menu bar; then choose the **Current Page** option, and click **OK.** It might take one or two tries to get the result you want.

(Continued on the next page)

Create Other Types of Watermarks (Optional)

If you would like to try using text, a WordArt object, or an AutoShape as a watermark, here are some brief instructions for additional practice. Otherwise, you can skip to the last step in this exercise and close the document.

13. Choose **View→Header and Footer** from the menu bar.

14. Click the Show/Hide Document Text 🖹 button on the Header and Footer toolbar.

15. Click on the *Draft* image in the middle of the page; then tap the (DELETE) key.
    Notice that the text box that contained the image is also deleted. In the next step, you will place an AutoShape on the page. You can place AutoShapes directly on the center of the page. There is no need for a text box as there was for the picture image.

16. Click the **AutoShapes** button on the Drawing toolbar; then choose an AutoShape such as a star. Draw a star in the center of the page. While the AutoShape is still selected, choose a light line color; then click the *Print Preview* button to view the printed page.

17. Close the print preview window; then choose **View→Header and Footer** from the menu bar, and click the **Show/Hide Document Text** button on the toolbar.

18. Select the AutoShape; then tap the (DELETE) key.

19. Create a text box in the center of the page; then set the *Line Color* to **No Line**.

20. Type some text in the text box, such as **For Internal Circulation Only**.

21. Select the text, and apply a light font color. You may also want to change the font size of the text. When you are done, use *Print Preview* to preview the page.

22. Close the Print Preview window; then return to the *Header and Footer* view.
    Next you will use a WordArt object as a watermark. As with AutoShapes, there is no need to insert a WordArt object within a text box as you did with a picture previously. You can place WordArt images directly on any part of the page.

23. Delete the text box; then click the WordArt 🔷 button on the Drawing toolbar. Create a WordArt object on the page with text such as **Draft Copy**; then preview the page.

    Notice how the background of the WordArt image is probably too dark. It may be difficult to read text that appears over the image. You might not want to place a WordArt object beneath a part of the page where body text would appear. You can always place a watermark in the header and/or footer sections of the page. This will prevent it from printing in the body area of the document.

24. Close the Print Preview window. Save 🖫 the document; then close ⊠ it.
    You are done with the final lesson! If you have gone through the entire book and understand the material, you should be ready to take and pass the Microsoft Word Expert User certification test. Good luck!

Concepts Review

True/False Questions

1. The Track Changes feature can automatically mark every change you make to a document. TRUE FALSE

2. The Track Changes feature cannot indicate which author made a particular change. TRUE FALSE

3. The *Protect Document* command can prevent unauthorized users from opening a document. TRUE FALSE

4. A workgroup template folder can automatically place new document templates in your New dialog box. TRUE FALSE

5. If you open an old version of a document and give the *Save* command, it will overwrite the current version of that document. TRUE FALSE

6. A bookmark lets you mark any spot in a document for quick navigation from the bookmarks menu. TRUE FALSE

7. You cannot create a hyperlink to a bookmark, you must use the cross-reference command instead. TRUE FALSE

8. Since watermarks are placed in the Header/Footer view, they may only appear at the top or bottom of a document. TRUE FALSE

9. When you review tracked changes, you cannot navigate within the document—you must use the *Find* buttons instead. TRUE FALSE

10. You can merge tracked changes from one document into another document. TRUE FALSE

Multiple-Choice Questions

1. What happens when you merge two documents?
   a. The contents of both documents are inserted into a third document.
   b. The content of the merged document is added to the end of the document from which the merge command is issued.
   c. The highlighted changes in the merged document are inserted into the document from which the merge command is issued.
   d. None of the above

2. Which of the following best describes a document version?
   a. An archived copy of the document that is stored within that document
   b. A backup copy of the document that is stored in a separate folder
   c. A document with a version number added to the filename
   d. None of the above

3. What can you do if you forget a protect document password?
   a. Send the file to Microsoft for decoding.
   b. Use the open document password.
   c. Run a shareware program on the file to list the password.
   d. Nothing. You cannot unprotect the document.
   e. None of the above

4. Which of the following items may be used as a watermark?
   a. Text boxes
   b. WordArt objects
   c. Images
   d. AutoShapes
   e. All of the above

Index